Loud and proud

MANCHEStER
1824

Manchester University Press

New
Ethnographies

Series editor
Alexander Thomas T. Smith

Already published
The British in rural France:
Lifestyle migration and the ongoing quest for a better way of life
Michaela Benson

Ageing selves and everyday life in the North of England: Years in the making
Catherine Degnen

Chagos islanders in Mauritius and the UK:
Forced displacement and onward migration
Laura Jeffery

South Korean civil movement organisations: Hope, crisis and pragmatism in democratic transition
Amy Levine

Integration in Ireland: The everyday lives of African migrants
Fiona Murphy and Mark Maguire

An ethnography of English football fans: Cans, cops and carnivals
Geoff Pearson

Iraqi women in Denmark: Ritual performance and belonging in everyday life
Marianne Holm Pedersen

Literature and agency in English fiction reading:
A study of the Henry Williamson Society
Adam Reed

International seafarers and transnationalism in the twenty-first century
Helen Sampson

Devolution and the Scottish Conservatives:
Banal activism, electioneering and the politics of irrelevance
Alexander Smith

Exoticisation undressed: Ethnographic nostalgia and authenticity in
Emberá clothes
Dimitrios Theodossopoulos

Immersion: Marathon swimming, embodiment and identity
Karen Throsby

Enduring violence: Everyday life and conflict in eastern Sri Lanka
Rebecca Walker

Performing Englishness: Identity and politics in a contemporary folk resurgence
Trish Winter and Simon Keegan-Phipps

Loud and proud

Passion and politics in the English Defence League

Hilary Pilkington

Manchester University Press

Published by Manchester University Press
Altrincham Street, Manchester M1 7JA

www.manchesteruniversitypress.co.uk

British Library Cataloguing-in-Publication Data
A catalogue record for this book is available from the British Library

Library of Congress Cataloging-in-Publication Data applied for

ISBN   978 1 7849 9400 6   hardback
ISBN   978 1 7849 9259 0   paperback

First published 2016

Typeset in Minion by
Servis Filmsetting Ltd, Stockport, Cheshire
Printed in Great Britain by
CPI Group (UK) Ltd, Croydon, CR0 4YY

To the future, which may, or may not, last a long time

Contents

List of figures viii
List of boxes ix
Series editor's foreword x
Foreword by Anoop Nayak xi
Acknowledgements xv

Introduction: Transgressing the *cordon sanitaire*: understanding the English Defence League as a social movement 1

1 The contagion of stigma: the ethics and politics of research with the 'far right' 13

2 Tommy Robinson's barmy army? The past, present and future of the English Defence League 37

3 Doing the hokey-cokey: everyday trajectories of activism 60

4 'Not racist, not violent, just no longer silent': aspirations to non-racism 92

5 'Their way or no way': anti-Islam and anti-Muslim sentiments 125

6 'Second-class citizens': reordering privilege and prejudice 154

7 'One big family': emotion, affect and the meaning of activism 177

8 'Loud and proud': piercing the politics of silencing 203

Conclusion: passion and politics 222

Appendix 1: Observed events 232
Appendix 2: Respondent set 234
References 238
Index 247

List of figures

3.1	Age of respondents	62
3.2	Declan: standing proud	63
3.3	Matt and Casey: teamwork	65
3.4	Educational status of respondents	66
3.5	Connor: 'Ain't bothered'	68
3.6	Employment status of respondents	69
3.7	Ethnicity (self-declared) of respondents	71
3.8	Lisa: seeing red	73
3.9	Rachel: fighting 'two-tier justice'	81
3.10	Jack: paying a high price (source: EDL News, http://edlnews. co.uk/index.php/latest-news/latest-news/853-edl-walsall-demo-turns-into-violence)	84
3.11	Kurt and the infamous flag	86
4.1	'Not racist, not violent, just no longer silent'	93
4.2	'Racist EDL': counter-demonstrators' placards, Manchester demonstration	97
4.3	'We love Hindus and Sikhs': EDL placard, Rotherham protest camp	100
4.4	EDL Angels 'stand *beside* their men' (courtesy of the EDL)	120
5.1	'No more mosques' flag, Leeds demonstration	138
5.2	Islamophobic and proud (courtesy of the EDL)	149
7.1	Crusaders?	188
7.2	Rachel's EDL tattoo	189
7.3	Chas in his Union Jack onesie	190
7.4	Being seen for who you are: personalised hoodies	191
7.5	Performance in protest	192
7.6	Symbolic violence in protest	194

List of boxes

1	Feeling the affect… Walthamstow, 1 September 2012	18
2	Help? The questions 'informed consent' cannot answer	25
3	Declan	63
4	Matt and Casey	64
5	Connor	67
6	Lisa	73
7	Rachel	80
8	Jack	84
9	Kurt	86

Series editor's foreword

At its best, ethnography has provided a valuable tool for apprehending a world in flux. A couple of years after the Second World War, Max Gluckman founded the Department of Social Anthropology at the University of Manchester. In the years that followed, he and his colleagues built a programme of ethnographic research that drew eclectically on the work of leading anthropologists, economists and sociologists to explore issues of conflict, reconciliation and social justice 'at home' and abroad. Often placing emphasis on detailed analysis of case studies drawn from small-scale societies and organisations, the famous 'Manchester School' in social anthropology built an enviable reputation for methodological innovation in its attempts to explore the pressing political questions of the second half of the twentieth century. Looking back, that era is often thought to constitute a 'gold standard' for how ethnographers might grapple with new challenges and issues in the contemporary world.

The *New Ethnographies* series aims to build on that ethnographic legacy at Manchester. It will publish the best new ethnographic monographs that promote interdisciplinary debate and methodological innovation in the qualitative social sciences. This includes the growing number of books that seek to apprehend the 'new' ethnographic objects of a seemingly brave new world, some recent examples of which have included auditing, democracy and elections, documents, financial markets, human rights, assisted reproductive technologies and political activism. Analysing such objects has often demanded new skills and techniques from the ethnographer. As a result, this series will give voice to those using ethnographic methods across disciplines to innovate, such as through the application of multi-sited fieldwork and the extended comparative case-study method. Such innovations have often challenged more traditional ethnographic approaches. *New Ethnographies* therefore seeks to provide a platform for emerging scholars and their more established counterparts engaging with ethnographic methods in new and imaginative ways.

Alexander Thomas T. Smith

Foreword

Two years ago on a rare, sunny afternoon in North East England, I headed towards a seaside town where I had been conducting research with young Bangladeshi Muslims. As this was a weekend I would normally be going there for a coastal walk or bike ride. Usually I would feel a sense of impending excitement at the thought of visiting the beach, feeling the sand between my toes and the sun upon my skin. Today though, things felt different. Make no mistake – there was a feeling in the air that things *were different.*

Odd as it may sound, I was travelling to meet up and congregate with a rabble of people I didn't know. They were a patchwork group of Socialist Workers Party supporters, local councillors and residents protesting against the English Defence League (EDL) that were planning to march through the local area in the interior heartland where my research had been based. We expected trouble. The police had told the Muslim restaurant owners and shopkeepers to consider boarding up their establishments while the march took place and there was a sense of wariness around. The warm weather also meant the pubs were busy as people sat outside drinking and spilling out onto the street. As I hurried past the bars and pubs to the meeting point I averted my gaze from the groups of men hanging about. The North East has its fair share of shaven-headed blokes with bulked up biceps who enjoy a few pints. But my antennae were hyper-sensitive, pushing forward a single, undiluted thought – *were they EDL?*

Though I am no Einstein, like most ethnic minority people I am familiar with the following formula:

$$\frac{White\ masculinity \times n\ (where\ n\ is\ unknown) + alcohol + EDL\ leanings}{Brown\ skin} = \text{TROUBLE}$$

As it turned out, aside from a brief skirmish I witnessed between a group of youthful Asian men looking for excitement and a few EDL supporters, there was little violence on the seaside that day. The police had deflated tensions by stopping the EDL from marching directly through the main South Asian area in town near where we were stood. Little did I know at the time that Hilary Pilkington, the soon-to-be author of *Loud and proud*, was attending similar marches up and down the country, but on the other side of the *cordon sanitaire*. She was researching the EDL.

While accounts of those who have infiltrated the British far right can be found, the portrayal in popular books and undercover television documentaries tends to focus on the spectacular. Yet Pilkington reveals that much of the daily activity of many EDL members is relatively mundane. So what did Pilkington achieve in studying the EDL upfront and up close? In reading the book there is little doubt that *Loud and proud* gets beneath the skin of the EDL and conducts a full and thorough autopsy of what lies beneath. With surgical precision Pilkington slices away at many of the myths and assumptions that surround the organisation – who they are, what they stand for, how they are organised and their *raison d'être*. Representations of the EDL as homogeneous with regard to the composition of participants are laid bare. While the majority of members are male and unemployed they are not all ex-football hooligans and far right fascists. What Pilkington reveals is a far more complex picture of the movement that includes an LGBT (lesbian, gay, bisexual and transgender) division, members who refute and challenge fascism, as well as a not-so-silent majority who feel disenfranchised by the numbing banality of contemporary British politics and the lack of meaningful debate on social polarisation.

A key contribution of the study is that it moves beyond media representations to investigate the people at the heart of EDL marches. Pilkington describes the EDL as a street-based new social movement that coalesces around a number of issues and popular concerns. She reveals how the movement is organised, financed, recruits and further seeks to disseminate its disquieting message. By probing behind the mask she draws out some fascinating biographies that help us understand the profile of supporters and works to flesh them out in meaningful and humane ways. Here we get to see them not simply as racist extremists but as whole people with families, jobs, mental health problems, stressful relationships and so forth. If we are to better understand contemporary forms of racism and religious intolerance, and offer meaningful strategies to tackle these, we need to know who these people are, what they think and why.

What makes Pilkington's study unique is the sense of 'being there', delivered through the intimacy of her eloquent ethnographic writing. What is most impressive is the dedication Pilkington shows to the ethnographic method, travelling on early morning coaches to rallies, experiencing police regulation through 'kettling' practices, joining supporters for drinks and perhaps, unusually for a professorial academic, engaging with people 'not like us'. As the testimonies reveal, many of the members are more like us than we might choose to imagine. Although it is rarely discussed in methodology textbooks, this type of work involves a great deal of stamina and an interest in people that cannot be feigned. It is impossible not to be impressed by the sheer willpower and intrepid nature of the author. Pilkington's discussion on method and research ethics is fluently written and illuminating; it really conveys how research gets done. The study is seamlessly interwoven with first-hand experience of events, interviews, photographs and field-notes. For anyone teaching research methods to students, the systematic approach to ethnography and the detailed reflections on the ethics and the issues thrown up will provide exemplary case study material.

Notwithstanding this enormous ethnographic labour, the book is likely to be controversial. This is not wholly because it is an ethnographic study that centres upon what is a largely vilified section of the population. It partly rests with the way in which Pilkington refrains from bestowing moral judgement on the participants she encounters, recognising the value of forming a rapport with them, and empathetically being conscious of the way in which similarities and difference underpin all human relationships. She chooses to allow participants to speak for themselves, granting them greater agency than many studies permit, even if some of what they say may strike readers as contradictory or unpalatable. At times this can be a difficult circle to square, which prompted me to enquire if Pilkington regards the ethnographer as dedicated to the description of culture, or as someone who is an agent in the making of that culture. The reality is that most in-depth research of this kind presents difficult ethical situations, unexpected alliances, oscillating attachments and partial acts of representation and (mis)recognition. To listen without prejudice is no easy thing to do.

Pilkington reveals how EDL members perceive themselves as victims of the state and harbour grievances towards law and justice, the allocation of public housing and shrinking employment opportunities. While none of this is new, it is interesting that the distribution of welfare benefits is of such concern given that most EDL supporters are themselves primary recipients of Britain's benefit system. This does not stop them from weaving together narratives that allow them to self-present as victims, often at the expense of minorities who are viewed as structurally advantaged by the state. But how real are these testimonies, what purpose do they serve, for whom and why? Through the telling of these stories the privilege of whiteness is erased. In doing so the EDL can lay claim to whiteness as an embattled identity, that is constantly under attack and must be protected. This is not just a discursive strategy, but an affective disposition that is strongly felt and widely believed. Even the name, the English Defence League, suggests an identity under siege.

Like many far right social movements before them, the EDL repeatedly claim they are not racist. Indeed, Pilkington draws out instances where those giving Nazi salutes are criticised and points where colour-based racism and generic violence is roundly condemned. However, a focal point for the EDL is an obsession with what they perceive as the 'Islamicisation of Britain' and concerns that Muslims are 'taking over'. Here EDL members invoke discourses of democracy, pointing to what they regard as the premodern patriarchal aspects of Islamic culture they claim subjugate women, or broader forms of territoriality concerning the building of mosques in a supposedly Christian country. When Muslims are discussed confusion reigns supreme – slippages are made between 'extremists' and 'moderate' Muslims, Islam, Asians and Pakistanis. More disconcerting though is that the views of the EDL are not hugely out of line with evidence found in recent polls and national population surveys that also reflect intolerance towards those of Muslim faith. Maybe parts of the EDL are more like the general population than we would like to think? Moreover in believing I might be able to spot EDL protestors in pubs around the North East coastal town, I too was working on stereotypical assumptions. Indeed, much contemporary racism is often found hiding in the light.

In many ways Pilkington's study gestures towards the strain of liberal democracy in Britain where people continue to feel removed and detached from formal politics. Recent times have seen a coalition government come to power that no one voted for and that was later superseded. In a period of political apathy the rise of alternative parties and movements is strikingly apparent. The bubbling popularity of the Scottish National Party in the 2015 elections, the rise of the United Kingdom Independence Party and the election of the overtly socialist Jeremy Corbyn as the new post-election Labour opposition leader have much to tell us about how the wider disenchantment felt by the British public towards mainstream politics. It is within the fault-lines of liberal democracy that grassroots movements such as the EDL have sprung up, feeding on public political anathema, disenfranchisement and a desire to do things differently. Interestingly, the majority of EDL supporters are wary of the movement becoming established as a formal political party, feeling it would risk watering down their message and dissolve the energy of street protest. There is little doubt that supporters enjoy demonstrations, the feeling of being part of a collective and the opportunity to share time with like-minded individuals. The desire to keep the EDL on the edges of the political arena and therefore away from power perhaps speaks to something that is more inexplicable, personal and cathartic. The act of being 'loud and proud' is about feeling, affect and emotion: a primal scream at the very core of British society that seeks to be heard. Pilkington is practised in the ethnographic art of listening and acts as an interlocutor who enables the primal elements of this scream to become intelligible.

Loud and proud is a terrific piece of scholarship that demonstrates a real commitment to the ethnographic method. It challenges many of the outward perceptions of the EDL, by listening to those who are at the heart of the movement. The writing is compelling throughout and the analysis is never overstated. The work is a real accomplishment, and like many of the best books, it will agitate and inspire in equal measure. Hilary Pilkington delivers what is ultimately a highly original, rigorously researched and thought-provoking account of the EDL. It is an unflinching ethnography of the EDL that is bold and humane in its approach.

Anoop Nayak

Acknowledgements

I would like to thank the commissioning editors and production team at MUP for their support and enthusiasm for a challenging project as well as their consistently professional, timely and friendly technical assistance. I would like to acknowledge also the financial support of FP7 OpenAire and the University of Manchester, which allowed the book to be made available through Open Access.

I am grateful to numerous friends and colleagues – especially from the MYPLACE project and the ESRC Research Seminar Series on Right Wing Extremism in contemporary Europe – who have listened to my dilemmas and concerns and responded kindly to draft papers as I tried to make sense of the research behind this book. I am indebted in particular to Anoop Nayak for his thoughtful and critical comments on a first draft of the manuscript and James Rhodes for being so generous with his time and knowledge as I struggled with the trickiest sections to write. The book has benefited greatly from their advice, although neither is responsible for the content of the final publication.

Financial support for the research that led to this book was provided by the European Union Seventh Framework Programme as part of the larger MYPLACE project (Grant Agreement number FP7-266831). I am grateful to the Commission for the faith shown in what was a hugely ambitious project and in particular to our Research Programme officer, Sylvie Rohanova, for her patience and support. I would like to thank also the whole MYPLACE team for their intellectual engagement, collegiality and good humour. The research findings, and their interpretation, in this book remain the responsibility of the author alone.

I want to thank all those who shared their time and experience with me in the course of researching this book but especially 'Rachel' and 'Kurt' whose support and friendship went well beyond consenting to take part in the research. There will be much in the book that they, and others, will disagree with but I hope that I have not misplaced their trust to 'tell it like it is'. This is how I saw it.

The research and writing of this book were never easy. Life intervened, sometimes brutally. I would like to thank my family and friends, in particular Ellie and Jim for being my purpose, Tony for caring beyond the call of duty, my mum and sisters for being there (as always) and Janet and Lena for their unwavering loyalty.

I have learned that Althusser was wrong – the future does not necessarily last a long time – but also that the present can be lived by the (Northern) light that glimmers at the end of the tunnel.

Introduction

Transgressing the *cordon sanitaire*: understanding the English Defence League as a social movement

This book is political – but not by design. It is rendered so by its object of study (the English Defence League) and its context – the rise of a new 'far right'[1] and 'populist radical right' across Europe and, more recently, America. It argues that establishing an academic '*cordon sanitaire*' (Mouffe, 2005: 72), in the form of typological and classificatory approaches that focus solely on the ideological dimensions of such movements and confine them to the ghetto of studies of the 'far right', is neither an adequate nor an effective answer to the questions raised by their emergence. It recognises that to do otherwise – to treat such movements as articulating not only the ignorant prejudice of the marginalised but their experience and perceptions of justice and injustice, equality and inequality – has political implications also. Those implications, it is argued, however, are not the condoning or legitimation of racist or Islamophobic attitudes. Transgressing the *cordon sanitaire* signals, rather, a commitment to the reclamation of 'politics'; the relinquishment of its quest for universal rational consensus through attempts to design institutions capable of reconciling all conflicting interests and values (Mouffe, 2005: 3) and its reconfiguration as a space for the legitimate expression of such conflict. This comes with real costs; uncomfortable views, and those who express them, have to be treated seriously, academically and politically, rather than dismissed, caricatured or ridiculed (Back, 2002: 39; Kenny, 2012: 32). Some will consider that too high a price to pay.

This introductory chapter sets out an approach to understanding activism in the English Defence League (EDL) from within social movement studies. It places the EDL alongside populist radical right rather than classic 'far right' movements on the political spectrum and outlines a provisional rationale for characterising it as an anti-Islamist movement. Prefacing the theoretical discussion in subsequent chapters of the book, it contextualises claims by the EDL that the organisation is 'not racist' but 'against militant Islam' within contemporary theories of 'race' and racism and in relation to empirical evidence of rising 'Islamophobia' among the wider UK population. The chapter describes the ethnographic approach adopted in the book, which is distinguished by a focus not on organisational structure and ideology but individual activists. The analytic emphasis on the meanings individuals attach to activism, it is argued, not only brings insight into how politics and passion are intertwined in the movement but, in so doing, may open avenues for challenging prejudices and stereotypes that constrain and distort political dialogue.

Far right? Placing the EDL on the spectrum

Britain, until recently, has felt itself to be comfortably immune from new right politics. Electoral support for radical right parties in national parliamentary elections has remained lower than in other western European states. No extreme right party has succeeded in having a representative elected to national parliament and, between 1923 and 2001, extreme right parties took only five seats even at local government level (Goodwin, 2011a: 5). Electoral results from 1980–2012 show that support for such parties[2] in the UK did not rise above 1 per cent until 2010–12; even then, at 1.8 per cent, support remained well below that in neighbouring countries such as France (13.6 per cent) and The Netherlands (12.7 per cent) (Minkenberg, 2013: 20). The reasons for this are explored in more nuanced ways by others (see Goodwin, 2011a) but might be summarised as resulting from a combination of: the first-past-the-post electoral system, which significantly reduces the incentive to vote for candidates with little chance of securing victory in a given constituency; and the failure of the British National Party[3] (BNP) to move in the direction of a 'renewed' radical right of the kind that has emerged elsewhere in Europe (Minkenberg, 2013: 17), continuing instead to mobilise racist and racial supremacist discourse thinly disguised in the notion of indigeneity (Williams and Law, 2012).

This immunity is far from absolute. The European Value Survey (1999–2000 and 2008–09 rounds) found base levels of xenophobia[4] in the UK to hover around 20 per cent; this is typical of western European countries although lower than most eastern European countries (Minkenberg, 2015: 40). On the single measure of anti-immigrant prejudice (1999–2000),[5] the level in the UK is actually higher (15.9 per cent) than the mean for western European countries (10.7 per cent) (Strabac and Listhaug, 2008: 277). Given that evidence suggests hostility to immigration is the most powerful predictor of support for populist extremist parties (Goodwin, 2011b: 9), it would appear that the same potential base of support for the populist radical right exists in the UK as elsewhere in Europe. Moreover, while proportional representation may be off the political agenda in the UK following the defeat of the referendum on electoral reform (May 2011), the political space is changing nonetheless as populist radical right and Eurosceptic parties, somewhat paradoxically, realise the potential for their voices to be heard in the European parliament. The BNP gained two seats in 2009 while the 2014 European parliamentary elections were won in the UK by the populist anti-EU United Kingdom Independence Party (UKIP), which took 27 per cent of the national vote.

To date research on the far right and populist radical right has been undertaken largely from a political science perspective drawing on statistical data on voter preference and behaviour, or the analysis of official programmes and statements, to understand the ideology underpinning such parties, their capacity and strategies for mobilisation and their electoral viability and prospects. Its outcome often has been the typologisation of parties and movements based on their connections with fascism and National Socialism, current constituencies of support and ideology/policy. Characterising trends across Europe, Wodak (2013: 26) suggests the radical right scene in the UK mobilises support by emphasising the danger posed to national identity from ethnic minorities (rather than appealing to a perceived threat from Islam or a national fascist heritage). However, assessing the appeal of radical right parties on the basis of election results alone can be misleading, especially in the case of the UK, which, like Germany and Sweden, has weak radical right-wing parties but a strong movement sector (Minkenberg, 2013: 9, 22). Moreover, no national political scene is monopolised by a single 'type' of party and many parties demonstrate elements of different types. Thus, the BNP has employed anti-Islam as well as anti-multiculturalist messages in its campaigns while the EDL is a single-issue anti-Islam movement close, ideologically, to parties such as Geert Wilders's Partij voor de Vrijheid.

Thus a focus on electoral parties or on classic ideological strands associated with the far right may fail to identify, or explain the appeal of, emergent movements and more diffuse or complex coalitions of ideological strands of thought. This, it is suggested here, is because such approaches fail to give due attention to either the politics or the passion at the grass roots of such movements. This leads, first, to a limited understanding of the complex intertwining of rational and emotional dimensions of activism. Second, dismissing individuals participating in such movements as blinded by 'fascist' or 'racist' ideology and thereby excluding them from what constitutes the political (through the erection of a *cordon sanitaire*), reduces the emotion and politics of resentment (Ware, 2008) to crude authoritarian populist mobilisation enacted upon a passive (white, working-class) population. Through the focus of this study on individuals active in a movement widely perceived to be 'racist' and/or 'Islamophobic', this book, in contrast, does not elide the agency and choices made by EDL activists whilst, at the same time, seeking to understand them in their full complexity.

What is the English Defence League? The politics of nomenclature

There is conditional consensus in academic literature to date that the EDL is 'not an archetypal far-right party or movement' (Copsey, 2010: 25). For Copsey this is because the EDL 'is not driven by a fascist or neo-fascist ideological end goal', while for Allen (2011: 294), the movement's successful inclusion of 'some Jews, gays and others normally excluded by the far right' is the distinguishing factor. What it 'is', however, remains an object of academic, and political, dispute. Jackson (2011a: 7) recognises that the EDL's self-representation as not traditionally far right, not anti-Semitic and having a multicultural constituency of support and membership is true 'to an extent', but he characterises the movement as '*new* far right' in as much as it has switched the object of demonisation from ethnic minorities (the target of the traditional far right) to Islam or Muslims.

Thus he calls the EDL a social movement with a 'new far right' ideology combining 'ultra-patriotism; a critique of mainstream politics; and an aggressive, anti-Muslim agenda' (2011a: 5). Copsey's (2010: 5) preferred definition is similar; the EDL is an 'Islamophobic new social movement'. Moreover, the identification of the movement as anti-Muslim or Islamophobic allows its differentiating features – the absence of anti-Semitism and homophobia – to be interpreted as strategically deployed rather than genuinely held principles, on the basis that 'enemies' of Islam (Jews and sexual minorities) are 'our' allies. Bartlett, Birdwell and Littler (2011: 29) conclude, rather differently, that the EDL is a 'populist street movement'. In place of an adjectival qualifier characterising the political or ideological nature of the movement, Bartlett, Birdwell and Littler simply note the gap between the EDL's own casting of its objectives in the language of human rights and the assertions by its critics that the group is 'racist' and 'Islamophobic'.

The interpretivist approach – which seeks to know the social world through understanding the meanings actors ascribe to it – underpinning the research conducted for this book would provide epistemological justification for taking a similar position to Bartlett, Birdwell and Littler or, indeed, adopting the self-ascription of the object of study. The political implications of simply accepting the EDL's description of itself as a human rights organisation protesting against radical Islam, however, rule out that option in this case. Rather, the self-understandings of the organisation and its members are treated as objects of critical analysis themselves (see Chapter 2 and Chapters 4–6) and, on the basis of this, the EDL is referred to in this book as an anti-Islamist movement. While not wishing to pre-empt the discussion in those later chapters of the rationale and evidence for, as well as the conditionality of, this characterisation of the movement, it is rooted in two principal judgements. The first is that the EDL is a movement of the 'populist radical right' rather than 'extreme' or 'far' right. This is based on the typological distinction drawn by Mudde (2007: 25) according to which 'populist radical right' characterises parties and movements that are nominally democratic (although oppose some fundamental values of liberal democracy) whilst upholding a core ideology combining nativism, authoritarianism and populism in contrast to movements of the 'extreme right', which are inherently anti-democratic (2007: 31). The argument for this, detailed in Chapters 2 and 8, is that, although sharing with more extreme right movements an ultra-patriotic agenda, and being populist in its claims to promote the concerns of 'ordinary people' against a liberal elite political hegemony, the EDL does not reject the principles of a democratic constitutional state or of fundamental human equality, does not uphold an ideology of racial supremacy and promotes women's and LGBT rights. It reflects, secondly, that amidst wide political and ideological diversity within the movement, frequent slippage between official positions and everyday talk and the conceptual ambiguity and confusion embedded in terms such as 'Islamophobia', the common denominator identifiable among EDL activists in this study is anti-Islamism. This characterisation of the movement is not without precedent (see Quilliam, 2013)[6] and is discussed further in Chapter 5.

'Accepted racism'? Islamophobia, racism and 'race'

For many, not applying the descriptor 'racist' or 'Islamophobic' to the EDL will appear a political misjudgement. It is done, however, in the knowledge that viewing racism as exceptional – the expression solely of the 'extreme right' – risks reinforcing 'the status quo of exonerated, guiltless institutional forms and responsible individuals' (Goldberg, 2006: 353) and making racism 'the problem of the ignorant working class' (Lentin, 2008: 500). Racism is not the property of extremist groups or misguided individuals but of us all. That racism remains a defining dimension of social relations is self-evident. The issue of contention is how racism, or more accurately the political struggle against racism, relates to the notion of 'race'. The fact that 'race' is socially constructed – bereft of any sustainable biological foundation – is well established and has led to the recognition that the social phenomenon we are dealing with is not different 'races' but 'the *racialization* of different "groups" that are culturally, socially and historically constituted' (St Louis, 2002: 652). At the same time, 'race' continues to have a '*social materiality*, "real" or "imagined"' (2002: 653) as well as the capacity to order social relations through its social product, that is, racism. In this sense the terminology of 'race' 'is an inescapable predicate for the discussion of anti-racist and post-racial possibilities' (2002: 654) as well as a politically powerful way to speak loudly how racialisation continues to impact on real lives. The danger is that, by holding on to 'race', we allow it to take on a reified status (Nayak, 2006: 414), grossly reduce the complexity of individual and collective identities and hinder movement towards a political future not constrained by 'race'. Since the reproduction of 'race' is a prerequisite for racism, arguably the first step towards a more progressive politics, capable of not only fighting but dismantling racisms, might be the excising of the discourse of 'race' (Paul, 2014: 704). These arguments for and against a conscious renunciation of 'race' are returned to in Chapter 4.

The connection between racism and Islamophobia is, according to Garner and Selod (2015: 11), already 'definitively made'. 'Islamophobia' can be operationalised to understand 'a set of ideas and practices that amalgamate all Muslims into one group and the characteristics associated with Muslims (violence, misogyny, political allegiance/disloyalty, incompatibility with Western values, etc.) are treated as if they are innate' (2015: 13). Thus Islamophobia constitutes a form of racialisation (Vakil, 2010: 276; Klug, 2012: 675). Both the robustness of Islamophobia as a concept and its connection to racism and anti-Muslimism (Halliday, 1999) are central to understanding and evaluating claims by EDL activists that they are 'not racist', and this is discussed in detail in Chapter 5. Here it is noted simply that the use of the term 'phobia' (denoting an individual pathology) risks presenting anti-Islam or anti-Muslim sentiments as individual and psychological rather than social, structural or systemic (Garner and Selod, 2015: 13), generating the same effect as in the dismissal of racism as an 'exception' noted above. However, for now the term is employed as if unproblematic in order to contextualise EDL activism within a wider rise in Islamophobia in the UK.

Islam is an established part of society and culture. Census data (2011) for the population of England and Wales show that 2.7 million people (4.8 per cent) identify themselves as Muslims,[7] making it the second largest religious identification and Islam the fastest-growing religion (Jivraj, 2013: 16). This mirrors the wider European picture; around 5 per cent of 425 million EU inhabitants are Muslim (Helbling, 2012: 2). However, the intense political, media and police scrutiny of Muslims has also become an established part of society, marking Muslims out as distinct from the larger political, social and cultural landscape, whilst simultaneously homogenising them in 'a single category or "community" defined solely through faith, which is itself a shorthand for a range of pathologies' (Alexander, 2013: 3). This, it is argued, has meant that 'Islamophobia has somehow become a kind of "accepted racism"' (Hafez, 2014: 479).

Islamophobia in the UK appears to be widespread and increasing. A meta-analysis of the findings of 64 opinion polls (2007–10) on attitudes toward Muslims suggests that Islamophobia is by far the most pervasive form of religious prejudice in Britain and is higher than it was in 2001–06 (Field, 2012: 158). According to Field, depending on the specific question asked, between one-fifth and three-quarters of the UK population hold anti-Muslim or anti-Islam attitudes. One explanation for these perceptions is that they are driven by the impact of 9/11 and other terrorist attacks, or more specifically, by subsequent media debates and policy responses. While there is clear evidence of an immediate rise in anti-Muslim and anti-Islam sentiments following major events (Strabac and Listhaug, 2008: 274), a series of studies suggest that, across Europe, attitudes and policies show more continuity than radical break, pre- and post-9/11 and that thus 9/11 had an immediate but short-lived impact on public attitudes to Muslim migrants (Helbling, 2012: 12). Another explanation might be that the growth in the Muslim population leads to growing hostility, not least in times of economic crisis. While, at country level the evidence does not support a general correlation between size of Muslim population and anti-Muslim prejudice (Strabac and Listhaug, 2008: 268), within-country differences may be obscured in nationally representative survey samples; in the UK, for example, relative density of Muslim populations varies significantly across localities with a number of urban centres having Muslim populations of 20 per cent and localities with the highest densities standing at 35 per cent (Jivraj, 2013). This has led to suggestions – most notably in the Cantle report (2001), which followed the inquiry into civil unrest that took place in some northern English towns – that Muslim communities have a tendency to lead 'separate' or 'parallel' lives (Meer and Modood, 2014: 659). This argument underpins much of subsequent government policy designed to increase 'social cohesion'. However, the 2011 census shows that the Muslim population is relatively evenly spread through England and Wales; in 2011, the Index of Dissimilarity was 54 per cent,[8] a decrease in the separation factor by two percentage points since 2001 (Jivraj, 2013: 17–18). Moreover, the fact that Muslims tend to live in areas that are diverse in terms of ethnicity and religion – Muslims live in areas where on average there are only 15 per cent Muslims – undermines claims of a tendency to self-segregation.

At the level of identity, empirical data also show that Muslim communities are well integrated on indicators measuring support for democracy (trust and efficacy) and sense of belonging to Britain (Sobolewska, 2010: 41). Citizenship Survey data show that levels of trust in British political institutions among Muslims are similar to, or higher than, those of non-Muslims (Bleich and Maxwell, 2012: 48). Notwithstanding the fact that Muslim respondents are most likely to claim that religion is an important, or the most important, part of their identity, these data also indicate that their levels of positive British identification are similar to, if not higher than, those of non-Muslims and the overall population (2012: 47–48). Heath and Demireva (2014: 171) also find, on the basis of the analysis of the 2010 Ethnic Minority British Election Survey (EMBES), high levels of British identity even in the first generation of ethnic minority groups and that the second generation is markedly more likely to feel British than the first generation (up by 25 percentage points). Those least likely to feel British, moreover, are not ethnic groups of Muslim faith but those of black Caribbean heritage (2014: 172). While this survey suggests that people of Pakistani and Bangladeshi background show the highest level of concern about intermarriage with a white person, they are no more inclined to reject integration into British society, to reject a British identity or to contemplate violent protest than are other ethno-religious groups (2014: 172–76).While Sobolewska (2010: 43) does identify a greater sense of alienation, exclusion and disaffection among young British-born Muslims than among their immigrant counterparts, this appears to be explained primarily by age; when Muslims under the age of 35 are compared with other (mostly white British) young people, the difference in the level of political alienation almost completely disappears. These results run directly counter to fears about Muslim alienation from the mainstream national community in Britain. Indeed, according to Clarke and Garner (2010: 203) it is not ethnic minority groups but the white English who are increasingly withdrawing from Britishness and retreating into a defensive space of Englishness.

This retreat by the white working class should be seen in the context of a series of backlashes against multicultural politics that have taken place in the UK in recent decades (Hewitt, 2005). It is accompanied by growing calls by, or on behalf of, them for recognition of the impacts of wider structural change on white working-class communities, which have experienced decreasing wages, reduced employment opportunities and declining social mobility for their children over the last three decades (Kenny, 2012; Lone and Silver, 2014: 178). White working-class resentment is cited as an explanation for racist or anti-social attitudes and represented as an unfortunate but inevitable outcome of inequality and injustice frequently related to the proclaimed failure of multiculturalism (Ware, 2008: 2). This is often expressed in the construction of economic migrants, refugees and asylum seekers as the undeserving beneficiaries of social resources who claim and receive welfare entitlements at the expense of majority ('indigenous') populations. A perception that such institutions favour immigrants over the majority population widens the opportunities for populist parties to propose simple messages that resonate with anxieties, thereby creating further tensions in the community (Lone and Silver, 2014: 181). The construction of immigrant, ethnic minority or Muslim communities as 'undeserving' beneficiaries of government resources has been shown to be central to the appeal of, and support for, the BNP in a number of local contexts (see Rhodes, 2010; Goodwin, 2011a; Ashe, 2012; Lone and Silver, 2014), and as Busher (2013: 72) suggests, the views of EDL activists can be broadly situated within this tradition of backlashes to multiculturalism. In constructing racialised 'others' as undeserving, white working-class communities are framed as excluded, discriminated and treated as 'second class', invoking notions of injustice and 'unfairness' (Ware, 2008; Rhodes, 2010). While this may constitute a well-intentioned attempt to 'put a face on' contemporary inequality, the very notion of a distinct social group of 'white working class' courts the danger of reframing disadvantage as ethnic identity (and thus obscuring class inequality) (Bottero, 2009: 14). In Chapter 6 these debates are returned to in order to evaluate arguments that at least some of the demands by, or on behalf of, sections of the white working class from which the EDL draws its support 'merit a more sympathetic hearing by the state' (Kenny, 2012: 24) against those who argue that such resentments distort the notion of fairness since they are articulated in contexts in which whiteness has historically conferred a guarantee of belonging and entitlement (Ware, 2008: 12) and are premised on assumptions of racially based inequality in which the natural order is one in which 'we', not 'they', are prioritised (Rhodes, 2009).

Transforming emotion into action: social movements and the 'far right'

This book proposes to understand the EDL through the prism of social movement studies. This is not without its challenges since empirical studies in this field tend to focus on progressive (and largely peaceful) forms of protest and evade engagement with more difficult far right and religious fundamentalist groups (Della Porta, 2008: 223) or 'distasteful' movements (Esseveld and Eyerman, 1992: 218). But it is not without precedent. Klandermans and Mayer (2006: 6–7), in their multi-country study of right-wing extremist activism, start from the premise that right-wing extremist organisations might be seen as 'a social movement obeying the same dynamics as any other social movement' and that activism in such movements 'is as equally rational as in any other movement or organization'. Moreover, as noted above, both Jackson (2011a: 7) and Copsey (2010: 5) have used the term 'social movement' to describe the EDL, and the notion of 'framing',[9] central to social movement theory, has been used to understand the relationship between ideology and collective action in both the BNP (Goodwin, 2011a: 157–70) and the EDL (Jackson, 2011a: 18).

What is novel about the approach taken in this study is twofold. First, it takes as its object of study the activism of individual grassroots supporters rather than the EDL as an organisation or movement. This forefronts agency significantly more than the notion of 'framing', which, although recognising the importance of the way in which individuals see the world, remains deeply embedded in the structuralist paradigm of political process theory which posits not social move-ment actors but the external environment (the state and its political institutions) as key factors in determining mobilisation (Edwards, 2014: 93). In contrast, this study starts from Castells's (2012: 12) argument that social movements are 'made of indi-viduals'. Second, the study conducted for this book is concerned with individuals not for what their socio-demographic profile tells us about the constituency of, and potential for, support for such movements but because the meanings attached by individuals to their activism are crucial to understanding contemporary social movements. The approach taken here builds on a recent re-engagement within the field of social movement studies with the affective dimension of activism; an approach that no longer sees emotions as necessarily opposed to rationality. Thus, the second theoretical starting point of the study is that 'social movements are emotional movements' (2012: 13) in as much as protest starts not with a pro-gramme or political strategy but with 'the transformation of emotion into action'.

While more theoretical discussion of emotion and 'affect' in social movements is undertaken in Chapter 7, here we consider briefly what and how emotion is transformed into action. Castells (2012) sees fear (a negative affect) and enthusi-asm (a positive affect) as the emotions of primary importance to social movement action. The process of the transformation of the former into the latter takes a number of stages in which other key emotions are evoked. The process starts with individual feelings of humiliation, exploitation, being ignored or misrepresented or anxieties and fear of external threats over which individuals feel they have no control. While anxiety and fear on their own have a paralysing effect on action, they can be overcome if transformed into anger, usually through the perception of an unjust action and the identification of the agent responsible for it. Anger, he argues, is neurologically associated with risk-taking behaviour and thus facilitates participation in collective action. It is through the expression of anger in net-worked social movements, and the 'togetherness' they generate, that individuals' fears are turned into outrage and outrage into hope (2012: 2–3, 14–15). Once the individual overcomes fear, positive emotions take over, as enthusiasm activates action and hope anticipates the rewards for the risky action.

Castells's somewhat idealistic view of this process may emanate from the par-ticular movements that form the focus of his study and is not a model that can be applied directly to the case of the EDL. There is also a good deal of slippage in the kinds of emotions he refers to and between individual feelings, their social expres-sion as emotions and the experience of 'affect' (see Chapter 7). Collins under-stands the process of how emotions are turned into action as one of the 'emotional dynamics' of social movements (Collins, R., 2001: 27). Drawing on Durkheim's concepts of collective ritual and 'collective effervescence', he argues that the success or failure of collective mobilisation is dictated by the degree of 'emo-tional transformation' that takes place as a result of collective rituals. Emotional transformations are of two kinds. They may amplify the original emotion, for example making an initial moral outrage stronger through becoming the object of collective focus. Alternatively, they may transform the initiating emotion into something else; an 'emotional energy' which arises out of the consciousness of being bound up within a collective focus of attention and fuelling a sense of solidarity. More emotional energy produces greater solidarity and thus likelihood of successful mobilisation of a movement (2001: 29).

However, emotions do not always produce positive 'affective solidarity' (Juris, 2008: 66). Protests are subject to ebbs and flows of emotion and protesters are often disappointed when protests fail to generate anticipated levels of emotional intensity (2008). Emotions and relationships can also be destructive; frustration, jealousy, envy, disgust and hatred can pull groups apart (Klatch, 2004: 489). Moreover, Collins's claim that understanding the levels of emotional energy generated allows us to predict whether movements will succeed or fail attaches too much weight to agency and emotions. It is argued in this book that, in the case of the EDL, while activism generates high levels of emotional energy, the degree to which emotional transformation is possible is tightly constrained by structural factors, especially the relationship of the movement with the external political realm. If societies are mechanisms for the distribution of hope (Hage, 2003: 3, cited in Ware, 2008: 9), disconnection from society means dispossession of hope. Thus, in the case of the EDL, while individual anxieties, through togetherness, are transformed into outrage or anger, the subsequent translation of outrage into 'hope' through activism in the movement is not accomplished.

Individuals in focus: the research design

This study of the EDL was undertaken as part of the MYPLACE (Memory, Youth, Political Legacy and Civic Engagement) project.[10] It was one of forty-four ethnographic case studies conducted in fourteen European countries designed to explore the meanings attached to activism among young people engaged in organisations and movements ranging from student self-organisation and youth sections of political parties through anarchist and Occupy groups to radical right-wing movements. While the youthful profile of the EDL was a key motivating factor for selecting it as a case study, this study is not restricted to *youth* activism. Although recruitment to the survey and interview elements of the MYPLACE project was strictly confined to the target group of 16–25 year olds, this was relaxed for ethnographic studies due to the importance of older gatekeepers or authority figures in accessing and understanding the groups researched. Thus, while there is an 'oversampling' of young people in this study, respondents ranged in age from 15 to 49 years (see Chapter 3).

Ethnographic case studies were employed, in the wider research design, to elucidate the meanings attached to activism by those actively engaged in movements or organisations. It follows that the object of analysis was the individual, not the organisation or the ideology of the movement. While the importance of hearing individual voices in the context of the ideological traditions of movements in which they are expressed (Billig, 1978: 9) is acknowledged, given the contemporary state of scholarship on the 'far right' – which focuses on the study of party and organisational ideologies, while individuals feature primarily in terms of the socio-demographic constitution of 'supporters' of such movements – the approach adopted here was to forefront individual activists and understand members of such organisations 'as individuals with real lives' (Ezekiel, 1995: xxxv). The politics and ethics of researching 'distasteful' groups in such a 'close up' way is complex and contentious; a thorough discussion of these issues is undertaken in the following chapter.

Conclusion

Understandings of, and responses to, movements such as the EDL, while on the surface politically charged, in practice may be politically complacent. The UK has often felt itself comfortably immune from political challenges from the far right, seeing the polity as protected by a weak fascist political heritage and a first-past-the-post political system. Placing a movement such as the EDL on the extreme right and seeking to understand its activism through the paradigm of far right studies allows it to be dismissed politically, as well as condemned morally. However, base levels of xenophobia and anti-immigrant prejudice in the UK are similar to those in most western European countries, suggesting that the same reservoir of support for the populist radical right exists in the UK as elsewhere in Europe. Moreover, having more in common with populist radical right than classic 'far right' movements (Mudde, 2007: 25), the EDL presents a new challenge to politics in the UK in as much as the attitudes and views articulated constitute a radical variant of views found in wider society rather than 'a "normal pathology" unconnected to the mainstream' (2007: 297).

This book takes the EDL seriously, academically and politically. In Chapter 1, it sets out the rationale for conducting ethnographic research with movements of the far right and in Chapter 2 gives an overview of the origins, trajectory and structure of the EDL as an organisation. In Chapter 3 it introduces the activists participating in the study, setting their participation in the EDL within whole lives and considering their personal trajectories in and out of activism. In Chapter 4 claims to non-racism by activists are critically explored. Since key arguments underpinning such claims are that 'a religion is not a race' and that the EDL is anti-(militant) Islam not anti-Muslims, Chapter 5 analyses in detail attitudes to Islam and Muslims among grassroots activists. The analysis in these two chapters is set in the context of theoretical debates about 'race', racism and post-racialism as well as whether Islamophobia should be seen as a distinct phenomenon or the latest manifestation of 'new' or 'cultural' racism. Chapter 6 turns the gaze away from the Muslim 'other' and towards EDL activists' construction of 'self' as devalued and discriminated white working class in the narrative of 'second-class citizens'. In Chapter 7 the emotional and affective dimensions of EDL activism are explored through the pleasures of the 'demo buzz' and the ontological security generated by relationships formed in the EDL 'family' whilst recognising the intimate connection between emotion, affect and *meanings* attached to activism at the cognitive level. This, it is suggested, is epitomised in the understanding of EDL activism as standing 'loud and proud' in an emotional expression of the rational demand to 'be heard'.

Notes

1 The terms 'extreme', 'far', 'radical' and 'populist' are often used interchangeably to refer to that part of the political spectrum that rejects wholly, or in part, hegemonic notions of liberal democracy. In this book, when citing published literature, the terms used in the original works are retained. I refer to the English Defence League as 'populist radical right' rather than 'extreme' or 'far' right based on the typological distinction drawn by Mudde (2007: 25) discussed below.

2 Those included in the UK case are the British National Party, the National Front and the Democratic Unionist Party.

3 The British National Party (BNP), founded in 1982 as an outcome of one of the splits in the National Front, has had more success than any other party of the far right in Britain, winning 6.2 per cent of the vote (although no parliamentary representation) in the 2010 General Election (Goodwin, 2011a).

4 Respondents are classified as 'xenophobic' if they include one or more of the categories 'Muslims', 'immigrants' or 'people of a different race' among those they say they would not like to have as neighbours.

5 This figure is based on EVS data for 1999–2000 using the proportion of respondents naming 'immigrants' as people they would not like to have as neighbours.

6 Quilliam (2013) describes the EDL as an 'anti-Islamist group'.

7 This question on religious affiliation is voluntary and has been included only since the 2011 census. Its introduction was advocated by the Muslim Council of Britain with the aim of facilitating policies to tackle inequalities experienced by Muslims (Meer and Modood, 2014: 12).

8 The degree of residential separation measured using the Index of Dissimilarity compares the percentage of a group's total population in England and Wales that lives in a local authority with the percentage of the rest of the population living in that same local authority. The absolute differences in percentage are added up across the 348 LAs of England and Wales, and then halved so that the Index is between 0 and 100 (Jivraj, 2013: 18).

9 'Framing' is a concept drawn from Goffman's understanding of the way in which experience is ordered and constructed to render it knowable (Edwards, 2014: 93).

10 The research was funded under the European Union Seventh Framework Programme (Grant Agreement number FP7-266831). The project employed a mixed method (survey, interviews, ethnographies) and case-study approach to map the relationship between political heritage, current levels and forms of civic and political engagement of young people in Europe, and their potential receptivity to radical and populist political agendas. The project coordinator was Hilary Pilkington.

1

The contagion of stigma: the ethics and politics of research with the 'far right'

Reading the American literature on the extreme Right, it is impossible not to acknowledge the tone of universal disapproval. The conviction prevails that there is something 'weird' or 'alien' about the extremist. (Fielding, 1981: 15)

Fielding attributes this disapproving tone to lack of sympathy towards members of far right groups rooted in the 'clash between a positivist and a Verstehen methodology' (1981: 16). Three decades on, interpretivist approaches are well established in the social sciences and yet the same tone prevails. This suggests that there are more than methodological issues at stake. As Blee (2007: 121) puts it, few academics '*want* to invest the considerable time or to establish the rapport necessary for close-up studies of those they regard as inexplicable and repugnant, in addition to dangerous and difficult' (my emphasis). The problem is rather one of how to study social movements which are 'distasteful', that is 'those individuals and groups with whom the researcher shares neither political orientation nor way of life and whose politics and/or way of life are found objectionable' (Esseveld and Eyerman, 1992: 217). Of course such movements are not only of the far right; substance users, sex workers or criminal gangs might be included among those with a distasteful 'way of life'. However, while there is an extensive literature on the latter, sustained engagement with far right activists for the purposes of academic study remains rare (exceptions include: Billig, 1978; Fielding, 1981; Ezekiel, 1995, 2002; Blee, 2002; Simi and Futrell, 2010; Pilkington, Omel'chenko and Garifzianova, 2010; di Nunzio and Toscano, 2014).

One way of managing close-up research with distasteful groups has been for researchers to distance themselves from those researched either through the adoption of theoretical frameworks that pathologise those studied or of research techniques – through the use of autobiographies, self-complete questionnaires or analysis of secondary material – that keep researchers' hands clean (Esseveld and Eyerman, 1992: 218). In studies of the far right this has been accomplished most recently through studies of how such groups use the Internet and digital media to recruit followers and disseminate ideas (see Back, Keith and Solomos, 1998; Atton, 2006; Bartlett, Birdwell and Littler, 2011; Jackson and Gable, 2011; Simpson and

Druxes (eds), 2015). Such studies allow covert research and thus minimise the 'contagion of stigma' (Kirby and Corzine, 1981) through personal contact.

In this chapter I make a case for conducting 'close up' research with groups perceived as far right notwithstanding the difficulties that this presents to both researchers and audiences. The argument has three components. First, there is no methodological obstacle to such research; the experience of access, formation and management of relations with respondents in this study demonstrates that it is possible to develop the quality of relations necessary to do meaningful ethnographic research with distasteful groups. Second, to generate such relations does not require unacceptable epistemological (claiming an 'objective' position) or ethical (feigning sympathy) compromise. Respondents accept that research can be undertaken in the interests of understanding how they make sense of the world regardless of the researcher's own political alignment. Sustained engagement is the crucial factor here; it generates confidence from both sides and renders the relationships increasingly able to withstand challenge and debate. Finally, if the first two contentions are confirmed, then what constrains us is not a lack of fit between the values of researchers and researched but an institutionalised distaste for close-up research with the far right. This is compounded by pressure to forefront, and make explicit, political intention in research practice in a way that threatens to place subjects with whose political views we do not agree 'out of bounds' (Esseveld and Eyerman, 1992: 15). The 'contagion of stigma' – whereby moral condemnation is attached to the research or researchers through a process of 'guilt by association' (1992: 4) – constrains the space for ethnographic research with far right groups and thus, it is argued here, our knowledge, understanding and capacity for changing the social world.

Listening to the EDL: collecting and analysing data

'Close up' research for this study was conducted over more than three years (April 2012–July 2015). Observation was carried out during participation in a range of EDL events: demonstrations, divisional meetings, informal social occasions and the Crown Court trial of two respondents (see Appendix 1 for details). Notes from observations and interviews together with summaries of any particular events or significant informal communication between events were recorded in a field diary. This field diary – 136,000 words long and divided into 65 individual diary entries – was anonymised before being coded alongside interview transcripts.

A total of twenty demonstrations were attended of which fourteen were national demonstrations,[1] two were local and four were 'flash' demonstrations. National demonstrations were viewed by many respondents as 'a good day out' and travel to and from them, usually by hired coach, afforded the opportunity to observe social interactions as well as a wide range of cultural practices (around alcohol, drugs, food and money) and to chat about everyday life. Time spent in the pub designated for EDL demonstrators to gather prior to the march allowed me to experience the 'build-up' to the demonstration and some of its affective dimension described in Chapter 7. Local demonstrations were rarely attended by respondents (outside their own area), although the documentary film *Loud and proud: listening to the EDL*[2] made as part of the study was filmed primarily at one such event. 'Flash' demonstrations were relatively infrequent and, since they were not pre-arranged with the police, communication about them was exclusively by mobile phone; venue and time were disseminated usually only hours in advance. The leaking of information, or an unpredicted change of circumstances, meant that, on two occasions, the planned 'flash' did not go ahead. Some key informants did not attend flash demonstrations on principle because they disapproved of this kind of 'direct action', although all the flash events at which I was present were non-violent.

Divisional meetings were infrequent, partially due to the temporary loss of an 'HQ' where the meetings could be held. HQs were pubs where sympathetic owners allowed the EDL to use the function room for the meeting. HQs were also used as meeting points before or after demonstrations; in some cases the pub would open especially for the EDL (including outside normal licensing hours). Because of this, and in order to protect the owners of the pub from threats or aggression from opposition movements, members were warned not to use the name of the pub in communications. Divisional meetings were not only infrequent but often insubstantial. However, they did allow an opportunity to meet and chat to people in-between demonstrations and to arrange interviews. Towards the end of the research, more substantial regional 'meet and greet' events were attended as well as a planning meeting between EDL leaders and police contacts ahead of a national demonstration. Observation was also carried out over four days of the Crown Court trial of two EDL members prosecuted for 'violent disorder' at an EDL demonstration. I was present also at a number of EDL social occasions and met individual respondents socially in their homes or in pubs especially during a lengthy period of withdrawing from the field.

Individuals were approached for interview either following contact with them at demonstrations or after an initial approach by a key informant. A total of thirty-one interviews – twenty-six audio, five video – were conducted in a range of venues, including: respondents' homes; the divisional 'HQ' or other pub; fast-food restaurants and supermarket cafes; and a public park. The interviews were conducted as conversations and thus varied significantly, although the employment of a common interview scenario ensured the inclusion, at some point in the conversation, of questions relating to six broad themes. These were: how the respondent became involved, and how they now participated, in the movement; views on the EDL as an organisation (structure, ideology); experiences of participation and activism; the role of activism in wider life; sources and transmission of political values (family, peers, inspirational figures); and views on wider society and the political system. Interviews lasted, on average, just over 90 minutes and both audio and video interviews were recorded and transcribed.

This study was designed as a classic face-to-face ethnography. However, online spaces were incorporated into the study as another site of everyday practice, communication, self-presentation and bonding of respondents (Hallet and

Barber, 2014: 309). Virtual spaces of EDL interaction were engaged with for communication and observation purposes only. Thus, I responded positively to 'friend requests' (if the person was known to me or verified by key informants) and communicated with individuals via private 'inbox' messages. I never posted to EDL divisional or members' personal pages (or even to my own personal page) and never engaged in discussion in these shared spaces. I accepted no non-EDL friend requests to the page in order to draw clear online boundaries between personal and professional life but also to ensure the anonymity of respondents, agreed as part of the informed-consent process. Accepting and making 'friend' requests allowed respondents to see with whom I was already in contact and thus build trust and openness.

Newsfeeds from 'friends' generated important contextual information about current issues of concern as well as changes in 'status' and personal events in respondents' lives. This was an important mechanism for keeping in touch between physical meetings and provided insight into the creation of community through the sharing of materials, responses to them and support of those experiencing difficulties. The systematic analysis of the huge amount of text and images generated from these virtual spaces is beyond the scope of this book. Of particular interest for future study might be the 'call and response' mode of much online engagement that often ratchets up tension not only between EDL supporters and 'trolls' but also between EDL activists. The petty but divisive squabbles generated in online spaces would simply have got 'sorted' had the contact been face to face (see Chapter 2).

A total of 593 still photos and 130 video clips were taken during the research and some of this visual data was included in documentary film or in the data set for analysis. Images in this book were taken by the author unless otherwise stated. Photos and video links were provided also by respondents. Other textual materials gathered included: leaflets produced by local EDL divisions; police flyers detailing demonstration regulations; flyers produced by counter-demonstrators; and a large number of media (mainstream and EDL oppositional) reports and posts on EDL-related issues.

Interviews and diary entries were transcribed and anonymised so that all key respondents (thirty-nine in total)[3] were referred to by assigned pseudonyms (used throughout this book), while the names of any other group members or family and friends mentioned by respondents were removed. References to place names (including names of schools, pubs, districts) that might make an individual identifiable were also deleted. The only real names given are for individuals in the movement who held openly public positions, that is, the leadership and inner circle who appeared with their real names (or own chosen names) on the website and at demonstrations. In cases where individuals were encountered (and assigned pseudonyms) as respondents but later became public figures within the movement, they are referred to by pseudonym in relation to information provided in their capacity as informant while material taken from the Internet or speeches at demonstrations, where they appeared as public figures, is referenced using their real names.

Data were analysed using Nvivo 9.2 software following a set of common principles designed for the larger MYPLACE project (Pilkington, forthcoming). This involved the use, initially, of a two-level thematic coding strategy: data were coded to over a thousand Level 1 (child) nodes grouped under thirty-eight Level 2 (parent) nodes. A number of theoretically informed 'themes' were generated following this initial coding and these 'themes' or 'metaphors' structure the empirical analyses underpinning Chapters 2–8 of this book.

Making friends with the EDL (and other unspeakable acts): access, trust and relationships in contentious research

On 1 September 2012, the EDL conducted a legally sanctioned demonstration in Walthamstow, East London. It was roundly declared by demonstrators to be 'the worst demo ever'. As they marched they were on the receiving end of a barrage of eggs thrown by counter-demonstrators who also occupied the designated space for speeches by EDL leaders, thereby preventing them from taking place. EDL supporters were kept within a tight police containment cordon from approximately 12.30 p.m. to 10 p.m. on a hot day without access to toilets, water or food. As night fell, they were arrested two-by-two under Section 60 of the Criminal Justice Act (breach of peace), regardless of whether individuals had participated in any public order offence.[4] Walthamstow was just the third demonstration I had travelled to with the EDL. It was my first weekend off intensive radiotherapy treatment and it proved to be a long and tough day. Its final stages are described in this excerpt from a much longer diary entry (see Box 1).

I start with this diary excerpt not because being designated 'one of the boys' is a badge of honour or marker of the acquisition of the trust needed to undertake ethnographic research. As discussed below, being 'accepted' by research subjects when those subjects are 'distasteful' is accompanied more often by a sense of guilt than of professional achievement. The story starts here because it captures the moment when the research *became* ethnographic. Ethnography demands neither sympathy nor empathy with those being researched, but it cannot be conducted without emotional engagement. Sharing feelings of nervousness and frustration, expressing anger and relief and experiencing the 'affect' of collective arrest signalled the start of the ethnographic process.

Access: time tells

Research with the far right, it is claimed, is fraught with difficulties of 'access', 'hostility' and mutual 'fear'; groups tend to regard academics as untrustworthy or hostile and seek to prevent entry to their groups or access to members (Blee, 2002: 14–17). In this research, access proved less problematic than anticipated. Approval by a Regional and a Division Level Organiser – both of whom were prepared to 'vouch for' me – generated wider acceptance. Of course the 'far right' covers a wide spectrum and the relative lack of hostility encountered in this case

Box 1: Feeling the affect ... Walthamstow, 1 September 2012

We are being processed very slowly still. Eventually – sometime after 9 p.m. – they open up a second exit point to process from and things speed up. When we finally get to the front of the queue there are no women police officers so we wait while about 20 blokes go ahead of us. We say we don't mind being searched by a male officer but we are told that would be 'wrong'. I point out it would be less a violation of rights than that endured over the last few hours. The police officer smiles wryly. About 9.30 p.m. we are finally 'processed'. The police officer tries to engage me in the eye and read me my rights. I am furious. An irrational response – the officer is just doing her job – but it positions me as somebody who has done something criminal and I resent that. I reach into my bag – I want to show her the project information sheet so she knows that I am there as an observer – and she clearly interprets this as a move to get some weapon and she starts to pull at my hands. Two male officers immediately move in and grab my arm. My anger and sense of injustice is rising and I start to understand why so many people are charged with resisting arrest. ... I manage to contain the anger and explain the research story. The woman officer offers to give me a copy of the arrest note and the name of the commander in charge to make a formal complaint. I am then told I need to get on the bus ... We will have to get the train back. ... The journey to Victoria seems to take forever. ... Eventually we are let off. It is almost 10 p.m. We have been without access to food, water and toilets now for nine and a half hours. ... Once on the train we buy a couple of half bottles of wine from the buffet car and sit together and begin to laugh about the day. This has a strong bonding effect. We discuss the rights and wrongs of leaving Richard, [names other EDL member] and Rachel; they had asked us to wait and go with them on a train at 1 a.m. [because it would be cheaper] ... The four of us have family to get back to though and we show each other photos of our kids on our phones. I remember that Jack always takes a present back for his daughter. ... He hasn't managed to this time ... When they get off at [names neighbouring city], Jack gives me a big hug and says 'You're one of the boys now'. (Field diary, 1 September 2012)

may say more about the EDL as a movement than about my research practice. Moreover, openness and lack of hostility are not necessarily benign; motivations for participation may be instrumental (see below).

My access to the field was facilitated by the personal contacts of another researcher through whom an initial meeting with a potential gatekeeper was arranged and who attended some observed events and interviews (April–July 2012).[5] The first meeting with the gatekeeper was approved by her Regional Organiser (RO), after which we were invited to attend demonstrations and local division meetings. Thus, reflecting the flat structure of the organisation and relative autonomy of divisions (see Chapter 2), there was no formal process of authorisation of the research at national level. The flip side of this was that access was not a single moment but required repeated negotiation and affirmation. The original gatekeeper, who had promised to ensure introductions to relevant people at the first demonstration, did not attend the demo and, soon afterwards, 'stepped back' from the movement altogether. This had consequences. Without the anticipated introductions, some supporters on the coach raised concerns with a Divisional Organiser about the presence of 'reporters' taking photos. The situation was defused by sitting down with the divisional leader and showing him the photos taken; the word then went around that the material being collected was not harmful (field diary, 14 July 2012).

Members of stigmatised groups show a heightened sensitivity to any potential threat to the group and often react protectively when asked to participate in research (Crowley, 2007: 607). The fear that research might lead to the public denigration of the group can lead potential respondents to subject the researcher to extensive checking out to ascertain whether he or she might be open (or hostile) to their cause before agreeing to (or rejecting) the request to participate (2007). While I have no doubt that respondents routinely 'googled' me, this verification process in my case was non-threatening and often good-humoured. At one divisional meeting, I was, unexpectedly, asked to explain plans to make a video documentary at a local demo. Introducing me to the group, the Divisional Organisers joked that they had checked me out and that I was 'not UAF' (Unite Against Fascism) (field diary, 19 October 2012).[6] Indeed, this was a practice that I encouraged. I opened a Facebook account in my real name and with a genuine profile and when inviting people to be interviewed I suggested they talk first to their Divisional Organisers or any common Facebook friends. This followed the internal group practice of 'vouching' for people. On only one occasion was there any covert attempt to check me out. This followed a conversation with a group of youth division members from another city whilst attending the EDL/NWI Manchester demonstration. We swopped phone numbers and subsequently agreed to meet up in their home city for an interview. On the night before the scheduled interview, I received a text from one of the group saying he had been told by other members not to talk to me because 'It safety as we had many do before and turned out UAF'[7] (field diary, 8 March 2013). A little later I received a call to my mobile phone from a woman asking if I wrote books; clearly some kind of 'test'. Logging on to Facebook, I saw a local youth division leader, Connor, had intervened and posted a message saying, 'The [names city] youth who are meeting that women tomorrow … she's doing research on why EDL youth want to get involved within things like the EDL' followed by a series of posts in which Connor and Chris stated that they had been 'working with her … for the last year' and confirming 'she's no informer or nuffin trust lads' (Facebook communication recorded in field diary, 8 March 2013).

The interview did not happen but I learned from the process that the most crucial aspect of gaining and maintaining trust was simply time. The longer I was around, and had not, as some feared, exposed individuals or the movement to the media, the more people trusted that this was not my agenda. Thus, by the time I arranged to interview a local RO in October 2013, he laughed that he had not needed to ask permission from national leadership to talk to me since I had 'been to fucking more demos than most fucking members I got' (Ed).

Consent: what am I agreeing to?

This research was conducted overtly. I introduced myself to people as a researcher interested in understanding why people became involved with the EDL as part of a wider project about youth activism in Europe. I made it clear that I was not a journalist and sought a sustained engagement with the group in order to understand grassroots members' perspectives. Of course this raises myriad questions about honesty, instrumentality, positionality and politics, which are discussed below. But there are also practical challenges to sustaining a completely overt stance. The 'mass' nature of some observed events meant that not all individuals, for example members of other divisions encountered at demonstrations, were aware of my status. These situations were handled on a case-by-case basis guided by a principle of not lying. I never used a cover story or pretended to be a member of the EDL and I did not elicit information from demonstrators if they did not know I was a researcher. If the conversation was sustained, I looked for a natural opportunity to explain my own reason for being at the demonstration. Sometimes this elicited interest and dialogue; in other cases it closed down the discussion (field diary, 2 March 2013).

Such situations demonstrate the inadequacy of formal ethical procedures for ensuring informed consent in ethnographic research. In this study, an information sheet and written consent form were used with all respondents engaging in interviews. In no case did a respondent refuse the request to sign a consent form and, since the researcher was well known to them, they were able to raise additional questions and concerns afterwards (via Facebook or text messages). However, while signed consent forms provide an institution-friendly paper trail, they are of little help in the day-to-day business of ethnography for either researchers or respondents. They work on the principle that they empower respondents to act in their own best interest and presume that this will be dictated by rational desires to minimise harm to themselves from engagement with the research. However, this is not always the case. When respondents were asked if they consented to photographs of them being used and, if so, whether they should be pixelated prior to use, for example, they responded in almost all cases with bravado. A typical comment was that since their faces were already all over the Internet as a result of police, media and other video footage taken at demonstrations, they had 'nothing to lose'. In other cases, 'being seen' constituted part of the cause (see Chapter 8). This issue was of particular concern in relation to younger respondents. Connor, for example resisted assurances about anonymisation, saying that he wanted the name of the youth division he ran to feature prominently in whatever I wrote. He also insisted, as a matter of principle, that any photos or videos used should not pixelate his face; 'I don't want my identity changed' (field diary, 18 July 2012). In this situation, I found myself urging him to think not only about the present but also the future and the possibility that he might regret the notoriety he sought now. Another respondent, after reading an excerpt from the manuscript, asked for his real name rather than the assigned pseudonym to be used; I replaced the pseudonym with a name with which the respondent was more comfortable.

Formal ethical rules are crude instruments in the navigation of the 'grey areas' of research. Anonymity was formally assured but practically pointless if individuals agreed to give video interviews for the documentary film. Not revealing the locations of divisions and regional organisations to which members belonged is academic when cited interview material contains distinctive regional speech patterns.[8] Moreover, consent forms are signed usually when respondents conduct their first interview while sustained engagement with respondents blurs the sense of what is being consented to. Outside of the interview situation (on the coach, in the pub, through Facebook) I was privy to personal and non-EDL-related information and could never be sure that respondents understood that personal stories and 'whole lives', as well as movement-related issues, would be treated as ethnographic 'data'. Thus, when anonymising the field diary and interviews, I highlighted text I felt should not be cited without re-contacting the respondent and the personal stories included in Chapter 3, as vignettes were given to individuals to check before inclusion. The fact that in one case this led to the exclusion of the vignette, confirms that consent requires an ongoing process of discussion, reflection and renegotiation of trust throughout the research (Duncombe and Jessop, 2002: 111).

Mutual manipulation? Rapport, trust and friendship in a research context

Smyth and Mitchell (2008: 442) argue that there is an erroneous assumption that 'rapport' between researcher and research subjects is essential for successful qualitative social research because it maximises respondent disclosure and enhances understanding. Based on their own work with groups with whom they feel no empathy (anti-abortion activists and conservative evangelicals), they argue that rapport is not inherently positive either epistemologically (understanding is not a consequence of empathy) or ethically (rapport can lead to the exploitation of research subjects). While I would agree with the epistemological argument that understanding is often facilitated best by challenging and interrogating, the notion of rapport provides too limited, and utilitarian, a description of a research relationship which, at least in the case of ethnographic research, is rooted in a range of emotional and sensory experiences that generate affective bonds regardless of whether the researcher shares beliefs, values or behaviours with respondents. The very notion that rapport can be constructed in order to generate trust and encourage disclosure is not only instrumental, it is also transparent to the interlocutor who is a knowing subject, and, especially in the case of stigmatised groups, alert to the possibility that this is the motivation of any apparently interested outsider. Moreover, in establishing a relationship with people to whom one does not feel akin, the usual rapport-building techniques of demonstrating appreciation of respondents' viewpoints are not available to the researcher since they seek to avoid the impression that they agree with those views (Team Members, 2006: 63).

In this context, trust and camaraderie emerges not from consciously generated rapport but everyday moments of mutual support, concern, attention and care. When I nearly faint on the overcrowded tube as we travel to the Walthamstow muster point, Jack catches me before I fall and finds me a place to stand nearer the police-guarded door where there is at least a hint of air. When I am travelling abroad and money for the coach has to be paid for the next demo, (unemployed) Kurt simply pays for me too (field diary, 10 May 2014). When I was subjected to verbal abuse by someone from another division for filming an incident with a counter-demonstrator at the Norwich demonstration, Rachel and Lisa tell the guy to back off (field diary, 10 November 2012). When Jack, at the start of his trial, has to make an important decision about his plea, I sit with him as his counsel explains the options and he works through the implications. These incidents – which litter the research diary – may be banal and unreflected, but they are the substance of social relationships and it is the entering into social relationships with those we want to understand that underpins the ethnographic method.

Is this friendship? Or faking it? Duncombe and Jessop (2002: 118–19) argue that by 'doing rapport' researchers create 'faked friendship' which may be subsequently exposed when respondents read the relationship as one of friendship while researchers view it as 'doing their job'. This they suggest might even call into question the ethics of such research since consciously fostered rapport might result in respondents disclosing incidents and emotions of a very personal nature that they had not anticipated when they gave 'informed consent'.

While this is not the place for a detailed discussion of the meaning of friendship per se, it seems unhelpful to talk of real and staged friendship. All social relationships have elements of front and back stage (Goffman, 1990: 32). In the case of relationships generated through close-up research, the bonds are first and foremost situational. But so too are workplace friendships or those with parents of our children's friends. As I started preparing to exit the field – a process which lasted more than 18 months – I found myself saying that I would 'keep in touch with those who are my friends', while struggling myself to know what friendship meant in this context (field diary, 18 May 2013), and have remained in social contact with a few respondents. Perhaps it is more helpful, therefore, to think about relationships not as either real or fake but as on a continuum where some have the potential to continue beyond the situation.

Entering into close social relationships with research respondents necessarily entails ethical challenges and risks. The most common criticism faced by researchers studying stigmatised groups is that, consciously or unconsciously, they become a legitimising mouthpiece for the organisation or cause being researched. This concern is rooted in a questioning of the reasons why activists may want to participate in social research; for stigmatised groups, being the subject of a 'scientific' study may provide visibility and possible legitimation, especially if the researcher is thought to be 'empathetic' (Esseveld and Eyerman, 1992: 229–30). In this study of the EDL it is true that, in the context of a belief that it is almost impossible to get even factual coverage of the organisation in the media (see Chapter 2), I was seen as a potential alternative channel for 'telling it as it is'. Discussing the police kettling at the Walthamstow demonstration, for example, one young respondent commented, 'that's what we need. More people like you in there, like inside' (Jason). Such suggestions that I might be used as a counterbalance to the negative coverage the EDL received in the media, however, were often rejected by close respondents before I could answer for myself. Highly aware of the stigma attached to the organisation and sensitive to my position, they made it clear to others that I was not there to 'put our side'. Only on one occasion was I asked to engage in activities – researching a planning application – that would help the EDL. I declined the request (field diary, 12 October 2013).

This does not mean, of course, that a researcher's presence and interventions are never used for representational purposes. Illustrative here is an incident following a day spent with the EDL's LGBT division leader (Declan). While the purpose of travelling to the town had been to interview Declan, the day had turned into a series of social occasions and the following day I inboxed Declan to thank him for his time and sent him a group photo I had taken on the seafront. A couple of days later, checking Facebook, I see that he has posted it to his personal Facebook page with the comment 'The far left call the EDL "homophobes." Let's see now, a married straight woman, a straight teenager and a gay couple holding the EDL flag. Call us homophobes now! ;-)' (field diary, 23 March 2013). The field diary entry captures my concerns and reflections on how my presence in the group produces material and symbolic artefacts which have consequences; in this case this photograph was used to undermine stereotypes of the EDL being anti-gay and I wondered whether I had been naive to send it. However, the posting made no reference to any 'authority' lent the representation because the photo had been taken by an outsider, and the image was a genuine representation of the people and their relations to one another as I had encountered them that day. Another potentially difficult moment arose when Jack, who had been charged with 'violent disorder' following the EDL national demonstration in Walsall in September 2012, asked me whether I would act as a character witness for him. Having been present throughout the demonstration, physically positioned on the EDL side of the police lines yet not an EDL supporter, potentially lent some authority to any statement I made. I had not seen Jack act violently or encourage others to do so and I could vouch for his peaceful behaviour at demonstrations I had attended with him previously. At the same time, I was conscious that acting on his behalf would draw attention to my presence at a number of events and the fact that I had notes, photos and video from them. If the police had reason to suspect that this material might provide evidence of unlawful action, they would have the right to request I surrender it; this carried implications not only for Jack but others in the movement. We agreed that his solicitor would ring me if he thought that it was still a good idea to ask me to act (field diary, 4 April 2014). The solicitor did not call.

A second criticism of researchers working with stigmatised groups is that they may themselves exploit the stigmatisation to deceive respondents into thinking the researcher is supportive of their cause in order to fulfil their own research needs. This often capitalises on the will among some groups to believe that, even when the researcher is overt, they may be a potential convert to the cause (Esseveld and Eyerman, 1992: 228). For this reason, Blee (2002: 11) states that 'from the beginning ... I explicitly said that my views were quite opposed to theirs, that they should not hope to convert me'. My own approach to this issue – usually encountered when respondents, often jokingly, looked for confirmation that the researcher had some sympathy with the movement before agreeing to be inter-viewed for example – was rather different. Typically I responded to such chal-lenges by making clear that the EDL was not a movement I would ever join but in a reciprocally light-hearted rather than aggressive or didactic way. I stressed always that my aim was 'to understand' rather than represent the movement either in a positive or negative light. This was an honest statement and, in as much as a research relationship can ever be 'equal', it established some shared goals to engagement in the research. In order to conduct the research, both researcher and respondents were required to suspend prejudices about the 'other': in the case of the researcher the media image of the EDL as 'racist thugs'; in the case of respondents, the common view within the EDL that universities were 'training grounds for the UAF'.

Finally, there is a danger that close personal rapport with respondents, espe-cially those experiencing difficult personal situations, can develop into quasi-ther-apeutic interviews, which may result in respondents disclosing more than they might have chosen to (Duncombe and Jessop, 2002: 111). While this study of EDL activism did not research difficult emotional or relationship experiences specifically, a number of respondents talked about such experiences. The ethical issues arising from this relate primarily to how far these data can or should be used. Recounting very specific personal situations runs the risk also of allowing individuals to be identified and thus the potential for 'doing harm' to respondents by using these details in publications is real. On the other hand, the sanitisation of EDL activism by considering it in isolation from the whole lives of activists obscures, or even distorts, its understanding. Thus, as noted above, once people start to talk not as interviewees the question of consent is reopened.

In most cases the discussion of personal issues was reciprocal and commen-surate with the relationship with the individual respondent; Kurt and I joked, for example, that coach journeys to national demos – when we often sat together – were more like mutual therapy sessions. On one occasion, however, an interview with a young man I had met only once before revealed a real need for professional help and left me feeling anxious and inadequate (see Box 2).

Blee (2007: 121) argues that the lack of 'shared values' between scholars and far right movements means the 'methodological bridge' facilitating trust and mutual understanding between researchers and participants is 'missing'. In this research, in contrast, I felt a genuine sense of shared experience and mutual care and friendship between myself and a number of key informants and I have argued here that it is possible to achieve the quality of relationships necessary to secure understanding. Klandermans and Mayer also conclude from their experience of

> **Box 2: Help? The questions 'informed consent' cannot answer**
>
> We first went together to pick up his Subutex prescription. Then we sat in McDonalds. ... As we sat he talked awkwardly about the EDL stuff. I felt he thought I was testing his knowledge because he was a 'newbie'. I wasn't ... The conversations around were intruding too much (to one side, a mother telling her kids off and, to the other, a growing party of hyper-demonstrative teenagers). While I felt increasingly uncomfortable, he withdrew into himself and shut it out. And once he had reached that space, he began to talk again about what was really going on for him. ... I am not a trained counsellor and his experience is way beyond mine. God knows what damage my responses might do, no matter how well intended. He commented, as we talked, how strange it was that this was the second time he had met me and I probably knew more about him than almost anybody else. ... he is clearly ready to talk about some of the really heavy stuff he is dealing with and he needs someone to do that with ... So, do I try and help him access that help? Do I walk away and protect myself? And what do I do with all this stuff which is now recorded? Of course all the formal (informed consent) boxes are ticked but it means nothing when you sit and think about this stuff. Of course he is an adult and he has basic access to services (hostel place, income support, the Subutex prescription) but that is never going to get him out from where he is mentally – what he needs is sustained coun-selling, what he has is a key worker who hasn't made a scheduled meeting in the last month. I felt really useless ... And what do I do with his story? Strip it back to 'variables' (no education, unemployed, criminal record, sustained substance abuse issues, failed relationship, victim of domestic abuse, disability issues, own problems with violence ...). What do we learn from that? None of them is a causal factor for joining the EDL. But EDL, like his daughter, like the gatekeeper/surrogate mother via whom he got into the EDL, are foci, points of solidity that might just help him pull himself out of the place he is in. What does that make the EDL? (Field diary, 20 November 2012)

conducting life-history interviews with far right activists that sufficient rapport was achieved to ensure 'reliable and valid interviews' (Team Members, 2006: 58). However, I have suggested that to think about 'rapport', 'trust' and 'friendship' as commodities that can be acquired and exchanged during research in order to achieve one's aims is to misrecognise what underpins ethnographic research. I argue, rather, that an ethnographic approach requires an emotional engagement with respondents that does not simulate friendship but takes a variety of situa-tional forms that may, or may not, transcend the research context.

Positionality: beyond researcher guilt

While the quality of relations necessary for successful research may be possible, some would argue that it is achieved only at a cost to the researcher's own position-ality or 'speaking position'. Back and Solomos (1993: 195) reflect that their strategic adoption of a 'value-free' position (as objective, outside experts) at points in their research compromised their 'anti-racist' project. Smyth and Mitchell (2008: 448) talk about the 'guilt' experienced as a result of 'not telling the whole truth' about their pro-choice views to anti-abortion activists being researched. As explained above, in my research I did not offer up my 'position' as a starting point, but when asked about my views I responded. I found that, in a similar but inverse way to that described by Back and Solomos (1993), my 'speaking position' shifted over time. As the research progressed, open discussion and challenge became increasingly possible and I came to understand the research as guided not only by an intellectual desire to understand how respondents understood their activism but a political desire to find a language through which to talk about the issues that concerned them. This shifting subject position is reflected in the writing of this book too, as the author's voice moves from something close to a 'neutral observer' in recounting the origins and trajectory of the organisation (Chapter 2), through that of a questioning interlocutor (Chapters 4–6) to a more emotionally (Chapters 3 and 7) and politically (Chapters 8–9) engaged narrator. Below I explore how I, and respondents, managed this shifting subject position in the course of fieldwork.

'Typical UAF'

On a long coach journey back from a national demonstration, a conversation started amongst a small group of people about how removed politicians are from ordinary people's concerns and strayed into a discussion of the Labour Party. One of the group commented that although his parents 'were Labour', he would never vote for them now, 'not since Blair sold out the country'. When, in the course of the ensuing conversation, he challenged me about being a 'lefty', I said that I was indeed on the left. The following day, a core respondent, Ian, rang me and warned me to be more careful what I say. After I got off the coach, he said, he had had to defend me from people saying I was UAF because I had told them I voted Labour (field diary, 25 May 2014).

While I took multiple subject positions into the field – gender, ethnicity, age, sexuality, educational background and professional identity – the most threatening to the management of relations with respondents was my political position. The solution proposed by some is to simply not disclose one's own views. Crowley (2007: 619), in her work with Fathers' Rights activists, refused to answer questions about herself, interpreting them as the 'highly motivated pursuit of personal information about me as a way of regaining control in the research context'. I both understood such questions and responded to them differently. When, at the end of a long interview, Matt asked me whether I was 'sympathetic' to the EDL, for example, his question seemed a legitimate attempt to get a sense of how I might interpret what he had said and what risk there was that it could cause harm to him or the movement. I responded as honestly as I could at that early stage of research. I said I was a Labour voter and would never join the EDL but that the research to date had led me to question whether people in the EDL were as simply 'racist' as portrayed in the media (field diary, 19 August 2012). Thus, in contrast to Crowley, and partially as a way of allowing the renegotiation of consent in the course of the interview (Duncombe and Jessop, 2002: 111), I encouraged respondents to ask questions. At the end of interviews, I asked if they had any questions they wanted to put to me. In response to this invitation, Ollie asked whether I personally identified with any political ideology. I answered that I was not sure if I signed up to any particular 'ideology' any more although I had been more involved in political activism when I was younger. When he asked whether that activism had been 'left wing, or right wing' I replied that it had been left wing and talked about some of the types of activism in which I had participated.

These exchanges can be unnerving, especially at the start of research, but as relationships with respondents develop, disclosure of difference and the maintenance of outsider status can provide space for the discussion of issues and feelings that respondents might not necessarily share with those on the 'inside' (Bucerius, 2013: 715). The next time I saw the respondent who had called me 'a lefty' in the incident on the coach described above, for example, he started to tell me animatedly about some research he had been doing on the left's position on animal rights and halal meat (the issue that had led him into the EDL in the first place). Recognising me as 'the other' amongst them thus sometimes opened up rather than closed down space for dialogue. When, during an interview with three youth division members, Chris commented that my audio recorder 'looks like a UAF tool to me', Ray responded, 'It doesn't bother me. What I would like to do is sit down with them and see their views on why they are against us.' In this way 'UAF' shifted as a signifier for counter-protestors to the researcher and her tools and, in the process, was divested of its threat and became a space for potentially meaningful debate.

Field observer: 'simples'

In November 2013, after I had warned key informants that I was withdrawing from fieldwork, Kurt turned up to a social event with a 'leaving present' for me. It was an army-style 'dog tag' inscribed with my name and status; the latter read simply 'Field observer'.

There is a danger in methodological writing that researchers over-problematise communicative interaction and social relations through extensive reflection on positionality. Most respondents had a straightforward and reasoned understanding of my position: I was there to 'report' what I saw. If that role was performed honestly, fairly and without prior prejudice, the fact that I had different views was not an issue. Respondents made no assumption that what I would report would be wholly positive – they were sometimes critical of the movement and certain individuals in it themselves – but they believed that I would see things 'as they are' and that this provided a counterbalance to intentionally negative media reporting. They often described this as being 'neutral' or 'neither for nor against' (field diary, 19 October 2012).

This is not to say there were not moments of tension and challenge but, as a rule, respondents understood the difficulty of my position and could empathise with it. One local division member commented that people in the movement appreciated that I was somewhere between a rock and a hard place and that they understood that what I would subsequently write could not be exactly what they say (field diary, 21 April 2014). The study had no systematic dialogic element, although I have talked through some of the provisional findings, and shared excerpts from the book manuscript, with individual respondents. I also showed the documentary film to a small group of respondents; their conclusion was that it was 'honest' (field diary, 31 August 2014). I discussed with respondents some of the presentations I had made to non-academic communities whilst still conducting fieldwork. In one case, this was to inform them that I had done a presentation at an anti-racist NGO event and, in a second case, I sounded out core respondents prior to accepting an invitation to present research findings to the police (at a Prevent programme training event). In both cases, the response was positive (field diary, 4 May 2013).

Challenging racism

Acceptance as 'other', of course does not resolve issues relating to researching 'distasteful' movements. On the contrary, the more I became accepted for who I was, the more I found myself in situations in which large amounts of alcohol were consumed and racist and sexist comments were freely traded. The fact that this is done as 'banter' or 'wind up' does not alleviate any of the discomfort. Discomfort was experienced also on a number of occasions when interviewing respondents in public places such as cafes or bars where I was extremely conscious of the presence of members of the public who might be able to hear the conversation and find it offensive or even intimidating. In these situations the researcher is caught between conflicting demands. On the one hand ethnographic empathy extends not just to the interlocutor but to those sitting nearby. On the other, any intervention would clearly alter the respondent's openness and responsiveness and thus inhibit understanding.

How should the researcher respond to such situations? Back and Solomos (1993: 188) view the range of possible responses as inadequate and ask whether non-response to racist comments or ideas communicated to researchers during fieldwork effectively legitimises these ideas through silence. In this research I rarely chose not to respond at all; where this option was taken it was in situations when comments or actions were judged to be primarily demonstrative and designed to test whether I would conform to the 'liberal left elite' type. This is captured in the following diary entry after a day spent with a group of youth division members:

> ... it was a tough day. Partly because they are young, partly for demonstrative purposes I think, Connor constantly made strongly racist remarks and sometimes in earshot of those he was abusing. These moments were really difficult to handle and I found myself moving away, looking away, cringing frequently but not intervening because I felt I was being tested both as an adult (always telling

kids off) and an outsider (when will I crack and reveal UAF colours?). I suspect Connor knows what he is doing. (Field diary, 2 February 2013)

Moreover, not responding immediately, in a way that will heighten tension, is not no response. Later that day, when Connor was on his own, for example, there was an opportunity to talk to him more seriously and point out the racist nature of generalising about groups of people based on cultural markers (such as religion) as well as skin colour. As part of my response to his question about whether I 'agree with EDL views', I say that it disturbs me when some people in the EDL talk about Muslims as 'this' or 'that' and he responds by saying 'to be honest I have seen a lot of racists at EDL demos, including people doing Nazi salutes' (field diary, 2 February 2013).

Another way of engaging in this debate was during interviews when, in discussing their experience of demonstrations, I routinely asked respondents if they felt uncomfortable with any chants and/or whether they felt some chants contradicted claims by the movement that it was 'not racist'. Often I would share my own discomfort with what was being chanted or said around me. I also felt that it was appropriate to correct statements that were blatantly inaccurate (accepting that many urban myths circulated might also have been challenged). One example of this was Connor's claim during interview that 'The English language is actually the second spoken language in England now.' This was clearly a misrepresentation of data from the 2011 census released that day, which had shown that Polish was the second most-spoken language in England and Wales after English. I told him this and suggested he go back and check his source. During informal communication – 'banter' – however, I usually responded immediately and in kind, by making pointed but not didactic comments about the gap between on-message (not racist) and off-message talk. The use of the term 'Muzzie', in particular, would prompt me to challenge respondents to think about whether terms used to refer to Muslims, or generalisations made about them, were really that dissimilar from the 'racist' comments they disapproved (field diary, 16 June 2013).

On one occasion during fieldwork I considered whether the appropriate response might be to turn to the police. This was following an interview with Andrew (an Infidels member on the extreme fringe of the EDL) who recounted his empathy for Anders Breivik and his feeling of being 'similar' to him. Given that Andrew worked as a teaching assistant, I considered whether something had been disclosed that indicated the threat of harm to others and warranted overriding the confidentially agreement with the respondent (as provided for in the ethics framework of the project). On reflection I decided it did not. Since Andrew had been suspended from his position at the school because of media coverage of his views and he was already being monitored by police, no additional measures to prevent harm to the public could have followed from me reporting him. I also chose not to pursue contact with this respondent (or indeed the other two Infidels members) beyond the interview.

Perhaps an even greater challenge is presented in the interpretation and presentation of respondent narratives. Allowing respondents to tell their stories as they understand them is a key principle of the ethnographic approach. Uncritically accepting and re-presenting these stories when working with 'distasteful' groups, however, opens the researcher to accusations of legitimating or condoning the views expressed. As Fielding (1993: 149) argues, analysis is also limited if 'it is informed first and last by scepticism', since if the fieldwork begins with an attempt to catch members out, rather than attempting to see why a worldview appeals to a particular group, the analysis will never be able to take members' beliefs seriously. Finding the right line to tread here has been extremely difficult, especially in cases where respondents present confirmation of 'urban myths' through reference to their own experience. Through subsequent chapters of this book, therefore, I have treated respondents in the same ways as I have those in other ethnographic studies; I have presented their stories as they have told them and reflected where appropriate on whether their accounts can or cannot be confirmed by observation or other evidence. The objective of the research is to understand how EDL activists interpret the social world rather than to judge whether those interpretations are 'true'.

Who are you? Constraints on research relations

The positionality I took into the field in terms of gender, age, ethnicity, educational background was secondary to the political markers discussed above in terms of affecting field relations. However, even if none of these factors had a particularly inhibiting impact on the research, they need to be taken into account.

Gender shaped research relations. Relatively few women attended demonstrations and thus, even though being a woman did not prohibit access to the movement, any new female face attracted attention. The most constraining aspect of gender identity was that many women were in, or had been in, relationships with men in the movement. While my position as a researcher meant that mostly I escaped this labelling, the high turnover in the movement, and the impossibility that all people knew who I was, meant that I was also subject to rumour and assumptions. I was fortunate to have two close female respondents whose activism was completely independent of any men and this created a secure space for the expression of female solidarity in amongst the unremitting sexual banter (field diary, 29 September 2012).

One role that attached to being a woman in the group was that of 'emotion work' (Duncombe and Jessop, 2002: 107). While this affected EDL activists more (see Chapter 3), it was something that I experienced also. This often took the form of 'talking down' men from potentially violent exchanges. One evening was spent responding to a series of emotional messages (personal inbox) from a core respondent to prevent him getting into a violent dispute with a neighbour and fellow EDL member. I wrote this up in my field diary the following day as feeling like 'me setting him boundaries and him looking for some reason to take control of himself' (field diary, 29–30 April 2013). A month later, I recorded a similar feeling of being 'like a typical girl playing the role of pulling the lads away from fights' following participation in a flash demonstration when limited police presence led to direct engagement with the opposition (field diary, 18 May 2013).

In this study, whiteness was not a prerequisite for accessing the group but carried the advantage of 'majority' status that did not need to be explained or justified (see also Back, 2002: 48). However, as the work of both Nayak in the UK (1999, 2005) and Ezekiel (1995, 2002) in the USA demonstrates, 'close up' research on white racist subcultures does not require common ethnic or religious background to produce insight into the social construction of whiteness (Back, 2002: 48). As indicated by the chant often directed at UAF counter-demonstrators of 'You're not English any more', exclusion from the category of 'us' among EDL supporters is based first and foremost not on race, ethnicity or religion but on alliance with what is perceived to be a hegemonic liberal elite that blindly pursues a mantra of political correctness and fails to stand up against Islamic extremism.

The potential for my assignment to this last category, given that universities are seen as the 'breeding ground of UAF' (field diary, 12 January 2013), and how that might impact on the research, was discussed above. Returning from a break in attending demonstrations for health reasons, I found the significant turnover in membership meant I had to regain acceptance, recording in my field diary that 'I feel a bit self-conscious at the start with people I don't know. I realise that I talk differently – both [regional] accent and vocabulary' (field diary, 10 May 2014). However, given the huge difference in opportunity that I had from educational background and employment, and that, in terms of my regional identity, I am an 'outsider', the hostility, even banter, I was subjected to on this front was less of a barrier than anticipated. It is possible that gender is a mitigating factor here, making me less threatening to male status. Or perhaps it is simply the failure to live up to stereotype that disarms. Bucerius (2013: 716) notes that in forging relationships with young male Turkish drug dealers in Germany, it was important that she defied their stereotypes of a 'typical German robot woman' who cares only about her career, while Ezekiel (2002: 63) found that when he failed to conform to respondents' images of a medieval Jew they responded positively to him as somebody who listened to them and showed, by attention and action over time, that they matter. Over and above any socio-demographic variable that either facilitated or hindered the research, this is the crucial factor. Time spent in the field builds trust that the researcher is who they say they are; who that is, is secondary.

Politics, ethics and the academic community

The experience of conducting this study suggests that individual researcher 'distaste' for the community being researched is sufficiently surmountable to mean that ethnographic methods can produce new and important knowledge about those studied. Indeed, the sustained contact and presence in the everyday lives of respondents that ethnography entails reveal that the behaviours which make subjects outcasts usually constitute a small part of their everyday lives (Kirby and

Corzine, 1981: 10). Being part of the whole lives of research respondents thus allows a range of subject positions other than 'member of far right organisation' – shared class allegiances and political origins, gender and a number of life-course experiences – to become (albeit sometimes slippery) stepping stones to mutually trusting and respectful relationships. This suggests that what constrains our knowledge is not only a lack of shared values between researchers and these particular communities but a wider problem – within and beyond the academic community – of placing subjects whose political views we do not agree with as 'out of bounds' for research (1981: 15).

This is far from a new phenomenon. In an article published more than three decades ago Kirby and Corzine (1981: 4) recount how their early research on gay subculture attracted moral condemnation in a process of 'guilt by association' (1981: 4). Their honest and open explication of the hostility they encountered to their research (among the academic community as well as the broader public) resonates with my own experience. My previous ethnographic studies with marginal or marginalised groups (including refugees and forced migrants, drug users, punks and skinheads) had attracted constructively critical responses from academic colleagues on methodological questions (field relations, mutual responsibilities and obligations between researcher and research subjects, trust and verification, exit from the field etc.). This time the very act of ethnographic engagement with the EDL seemed to evoke moral indignation. I found myself accused of not taking a significantly 'critical position' in relation to my research subjects and of 'implying' my support for EDL views.

Clearly the study of groups such as the EDL is not 'out of bounds' per se; there is, after all, an established subject area of 'far right studies'. What seems to be beyond the pale is the application of *ethnographic* research methods to this social phenomenon. Unlike studies of voting intentions or electoral support for far right parties using either survey or qualitative interview methods, ethnographic research requires 'direct and sustained contact with human agents, within the context of their daily lives (and cultures)' (O'Reilly, 2005: 2). As Kirby and Corzine (1981: 13) point out, the contagion of stigma relates not only to the initial moral discomfort with the group studied but there is 'an additional stigma that arises from personal contact'. While they understand this as the extension of 'labelling' – as researchers come to be seen as members of the group being studied – I would argue that the problem is less the label than its 'stickiness' (Ahmed, 2004: 117–19). Stickiness, Ahmed argues, ensues from the emotions that circulate between bodies and signs and align individuals with communities (or bodily space with social space). It was this personal contact, the sharing of this affective space, that made the research possible; it marked me as 'the researcher bird' (accepted outsider) rather than 'journalist' (threatening outsider). At the same time, by engaging in that emotional space, the researcher becomes a player in its 'affective economy' (Ahmed, 2004) and suspect to the outside world since it calls into question the researcher's ability to regain sufficient distance to take up the necessary 'critical position'. As Back (2002: 34) reflects, in relation to the moment he moved from an Internet-based study of nationalist movements to a face-to-face interview with Nick Griffin (later to become leader of the British National Party), 'the stakes change when one decides to look into the face of racial extremism'. Criticisms are rarely made 'in principle' but are voiced in terms of individual researchers' failure to state their own political position, to take a sufficiently critical stance towards respondents' views (both in and after the field) or to consistently 'other' research subjects when talking about shared field experiences. This raises the crucial question of the relationship between politics, ethics and research.

There is a growing trend within social movement research for research ethics to explicitly include a statement of the political objectives of the research (Gillies and Alldred, 2002: 48) and for academics to consciously take on the role of 'activist-scholars' (Gillan and Pickerill, 2012: 135) or conduct politically engaged research through 'militant ethnography' that rejects the divide between observer and practitioner (Juris, 2008: 64). Such approaches, however, assume at least a broad political alignment between the researcher and the movement studied, which becomes deeply problematic – and likely to meet profound critique from the same activist-scholars – when the movement concerned is perceived to be 'racist' or 'far right'. That sociological research cannot be value-free is widely accepted and in many traditions, researchers explicitly align themselves with relatively powerless social groups (Smyth and Mitchell, 2008: 441). However, in studies of far right activism, such side-taking feels wrong:

> On a pivotal afternoon very early in the project, I was driving to Detroit to continue our conversations and thinking about the life of one of the young men. I had been getting a sense of what his life had been and what its onward trajectory was likely to be. What could be done, I asked myself, that would help him have a more competent sense of himself, that would encourage him to take a firmer grasp on his life – to begin to understand that his life mattered and that it could be directed in a hopeful way? I pondered and abruptly shook myself: 'What am I doing, worrying about a Nazi?' I thought about it. And then from my gut came the reply: 'He is also a kid. It cannot be wrong to be concerned about a kid.' (Ezekiel, 2002: 63–64)

Indeed, Ezekiel has a long-standing concern about kids; earlier published work had highlighted poverty among African American communities in inner-city Detroit. In this later study of poor white kids who turned to racist organisations to give them a sense that their lives had some meaning, he reveals continuities between the cases in terms of the stigmatisation of the poor, the failure to tackle long-term deskilling and unemployment in inner-city areas, lack of personal connectedness and warmth that gives meaning and prospect to life (see also Pilkington, Omel'chenko and Garifzianova, 2010: 229). The difference is that in the first case, as the victims of racism, research subjects are perceived to be a legitimate, powerless group with whom the social scientist may 'side'; in the latter case, as the perpetrators of racism, the research becomes dirty and the researcher guilty of failing 'to keep his subjects at arm's length'[9]. This moral overdetermination of power and powerlessness obscures a more complex understanding of social relations in which the oppressed can also perpetuate oppression. Of course not all socio-economically and educationally disadvantaged people take political paths that oppress the rights of others, but that does not take away their own disadvantage or make it unworthy of social research; if this is a possible outcome of it, indeed, it becomes all the more important to understand.

Accepting that research is not value-free and that political intent should be openly acknowledged and effective interventions sought, who decides what constitutes an appropriate or acceptable political position? In a highly reflective piece that engages directly with the experience of conducting anti-racist research, Back and Solomos (1993: 196) recognise that there is 'no easy way for research on racism that is not in some way political'. Yet, in the absence of concrete strategies for effecting change, they reflect, it is also all too easy for researchers to construct 'an elaborate form of credentialism where one simply identifies oneself as doing "anti-racist research"' when what is needed is a more flexible approach (1993: 196). Thus the anti-racist political agenda of research needs, sometimes, to be strategically shelved in favour of a speaking position as an 'impartial academic' in the interests of making a more effective long-term intervention (1993: 194).

This raises the possibility that rigid standpoint positions – where they lead to the moral condemnation of non-standpoint positions – may constrain what we know about the world and thus what we can change in it. 'The contagion of stigma', Kirby and Corzine (1981: 14) argue, 'has an effect on the overall level of research on homosexuality and other sensitive topics'. In the case of far right groups, not allowing 'subjects to give their own account' has effectively narrowed and impoverished the field of study, reducing it to macro-scale correlations between, for example, social class and political belief and leaving unexplored questions of the connection between beliefs and activism (Fielding, 1981: 15–18). The problem is, as I have argued above, not so much that researchers are unable to develop the trust with respondents necessary to facilitate that 'own account'-giving process but that this requires a level of subjective engagement that is experienced as politically and ethically uncomfortable.

Conclusion

Why undertake ethnographic study if it blurs boundaries and disrupts the moral norms of the academic community? First, it has been argued here, employing an ethnographic method in the study of far right groups extends the parameters of what we know and problematises and expands our understanding of the phenomenon. The sustained contact and presence in the everyday lives of respondents that ethnography entails reveals that ideological concerns may be secondary to other practices, particularly among young members of far right groups (Nayak, 1999, 2005; Kimmel, 2007; Pilkington, Omel'chenko and Garifzianova, 2010; Pilkington, 2014a; Garland and Treadwell, 2011). This raises questions about the desirability of employing standpoint positions or declaring the researcher's political intent at the outset of research. While in some cases this may forge rapport with research subjects and enhance knowledge, it also risks confining findings to the question of ideology and reducing the capacity of qualitative research to adapt and develop with the research process in order to understand the object of study as it is found rather than as it is imagined. This is not a call to revert to a naturalistic version of ethnography which denies subjectivity in the research process (Willis, 1997: 247) and makes false claims to scientific objectivity (Clifford, 1986: 2) but to employ a form of 'epistemic reflexivity', which not only acknowledges the social and personal drives of the individual researcher but forces us to scrutinise the very act of construction of the object of study in the theories, problems and categories of scholarly judgement (Bourdieu and Wacquant, 1992: 38).

Second, existing research on the far right in the UK continues to emanate primarily from a political science perspective and draw its evidence from statistics on voter preference or the analysis of official programmes and statements (Copsey, 2010; Goodwin et al., 2010; Allen, 2011; Goodwin, 2011a). The recent Internet-based survey of EDL supporters conducted by Demos (Bartlett and Littler, 2011) has filled in some of the gaps identified by Allen (2011: 285) in our knowledge about the profile of EDL supporters. However, this and other studies based on the social media (Jackson, 2011a, 2011c), whilst illuminating, are able to answer questions about the significance of social media for resource mobilisation and social network development better than they can address questions of what motivates and sustains movements like the EDL. While there is a small body of work that includes qualitative interviewing (Klandermans and Mayer (eds), 2006; Garland and Treadwell, 2011; Rhodes, 2011), ethnographic research is extremely rare (the exception here is Busher, 2012, 2013). The 'real people' missing from academic research in the field are substituted by literature based on investigative journalism (Trilling, 2012) or authored by oppositional political activists, including those who were formerly members of far right movements (Hann and Tilzey, 2003; Collins, M., 2011). In this sense we have moved little nearer to resolving the absence of any 'humanistic account of an extreme Right movement' (Fielding, 1981: 16), as noted by Fielding more than three decades ago.

Third, while there is a clear preference among researchers for studying those communities with which they empathise, there are no insurmountable methodological obstacles to conducting 'close up' research with 'distasteful' communities. The experience of this study, and others, has shown that sufficient trust and mutual respect can be built to allow meaningful research that extends our knowledge. As Ezekiel (1995: xx) states simply, 'I hate racism, which sunders the world I want to live in and harms great masses; but I have no trouble knowing that the racist is a comprehensible human: We went to school together.' The continued paucity of ethnographic studies on the 'far right', it has been suggested, therefore is not simply a problem of individual mismatch between researchers and subjects, but a wider problem of the 'contagion of stigma' attached to research with such groups. While this is often voiced through the critique of individual researchers for their lack of political standpoint, it reflects a wider tendency when it comes to issues around the far right – specifically fascism or the Holocaust – to view social phenomena as aberrations dispossessed of any rationally graspable cause and, as a result, 'condemnation replaces explanation' (Laclau, 2005: 249). Not only does this substitution impoverish the substantive and methodological knowledge base of the social sciences but, whilst posturing as a critical political stance, in fact it constitutes one of the main forms of contemporary political 'faintheartedness' (2005: 249).

Notes

1 One of these was an English Volunteer Force (EVF) demonstration. Another was formally organised by the North West Alliance. See Appendix 1 for full details.
2 See https://myplaceresearch.wordpress.com/films.
3 Of these, thirty-five are considered the core respondent set (see Appendix 2). An additional three were assigned pseudonyms because they are mentioned frequently in the fieldwork diary although they are not included in the formal 'respondent set'. The final respondent, the Chairman of the EDL Management Group at the time, was interviewed as an 'expert' rather than as a grassroots activist and is referred to by his real name.
4 These arrests, but not their indiscriminate nature, are noted in: www.guardian-series.co.uk/news/wfnews/9906196.print. Accessed: 26.08.2015.
5 This researcher prefers not to be named.
6 Unite Against Fascism (UAF) is an umbrella organisation of anti-fascist groups closely linked to the Socialist Workers Party. It is the organising body of most of the counter-demonstrations to EDL national demonstrations and is used as shorthand by EDL members to indicate the 'main enemy'.
7 All communications are reported verbatim, including syntax and punctuation.
8 For this reason the decision to leave text from interviews exactly as spoken was an extremely difficult one and was taken because this is also part of respondents' identities and its 'correction' would have been disempowering.
9 This is a phrase employed in one review of Ezekiel's *The Racist Mind* (1995). See www.kirkusreviews.com/book-reviews/raphael-s-ezekiel/the-racist-mind. Accessed: 13.01.2015.

2

Tommy Robinson's barmy army?
The past, present and future of
the English Defence League

This chapter introduces the EDL as an organisation: its origins, shape and trajectory. While ostensibly a straightforward exercise in ethnographic description, the EDL proved to be a slippery object of study. This is, first, because the movement itself is currently in a 'state of flux' (Eddowes, 2015) as it seeks to simultaneously stabilise and transform following its so-called 'decapitation'[1] in October 2013 when its co-founders and leaders unexpectedly resigned. Second, it is because to write about the EDL is not to simply describe a contemporary social movement but to navigate a representational battlefield where one-dimensional reporting of the organisation competes with the movement's own defensive self-presentation. The chapter is thus rather the story of the shifting constitution of the EDL as the outcome of its reflexive engagement with external representations and its internal struggle to create a structure and purpose beyond the street protests of 'Tommy Robinson's barmy army'.

Founding myths: the origins of the EDL

The EDL was founded on 27 June 2009 as a response to street protests against British troop homecoming celebrations[2] in Luton by an offshoot of the Islamist group al-Muhajiroun, Ahlus Sunnah wal Jamaah, led by Sayful Islam (Copsey, 2010: 8). It built on long-standing tensions in the town, which has a population that is 18 per cent Muslim and a history of Islamist recruitment and activism (2010: 8), and drew on links not with traditional far right parties but a number of ultra-patriotic 'anti-Jihadist' organisations evolving from within the football casual subculture (2010: 9). Thus, the EDL was originally a single-issue movement, protesting against 'extremist Islam' and disrespect for British troops. At its outset its aim was to force the government to get Islamic extremists 'off the streets' (2010: 11).

This single-issue focus – and absence, for example, of a more general anti-immigration stance[3] – has been a persistent source of criticism from more traditional far right groups and individuals on the periphery of the EDL. For mainstream EDL supporters, however, it remains an important founding myth that the EDL 'started up in response, as a protest group, to basically demonstrate ... to the government against things like this attacking of the troops happening' (Tim). Many also recognise the importance, especially at the start of the movement, of the links with football firms – 'when it first started … it was all football fans' (Matt). Indeed, Matt was organiser of a city division of the EDL that had been originally constituted not in the name of the city but of one of its football teams and continued to hold its 'HQ' and divisional meetings in a pub close to its ground.

The EDL presents its objectives in its mission statement,[4] which conceives of the movement, first and foremost, as raising awareness of the perceived threat of Islam to British culture and society. That statement sets out the EDL's mission as one to promote: human rights against 'religiously-inspired intolerance and barbarity that are thriving amongst certain sections of the Muslim population in Britain' (specifically the denigration and oppression of women, the molestation of young children, 'honour killings', homophobia, anti-Semitism and support for those committing terrorist atrocities); democracy and the rule of law (by opposing Sharia law, especially its implementation and the operation of 'Islamic courts'[5] in the UK, and the extension of the sale of halal meat without non-halal alternatives); public debate on Islam that is balanced and not 'sanitised' by politicians or that labels any discussion of the link between Islamic teachings and the activities of Islamic radicals and criminals as racist, xenophobic or Islamophobic;[6] the respect of the traditions and culture of England both within public educational institutions (which are seen as prioritising minority cultures) and by those who migrate to the country; and an international outlook that allows the movement to work in solidarity with others around the world.

This official 'awareness raising' objective was referred to spontaneously by respondents and is ostensibly embedded in the primary form of activism of the movement – street demonstrations – which are held always 'for a reason' (Kane). When the local community see and hear the demonstrators, Chas believes, 'they'll click in their head "so this is happening in our local community"'. However, in practice, there was little discussion or knowledge of the particular issue about which awareness was being raised in advance of national demos to which respondents travelled; information about the purpose of the demonstration was often shared only on the coach. Observation at divisional meetings suggested that the location of national demonstrations was determined as much by Regional Organisers' desire to profile the region as the 'reason' for holding it there (field diary, 4 April 2013). Discussion of potential foci for demonstrations, however, also revealed organisers sought to avoid purely opportunistic demonstrations; for this reason two local tragedies (a murder and a suicide) were ruled out as legitimate reasons for protest (field diary, 4 April 2013).

Another key foundation myth was that the EDL was not a traditional far right party. Differentiation of the EDL from other movements on the far right of the political spectrum, especially the BNP (which the EDL leadership and many grassroots members denounce as 'racist' in its policies and membership rules) is central to definitions of 'self' for EDL members (see Chapter 4). The defensive nature of this narrative is explained not least by the fact that both Tommy Robinson and Kevin Carroll had been members of the BNP formerly. When these connections are pointed out, respondents explain that 'Tommy Robinson said himself, the reason he joined the BNP is because … he was that desperate. There was nothing else you could turn to' (Tina). While these links are far from confined to the former leadership, nor are they universal. Of the thirty-nine respondents in this study, only two had been members of the BNP and one had 'been to a couple of talks' held by the party although not joined. Ed, a Regional Organiser (RO) of the EDL at the time of fieldwork, had been a BNP organiser and member of the security team (from 2005) and had stood for election in the local council elections in his area three times. When the EDL became a 'proscribed organisation' in the BNP in September 2009, Ed was given an ultimatum to 'choose' between his BNP and EDL affiliation and 'chose the EDL'.

The development and trajectory of the EDL: turning points

The EDL has no formal membership making it difficult to estimate its level of support. The current number of 'likes' on the national Facebook site stands at 181,000; while this is a fraction of the 816,000 Britain First boasts, former EDL Chair, Steve Eddowes, emphasises that, unlike for Britain First, support for the EDL 'ain't bought' (Eddowes, 2015). The number of *active* members is estimated to be 'at least' 25,000 to 30,000 according to a Demos survey of its Facebook users (Bartlett and Littler, 2011: 5). If we take attendance at demonstrations as a measure of activism – using Copsey's (2010: 27–29) data on the thirty EDL (co-)organised demonstrations between July 2009 and October 2010 – then the trajectory of the movement shows a rise in attendance to a peak of around 2,000 (January–April 2010) followed by a decline to around 800 to 1,000 during the second half of that year. This pattern is confirmed by this study; demonstrations such as that in Stoke-on-Trent (January 2010) are remembered with particular nostalgia (Chas, Tim) while the decline noted towards the end of 2010 continued. When fieldwork for this study began (April 2012) numbers at national demonstrations were routinely in the hundreds (between 300 and 700 people) rather than thousands. Thus a climate of despondency characterised the first year of the research as numbers of people attending demonstrations were 'dying' (Tim) and the movement itself appeared to be in a serious crisis of leadership, strategy and recruitment. This was partially a result of the absence of Tommy Robinson who was arrested in October 2012 (released at end of February 2013) for the use of false identity documentation during a trip to the United States (Gover, 2012), which provided the space for in-fighting, leadership challenges and a general uncertainty about the future of the movement.

May 2013 marked the first of two turning points in the movement's trajectory when the external environment was significantly altered by the murder of soldier Lee Rigby (22 May 2013) in Woolwich, London. The media reported a number of flash demonstrations by the EDL immediately after the killing and accused the movement of 'exploiting' it for its own Islamophobic aims as well as being responsible for a series of attacks on mosques and Islamic cultural centres. While this raised the profile of the movement in a negative way, the ferocity of the murder and the perpetrators' own declaration that it constituted legitimate revenge for the death of innocent Muslims resulting from British military action abroad, aroused popular interest in the movement. Local divisions of the EDL reported numbers registering through their webpage as tripling within 48 hours of the murder. The first national demonstration after Lee Rigby's murder (Newcastle, 25 May 2013) saw the movement able to mobilise at least as many demonstrators as at its former peak. Indeed, Ed, who had been attending EDL demonstrations since the start of the movement, claimed it was 'bigger than any demo I've been on' and estimated the number of demonstrators at 7,000. Perhaps more significantly, the events of May 2013 triggered a resetting of the movement's frame to emphasise, as it had done at its inception, a primary concern with the denigration of British Armed Forces. As Tommy Robinson said in his speech at the Newcastle demonstration – over the four years of its existence, the movement had 'swayed from our course' but these events had 'brought it back together' (field diary, 25 May 2013). If, prior to the murder of Lee Rigby, the EDL was far from being a household name, the situation after May 2013 was very different.

It was internal shock waves that caused the second turning point. On 7 October 2013, just four and a half months after the Lee Rigby murder and when the movement seemed to have been given a new lease of life, Tommy Robinson and Kevin Carroll resigned. The resignations were given particular dramatic effect because they were announced at a press conference organised by new 'partners', the Quilliam Foundation.[7] Moreover, even to ROs in the movement, the news 'came as a bit of a shock' (Ed). While the links with Quilliam were known about, the talks the leadership were in had been thought to be about 'bouncing ideas off each other rather than actually sitting at the same table' (Ed).

At grassroots level, response to the news was raw and mixed. On the day of the resignation I was in Crown Court attending the trial of one of the respondents (Jack) accused of 'violent disorder' at an EDL demonstration more than a year previously. The irony of the situation was not lost on either the respondent or the court officials. Between proceedings the prosecution and the defence counsel joked with each other that, mirroring Tommy Robinson's move, Jack's defence counsel, who was Muslim, would be 'the next leader of the EDL' (field diary, 8 October 2013). The resignations impacted negatively on morale and numbers at demonstrations declined once more. At the national demonstration in Bradford on the following weekend, members expressed mixed emotions. One, very drunk, demonstrator pronounced that the former leadership had been 'bought off' and at one point the familiar chant of 'Tommy Robinson's barmy army' (see Chapter 7) rang out as 'Tommy Robinson's Muslim army' (field diary 12 October 2013). Alongside the anger there was widespread recognition of the pressures the leadership had been under (from past and pending prosecutions, threats and intimidation and financial difficulties). Indeed, it was not so much the decision to resign that shocked people but the suddenness and manner in which it happened. Tina encapsulates the emotions this evoked in interview a few days later: 'when it first come out ... I just thought, "You absolute traitor" ... especially when I seen him on the Sky news, sitting in between two ex-jihadists, calling us extremists. I just thought this guy's been had by the balls' (Tina).

The facilitation of the resignation by Quilliam jarred. People were also angry that at both this initial press conference and in subsequent interviews (on BBC's *Newsnight* for example), Tommy Robinson suggested that the reason he had resigned was that the movement remained home to 'extremist' elements. He cited specifically his horror at seeing White Pride flags flown at the Manchester demonstration, which he had attended while on tag.[8] Respondents reported that on a BBC *Look East* programme he had also claimed the EDL would be 'dead before Christmas' without his support, and this provoked determination to defy the prediction (field diary, 12 October 2013).

The accusations of treachery were fuelled by rumours that the leadership had passed on the details of EDL members to Quilliam and the police (field diary, 12 October 2013) and initially were echoed by a number of ROs. However, following a meeting of ROs at which a new collective leadership was agreed, the line was taken that 'We still a hundred per cent back ... Tommy and Kev' because they are not working 'for' but 'alongside' Quilliam (Ed). Ed, who had talked personally to the former leaders about their decision, goes on to suggest that those who were quick to point the finger should 'look at the bigger picture' since the resignation had generated significant publicity: 'He's been on more TV shows in the last fucking three weeks than he has been in four years. ... They turned him down in the past and now they want him on' (Ed).

At a meeting of ROs shortly after the resignations, it was agreed that the EDL should henceforth be run by a committee of the nineteen ROs with a rotating chair. This committee remained loyal to the former leadership, taking the line that the former leadership was simply 'going in a different direction' to 'get a bigger stage' (Ed). The decision to run the movement through a 'Management Committee' was partially designed to relieve the pressure on a single leader, allowing the Chair to 'step back' when they began to feel the pressure from the 'hounding' any leader of the EDL would be subject to (Ed). The initially appointed Chair, Tim Ablitt, was replaced on 8 February 2014 by Steve Eddowes, previously RO for West Midlands and Head of Security. Eddowes himself stepped down as Chair and RO in autumn 2015 due to competing commitments. He returned to running security for Tommy Robinson, who launched the (official) Pegida UK movement in December 2015, although is not affiliated with the new movement (Eddowes, 2016). Ian Crossland was elected leader of the EDL in December 2015 and Alan Spence became Chair of its Management Committee.

The humiliation of the resignation and realignment of Tommy Robinson and Kevin Carroll left the movement vulnerable. By January 2014, the initial spike in numbers following the murder of Lee Rigby had gone 'flat'. The potential to scoop a ready-made street army was not lost on emergent parties of the far right who, according to Eddowes (2015), saw the opportunity to snap up 'brand EDL'. The most obvious attempt to court EDL activists was by Britain First, founded in May 2011 by a number of former BNP activists (including Jim Dowson and, current leader, Paul Golding). A video released in November 2014 by the party directly compares the record of the EDL and Britain First and criticises the EDL for lack of direct action, for cooperating with the police over planned demonstrations, not recognising that real change could only come about through being part of the political process and for wasting time idolising their old leader who had betrayed them.[9] The hostility between Britain First and the EDL is mutual. Ed, who had known its founders personally from his own previous BNP activism, called them 'horrible people' holding racist views while Eddowes (2015) dismisses the party as 'all spin … all marketing'. At the same time, old alliances such as that with Paul Weston, leader of Liberty GB and former leader of the British Freedom Party, remained in place. Paul Weston subsequently became official leader of Pegida UK[10]. The earlier strategy of extending international links with the broader 'counter-Jihad' movement including the Pax Europe Citizens Movement, Stop Islamisation of Europe, and its American affiliate, and the formation and links with Defence Leagues[11] in a number of north European and Nordic countries (Copsey, 2010: 24) has also suffered from the wider instability. While there remains a commitment to international collaboration, such links are on the back-burner until 'we've got our own house in order' (Eddowes, 2015).

'Every single one of you is a leader': organisation and structure

Existing literature on radical, right wing and populist parties suggests that they 'usually have a hierarchical structure with (male) leaders who exploit modern trends of the political profession to perfection' (Wodak, 2013: 28). This is rooted in a wider understanding of extremist groups as rigidly and hierarchically structured with a clearly delineated chain of authority and limited tolerance of internal dissent and criticism (Hogg, 2012: 25). However, the evidence for this argument in relation to radical right parties and movements is based on a relatively insubstantial body of work due to their empirical inaccessibility (Kitschelt, 2007: 1195). For this reason, the discussion below focuses on the insight that ethnographic data and interview material lend to understanding how the movement is experienced organisationally by its grassroots members following a brief outline of the formal structure of the organisation.

'No one is bigger or better than anyone else': structure, function and hierarchy

Even formally, the EDL is characterised by a relatively flat structure. Until the resignation of Tommy Robinson and Kevin Carroll in October 2013, the structure consisted of Robinson and Carroll as co-leaders (often described as 'spokesmen' by activists) supported by ROs heading up nineteen geographically delimited regional organisations. The regional organisations preside over myriad local 'divisions', which are the basic unit of grassroots activism. These divisions are territorially structured although very fluid in terms of their activeness; 'divisions' may cover whole cities or counties in some cases while in others there may be more than one division for a single postcode area (field diary, 3, 7 September 2013). This unevenness stems from the rapid turnover in members, especially 'admins' (those who run the Facebook pages for the division and organise fundraising events and travel to demonstrations) as well as being the product of personal disputes between admins (leading to the proliferation of divisions to appease 'egos'). Division names are often displayed on the back of EDL hoodies, along with other customised slogans (see Figure 7.4). There are also a number of 'divisions' that cut across the territorially rooted structural organisation of the movement. While these divisions vary in size, stability and degree of 'real' as opposed to virtual existence, over the life course of the EDL they have included dedicated divisions for supporters who are Sikhs, Hindus, Jews and Greeks/Cypriots. The movement also has long-standing women's ('Angels'), LGBT and Armed Forces divisions. Some divisions have dedicated 'youth divisions' attached to them, although there is no youth division coordinated at national level. In this study a number of respondents had established and run a 'youth division' attached to their town division and saw it as important in ensuring their voices were heard:

> … because it's good like to let the youths get to voice their opinion. Cause really if you're part of like say our [names home town] youth we can do our own thing like with the public and that. We don't have to run it through the olders. We can just like get the lads together and like say 'Lads we are leafleting'. We are doing it as youth, do you know what I mean? (Connor)

However, some older members resisted the need for youth divisions, suggesting that younger members were 'hard work', jumpy and defensive. Intergenerational tensions – around the form and pace of activism (Brown and Pickerill, 2009: 30) – emerged from time to time. A dispute had developed between the leader of a local youth division and a Divisional Organiser over control of the youth division web page (Connor) and the same youth division had been the subject of disciplining by older division leaders following their 'loud' and aggressive behaviour travelling to a demonstration (see Chapter 8).

Divisional meetings are infrequent and generally poorly attended. Those at which I was present had between twelve and twenty-five people in attendance, although there were larger 'meet and greet' events too. Meetings were unstructured and supported by neither a formal agenda nor minutes. Although, in principle, 'any good idea will be listened to' and participants are asked if there are any 'questions' at the end, meetings are mainly an opportunity for Divisional Organisers to inform people of decisions and there is no apparent procedure for raising agenda items or motions, making points or reaching decisions (field diary, 31 August 2012). Issues discussed at various meetings included: the planning of future demonstrations; potential flash demos; the organisation of travel to demonstrations (finding coach companies prepared to transport the EDL was a perennial logistical problem); merchandising; recruitment; and matters of discipline. Guest speakers were invited sometimes; on the occasions I witnessed this, one was a spokesman for the Sikh Awareness Society, the other a member of the Sikh division of the EDL and in both cases they talked about their concerns about

Islamism from the perspective of the Sikh community. Only once was a vote taken. This concerned whether a member accused of having acted violently at a demonstration should be allowed to stay in the movement. That voting took place rarely was evident from both how this vote was conducted and the fact that the results continued to be disputed afterwards as individuals complained that some people who did not even know the person in question had voted. Meetings were held in what was referred to always as 'HQ' (in order to protect the pub landlords), often coincided with other 'social events' and were always preceded and followed by liberal alcohol consumption.

Functions and hierarchies are unclear. One local division leader laughed that 'ROs they don't do nothing' and at early divisional meetings, it was indeed the two division leaders who took the stage while ROs for the wider region (if present at all) remained in the background, commenting only where necessary. From April 2013, however, one of the ROs for the region took a much greater directional role and started to chair the meetings. This is not unusual – visibility and positioning as well as 'stepping back' occur frequently, especially when individuals need to adopt a low profile either because of legal investigations or for personal reasons. However, moments of crisis exposed the 'loose and chaotic structure' (Copsey, 2010: 6) of the movement. When it was decided that a committee of the ROs would lead the movement, following the resignation of Robinson and Carroll, for example, it transpired that there was not one but four ROs for the region as individual town or city 'divisions' had named ROs (field diary, 12 October 2013).

This proliferation is a product of the informality and lack of strict hierarchical structure of the movement. Many of those in division leader or 'admin' positions narrate this as a passive process: 'somebody gave me the [names city] division I just run it since then like' (Matt). Theresa described how 'I've been left to run [the division]' after the previous admin had had some personal problems. An exception to this rule was recounted by Euan. To avoid the practice of what he called 'self-appointment', when his division leader had died, a voting procedure had been instigated to choose his successor and the three people with the highest number of votes decided to work together as a 'committee' to run the division (Euan). Moreover, the positive side of this informality is that, alongside a good deal of banter and irreverent complaining about local division and regional leaders, there is a genuine sense that the role of leaders is to facilitate and initiate rather than 'lead'.

> I aye[12] a leader, do you know what I mean? Everyone's in there. If I wanna do something, like today, I asked everyone for their opinions on doing it. ... I day just go yeah we are doing it, you aye got a choice. ... We're all in it together. That's the way I see it. (Connor)

Matt also sees everyone as equal in the movement regardless of how long they had been in it: 'a new person could join tomorrow and like he's the same as me. ... [N]o one is bigger or better than anyone else, apart from Tommy and Kevin' (Matt). This raises the question of leadership at the national level; are some, in fact, more equal than others?

Leading the 'barmy army': mediating opinions and talking sense

Until October 2013, the EDL was co-led by Tommy Robinson and Kevin Carroll (themselves cousins). Most members saw the two men as playing equal but complementary roles in the movement; Tommy Robinson's 'passion' and 'drive' (Eddowes, 2015) made him a motivating street leader while Kevin Carroll sought to steer the movement towards a more political route by pursuing an alliance with the British Freedom Party and standing in the 2012 Police and Crime Commissioner elections (Kelly, 2012). The movement was not 'leaderless' (Castells, 2012: 170), therefore, but there is equally little evidence of the 'cult of leadership' normally ascribed to far right political parties (Ignazi, 2003: 106). At demonstrations, people applauded and often posed for pictures with the co-leaders and sometimes a chant of 'Tommy Robinson's barmy army' could be heard (field diary, 29 September 2012). Speeches were passionate but not rabble-rousing and an effort was made to include local speakers, women speakers[13] and, increasingly, young speakers rather than focusing on a single, charismatic leader. Some respondents articulated an emotional attachment to Tommy Robinson – 'I will march into hell for Tommy' (Declan). However, most talked rationally about their 'respect' for him, in particular for the fact that he 'knows his stuff' and that he had carried on despite the pressures on him and his family that accompany the leadership role. At the same time, neither leader was beyond criticism. There was scepticism about some of the stories of hardship and persecution endured by the leaders (Ian, Tim) and one respondent felt Tommy was 'way over his head' with his ambitions to move into politics (Michelle). Thus, when the movement was effectively functioning without either of its leaders in late 2012 (while Tommy Robinson was in prison and Kevin Carroll on bail conditions that did not allow him contact with other EDL members), Local Organisers remained unconcerned since, for them, the EDL was never a top-down organisation anyway (field diary, 18 November 2012).

Particularly valued in the leadership is the quality of 'telling it as it is'. Jason believes that both Tommy Robinson and Kevin Carroll 'speak their minds' and 'tell the truth' while Tommy Robinson 'always speaks sense' (Kane). This, according to Chas, is because he is 'one of us':

> ... the thing which I always liked about him was that he was just one of us. He would talk to you like he was one of us. He wouldn't look down on you. He wouldn't say like 'you don't know this, you don't know that'. ... I always liked Tommy for that. He was a typical bloke off a council estate which most of EDL began as. (Chas)

The point of contrast here is of course mainstream politicians who are characterised as privileged and detached: 'They've not lived in the real world' (Lisa). The lack of 'real-life experience' of politicians seriously undermines their capacity to govern: 'David Cameron, for instance, right? Why would a person like me wanna let him tell me what's best for me when he's never lived my life?' (Tina). Thus, what politics needs, according to Chas, is precisely a Tommy Robinson figure: 'It needs ... not someone's who's been like at Eton school who's had like everything done for 'em who's had all this. It needs somebody who's actually grown up on the streets.' Comparing Tommy Robinson (at the time of interview serving a prison sentence) to Nelson Mandela, Lisa says he is the kind of leader who is persecuted for 'speaking up for the people' (Lisa). In contrast, mainstream politicians are not out to do things for 'the people' but 'just there to fill their own back pockets' (Michelle). Encapsulating what Hay (2007: 39) cites as one of the three key sources of voter distrust of politics – the (perceived) tendency of political elites to subvert the collective public interest in the narrow pursuit of party or self-interest whilst proclaiming themselves disingenuously to be guardians of the former – Tina declares that the problem with the main political parties is that 'they act like they're, they're so good to the public, and everything's for the people when nothing is'.

That the movement is not dependent on a single charismatic or strong leader appears to have been confirmed in the restructuring of the movement following the unexpected resignations of Tommy Robinson and Kevin Carroll. The candidature of a potential replacement 'leader', Tony Curtis,[14] was rejected in favour of a committee of ROs, because Curtis saw himself as 'some self-proclaimed messiah' (Ed).

The move to a committee structure incurred some grassroots criticism of the undemocratic nature of the transfer of power. When Ivan Humble announced at the Bradford demonstration (October 2013) that the ROs would take things forward and that ordinary members should make their voices heard by talking to their ROs, an EDL demonstrator was heard to grumble 'but nobody elected them, they were appointed by Tommy. It's not democratic' (field diary, 12 October 2013). The Chair of the committee rotated from the initially appointed Tim Ablitt to Steve Eddowes (February 2014) who, from the outset, stated he was not interested in becoming the face and voice of the movement. Eddowes (2015) saw his role as one of mediating between 'strong personalities and a lot of strong opinions' and being prepared to take responsibility for the final decision. This led him to focus on a behind-the-scenes role, allowing others such as Paul Weston, leader of Liberty GB, and former leader of the British Freedom Party, and 'freelancer' Dave Russell ('DJ Bossman') who also had no official position within the EDL, to deliver speeches at demonstrations. Collective leadership was absorbed into the ethos and mission of the movement. Following criticism of a 'leaderless' EDL, Eddowes declared, in a speech at the Birmingham demonstration (11 October 2014), that what had been learned from the process of picking up the pieces of the EDL after the resignations of Robinson and Carroll was that 'there is no way in the world this precious thing of ours could ever be allowed to be in one person's hands again'. Calling on grassroots members to recognise that this 'committee' is just a name for the old ROs who had always made the movement function, he declared, 'Leader? Yeah, I'm a leader, they're [ROs] leaders, stewards are leaders, security are leaders. But most importantly, every single one of you is a leader.'[15] While this may appear to be populist rhetoric, the accessibility and proximity of leadership at both local and national levels, based on the evidence from this study at least, translated into a sense among grassroots activists that they could, and, if the opportunity arose, would, take a leadership position in the movement.[16] Although from December 2015, the EDL once again had an official 'leader' – Ian Crossland – grassroots activists participated in his election through social media and the Management Committee remains in place with a new Chair.

Stepping out of line: hierarchy and discipline

In theory the EDL is governed by a 'code of conduct' stipulating that all members must adhere to the correct chain of command (division leader, RO, national leadership) (Copsey, 2010: 19). Long-standing activists recognised that the movement had become more structured than in the early days when 'It was just like ringing up twenty lads, and twenty lads turn up in the boozer, jump on the coach' (Ed). However, while there was a formal chain of command, it was not one that people necessarily observed. Ed noted that he himself had flouted the official code of conduct by not taking my request to interview him further up the chain of command, opting to informally consult a fellow RO instead.

Indeed, there appear to be more grey areas than clear lines to cross in the EDL chain of command. One member had been pulled into line when he had suggested – because of his profile in one of the cross-cutting divisions – that after the leadership resignations he felt that he did not know whom he should answer to; Ed told him straight that if he is 'in [names region] division' he answers to their ROs (field diary, 31 October 2013). When Rachel was told to leave the movement when she challenged the right of a new division leader to order her about, other division leaders and the RO backed her, as a long-standing local division admin, over the highly active but new division leader (field diary, 22 November 2014). The next day the new division leader posted a statement that he had decided to step down from leadership of the division.

Just who had the authority to 'kick out' someone from the movement is unclear. Early in the research, the case for and against 'kicking out' one member of the local division had been discussed at a divisional meeting (see above). However, later cases of individuals who were local admins and, in one case, an RO who apparently had been 'kicked out' had not been discussed by the division (field diary, 10 May 2014). This internal 'infighting' or 'factioning' is perceived by members as one of the main constraints on the efficacy and future of the movement (see below) and the lack of transparency in hierarchy and authority exacerbates the tension.

Disciplining through exclusion is discussed most frequently in relation to the non-tolerance of neo-Nazi elements; a policy promoted by the leadership, demonstratively pursued at public events and spontaneously enacted at grassroots level (see Chapter 4). Flushing out 'closet neo-Nazis' requires extensive networks of people with their ear close to the ground and their eyes open since the contemporary 'dark network' is much harder to identify than the old enemies such as Combat 18 (Eddowes, 2015). Those who 'cause trouble', by getting drunk and starting fights especially at demonstrations, are also disciplined. People were thrown out of the organisation, according to one respondent, primarily not for ideological reasons but 'because they're absolute idiots' (Tim). Others argue that there is already too much discipline and say they would prefer 'a more laid back approach' (Chas). Since younger EDL members like Chas are perceived as unruly, prone to 'kick off' at demonstrations or to use inappropriate language in posts to social media sites, they are also often the object of disciplining or exclusion. A particular incident in which members of a local youth division were perceived to have acted out of line while travelling to an EDL demo (see Chapter 8) resulted in them being given an official warning by a Divisional Organiser that 'if they can't toe the line then we don't want to stand with them' (Matt). Whom the movement should 'stand with' and whom it should exclude is discussed further below.

Who finances the EDL?

There has been considerable speculation and dispute over the origins of funding of the EDL. Copsey (2010: 15) suggests that Alan Lake, a millionaire IT consultant from north London and founder of the website 4freedoms.com, has provided generous financial support to the movement. This is a persistent allegation by the BNP and UAF. In September 2009, Lake came forward as a key figure working behind the scenes for the EDL, although rumours that he bankrolled the EDL to the tune of millions of pounds remain unsubstantiated (2010: 15). Eddowes (2015) admits that, at the start, 'there were people who were putting funds in' but notes that any such funding is 'long gone'. At grassroots level, the few comments on financial issues encountered, rejected the idea of an external funder, comparing what they perceived as the 'working class' basis of the EDL to the privileged position of opposition groups who, it is claimed, are government-funded:

> They've got big offices and they employ people to work there, so how can the UAF afford that? They have got to get some funding. They said the EDL are funded by BNP and Pamela Geller. We get nothing. Every march, every bit of merchandise is out of our own pockets. I mean it's so hard. … Because we are a working-class movement. I mean everybody who you see on an EDL march is working, unemployed, students. (Declan)

Evidence from grassroots level is that although Lake's anti-Islam discourse has a number of common tropes with those found in EDL statements and narratives, as a figure he has no visibility. Few members in this study had heard of Lake or his website although since I was approached and given a card with the website address on it at the EDL demonstration in Bristol, it might be presumed that respondents had also encountered those promoting the site (field diary, 14 July 2012). After a failed attempt to persuade the EDL to align itself politically with

UKIP in May 2010, Copsey suggests, Lake ceased putting himself forward as an EDL spokesperson (2010: 18).

Following the resignation of Kevin Carroll and Tommy Robinson, the new governing Committee of ROs responded to rumours about what previous leaders might have gained from the organisation financially by creating a limited company and keeping proper accounts of all donations and other income (Eddowes, 2015).[17] However, in contrast to movements such as Britain First,[17] the EDL continues to have no income from membership subscriptions and remains donation-light. In reality, Eddowes (2015) claims, those in senior positions put money in – to maintain websites and pay for security – rather than take it out of the movement.

Since there are no membership fees or obligatory donations, at local divisional level, the only funds in evidence are those generated locally through the sale of merchandise, collections for coach trips and from fund-raising activities such as barbecues. Local divisions in this study were described as having from 'nothing' in their kitty currently to, the most well-fleeced one, having 'three-and-a-half grand' (Ed). Another local Division Organiser confirms 'there's no finances basically. No financial backing, no nothing' (Euan). If money does accrue in the division pot (if for example the coach is filled completely rather than just to the number that covers the outlay), then it is put back into the division and used, for example, to help those who get arrested or who cannot pay for a coach ticket because of difficult financial situations. This 'looking after your own' though applies only if the arrest is considered to be unwarranted; if a member is judged to have brought it on themselves, they are not helped.

'No surrender': looking to the future

In 2010 Copsey (2010: 5) concluded that 'the future trajectory of the EDL is uncertain'. While, on the one hand, he argues, the 'threat' posed by the EDL 'to our country, our values and our communities, should not be taken lightly', on the other, its loose and chaotic structure may mean it will quickly 'run out of steam' (2010: 6). Despite the five years that have elapsed since that conclusion, the future of the movement remains uncertain. Public opinion data suggest that the EDL continues to be a marginal group in terms of its visibility and popular appeal. A poll conducted by Extremis/YouGov in October 2012 showed that only a third of respondents in the survey (n=548) had heard of the movement and knew what it stood for and of those who had heard of it, only 11 per cent would consider joining. This leads the authors to conclude that 'similar to the reaction of the British public to other far right groups, we find that a clear and overwhelming majority consider the EDL to be a political pariah'.[19]

Nonetheless, the movement persists and has withstood a series of major challenges and, in this final section, an attempt is made to explain its tenacity. It explores, first, the ongoing struggle with the media in which EDL activists perceive themselves to be locked and how new and social media may provide a means of partially compensating negative or absent mainstream media exposure. It goes on to discuss the extent to which participants in the movement feel they can effect change and the challenges and obstacles to efficacy. Concluding that there is little evidence of hope that they can shape the future, it is suggested that the EDL is fuelled rather by a sense of collective duty to have 'at least tried' and by a 'no surrender' ethos.

'The only attention is bad attention': navigating the media

The media are viewed first and foremost as a site of 'misrepresentation'; of all statements by respondents about the media a third accused the press, and especially the BBC, of misrepresenting the EDL. The most common complaint is that the media are selective about what they report, resulting in 'the only attention we get is bad attention' (Rachel). Positive actions (e.g. charity work) of the EDL, it is claimed, are not publicised while the EDL is blamed in the press for the actions of others. This selectivity is felt to be evident in the way the media fail to show the diversity of the movement (never featuring ethnic-minority or gay members for example) and for 'interviewing those who are drunk just so they can keep their little manifesto of EDL drunken thugs' (Declan).

> RAY: The press thingy like. They pick out the worst ones …
> CHRIS: They look for someone who's not all there, a bit slow in the head, or someone who's drunk. They find someone who's drunk and start asking questions.
> RAY: Then they're going to give 'em stupid answers.

This representation of EDL supporters as 'chavvy, uneducated, yobbos' (Tina) is translated into wider public perceptions – not least through popular culture in the form of comedy sketches or spoofs of EDL actions and supporters by comedian Russell Howard and in Heydon Prowse and Jolyon Rubinstein's BBC 3 satirical comedy show *The Revolution Will Be Televised*. A classic illustration of the cycle of production, reproduction and reworking of such representations is the infamous 'Muslamic ray guns' video.[20] This image is encountered directly by respondents at demonstrations where placards held by counter-demonstrators include those declaring, 'If you can read this, you shouldn't be in the EDL' (field diary, 14 July 2012).[21]

By far the most common frustration, however, is that the media misrepresent the organisation as 'Nazi' or 'racist' (Tim), leading to crude equations in the public mind between 'Nazi' or 'fascist' ideology and the EDL. The media are accused of fuelling misperceptions through inaccurate reporting; a chant at the EDL national demonstration in Birmingham in July 2013 of 'There is only one Lee Rigby' was reported by local news subsequently as 'There is only one Nick Griffin' (field diary, 20 July 2013). Perceptions of the EDL as racist are also blamed on the media's tendency to focus on demonstrative acts such as individuals sporting Nazi symbols or performing Nazi salutes at EDL marches. For some respondents such acts were the work of either UAF or National Front[22] 'infiltrators' aided and abetted in misrepresentation by the media (Declan, Mike). However, others recognise the responsibility of a minority 'within', which provides the opportunity for the media to tar all supporters with the same brush.

The negative image of the EDL is a cause of deep concern for many and managing the image of the movement is the second most frequently mentioned issue in relation to the media. There is little confidence, however, that there is any possibility for a movement like the EDL to counter either negative or simply absent mainstream media exposure. This encourages a certain nostalgia for 'the old days' when violence at demonstrations appeared to be more effective:

> Yeah because the thing was when it was kicking off all the time straight away it was on all the news. It was being heard. People were seeing it on the telly. … People was listening. And then when they started, they went peaceful you know, nothing was happening, nothing kicking off it day even make page eight in the [names local town] News, do you know what I mean? You don't even get nothing. Not a mention. Total media blackout. (Euan)

The trade-off to be made is thus between 'spectacular' actions, which attract media attention albeit of a negative kind, or peaceful demonstrations which are simply ignored (Juris, 2008: 84).

Trolls and other deadly beasts: social media use

One mechanism for circumventing negative representation in the media is to actively use the opportunities provided by new forms of media. This has been a hallmark of the EDL, which is considered one of a new generation of movements for whom new social media (specifically Facebook) is the 'central communicative and organisational tool' (Bartlett and Littler, 2011: 3).

In this sense, the use of the new media in the EDL is more akin to how such media have been employed in new social movements to generate and communicate within social networks (Castells, 2012) than its top-down use in traditional far right parties such as the BNP (Atton, 2006: 573; Jackson, 2011b: 73; Jackson, 2011c: 30). This is confirmed by evidence from this ethnographic study, which showed that the EDL national page is rarely used by respondents. Even official EDL pages at divisional level are used by admins as a site for posting only general information about forthcoming events; in the interests of security, details of meetings and pick-ups for demonstrations or notification of flash demonstrations are passed by phone or personal 'inboxing'. More important are personal Facebook pages, which are used to network and to share and 'like' images and reports related to key campaigns, photos and videos taken during demonstrations, promos for forthcoming demos or home videos of local divisions 'on tour' as part of a bonding practice that sustains the EDL's 'one big family' ethos (see Chapter 7).[23]

However, social media is also a double-edged sword. While it has allowed the movement to generate and maintain extensive grassroots networks (Jackson,

2011b: 72), it opens the movement to 'trolls' and other dangerous beasts and is frequently the place where internal squabbles are played out in a destructive manner. Kane had stopped accessing Facebook, except to find out information for participating in demonstrations, because too many personal issues and 'arguments' were encountered there and such 'infighting' is cited frequently as the cause of supporters leaving or 'stepping back' from the movement.

Thus, while social media are central to EDL activities there is much more scepticism about Facebook than one might assume from the existing secondary literature. Individual members often change their pages or have multiple accounts in anticipation of being temporarily banned from the site; Michelle said she had had almost fifty accounts 'disabled by Facebook'. Others, in contrast, are simply 'not a Facebook person' (Lisa) and use it only as a necessary evil.

Security is another source of tension over the use of Facebook, eliciting practices of 'vouching' for someone before accepting a friend request (Rob). EDL activists are on permanent 'troll' patrol and complain that Facebook is 'where UAF get their information from' (Declan). The 'troll factor' is more than paranoia. Bartlett and Littler (2011: 35) estimated that around '10 per cent of the EDL's Facebook group supporters could be trolls'. Examples of 'trolling' recounted by respondents included the setting up of fake Facebook accounts to expose the EDL, being reported to Facebook by those objecting to the content of pages and the hacking of Facebook accounts and posting of false information. Failure to protect oneself on social media could have real consequences. Jordan had been suspended from work, and subsequently told he would be sacked if he did not voluntarily resign, following routine surveillance of employees' Facebook profiles that revealed his EDL links. Damon was charged and bailed when 'a joke' post to Facebook – in which he said that he would pay £100 to anyone who would knife a leader of the UAF – was reported to the police (although subsequently charges were dropped) (field diary, 4 May 2013). Threats of violence, including death threats, are also received by EDL supporters. Indeed they are so routine, youth division activists claim, they no longer take them seriously (Connor). Another 16-year-old member noted that he had stopped using Facebook since photos of him at a recent demonstration had found their way into the media and he had received a death threat to his phone:

> They put. 'I'm gonna tie you to a chair and slaughter your mother, little sister and father, rip their throat out and leave them to bleed to death in front of you. We're going to burn your house down with you in starting from upstairs down. You've got until the seventh, Brett, the clock's ticking.' (Brett)

Thus, while some respondents imagined 'banter with the opposition' (Ray) via social media to be at least some proxy for being listened to (see Chapter 8), in practice the social media can act to close down as much as open up political debate as it becomes a space for confirming rather than challenging prejudice and for disparaging rather than engaging with the opinions of others (Herring, 2001).

A losing battle? Efficacy and activism

CHRIS: We don't want to have to go to demos to stop our country being taken over but it's the only way we can try and do anything. We won't succeed.
RAY: Fighting a losing battle.
CHRIS: The government are so up their fucking arses. They aren't going to get nowhere but it isn't going to stop you trying. ...
INT: Is it worth trying?
CHRIS: Yes, as long as you're still trying they know there are still people out there that don't agree with them.

A concern about lack of efficacy runs through the narratives of EDL members in this study. As evident from the exchange between Ray and Chris above, demonstrations are felt to be a channel for raising the profile of the movement by making sure 'You've got your word out' (Chris). However, more respondents thought demonstrations were an ineffective rather than effective form of activism, leading even these youth division members to think about them as little more than visible evidence that 'you're still trying' (Chris). Casey is similarly doubtful about 'whether they get listened to or not' but thinks the demonstrations are worth it because 'they're going to try to do something for the country ... they're trying to make a stand'. Tim reports that 'a lot of people say "Well what difference are you gonna make?" and it's like we might make none but at least we'll know we've tried.'

Respondents did make positive suggestions about how to improve the efficacy of street demonstrations, arguing in particular that they would be more effective if they were less frequent but bigger (Connor, Matt). Lisa thinks the movement should extend its range of activities by leafleting the local area with flyers setting out the EDL's message. She also suggests the movement engage in community outreach: 'I'd love to do soup kitchens, you know, and helping like the young, like British youngsters, you know, yeah definitely I think it's not all about demos is it?' (Lisa).

For some, demonstrations did more harm than good since they revealed a lack of professionalism and seriousness; a criticism voiced primarily by those on the extremist fringe (see Chapter 4). Ollie calls EDL demonstrations 'chaotic' while Andrew notes that people turning up 'with their flags the wrong way round' and things spelled incorrectly on placards 'makes them a laughing stock'. However, the damage done to the movement by those who attend demonstrations drunk or high is noted by mainstream EDL members as well: 'I just look at some people and just think like yeah you're a bit of a clown' (Tim).

To improve efficacy, activists call for more discipline in the movement (Michelle). This is most frequently expressed as a need to 'kick out the racists' but there is also considerable criticism of the damage done to the movement by the continued violence at demonstrations despite efforts by organisers to 'keep out all the trouble makers' (Jason). Andrew's conclusion after attending the national demonstration in Manchester and organising his own small flash demo is that 'it needs intelligent people within these movements. I say that us four who went out on Monday did more and created more of an impression than what those 600 or so EDL did' (Andrew). Lisa also sees the need for greater purpose and fresh ideas:

> I think you have got to have a goal. What do you want to achieve at the end of this? You can't say 'get rid of all Muslims'. Fucking not gonna happen and that's not what the problem is or the issue. So yeah I would like definitely, you know, I would like, would love to be sat at the front there and coming up with ideas. (Lisa)

Divisional meetings are also criticised for being called or changed without sufficient notice (Michelle) and for being 'not structured at all' (Lisa).

Another perceived hindrance to the effectiveness of the movement is internal dispute. Here there is a palpable tension between the desire and need for 'unity' for the success of the movement and the everyday 'in-fighting' that disrupts the achievement of its goals and undermines commitment to the group. The EDL has a history of factioning, most notably related to the formation of more radical 'Infidel' groups and to manoeuvrings for power while Tommy Robinson was in prison. Referring to rumours of attempts to take over the movement at one such time, Connor complains, 'You should not argue like in the public ... You should stand together. ... [L]ike the way I see it is if we don't stand closer together now, the EDL's gone' (Connor).

The question organisationally is how best to handle such factioning in order to minimise the harm done to the movement; grassroots opinion on this was divided. For some, tensions were resolved by setting up either a new division of the EDL or a new movement. Respondents in this study included three who were primarily affiliated to a local 'Infidels' group and one who had moved from the EDL to the newly formed English Volunteer Force (EVF). This itself creates a new problem of determining which groups the EDL can 'stand with' and are thus welcome at EDL events and which should be excluded as it seeks to distinguish itself from the 'far right'. Illustrative here are differing opinions on the public physical attack by Tommy Robinson on a prominent member of the National Front attending an EDL demonstration. For Rob, who at the time of interview had himself left the EDL and become Local Organiser for the EVF, this had signalled the start of the end of the EDL which should, to his mind, embrace all like-minded people. In contrast, for Chris, Tommy Robinson had acted correctly, since he was responding to the National Front member doing 'the Hitler salute'.

Criticism of the (national and regional) leadership of the EDL was expressed only by one respondent (Michelle), although Connor notes that 'disrespect' shown for the leadership (as well as Tommy Robinson's absence from demonstrations while he was in prison) had had a negative impact on the movement.

The continuation of this dilemma into the post-Robinson era of the movement is evident in press releases by the new leadership in January[24] and September

2014.[25] On 16 January 2014, the new committee of ROs running the EDL issued an explicit statement declaring that the Management Group did not want 'to have unity' with a range of named splinter groups – Britain First, South East Alliance, North West Infidels, North East Infidels, English Volunteer Force, National Front, Combat 18 and White Pride – because they 'are openly White Pride and racist' and/or 'are against our Jewish and LGBT community'. In interview Eddowes (2015) defined these groups as 'those whose strings are being pulled by far right movements'. The EDL management, the statement went on, 'are happy to stand with any like-minded patriots who do not discriminate against creed/colour, we will not stand with groups that do discriminate and are racist'. The dilemma is that on the one hand the new leadership 'recognises that there is a need to collaborate with like-minded organisations' but fears that 'People who are talking about "unity" are trying to push agendas of white pride and Nazism which we have spent five years trying to keep away.'[26]

Narratives of factioning among respondents tend to focus on individual and personal issues rather than ideological disputes, confirming that it is not only disagreements on strategy and tactics within groups that divide but that 'jealousies, hatreds, disappointments, and demonization foster schisms within movements' (Klatch, 2004: 489). Connor complains 'people are dropping out through backstabbing and egos … in-fighting is the fucking worst thing like what's putting us back' (Connor). For Euan, internal disputes and factioning often arise from personal relationships turning sour, confirming other research suggesting that the 'libidinal economy' of social movements both inspires and detracts from activism (Brown and Pickerill, 2009: 31). As division leader, he found himself often trying to 'sort out a lot of people's problems when they are having a fall out' (Euan).

There are also positive assessments of the movement. Matt, although admitting he sometimes wonders whether it is all worth it, notes that 'we're slowly getting noticed' and mentions small achievements, including objections to local planning applications that would not have happened 'if it wasn't for us' (Matt). While not perfect, demonstrations are seen to serve their purpose, if only very gradually, of raising awareness (Chas). Chris says attending demonstrations makes him feel 'You've got your word out' and Connor concludes that, even if only one person listens to what is said, 'You're still making a change.'

A small number of respondents enthusiastically claim the future of the movement is in expanding internationally – 'going global' (Brett, Neil, Jason). Others presume the external environment – new flows of immigrants, new mosques being built, more awareness about grooming gangs – means numbers joining the movement in the future will rise (Andrew, Chas). Nonetheless, respondents remain largely sceptical about their own efficacy. Tim perceives the movement to be on a downward trajectory as 'people are thinking there's not enough results to the amount of work that's being put in' (Tim) while Richard, who stopped attending demos, states starkly that 'You can do as much protesting as you want but I think it still don't make a difference' (Richard).

No surrender: duty not hope

I think you can't give up, can you? No surrender. (Lisa)

In the absence of hope that anything might really change, what sustains activism in the EDL? While the meanings attached to activism by respondents are considered in detail in Chapter 7, here it is noted only that activism is more than the outcome of the rational application of means in order to achieve specific aims. Ollie, for example, does not expect any outcome for himself: 'It's not that I'm doing it for myself, if I do something now and it just … makes it a little bit better for the people in the future then I'm still going to do it' (Ollie).

What is striking about narratives among grassroots EDL activists is that while emotions such as anger, hate, fear and respect pepper their narratives, 'hope' is directly mentioned only once and in relation to its absence (Andrew). Lisa notes that 'there's got to be light at the end of the tunnel' to give protests a meaning; although she does not say that she sees such a light.

In place of hope, respondents' voices are filled with defiance and a determination not to 'bow down':

> INT: And what do you think is the point of having these kinds of demonstrations?
> CONNOR: To prove a point like we am there and that we ain't gonna hide, we am gonna go out on the streets and we am gonna prove who we am. We am English and you aye gonna stop us really. You aye gonna make us bow down and like not listen to you, we are gonna do it whether you like it or not.

'No surrender' – originally associated with Unionist slogans of 'no surrender to the IRA' – is commonly encountered in EDL discourse. 'Nfse' ('no fucking surrender ever') is a frequent sign off on posts or inbox messages, while one of the core chants at demonstrations is 'No surrender, No surrender, No surrender to the Taliban' (see Chapter 7). Ed talked about a tattoo he was planning for his chest consisting of the acronym 'Sinao' ('Surrender is not an option').[27] Kane expresses his determination to 'never surrender' even in the face of declining numbers, 'cause I believe what they am fighting for and the reasons why we am normally there'. Expressing this in a more positive vein, Tim explains that the EDL for him is a way to 'stand up' for what you believe in and feel that at least 'we tried':

> I stand up for things and what I believe in. I've been in trouble in the past just for purely standing up for things like I remember the first time I ever got arrested I was 15 and it was because I'd seen an older lad … picking on one of my friend's younger brothers and I caught him doing it and I went over and I said 'I'm not gonna let this happen', and it's like 'if you wanna pick on someone try someone who'll fight back' you know. … Me, I'd rather be able to sleep at night knowing that I've tried than knowing that I didn't bother. (Tim)

Mouffe (2005: 69–71) has argued that right-wing populist movements in Britain today are able to exploit popular frustration by drawing on unacceptable mechanisms of xenophobic exclusion to provide people with some form of hope that things could be different. While at a deeper, existential, level, Mouffe may be right, the findings of this study provide little evidence that EDL activists are 'hopeful' about the future or, even less, have any sense that that future is in their hands. The movement is sustained, at the rational level, rather by a sense of collective duty to have 'at least tried' and a 'no surrender' ethos. The significance of the affective dimension in sustaining the movement is discussed in Chapter 7.

Conclusion

At the time of writing the EDL is in the process of reshaping itself from 'Tommy Robinson's barmy army' into a broader-based and stable organisation. Steering the movement through this 'state of flux' is not a simple task according to the EDL's Chair at the time, who was conscious above all of the need to 'stop it from morphing into something dark which is where it could well have gone' (Eddowes, 2015). The task is complicated further by the acute reflexive engagement of the movement with its own representation. The movement is routinely subjected to caricature and ridicule as racist, thuggish, drunken and uneducated and this is experienced as a major obstacle to efficacy; indeed the failure to rid the movement of this association is ostensibly the reason for the resignation of its founding leaders.

In contrast to the 'victim' relationship the EDL perceives itself to have in relation to traditional media, it has used new or social media extensively to organise, network and disseminate. However, this chapter has suggested that the relationship between the media, new and old, and the EDL is more complex than it appears in existing literature. While social media have been employed effectively to circumvent 'media blackout', it remains a site of tension; despite significant control over Facebook use being devolved to local divisions, the right to 'say it as it is' is a constant source of conflict between older and younger and between admin and rank-and-file members of the organisation. Moreover, although the social media do play a crucial role in everyday recruitment, bonding and organisation, many members are highly sceptical and often hostile to the medium. Trust and loyalty are valued above anything and those are gained only through face-to-face activities. Finally, the importance of the new media does not mean the old media have lost their significance; media representations of the movement confirm a sense of 'conspiracy' between political and cultural elites to silence 'working class' or 'ordinary' voices and concerns and thus serve a bonding function.

The EDL has, contrary to widespread expectation, survived – albeit in a diminished form – the resignation in October 2013 of its co-founders and leaders. Currently it is locked in a process of 'metamorphosis' in which new forms of organisation and strategy are engaged with on a basis of 'trial and error' (Eddowes, 2015). While its evolution into a more sophisticated political organisation is not impossible in the future, its current aim is modest; to survive as 'a platform for people to come to when they've finally had enough' (2015).

Notes

1 A phrase used initially by representatives of the Quilliam Foundation who facilitated and announced the resignations. See www.dailymail.co.uk/news/article-2449542/ Tommy-Robinson-quits-leader-EDL.html. Accessed: 26.08.2015.

2 A group of around twenty members of the group held inflammatory banners and shouted abuse at soldiers of the 2nd battalion of the Royal Anglian Regiment returning from a six-month tour in Iraq (Copsey, 2010: 9).

3 In February 2014, the EDL announced that 'mass immigration' would, in the future, be included in the EDL's mission statement (www.englishdefenceleague.org/edl-announces-new-chairman. Accessed: 28.03.2014). However, this materialised only in a new version of the mission statement released on 3 January 2016 (see Chapter 4).

4 See http://englishdefenceleague.org/about-us/mission-statement. Accessed 26.06.2012. It is this mission statement that is referred to throughout this book unless otherwise stated. The revised version was released only in 2016 and thus was not known to respondents.

5 'Islamic courts' is a phrase used by EDL members to refer to what they perceive to be an alternative legal system in operation in the UK. It is not clear whether they refer here to Sharia Councils, which provide legal advice and rulings primarily on marriage and finances based on Sharia law although have no legal authority in the UK, or to the Muslim Arbitration Tribunal, which is an alternative dispute resolution structure governed by the UK Arbitration Act.

6 This position also calls for the recognition that Islam has social and ideological aspects in addition to being a faith and that its principles, in some cases, contradict those of liberal democracy and therefore have implications for non-Muslims living alongside Muslims.

7 The Quilliam Foundation is a counter-extremism think tank chaired by Maajid Nawaz and funded, initially, under the UK government's 'Prevent' programme designed to counter (primarily Islamic) violent extremism (PVE).

8 See www.youtube.com/watch?v=9RTa0vmFCAY. Accessed: 14.04.2014.

9 See www.youtube.com/watch?v=YsfovbkDi0M. This video has been removed by YouTube because its content violated the company's terms of service.

10 See https://www.youtube.com/watch?v=F9zTQRFerII.

11 For the Memorandum of Understanding governing the collaboration of these European defence leagues, see http://englishdefenceleague.org/european-defence-leagues. Accessed: 26.6.2012.

12 As noted in Chapter 2, all quotes are cited verbatim from the interview transcripts or field notes including where regional speech patterns do not conform to standard English grammar. Where these patterns might obscure meaning, the standard English equivalent is noted. In this quote 'aye' means 'am not' and 'day' means 'don't'.

13 In sharp contrast, Ezekiel (2002: 54) notes that in seven years of study of the white racist scene in the USA he never heard a speech by a woman.

14 Curtis had been tipped to stand in for Tommy Robinson while he was in prison but had left the movement and flirted with the British version of 'Golden Dawn' and then the EVF.

15 See www.youtube.com/watch?v=c6fmJeYOiLQ.

16 Besides the 19-year-old leader of the LGBT division who already held a prominent position in the movement, a further eight respondents in this study (including two 16

year olds and two women) noted their desire to 'move up' the movement and be one of the people who organised rather than demonstrated.

17 See www.youtube.com/watch?v=c6fmJeYOiLQ). Accessed 11.12.2014.

18 See http://search.electoralcommission.org.uk/Api/Accounts/Documents/16078.

19 See http://extremisproject.org/2012/10/the-english-defence-league-edl-what-do-peo ple-think. Accessed: 5.05.2014.

20 It started when a YouTube video featuring an inarticulate EDL supporter at the Blackburn demo (the individual referenced in the discussion between Ray and Chris above) went viral (see www.youtube.com/watch?v=AIPD8qHhtVU). It began to be used by groups opposing the EDL to demonstrate the stupidity of EDL members before being reappropriated by EDL supporters and used as a resource for self-irony.

21 A photograph of this placard can be found at: www.thisisbristol.co.uk/pictures/Bristol-EDL-march-anti-EDL-protests/pictures-16536026-detail/pictures.html.   Accessed: 24.08.2015.

22 The National Front (NF) is a far right 'whites only' political party founded in 1967 and most active during the 1970s, when it secured just over 3 per cent of the vote in those seats contested in the 1974 General Elections, but splintered over the course of the 1980s following a decline in electoral success after the first Thatcher government came to power in 1979 (Goodwin et al., 2010; Allen, 2011; Solomos, 2013). As discussed below the NF is one of the groups from which the EDL is keen to dissociate itself.

23 Of course much non-EDL related material is also shared on these pages, including: information about causes supported by but not linked to the EDL, personal images and messages, pictures of new tattoos or haircuts and humorous 'motivational' posters, YouTube videos of favourite songs, updates on relationship status, arguments, plans for the evening, football results etc.

24 See www.englishdefenceleague.org/splinter-groups. Issued: 16.01.2014. Accessed: 25.11.2014.

25 See   www.englishdefenceleague.org/suspicions-raised-about-nationalist-demonstra tion-on-8th-october-and-neo-nazi-named-and-shamed. Issued: 19.09.2014. Accessed 24.11.2014.

26 See www.youtube.com/watch?v=c6fmJeYOiLQ.

27 There are clear loyalist connections to the use of these phrases and the links between EDL and loyalist groups is worthy of further researcher and discussion.

3

Doing the hokey-cokey:
everyday trajectories of activism

Social movements do not consist of 'one hero, accompanied by an undifferentiated crowd' (Castells, 2012: 12) but of rounded individuals whose diverse
trajectories in and out of activism are embedded in personal life stories. These
individuals are neither born nor aggressively recruited into EDL activism. They
are neither duped by a charismatic leader nor spring from the earth as authentic,
working-class anti-heroes. Their trajectories in and out of the movement are
prosaic rather than heroic.

This chapter opens with a broad-brush portrait of the socio-demographic
profile of activists in this study contextualised in existing data on the composition
of support for, and activism in, far right organisations. The chapter then considers
routes into (and often out of) the movement and the costs and consequences of
participation. While space does not allow the detailed profiling of all respondents,
the individual stories of eight activists are included as short vignettes. In this way,
it is hoped to evoke characters who are recognisable and 'live from chapter to
chapter' rather than reducing respondents to 'a bunch of disembodied thoughts
that come out of subjects' mouths in interviews' (Duneier and Back, 2006: 553).

This attention to individual agency (motivations, choices, turning points)
requires embedding in the socio-economic context of those lives at a more structural level; while macrostructural determinants may not be immediately visible
to the ethnographic eye, they remain 'inscribed in the material distribution of
resources and social possibles' (Wacquant, 2008: 10–11). Realising this aspiration
is problematic in this study for two reasons. First, it would require detailed discussion of the history and (post-)industrial development of the area in which the
study is located, which would reveal the geographic location of the study and thus
compromise the anonymity assured to research participants. More pragmatically,
while respondents mainly come from a single region (in terms of EDL organisational structure), they were resident in different parts of that region (up to
ninety miles apart); this made it impossible to conduct ethnographic observation
of respondents' everyday interactions with the formal and informal institutions
through which resources such as employment, education, housing and welfare
are accessed. Structural factors shaping paths into (and out of) EDL activism are
addressed here, therefore, only in so far as they are articulated by respondents

themselves in interview or conversation. This nonetheless provides some insight into the deeper social structural forces shaping participation in the movement beyond individual 'motivations'.

'Who are you?' EDL activists in profile

The EDL is said to be composed of mainly poorly educated, white, working-class young men (Copsey, 2010: 5; Ford and Goodwin, 2014: 79). Against such broad-brush portraits of EDL activists, the socio-demographic profile of respondents in this study is painted here in finer detail and set in the context of existing literature and more statistically representative data. For the purposes of this book, the 'respondent set' (see Appendix 2) are considered to be those who took part in recorded interviews, although the number of people who contributed to the researcher's understanding of the movement is much larger. They consist primarily of EDL activists from divisions within one regional organisation who travelled to demonstrations. Exceptions are: three members of the more extreme 'Infidels' organisation, who were from the same region and attended some EDL events whilst being critical of the EDL as a movement; two respondents who were members of a football firm of a nearby town and identified primarily as Casuals but participated in events organised jointly with the EDL; three respondents from a different part of the country interviewed after one of them was met at a national demonstration; and one respondent who was a family member of a key informant and who did not travel to demonstrations but was an EDL sympathiser.

Age

The EDL is described as a 'young' movement by Demos, whose Facebook-hosted survey suggested that 72 per cent of its supporters were under the age of 30 (Bartlett and Littler, 2011: 17). This contrasts the primarily 'grey-haired' support for the BNP (Goodwin, 2011a: 137) and UKIP (Ford and Goodwin, 2014: 175) and is in line with what we know more generally about the greater appeal to young people of subcultural or direct-action movements linked to the extreme right rather than formal political parties (Mudde, 2014: 4). In this study too, almost three-quarters (74 per cent) of respondents were under 35 years of age (see Figure 3.1).

While this might appear to confirm the youthfulness of the EDL suggested above, in fact young people were significantly less visible in the movement than expected and the achieved age distribution was driven by the focus of the larger MYPLACE project on *youth* activism and receptivity to radical political agendas (see the Introduction). Ethnographic observation suggested, in fact, that the proportion of those aged under 30 among active members of the EDL is significantly overestimated in the Bartlett and Littler study; almost certainly a result of the fact that the survey was conducted via Facebook, which is used more frequently by young people (Bartlett and Littler, 2011: 17). In contrast, the current study may have underestimated the proportion of virtually active young people since

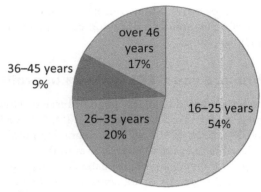

3.1 Age of respondents

it recruited respondents primarily through face-to-face acquaintance at demonstrations and meetings. Although many young supporters enjoyed the 'buzz' of demonstrations (see Chapter 7), their participation was inhibited by travel costs (Connor, Tina, Rob) and the crackdown by the movement on violence (Ray, Chris, Connor). Respondents also recognised that young people are disinclined to join the movement because it is represented in the media as racist (Ray, Connor). Indeed a recent Extremis/YouGov survey found that, of those who had heard of the EDL, only 5 per cent of 18–24 year olds said they would consider joining, while 13 per cent of 40–59 year olds could contemplate doing so.[1]

Gender and sexuality

Studies to date have shown that women are significantly under-represented in all extreme right groups from relatively moderate radical right parties to the most extreme neo-Nazi groups (Mudde, 2014: 10). This study confirmed that men significantly outnumbered women in the EDL; 77 per cent of the respondent set was male and 23 per cent female. This mirrors Klandermans and Mayer's study of extreme right activists in Europe where, even after deliberate oversampling of women activists, the proportion in each country sample ranged from a fifth to a third (Team Members, 2006: 52). It concurs also with the Demos survey of EDL supporters, which found 81 per cent to be male and 19 per cent to be female (Bartlett and Littler, 2011: 5). Although sexual orientation was not something that was asked when socio-demographic data were collected from interviewees, three respondents (two men and one woman) were open about being gay or lesbian (see Box 3).

When asked whether their minority position in the EDL concerned them, women activists in this study said they felt comfortable, accepted and equal in a male environment and that having men around made them feel safer (Tina, Rachel). Women were visible in the EDL online and physically in many 'admin' roles and as stewards and speakers at demonstrations. Women were included among the inner circle of Regional Organisers (Gail Speight) and top leadership

Box 3: Declan

When I first met Declan, at the muster point for an EDL demonstration in Manchester (March 2013) he was reluctant to give me his mobile phone number. He had, he said, had previous experience of being 'exposed' by a journalist. Yet, surrounded by EDL supporters, he had no qualms in telling me he was gay.

He had joined the BNP in 2005 at just 13 years of age – his parents were both BNP members – but, in 2009, he left and joined the EDL because he found it more open towards him as a young gay man. When we met for interview in March 2013, however, it was at the flat of a division organiser in a town neighbouring his home town. It transpired that a few weeks earlier, his own local organisation had held a recruiting day at which some members of the division had called him 'an embarrassment being a gay EDL member and said that the EDL should not allow gays'.

Declan is as much anti-communist or anti-left as he is anti-Islam and he criticises left-wing groups opposing the EDL for failing to be consistently critical of homophobia 'wherever they find it'. Due to an implicit hierarchisation of oppression he suggests that the left fails to challenge Islamic teachings which say 'gays should be taken to a top of a mountain and thrown off'. At the end of 2012, Declan was

3.2 Declan: standing proud

asked to take over heading up the LGBT division and he was visible at almost every national, and many local, demonstrations carrying his rainbow flag amidst the sea of St George's crosses.

When I interviewed Declan he had recently lost his job at a DIY superstore and was living on benefits of £112 per fortnight. Both his parents were long-term unemployed and the only member of his extended family working was one cousin. He had applied for over fifty jobs that week and joked ironically that he was competing with his own parents for jobs, since they applied for the same limited opportunities in their area. The situation was materially difficult; 'the house is clean you know what I mean but in the fridge there's very limited food ... the bills are piling up, the rent's going up'. Besides, he said, 'I can't not work. I'm just not that sort of person.'

(Helen Gower); a sharp contrast to the findings of Ezekiel's (2002: 54–55) study of neo-Nazi and Klan groups in the United States, where women were never encountered in leadership roles. Women activists demonstrated a range of trajectories into the movement, defying the stereotype of 'following a man into racism' (Blee, 2002: 10). Indeed a number of women had joined the movement on their own, or with other women, and did not develop long-term partners within it (Rachel, Lisa).

However, the authenticity and integrity of women's activism is nonetheless subject to question and dispute. Women are often described as 'girlfriends' of male members (Rachel) (see also: Ezekiel, 2002: 54; Kimmel, 2007: 207) or ascribe themselves a primarily 'supportive' rather than active role. Casey, for example, describes herself as 'on the side line' but she agrees with and supports her partner (a divisional leader) by managing his correspondence with the police because 'he's shit at things like that' (see Box 4).

Women in the movement are undermined above all, however, by claims that their participation is motivated by the desire to find a sexual or romantic partner:

Box 4: Matt and Casey

On the coach on the way back from my first demonstration, a local division organiser takes the microphone. He has an important question; will his girlfriend marry him? From my seat, and amongst laughter and taunts about 'how gay is that?', I don't hear Casey answer Matt's question, but the clapping suggests it is a 'yes'.

When I first met them, Matt and Casey lived together with Casey's 11-year-old daughter, two Staffordshire terriers, an impossibly large rabbit and a veritable menagerie of snakes, spiders, scorpions and tropical fish. Towards the end of the fieldwork the family grew again when they had a baby daughter together. Casey attended demonstrations when she could but saw her role primarily as to 'support' and 'help' Matt especially with organisational matters and sorting catering for meetings and socials.

3.3 Matt and Casey: teamwork

Matt has a strong sense of stigmatisation. His mum raised him and his brother alone and, although it is not talked about openly in the family, he suspects his dad was violent towards her. He thinks that being a one-parent family was why he and his brother got 'blamed' for low-level crime in the area (thieving, graffiti) and classed as the local 'rogues'.

Matt still strongly identified with his football hooligan past. At 16 he had started to support the local city team and become part of its firm. This had landed him in prison when he was younger but he said he had put all that behind him and not been in trouble with the police for more than three years. During the fieldwork, however, he was convicted of 'common assault' after an argument on a bus and served four weeks of an eight-week prison sentence.

Matt was very conscious that 'my face is known' locally, to the police because of his football past, and to the wider community because of his EDL activism. He had received a series of threats via Facebook and had a 'petrol bomb' thrown at him in the street.

Neither Matt nor Casey was in paid employment when we first met, although Casey later got a job in a school kitchen. Matt is often rushing around 'seeing a man about a dog' although he never tells me how he makes money. Two litters of puppies are sold in the course of the fieldwork, however, suggesting that, in this case, the metaphor is more literal than one might imagine.

'Most of the EDL lasses are in it for cock. I will put it straight; I do think some of them are slags' (Connor). This is a discourse, moreover, to which women contribute; Michelle proposes that 'sticky knicker brigade' would be a more appropriate name for the women's division than 'Angels'. When set alongside the observation that sexist 'banter' – language and jokes – is routine to the point of being invisible to many women activists (Tina), this suggests that despite the visibility of women in the EDL, they retain what Kimmel (2007: 207) terms a 'relegated status'.

The question of why women are less active is difficult to answer on the basis of a small ethnographic study. Respondents often referred to their responsibility for children meaning they had 'no time' to go on demonstrations (Carlie) or that the children simply 'came first' (Casey). In informal conversation, however, female respondents claimed other women in the movement were prevented from attending demonstrations by their male partners (field diary, 29 September 2012). There is also some evidence from data on electoral support for the extreme right that, in general, women are less attracted to radical right-wing parties, and more inclined to back the welfare state, due to their roles as primary caregivers and their more vulnerable labour-market positioning (Kitschelt, 2007: 1199).

Educational experience

Figure 3.4 details the current or achieved educational level of respondents (in absolute numbers of respondents) and paints a somewhat different picture to the findings of the Demos survey from which it was concluded that EDL supporters were 'more educated' than many would assume. Against a national higher-education participation rate of around 45 per cent and Bartlett and Littler's (2011: 18) finding that around 30 per cent of EDL members surveyed via Facebook were 'educated to university or college level', in this study only 6 per cent of respondents (two respondents) had completed, or were currently studying for, a higher-educational degree while 28 per cent had taken the vocational education route. Most striking of all is that almost 20 per cent (six respondents) had not completed secondary education, having left or been excluded from school before completion of exams. Two respondents had been educated, at least partially, in the private education system;[2] both were members of the more radical 'Infidels' splinter group and self-identified as 'national socialists'.

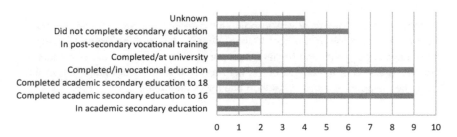

3.4 Educational status of respondents

Based on a respondent set of thirty-five, these figures are not representative of EDL activists more widely but they are indicative of some of the troubled educational experiences that dominate personal narratives. Nine respondents talked about their own exclusion or temporary suspension from school or college for a mixture of behavioural and political reasons. Sean was expelled in Year 10 'for blowing the science lab up'; he was, he said, 'bored' but 'good at practical work'. Michelle too felt that she could 'learn quickly' when it came to practical skills (she would have liked to train as a car mechanic) but had found school, where you have to 'sit down with a pen and pencil and piece of paper', deeply frustrating. Other stories were more directly linked to political views, although it is not always clear whether these incidents constituted a cause or effect of anti-Muslim views:

> when I was in [names school] a few years ago, Year 8, a Muslim lad smacked me over the head with a chair so I grabbed his head and smashed his head on the table. I got kicked out the school for it, and it was on camera him hitting me over the head with a chair. ... I got kicked out of school for a racial attack. ... I had to move school. (Brett)

At the time of interview, Connor was just 15 but neither in school, training nor employment because, he explained, when pupils were reallocated, following the closure of the school he was at, other schools in the area refused to accommodate him because he was known to be an EDL supporter (see Box 5).

More routine, but equally life-shaping, experiences involved low educational achievement due to the failure to complete school or truancy. For Ian, everything

---

Box 5: Connor

Connor was just 15 years old when I first met him at an EDL demo in Bristol with two other members of a local EDL youth division that they had founded. Soon after, when Chris was given a prison sentence and Ray, Connor's older brother, was too busy with college to continue organising the division, Connor took on leading the division himself. His enthusiasm often got him into trouble with older members of the movement but he was also effective in bringing younger people into the movement. He made his own poster and set up his own Blog Talk Radio show which he hosted in late 2012.

Connor was very active on Facebook, using it for personal issues, to access, and sell, things cheap as well as for EDL-related posts. At the start of fieldwork he also attended demonstrations regularly, but thereafter he was often absent. Sometimes he simply had no money to travel. Other times he blamed the negative attitude of older members to the younger ones' loudness for a decision not to travel with the older members of the division anymore. Periodically he also posted that he was fed up with 'backstabbing' or lack of seriousness in the movement and was 'taking a step back' from the EDL.

3.5 Connor: 'Ain't bothered'

Connor lived with his grandparents. He had contact with his dad, who, together with his uncle, had run a local division of the EDL. Neither he nor his brother Ray ever mentioned their mum. In my last communication with him, Connor said that he had not been out and about with the EDL recently because he was about to become a dad.

had started to go wrong when his granddad, who he described as 'basically my dad', had died when he was 14 and he 'just stopped going to school, started kicking off at football matches'. He now regrets not attending school since 'I know if I'd have gone to school more I could have done a hell of a lot more.' Richard reflects that he had the romantic belief he was going to be a professional footballer and did not need to do well at school. He left without any qualifications as he was excluded before his GCSE exams. Richard, who worked as a refuse collector for the local council, laughs that 'one of my teachers said if you don't try hard at school you're going to be a bin man [laughs]'. While Richard is one of the few full-time employed respondents in this study and happy with his job conditions and prospects, he also recognises the stigma it attracts; you get 'labelled a tramp' if you handle rubbish.

An important dimension of stories about school or college is personal experience of being bullied. Five respondents in this study said they had been bullied at school and their accounts of this experience are discussed in Chapter 6. Studies of participants in 'EXIT' programmes in Scandinavia and Germany also found that 'bullying was a common unifying theme' (Kimmel, 2007: 209) suggesting the role of bullying in the stories of young people's paths into extreme right activism, alongside domestic and sexual violence (discussed below), is an important and under-researched question.

Employment

The most striking dimension of the socio-demographic profile of respondents in this study regards their employment status (see Figure 3.6). While in the Demos survey, just over a quarter (28 per cent) of EDL supporters were unemployed (Bartlett and Littler, 2011: 5), in this study the figure was almost half (49 per cent).[3] A further 20 per cent were in either part-time or 'irregular' employment, which covers a range of statuses, including seasonal and occasional work, cash-in-hand employment or semi-legal and illegal trading activities. In contrast only 11 per cent were in full-time employment.

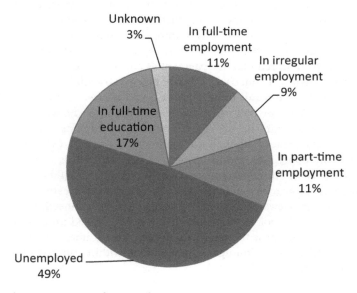

3.6 Employment status of respondents

There is a widespread assumption that unemployment, both at the national (macro) and the individual (micro) level, is correlated to extreme right attitudes since it is believed that marginalisation leads to political frustration and consequent extremism (Mudde, 2014: 8). Qualitative studies of extreme right activism also often reveal circumstantial evidence of the connection. Ezekiel's (2002: 58) study of members of a white racist group in Detroit showed most of the members to have no jobs and no prospect of work while those who did work, earned low wages or found occasional, manual work on an informal basis. However, there is also a growing body of evidence that support for extreme right parties and movements emanates not from the poorest groups but the lower middle class and skilled manual workers (Blee, 2002: 25; Kimmel, 2007: 207; Rhodes, 2011: 115).

Respondents in this study identified themselves as working class, or as Tina put it 'the normal working class that are struggling to get by' (Tina). Older respondents survived on a combination of benefits (often as a result of ill health) and informal work or irregular earning opportunities and everyday conversations frequently concerned material issues, debt and bills, benefit claims and sanctions. Younger respondents found themselves moving rapidly between insecure and low-paid jobs, in a similar trajectory to the 'downwardly mobile' young men in Kimmel's (2007: 207) study. Declan explains the competition for even low-paid jobs in his local area as 'if there's one job advertised they'll be 900 people applying for it and only 10 would get an interview'. Declan is no stranger to unemployment; his dad had been unemployed for 12 years and his mum had not worked since losing her job when he was a child. Tim, whose dream was to work in a job caring for animals, describes how, since the closure of a major employer in the area, work had become precarious. Despite being only 25 years of age, he had moved already between a series of construction and service industry-related jobs, for most of which he had no previous training, and from which he appeared to be laid off, conveniently for the employer, just before they would have been obliged to offer some form of redundancy payment (Tim). For Jordan, the fact that 'the work's not out there' explained why seven of his close friends had joined the army.

That the EDL commands more support from lower-class strata is confirmed by the Extremis/YouGov poll which found that, of those who were aware of the movement, people from the working classes and on benefits were more likely to agree with the values (although not methods) of the EDL (31 per cent) than those from the upper and middle classes (18 per cent).[4] This is not to explain away extreme right attitudes as the necessary outcome of either working-class status or deprivation; many more people in these structural locations do not align with extreme right views. Still less is it to suggest a direct connection between the unemployment and poor job prospects of these people and immigration flows. However, it is to recognise the intertwining of persistent unemployment and the permanent settlement of immigrant populations within patterns of 'advanced marginality' (Wacquant, 2008: 163).

Family status and background

Socio-demographic data on the family status of respondents captured basic information about whether respondents were married or living with a partner (29 per cent), single (54 per cent) or divorced/separated (17 per cent). The high proportion of 'single' respondents clearly reflects the skew towards younger people in the respondent set. Family background and childhood experiences were found to be very significant in shaping the lives and political trajectories of respondents and are considered below.

Ethnicity

Respondents were asked how they usually referred to themselves when declaring their ethnicity (for example when completing official forms). Figure 3.7 shows that 51 per cent referred to themselves as 'White-English', while 23 per cent called themselves 'White-British'.[5] This identification as 'English', ironically, is slightly less than for the general population; 2011 census data show that three-fifths of the population in England do not identify with a British national identity, and only see themselves as English (Jivraj and Simpson, 2013). In interview, moreover, the insistence on 'Englishness' is not as pronounced as anticipated from the name and symbolic representations chosen by the EDL. The main concern expressed is a resentment that, while other national groups in the British Isles routinely consider themselves to be 'Welsh' or 'Scottish' rather than 'British', it is considered 'taboo' or even 'racist' to declare yourself to be 'English' (Ed). This is echoed in Clarke

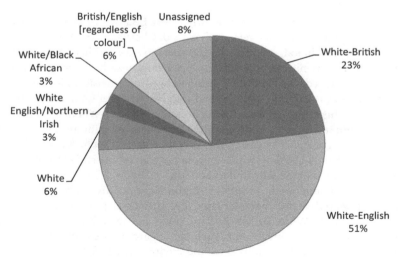

3.7 Ethnicity (self-declared) of respondents

and Garner's (2010: 203) study of white residents in Bristol and Plymouth who viewed enviously other constituent nationalities of the UK, whose identities were 'celebrate-able' without guilt. A particularly contentious issue is that on official forms, where you are required to state your nationality, there is no option to state you are English rather than British while it is possible to say you are Scottish and so forth (Ed). Both Ed and Ian complained that forms they had filled in had been returned because they had put 'English' where asked to state 'nationality' (field diary, 21 April 2013). Others acknowledge that although they consider themselves 'English', the use of the term in the name of the organisation is 'controversial' and might give the wrong impression (Tim). Moreover, among respondents there were equally strong commitments to the importance of maintaining a united Britain (Nick), feeling a primary allegiance to the Union Jack rather than the St George's flag (Lisa) and rejection of the special status of 'Englishness', seeing it as synonymous with 'British' (Kane) or viewing the differentiation between the two as a recent phenomenon (Lisa).

It is worth noting also that two respondents insisted on having their ethnicity recorded as either 'British' or 'English' but not as a subcategory of 'White' on the grounds that 'colour makes no difference to being British/English' (Declan, Carlie). Of course this is not the case for all. For other individuals, 'whiteness' was a key marker of identity:

> I grew up in a white community. I went to a white primary school. … Then all of a sudden I've gone to a secondary school and it was full of 'em. … I looked at the class and I was thinking, 'Wow, there's so many different colours' … it was a shock, I was just like, no I'll never forget that. (Jordan)

The only respondent of mixed ethnic origin was Lisa, who has African (on her father's side) and Italian (on her mother's side) heritage (see Box 6). Lisa had had a difficult childhood, spending several years in care and her contact with her dad had been intermittent and difficult, problematising her own knowledge of her heritage. Indeed, she said, since her dad 'was a Barnardo's kid', he was not sure himself of his origins. What he had told her was that he had been born in Islington, that his mum was from Mauritius and his dad from Somalia and that he had been 'adopted out by a white family' whom he lived with until he 'ran away with the fair' at the age of 14 (Lisa). Damon also tells me that he has Polish Jewish heritage – his family had fled to Britain from pogroms at the end of the nineteenth century and settled in the East End of London.

The socio-demographic profile of respondents in this study has identified a range of shared social characteristics and structural positions; respondents are predominantly White British/English, male, not in stable employment and with low educational achievement. Such factors are not determining, however; more people sharing these individual and environmental factors choose not to participate in, or to actively oppose, such movements. In the second half of this chapter, we thus consider what leads particular individuals to become active in the EDL.

Box 6: Lisa

I met Lisa at her first EDL demonstration (September 2012). She was nervous – not because of any potential risk (she had served in the British Army for four years and completed a tour in Bosnia) but was apprehensive about how she would be received 'because of my colour'. She also described herself as 'quite shy' and found social interactions that were heavily alcohol-fuelled difficult; she had stopped drinking herself following alcohol-related problems. After the demonstration she said that her colour 'wasn't an issue' and after 'about an hour' she had felt comfortable with other division members.

Lisa had had a difficult childhood. Her dad had been largely absent in her early years when she had been physically abused by her mum. When her mum attempted to kill her, at the age of 7, by giving her an overdose of tablets, she was taken into care and then fostered. When she was 12 her dad reappeared and she lived with him – although he was in and out of prison – until the age of 19 when she joined the army.

Lisa had been prosecuted twice for racially aggravated offences. The first occasion had been more than a decade ago when, after an argument with her dad, a brick she threw at his house had smashed a window of a West Indian club next door. She was prosecuted for racially aggravated criminal damage because she

3.8 Lisa: seeing red

had called her dad a 'black bastard' in the course of the argument. When we met she was being prosecuted for racially aggravated harassment following an argument in the street with some Polish neighbours; she was convicted and given a two-year suspended sentence. When narrating these episodes she does so with irony, pointing out her own experience of racism – 'When I was a kid we got chased by the BNP when they were all skinheads.'

Lisa reads widely and is critical of the haphazard form of EDL divisional meetings. She is keen to extend the kind of activism undertaken, suggesting producing leaflets that could be put through letterboxes locally.

Lisa does not work due to long-term mental health issues. She lives with her partner who encouraged her to join the EDL to 'channel the anger' that she was experiencing but whose own job in the public sector prevented her having any personal association with the movement.

Paths into the EDL

Explanations of receptivity to far right extremism at the individual level have sought to identify vulnerable personality 'types'. Theories of a fascist personality type, first found in the work of Reich and Fromm and later operationalised by Adorno *et al.* in their classic study of *The Authoritarian Personality* (1950), identified propensity to fascism (among 'ordinary' individuals) and attributed these psychological traits primarily to upbringing, especially relations with parents; the authoritarian is assumed to repress resentment against his or her parents and this resentment forms the basis of later prejudices (1950: 38). The authoritarian personality thesis has been robustly critiqued for suggesting inter alia that the contradictions of fascism are contradictions which exist within individuals rather than between individuals within movements (Billig, 1978). Later developments of the theory away from 'fascism' and towards a wider notion of propensity to 'authoritarianism' have suggested typologies of the 'open' versus the 'closed' mind (Rokeach, 2015) and the need for dichotomous categories to order the world (Allport, 1979); approaches that have come to underpin understandings of prejudice and Islamophobia. According to Billig (1978: 59–60), however, these theories rest on a central paradox of the concept of authoritarianism (as described by Adorno *et al.*), which defined the potential fascist as threatened by ambivalence and complexity but measured this through approval of F-scale statements that were essentially ambiguous. Thus, the potential fascist, far from being totally intolerant of ambiguity, is constituted as requiring ambiguities to express their intolerance.

The uncomfortable reality is that there is not one 'type' of person that is attracted to a movement like the EDL; rather decisions to start, continue and draw back from activism are set within a complex web of local environment and personal psychodynamics and family dynamics. Joining the EDL is not an 'end point' – the formation of the individual subject as part of an extreme right fringe of society that the latter tolerates as a 'pathological normalcy' of democratic society (Mudde, 2014: 8) – but one dimension of largely 'normal' lives and one that shifts in its importance to individuals as life circumstances change.

Using life-history interviews with thirty-six extreme right activists in the Netherlands (1996–98), Linden and Klandermans (2007) suggest there are three 'paths' into extreme right activism. These trajectories are characterised by: 'continuity' (where activism is a result of prior political socialisation and expresses itself in the life-long commitment to a movement, in the case of 'revolutionaries', or movement between organisations, in the case of 'wanderers'); 'conversion' (where activism marks a break with the past); or 'compliance' (when individuals are persuaded to become active by those already committed). For Linden and Klandermans these trajectories map on to three underlying motives for participation in social movements: *instrumentality*, characterising the ideologically motivated 'revolutionary' but also the angry 'convert' who seeks to fight injustice; *identity*, characterising both the 'wanderer', who is in search of a political home and like-minded others and the 'compliant' who remains in the movement primarily through identification with others there; and *ideology*, motivating those who want to express a view. What brings people to movements depends on which trajectory activists have taken and which 'type' they constitute.

While, as ideal types, these constructs are useful, both movements and individual participants combine elements of more than one type. In the case of members of the EDL in this study, while the prominent 'type' would appear to be the 'convert', drawn to the movement in pursuit of a struggle against perceived injustice, fringe members (including the three Infidels members) conform more to the 'revolutionary' type. Moreover, perhaps because the Linden and Klandermans's typology emerged from a life-history study, the notion of 'convert' places too much weight on a life-changing moment to accurately render accounts in this study. While some respondents narrate their pathways into the movement through particular instances of injustice, these are set within a strong pre-existing discontent or discomfort with the world around; a particular experience may provide a tool for narration of their path into activism but does not mean that it motivated it. Indeed, as Blee (2002: 33) notes, studies of right-wing extremists are prone to the assumption that dramatic life outcomes must have dramatic causes when, in practice, racist activism typically has quite mundane beginnings, and motives attributed often after the event should not be taken at face value (2002: 33). Moreover, while 'conversion' for Linden and Klandermans (2007: 185) marks 'a break with the past', often associated with critical events in individual life-histories, in this study paths into the movement are marked by significant continuity in respondents' wider lives rather than a radical break in them. Equally, while none of the respondents in this study could be described as primarily a 'compliant' – almost all had actively joined the movement through their own personal desire – a number had reached a point where they felt little ideological stimulation from participation and remained primarily because of the affective bonds they had formed.

Recognising the complexity and 'messiness' of individual narratives, I propose to consider below not 'motivations' for joining the EDL but the *contexts* in which individuals first became involved in the movement. This focus reflects the situational rather than life-history approach of the study and allows attention to questions of: *environmental factors* – locality, housing, material circumstances – which constitute important contexts for decisions to become politically active; *socialisation*, in particular whether the choice of political direction is shaped by a family 'tradition' of far right activism; and *personal and family dynamics* – family background, experience of violence and abuse, health and social integration – that emerge as central to the accounts respondents give of their whole lives.

'Seeing Islam': environmental contexts

When recounting how they became involved in the EDL for the first time, individuals often recall events that had been important in shifting their perspectives or making them want to be active. However, in distinction from the 'converts' in Linden and Klandermans's (2007) study, the kinds of stories told are not usually of a dramatic turning point in life-histories but of how particular, often external, events release a deeper, simmering anger or resentment that leads them into activism.

Some respondents associate their decisions to become active with a response to national and international events such as the terrorist attacks of 9/11 in the USA or 7/11 in the UK or the more recent murder of British soldier Lee Rigby (May 2013).

> KANE: It's been about a year and 3 months now. My first demo was Leicester. You know I got involved in that for just like seeing Islam. Just seeing, just look at it, first 9/11, then the double decker bus in London, then that making soldiers die in the streets, having their heads chopped off, that's Islam. Heads being chopped off. I've seen live videos in Pakistan of kids that have been randomly battered for no reason, age 3, being battered. It just makes me feel sick pretty much, just seeing a 3 year old being battered, slapped, punched across the room. That was on a live video thing that was. It just made me feel sick.
> INT: So it was just kind of seeing stuff like that then?
> KANE: Yeah and then I remembered the English Defence League got mentioned to me. I looked into it and … them fighting for the kids, them fighting for everyone. Them just trying to make this country a better place for our kids to live in.

The viewing of images and videos on the Internet, often shared through social media, is an important factor in framing fear and anger and identifying the EDL as a way of expressing it. However, individual events, as refracted through the media, do not cause but actualise longer-term frustrations. This is evident from both Tina's and Lisa's explanations of how they first got involved in EDL activism:

> I was just getting so annoyed with how the country's going. And … then obviously when Lee Rigby died, the EDL was on the TV, and that's the first time I'd heard of the EDL … I looked them up on Facebook. I liked their page, found out about the Birmingham demo, me and my partner went. (Tina)

> I was getting angry basically or frustrated, I should say, not angry, well yeah it was turning into anger and my partner was saying, you know, I think I saw it on TV and I said that's who I'm going to join, EDL. … So, I got in contact with EDL. (Lisa)

In both cases respondents do not become aware of the EDL through social media but use it to 'look up' and make first contact with the movement once particular events or personal experiences had evoked an interest.

Longer-term frustrations and accumulated 'anger' may be locally framed as a feeling of resentment towards the increasing visibility of Islam in the community. Chas had joined after encountering an EDL demonstration by chance while in the city centre and finding what he heard resonated with a feeling he had that 'I've seen this happen.' It is in these lived local environments that interest in the EDL is activated. These contexts are described as 'rough', 'poor' and dogged by crime and 'gangs' such that 'I don't feel safe walking around the streets anymore' (Sean).[6] For many young respondents, the locality was 'dead', offering little prospect of either employment or leisure. As Ray put it, 'The best thing you've got in our area is the swimming baths. ... And that's two foot deep and that's the deep end.'

The primary dimension of locality as narrativised by respondents in this study, however, is its relative multicultural or monocultural nature; a shift from the latter to the former is frequently the prompt for discussing this. These 'changed' environments are described as 'not English ... It's like driving somewhere else. In another country' (Brett). For Tina this is expressed through the changing ethnic composition of those on a particular bus route in her home district (see Chapter 4) while others experience 'shock' when they themselves move from one environment to another, as in Jordan's description (above) of his experience of moving schools. In his case this resentment is embedded within nostalgia for 'strong communities' in the past – before they became multicultural – found also in studies of BNP supporters (Goodwin, 2011a: 149).

> It was a rough area, poverty. If you asked people at [names district] they would say it was a shit hole. To be honest it was but the community I lived in everyone looked out for each other but you can't find that anywhere to be honest now. (Jordan)

However, younger respondents in particular can also be critical of mono-cultural environments, which they describe as 'racist' (Tina, Peter, Kyle, Ian). Peter notes that his home town is so racist that racist comments are directed even 'towards their own football players'. Both Peter and Kyle explain this as a product of residents' fear of change. For respondents in large urban conurbations too, however, the environment appears to be changing dramatically around them. The fear it evokes is exacerbated by the feeling that they themselves are static as their mobility is constrained by their dependence on the social housing system. Of the twenty-one respondents in this study living independently,[7] 57 per cent (12) were living in social housing compared to 17.5 per cent of the population in general (2011 census data).[8] Moreover, getting access to social housing for many had been a long and frustrating process; two single mothers complained of having to wait more than ten years to be allocated a house by the council. For Tina in particular this experience framed her vision of a society in which others' needs were being prioritised over hers and underpinned her EDL activism: 'Every single property that I went to view, Somalians got it, you know ... it really got me

angry.' Tina's story (told more fully in Chapter 6) is familiar from existing literature on support for populist radical right and far right parties. At the individual
level, it echoes respondents in Linden and Klandermans's study (2007: 194) who
ascribe their 'conversion' to anger about their own treatment by the Dutch social
security system when 'those foreigners get everything' while, at the wider community level, it is reminiscent of Rhodes's (2011: 108) analysis of how BNP voters
in Burnley constructed particular 'Asian/Pakistani/Muslim' areas of the town as
receiving 'a disproportionate share of council monies'.

'Them are EDL so best we're EDL': socialisation and solidarity

There is some evidence that family histories of voting for far right parties and
growing up in extreme right families are important in forming racist views (Nayak,
1999; Simi and Futrell, 2010). As noted above the Linden and Klandermans (2007:
184–5) study identified one type of trajectory into activism as being the result of
prior political socialisation ('continuity'). In this study, there are a small number
of cases where there was a strong family tradition of far right support leading to
participation in extreme right groups in early teenage years. The clearest case of
this concerned brothers Connor and Ray whose father, and subsequently their
uncle, had run a local EDL division: 'that's where we get our incentive from. Well,
them are EDL so best we're EDL.' (Ray). However, even in this case, the boys had
experienced a diversity of influences, not least because they had been brought up
by their grandparents who were, according to Ray, 'dead respectable' and would
discuss concerns they had about the movement with them.

Other respondents had backgrounds in older far right parties and movements.
Declan had joined the BNP when he was just 13. His grandfather had been a
National Front member when it was first formed and both his parents had been
BNP members. However, he had come to his own decision to leave the BNP for
the EDL when 'I was starting to realise that I was gay and I came to realise that I
couldn't be gay and in the BNP' (Declan). Jordan had been strongly influenced by
his grandfather who had been a National Front member while Kane also talked
about an influential grandfather who had always supported the BNP.

However, other respondents who had become active in their early or mid-
teens (Chas, Ollie, Nick) did not have a family history of far right support. This is
a pattern identified also by Blee (2002: 27) who found that more than a third of
the women she interviewed identified their parents as Democrats, progressives or
even leftists while many of the other two-thirds described their parents as moderate or non-political, and only a handful called them 'right-wing racist'. Indeed
among this EDL respondent set, there were cases where respondents' views or
activism were not only not supported at home but caused worry, embarrassment,
arguments and tension: 'If I talk politics at home, I'd either end up scrapping with
Dad, or Mum would call me racist' (Peter). Chris, 18 years old at the time of interview, reported having been thrown out of the parental home and having to move
into a hostel 'because my mum's against EDL. … [M]y mum don't agree with it.'

Surprisingly few respondents cite the influence of peers or friends in becoming involved in the EDL; the movement appears, rather, as a site for making new or 'real' friendships. This is in sharp contrast to Blee's (2002: 52) findings that both men and women come into organised racism in the USA primarily through social networks in the form of a friend or acquaintance (as well as a family member) and to Kimmel's (2007: 210) suggestion that points of entry into the neo-Nazi movement for teenagers in Sweden was often through social activities with friends, peers or relatives. However, some respondents noted that they had first heard about the movement from friends (Chris, Sean, Michelle, Rob, Kane) and attended first events together with them. Making a personal contact in the local movement was also instrumental in Lisa's route to activism. Although, as noted above, she had registered her support for the group via Facebook, she did not become active until she was approached directly by another member, Rachel, who identified her as a potential supporter from a hoody she was wearing around town bearing the slogan 'British jobs for British people'. As Lisa explained, her own lack of social confidence meant that without this personal contact, it is unlikely that her interest would have turned into active participation in EDL events.

Another common route to the EDL was via an existing crowd; the football firm. A number of respondents had previously, or currently, participated in football-firm activities (Matt, Peter, Kyle, Ian, Connor, Jordan, Richard). Rob had consciously replaced the 'buzz' of football hooliganism with EDL activism:

> ROB: just as I got banned from football the EDL started so guys that I knew that were banned as well says 'come along Rob, it's the same sort of thing'. ...
> INT: So what's the connection then? What makes it similar?
> ROB: Erm the singing, the drinking, the shouting, the chanting, the camaraderie, just being part of a family again, do you know what I mean? It just fell in line for me perfectly. I got banned one week and about 3 month later the EDL kicked in. So I thought, 'Oh I'll have a try at this.'

Finally, a number of respondents had pre-existing solidarities with the armed services, which they evoked to explain routes into EDL activism. Four respondents (Lisa, Ed, Jason and Mike) had served in the army themselves, and another two (Peter, Rob) had signed up but not passed basic training. A number of others expressed a desire to join the army either in the past or in the future. For Kane the army was a 'family tradition' – his granddad, dad, uncles and aunt had all served – and he himself had 'wanted to follow in my granddad's footsteps' but had been deterred because he suffered from asthma. Six respondents mentioned close friends or family who were serving in the army and four said that they had friends or family who had been killed or injured in combat. For Jordan, the loss of a friend in Afghanistan was central to his unconcealed dislike for Muslims (see Chapter 5) because, he said 'what killed my friend in Afghanistan were Muslims' (Jordan).

Personal and family dynamics

Even where family is not a direct or primary force in political socialisation, still less the training ground for the authoritarian personality, it remains central to the contexts that shape trajectories into the EDL. Family contexts described are rarely ones of stable, strong and protective environments. Two respondents had grown up living in a mixture of parental homes, children's homes and foster care. Rachel's story was particularly striking; despite having been separated from her siblings and having grown up largely in care due to her mother's alcohol problems, it was she who nursed her mother through terminal cancer (see Box 7).

Four respondents had been brought up by their grandparents rather than parents and another had lived with his mother and grandfather. These grandparents were talked about fondly and a number of respondents expressed appreciation of mothers or fathers who they felt had 'been there' for them even if familial circumstances had not been perfect. However, even Chas, who made one of the few positive references to his family being 'strong', noted that what he had gained from that was, 'You are taught how to fight for yourself' (Chas).

Box 7: Rachel

Rachel talked straight and always from the heart. It was infectious. I met her for the first time a few days before my first demonstration; within half an hour we had shared personal information that nobody but close friends knew. This was not strategic on Rachel's part – she was not testing me nor did she use what she knew against me – it was just how she was.

Rachel is separated from, but has a good relationship with, her husband. She has two grown-up children and three grandchildren about whom she is fiercely protective. She is also affectionately called 'mum' by Sean, a childhood friend of her son, who had a deeply problematic relationship with his own family and found a 'safe' space at Rachel's. She lives on her own in a one-bedroom flat, which was always immaculately clean and tidy. She scrapes by on benefits and casual employment. She enjoys her independence, going to music festivals and on holiday with female friends, although she occasionally tested the market for a new long-term relationship.

Rachel regularly attended demos and meetings and undertook much background organisational work to ensure a 'turnout' from her area. She was asked to become divisional 'admin', taking over responsibility for the website and organisation of travel to demonstrations. She later became an admin on the regional 'Angels' division page.

During a long car journey to a 'meet and greet' at the other end of the region, Rachel told her story. She and her three siblings had been taken into care as children (she was 7 years old) although subsequently her two brothers were adopted and her sister was taken back by her mother. She had only recently traced her brothers. Wanted by neither her own nor the adopting family, Rachel had stayed

3.9 Rachel: fighting 'two-tier justice'

in care. Despite this, it was Rachel who looked after her mother through the cancer that eventually caused her death.

Rachel's kind-heartedness could be abused and during fieldwork she ended a friendship with another division member who had started to exploit her generosity. Struggling financially herself, towards the end of fieldwork reluctantly she had taken 'a step back'.

The family thus often constituted in practice an all-too-thin layer of protection between internal and external worlds and is often narrated as a site of trauma and resilience. Experiences of abuse and violence within the family and family deaths appear as key influences in shaping respondents' lives. Eight respondents in this study talked about abuse they had experienced or witnessed in the family. One respondent was sexually abused by family friends, another had been sexually abused while in a foster family, and one respondent reported his sister had been a victim of a local grooming gang. In the first case, the perpetrators had been prosecuted and the process of the trial and associated publicity had taken its toll on the respondent's mental health: 'when it all came out ... I went through post-traumatic stress, depression' (Ryan). Two respondents had been physically (and psychologically) abused by their mothers when they were young children. One had been beaten by his father and traumatised by witnessing domestic violence between his parents:

> I mean I used to sit at the bottom of the stairs and listen to my Mom get beaten up and everything. ... Seriously. He used to beat the shit out of my Mom. ... Seeing my Mom wearing a pair of glasses walking to school. No. Taking a baseball bat to me at 13 years old. (Sean)

It is hard in the context of a research project to be able to draw any concrete connections between childhood abuse and trauma and trajectories into the EDL; discussions are fragmentary, not conducted by a trained psychologist and the experiences often still raw and unprocessed by respondents themselves. Here, just one case is highlighted as an example of how traces of these early experiences might seep through into the meanings attached to current activism. Kane recounted a series of violent and abusive episodes from his childhood in such a vivid way that it left no doubt that these memories remained very much part of his present.

> I think I was about 5, 6 but the memories are still there in the back of my head. There's memories that I'll never forget. I watched my Mom try to kill my Dad in the car just coming back from the cemetery from seeing my nan ... it's hurt me keep having these memories come back and come back and it's changed me in a way cause of my temper cause I snap sometimes, now and again ... like in Year 3 in primary school, say about 8 years old, my mum went on a chat website and she met a Muslim and started talking and that and the next thing he come down and started talking as a family friend, Dad day seen nothing of it, and he says, my mum turned round after he went and says 'I wanna go and live with him' ... and after that they started living with each other. And Mom tried to kidnap me with him, both chased me in the car. (Kane)

Kane's articulation of his route into the EDL was noted already above when he recounted a connection he made between violence towards children seen in radical Islamist videos on the Internet, which had made him 'feel sick', and activism in the EDL, which he saw as 'trying to make this country a better place for our kids to live in'. At a non-rational level, however, the EDL had become for him also the safe family space that he had missed in his own life:

> I do have flashbacks to what has happened in the past. That's the only thing that gets me down is stressing and everything. But I feel more safe with the EDL than what I do at home most times. Cause what I go through at home, it's unbelievable. ... Mom is the evil one to me. Hers abused me Mom has and then still today she works with kids. (Kane)

Kane's profound desire to protect other children is expressed frequently, stamped indelibly on his body in the form of the names of four of his nieces and his favourite aunt tattooed on his chest and is even projected into the future as he talks about his activism as motivated by the desire to make a safer and better society in which 'my kids' will grow up. While one might assume that the centrality of assaults on the body found by Blee (2002: 36) as central to women's stories of their routes into activism might be gender-specific, Kane's story shows that such experiences may be found among male activists as well. In discussion of childhood abuse, violence, sexuality and the breakdown of relationships there emerges a recurring theme of the EDL as a surrogate family and a focus for channelling feelings of anger or hopelessness.

Family deaths were also traumatic experiences discussed by respondents.[9] Tina, her partner and her four children had shared intimately in the final months of her father's life when the family was forced to move in with her parents while she waited for council housing. This traumatic experience subsequently became crucial to her interpretation of contemporary society being run as a 'two-tier system' (see Chapter 6). Jason also expressed an anti-system view as emanating from the experience of his granddad's death (he had been brought up by his grandparents), blaming the lack of funding in the NHS for his granddad not having been properly cared for in the final days before he died of cancer. Tim had lost his mother when she was just 50 and Richard had lost his dad (who had brought him up after separating from his mother) at 18. Neither blames these losses directly for their own state of being 'out of control' but both talked about these difficult periods in their lives and their impact on their education and future prospects. For Jason and his partner, the loss of twins (stillborn) was a life-changing event and the date of their still birth was tattooed onto the back of Jason's neck. Ian ascribes a complete change in his trajectory to the death of his granddad (see above); he found his death emotionally difficult to manage since he had never known his father and, while his mother worked to support the family, it was his grandfather who had looked after him.

Other personal problems or traumatic experiences that respondents link to their trajectories include: being bullied (discussed above), being socially challenged, being socially unskilled or feeling 'different' or 'judged'. This was articulated in an extreme form by Andrew, an Infidels member who also empathised with Anders Breivik and considered that they had 'a lot in common'. Andrew felt isolated in the community and at college and that he didn't fit in anywhere.

> I feel as if I belong in the 1920s ... I feel as if, as if my values and my way of looking at life isn't the same as what it is in this in this day and age, I feel like, [exhales] I feel as if I'm in the wrong place, as if I was born in the wrong time period. But I know, I know deep down, that this isn't our true culture, this is this is something that has degenerated over time, this isn't how things should be now, today. ... [I]t shouldn't be like this, it's not me who's out of place, I have to keep reminding myself – it's not me. (Andrew)

Six respondents have serious ongoing mental health issues. In two cases there has been a diagnosis but other respondents talked of struggling with trauma from childhood: 'I've got demons to fight still' (Sean). In addition to the violence experienced as a child, Sean's demons include issues related to an ongoing drug addiction and the temptation to slip back into his former criminal life.

In contrast, although prison experiences were common, they were recounted largely pragmatically and never as a 'turning point' in life. At the time of research all the respondents who had served time in prison had done so for non-EDL related offences, although towards the end of the research, Jack was convicted of 'violent disorder' following the violence which took place at the EDL demonstration in Walsall (September 2012) and sentenced to thirty-six months in prison (see Box 8). This demonstration, the ensuing prosecutions and how it confirms visions of society as unjust and weighted against 'us' are discussed in more detail in Chapter 6.

Box 8: Jack

On 17 December 2013 Jack was sentenced to 36 months imprisonment after his conviction for 'violent disorder' during the EDL demonstration in Walsall in September 2012. I had been sitting next to Jack on the bus from the station that day and he had asked me what kind of guy I thought he was. I responded 'a family man, a man passionate about what he believes in and honest'.

Based on what I saw of the violence at Walsall, what the CCTV showed (or failed to show) during his trial and what I knew of him from other events, I would

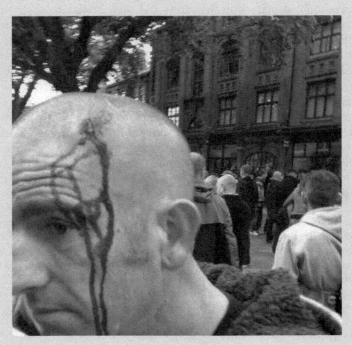

3.10 Jack: paying a high price

not change that description. When he pleaded not guilty and repeatedly said that he was not violent towards the police or counter-demonstrators nor had he incited anyone else to violence, I believe he was telling the truth. But, as he admitted himself, he had been an idiot to join those reacting angrily to counter-demonstrators when they became visible on the other side of the police lines and not to move away when missiles began to be thrown and police in full riot gear were deployed.

On the way to the demo, Jack had talked, as he usually did, about his partner and their 2-year-old daughter, for whom he always found a small present to take back with him. His partner had grown up in care and suffered domestic abuse in her previous relationship. She had never been abroad and he dreamed about getting married and taking her on honeymoon to the Caribbean. But he told me also that he would be 'prepared to die' for the EDL. Just over a year later, as the news came through in the midst of his trial that its leaders had just resigned and joined Quilliam, he rued the day they had formed the movement.

The fact is that, an individual is guilty of violent disorder even if they did not use or threaten violence themselves if violence involving more than three people is proven and the individual's actions can be said to have incited others to violence. What previously might have been interpreted as routine banter between demonstrators and counter-demonstrators, in the context of violence, becomes incriminating. He should have moved away. He didn't. He has just been released from prison on tag.

Finally, while in no case do respondents themselves connect their material circumstances with their trajectory into the EDL, it remains an important context for understanding life decisions. Respondents in paid employment were in the minority and those on benefits described how difficult it was to survive on benefits or (in the case of young respondents) how they were not entitled to any kind of benefit and rendered completely dependent on parents or other carers. Rent arrears were a problem faced by a number of respondents and three had been evicted, or were in the process of being evicted, from social housing in the course of the fieldwork due to rent arrears. One of these was Kurt whose situation had been compounded by wider circumstances (the death of his father, loss of job) and he had simply not taken in how imminent crisis was (see Box 9).

Gradual payment schemes to repay debt are discussed by many respondents and daily problems of keeping the household in food by some. It goes without saying that activism is profoundly affected by this; the inability to travel to demos or meetings because individuals do not have cash for public transport or the coach is a routine problem, for example.

Paths out of the EDL: 'stepping back' and the costs of activism

While the far right literature approaches withdrawal from activism as 'exits' – often risky moves requiring support and facilitation – movement in and out of the EDL was much less definitive, often articulated as 'taking a step back' for a period

Box 9: Kurt

When Jack is convicted of violent disorder and awaiting sentencing, Kurt gives him a 'going away' present; he has turned his own prison phone card into a key ring and inscribed it with Jack's name. It reminds me, with shock, that Kurt had also served time – four years – after he violently attacked the man he found his girlfriend cheating on him with. Kurt is the last person you would have expected to have a prison record. He is mild and affable although with a sharp sense of humour and ability to story-tell in an engagingly self-deprecating way. Recognising his struggle with modern communication technologies, he says of mobile phones, 'My method is to stamp on them.'

He was known by everybody by his nickname, which reflected that he always carried the division flag, mounted on a fishing rod inherited from his dad and always a few feet higher than any other flag. At one demo, even a police officer complimented him on it.

3.11 Kurt and the infamous flag

Unlike many other respondents, Kurt had had too much rather than too little parenting while growing up. He had four siblings and had been brought up in a strict Jehovah's Witness household which he described in ways that suggested physical abuse had been replaced by emotional cruelty.

When I first met Kurt he had been working as a quality inspector in a factory producing parts for high-end cars. He was a natural engineer – anything could be made or adapted to function in his hands – and in any practical crisis, he would have some item in his pocket that would 'fix it'.

Towards the end of the fieldwork, Kurt's life got increasingly difficult. His parents had separated and so when his dad became very ill and in need of extensive care, Kurt looked after him. It meant he frequently missed work and was eventually sacked. He survived financially because a long-awaited injury compensation claim was settled. But in a depressed state he failed to keep on top of bills and rent or sign the paperwork to transfer his dad's place after his death. When he missed a court appearance, he woke the next morning to find the locks on his door being changed. He was evicted with a carrier bag holding what he needed for that night.

Kurt moved back to his mum's, is finally getting therapy to help deal with his depression and structures his days by volunteering at a food bank.

of time rather than a once and for all departure. Chas described his relationship with the EDL as doing the 'hokey-cokey', he had moved in and out so often.

Such stepping back is often an outcome of the very high costs of EDL activism. Tim describes how he had 'stepped back' when he found himself 'getting in a lot of trouble' and his dad had become anxious that he would end up in prison. Others pulled back from participation for similar reasons – because bail conditions included a ban on attending EDL marches (Jack) or because they were too risky an environment to be in when on police charge or tag (Chas). This reflects Kimmel's (2007: 215) finding that the most common reason for leaving the Swedish neo-Nazi movement was 'burn out' due to the demands of drinking, fighting, constant arrests and violence. In this sense while other forms of political participation demand too little involvement, movement participation over a sustained period requires too much (Jasper, 1998: 419–20).

The costs or consequences of activism are cited frequently by respondents. Loss of, or being disowned by, family and friends because of their disapproval of the respondent's activism in the EDL is common (Chas, Chris, Ed, Jason, Tim). Respondents are also conscious of the 'worry' that their activism causes family, partners and friends who fear they will end up in prison or physically injured (Euan, Ed, Tim, Jordan, Kane, Lisa, Nick). This leads many to avoid discussing their activities with partners and families in order to protect them and to adopt a strategy of 'sorting' issues without involving anyone else. Thus when Chas is given a council flat and is able to move out of the family home, it is above all a relief: 'I don't want any trouble on anyone's door step. Now I feel much more secure now. I've got my own doorstep now' (Chas). Although it had not happened to anybody in this case study personally, respondents also talked about the threat of Social

Services removing children from their care because of their EDL activism. This was something they claimed had happened to others in the movement (Jason, Casey, Matt) and isolated cases have been reported in the media.[10]

Other consequences of activism that led to 'stepping back' included losing jobs and contracts. Andrew had been suspended from his post as a teaching assistant following the newspaper reports of his support for Anders Breivik and was told subsequently he would have to resign. Jordan was also first suspended and then forced to resign from his job at a supermarket chain because of material found on his Facebook page. Others mention friends who have lost employment due to association with the EDL (Declan, Euan, Jason, Matt), keep their own activism quiet at work for fear that the same fate would befall them (Jason, Tim) or take measures to prevent being identified on YouTube videos at demonstrations (Michelle). A number of respondents had been excluded or suspended from school or college for EDL-related activism or as a result of accusations of 'racism'. In addition to Connor's case (see above), Chas had been suspended for two weeks for wearing an EDL hoody and Tina chose to keep her affiliation quiet at university for fear she would be excluded. Kane had been thrown out of a supermarket store because of his 'offensive' hoody and the local library where he did much of his 'research' into EDL-related issues.

Physical injury or threats thereof were also a real concern for respondents. Brett reported that his brother's house, in a Muslim area of town, had been set on fire because, he claimed, 'he had the England flags on the front of his house' (Brett). Concern was expressed over the death threats received by Tommy Robinson and, in particular, the 'intimidation' of his wife and children (Declan) and attacks on his family home that had forced him to move house (Jack). Euan claimed Tommy Robinson routinely 'has the shit kicked out of him' if he goes out at night while Kane called him 'a dead man walking'.

Accounts of respondents' own or friends' physical injury were common. Most related to injury from clashes with the police, mainly associated with the Walsall demonstration (Connor, Jack, Rob, Declan, Tim). Others relate to 'opposition' or counter-demonstrators. Declan recounted a particularly emotive story about a 12-year-old boy having his 'head cracked open by a UAF brick' at the Manchester demo and his own actions to get him medical treatment:

> I didn't see the brick hit him. I just saw him after he was on the floor. Literally got him in my arms like this and [he] had all blood coming down here and took him out of the march. The police medic came along and I said to this police medic right 'you better see to him or that is gonna be it and I'm gonna lose it'. I had him literally in my hand like this. ... He got taken to hospital and I don't know how he got my number but he rung me up a couple of days afterwards saying '156 stitches' in his head. (Declan)

Ed recounts how a quiet and reliable member of the division had been beaten up by a group of four to five men in the HQ pub on the eve of the Bradford demonstration after being approached and asked, 'You're EDL ain't yer?' (Ed).

Threats were also a cause of concern. Ed had been issued an Osman warning[11] and many respondents had been made aware of their own vulnerability to attack following the prosecution of two men for attempting to plant bombs at the EDL demonstration in Dewsbury in June 2012 (Kane). Tina said she got nervous prior to demonstrations because she feared she would 'get stabbed or petrol bombed'. Indeed Matt reported having had a petrol bomb thrown at him from a moving car as he walked through a district of the city. Members of one local youth division routinely received threats of violence towards them via social media. Connor laughs these off: 'I get phone calls and everything me. I just answer them and take the piss out of 'em. Don't really take no notice of 'em. Don't bother me anymore.' Explicit death threats such as that received by Brett (see Chapter 2) were, none-theless, shocking.

Finally, as discussed further in Chapter 7, the strong emotional dimension of activism that binds and sustains social movements can also work to undermine them (Jasper, 1998: 419–20). A number of activists had left the movement due to personal disputes, frustration or disillusionment. Others were simply over-whelmed by work commitments, personal problems or 'life' in general. Of the thirty-five participants listed in Appendix 2, I know six to be still active in the movement, nine are active only occasionally or have taken 'a step back' while they prioritise other aspects of their lives and seven have left for ideological or personal reasons.

Conclusion

The previous chapter provided an understanding of the EDL as a movement; this chapter has focused on its constituent grassroots activists. Whilst prioritis-ing individuals and their trajectories, however, the analysis undertaken here has eschewed the attempt to discern 'the motivation of someone who becomes an extreme right-wing activist' (Klandermans and Mayer, 2006: 7). Rather it has traced shared social contexts and life experiences among EDL activists. This is, first, because classic psychological models explaining receptivity to movements such as the EDL as rooted in the formation of an 'authoritarian personality' as a result of particularly strong modes of parental authority are not substantiated by individual narratives in which parenting is often chaotic or absent rather than intrusive and constraining. Second, while more sociologically oriented ideal types of trajectories into extreme right activism suggested by Linden and Klandermans (2007) are useful for distinguishing between experiences, evidence from this study suggests that both movements and individual participants combine elements of more than one type. Moreover, the most appropriate 'type' for the majority of members of the EDL participating in this research – the 'convert' – places too much weight on a life-changing moment in charting paths into the movement. In practice, while some respondents narrate those pathways through instances of injustice, it would be inaccurate to conclude these are direct motivations for it.

It has been suggested here that there is not one 'type' of person that is attracted to a movement like the EDL; rather decisions to enter into, continue and draw back from activism are set within a complex web of local environment and personal and family psychodynamics. These environmental factors are captured both in the socio-demographic profile of the respondent set as well as in their individual narratives, which highlight, in particular, the importance of their perceptions and experiences of change in local communities. It is acknowledged that structural factors are underplayed in this analysis since the ethnography was not based in a single locality or neighbourhood and the respondent set is not sufficiently large to discern meaningful patterns in socio-demographic characteristics. However, these factors – the places individuals live, work, hang out – are nonetheless understood as indicative of more than the sheer 'accident' (Blee, 2002: 30) that draws people into extreme right activism. These sites constitute the structural contexts of trajectories into – and often out of – activism.

Personal and family psychodynamics are also explored through the narratives respondents construct of their lives. Traumatic and abusive experiences in childhood, as well as bullying, are identified as strong markers of individual pasts. Family histories of support for the extreme right are found to be present in some cases but not in others; thus both continuity and radical breaks in political socialisation are identified in different cases. One finding is that in this respondent set the emphasis on pathways into the movement through friends and acquaintances identified in other micro-level studies is not fully confirmed. Rather the movement appears to be a site for the formation of new affective bonds (of 'family', 'friendship', 'loyalty' etc.). This is returned to in Chapter 7.

Finally, in relation to trajectories out of the movement the study indicates a rather different pattern among EDL activists than found in classic far right movements. Rather than decisive entrances and exits, engagement with the EDL, as Chas puts it, resembles a 'hokey-cokey' in which members engage fully and 'stepback' as they marry the costs and consequences of participation with their wider, and largely normal, lives.

Notes

1　See http://extremisproject.org/2012/10/the-english-defence-league-edl-what-do-people-think. Accessed: 05.05.2014.
2　In one case this was a result of placement in an independent boarding school by the local authority due to the respondent's Asperger's condition.
3　This includes three respondents who were not employed because they were looking after children.
4　See http://extremisproject.org/2012/10/the-english-defence-league-edl-what-do-people-think. Accessed: 05.05.2014.
5　In addition to the eight respondents declaring themselves 'White-British', two respondents who identified as British rather than English are recorded separately because they also reported as being of mixed race or refused the label of 'White'.
6　Only one respondent describes his locality as 'middle-class' (Ollie).
7　The standardised socio-demographic data collection conducted included only whether respondents lived independently or with parents rather than whether they owned/

rented or were in social housing. The housing status of the remaining five living inde-pendently is unknown as is that for the fourteen respondents still living with parents or grandparents.

8 The ONS census data show 17.5 per cent of the population to be living in all forms of social housing while 9.4 per cent live in local authority rented housing ('council housing'). See www.ons.gov.uk/ons/rel/census/2011-census/detailed-characteristics-on-housing-for-local-authorities-in-england-and-wales/short-story-on-detailed-char acteristics.html. Accessed: 29.05.2015.

9 Ezekiel's (2002: 57) study also revealed three of twenty respondents to have lost parents in childhood due to death or other unexplained circumstances.

10 Darlington Borough Council was criticised by a judge of the Family Division of the High Court for removing a child from his father on grounds of his connection with the EDL See www.bbc.co.uk/news/uk-england-tees-31509391. Accessed: 26.08.2015.

11 A warning issued by the police when they have credible evidence that an individual is a terrorist target.

4

'Not racist, not violent, just no longer silent': aspirations to non-racism

The EDL is widely represented and perceived as a 'racist organisation'; it is considered to be such by three-quarters (74 per cent) of those surveyed by Extremis/YouGov in October 2012.[1] The EDL itself publicly claims to oppose racism, fascism and Nazism; this is encapsulated in the movement's core slogan, 'Not racist, not violent, just no longer silent' (see Figure 4.1).

There is a degree of academic consensus that the EDL is not a classic far right organisation (see the Introduction). Nonetheless, existing literature suggests that racism and Islamophobia are commonplace among the EDL's 'rank and file' (Garland and Treadwell, 2010: 27–30). This view appeared to be confirmed when, in October 2013, Tommy Robinson cited frustration at a long but unsuccessful struggle to rid the movement of racists and extremists as the reason for his resignation as co-leader.[2] Thus, for Allen (2011: 294), while the EDL might be 'more fluid and reflexive than other far-right organizations, it maintains an ideological premise that is typically discriminatory', while Garland and Treadwell (2010: 30) argue that claims to non-racist ideology by the organisation constitute a veneer of respectability only thinly covering more commonplace racism and Islamophobia among the EDL's 'rank and file'.

The research conducted for this book – whose ethnographic approach allows declarative statements to be evaluated alongside observed behaviour – suggests a more diverse and complex set of understandings of 'race' and racism among grassroots activists in the movement. This chapter starts with a brief discussion of core debates over the contemporary meanings of 'race', racism and post-racialism before the understanding of what constitutes racism and what it means to be racist is explored in the narratives of EDL activists. Notwithstanding the argument that hostility towards Muslim minorities constitutes a 'new racism', however, the exploration of attitudes to Islam among EDL supporters is postponed until the following chapter in order to allow a detailed and discrete discussion.

'Race': buried alive or artificially resuscitated?

How can the EDL appear a blatantly 'racist organisation' to those outside it and as passionately 'not racist' to those on the inside? The answer lies neither in media

4.1 'Not racist, not violent, just no longer silent'

misrepresentation of the movement nor manipulation by the movement but in the contested status of 'race' and its relationship to racism and the struggle against it. The issue is how we resolve (academically and politically) the tension between three somewhat contradictory 'givens'. The first is the consensus that 'race' is a constructed category with no biological foundation (St Louis, 2002: 652; Paul, 2014: 703) but constituted, rather, as 'a practice with no solid basis outside the discursive, material, structural and embodied configurations through which it is repetitively enacted, performed and, tenuously, secured' (Nayak, 2006: 423). The second is that racism – discrimination against those to whom 'other' racial characteristics are ascribed – continues to exist. It follows that, as long as the social effects of being 'racialised' are in evidence, then 'race' itself is phenomenally real (Paul, 2014: 705). The third widely accepted proposition is that racism extends beyond the biological characteristics accorded to 'race'. This is often referred to as 'cultural racism' or 'new racism' which, according to Barker (1981: 16), functions by using the notion of 'genuine fears' about immigration to imply that it (or 'difference' more widely) constitutes a threat to our 'way of life' or 'culture'. Thus 'cultural racism' dispenses with biological determinants and becomes rooted in frames of inclusion and exclusion (Allen, 2010: 154).

It follows from this that 'racism' is the most appropriate way to conceptualise discrimination and prejudice in relation to a range of ethnic and religious minority groups – whether or not they are ascribed 'racial' characteristics – as well as non-ethnically or religiously specific groups such as 'immigrants' or 'foreigners'. Contemporary racisms are viewed as taking plural and complex forms and are expressed not least through the coding of 'race' as culture (Solomos and Back, 1994: 155–56). Characteristics viewed as inherent to members of a group because of their physical or cultural traits – not limited to skin tone but also cultural traits such as language, clothing, and religious practices – emerge as 'racial' as an outcome of the process of racialisation (Garner and Selod, 2015: 12). The crucial property of these new elaborations of racism is that they can produce a racist effect while denying that this effect is the result of racism. The ideology of the EDL, Allen (2011: 293) argues, is one such form of 'new racism'.

The conundrum here is that the struggle to eliminate the justification of discrimination of people by reference to biological difference (between distinct 'races') is predicated on the deployment of the notion of 'race'. Academic and political argument thus turns on whether racism is best understood and combated by retaining or renunciating the discourse of 'race'.

Lentin (2008) argues that the conception of 'race' is being actively removed from political discourse by political actors not because it has lost its classificatory power but in order that societies are not *perceived* to be racist. While culture, ethnicity, religion, nationality and (but not always) skin colour can all stand for 'race' at different times, she argues, replacing 'race' with signifiers such as culture or ethnicity would obscure how racial difference has been fundamental to the very conception of Europeanness and non-Europeanness (2008: 490). What Lentin is suggesting is that while 'race' is discredited in terms of any biological scientificity, its power to order social relations remains intact through its social product, that is, *racism*. Indeed, in this sense racism may be seen as functioning independently of 'race', preceding even the stereotypes and discrimination embedded in the 'race' projects (slavery, colonialism, eugenics, genocide) of the eighteenth and nineteenth centuries (2008: 492).

The retention of the notion of 'race' is crucial, for Lentin, therefore, because it continues to be imposed upon, and experienced as racism by, non-whites and non-Europeans and thus its recognition is essential to the struggle to remove its consequences (racism). In this way 'race' stands not for the invocation of differences in human biology but the crimes for which it is responsible (2008: 497). Any move to replace 'race' with alternative signifiers, moreover, would constitute an act of dissociating Europe from the problem of 'race' and of 'giving race back to its bearers', that is, those who have been racialised in the first place as part of the process of constructing Europeanness (2008: 500). The retention of 'race' is, in this way, also central to exposing its role in the conception of the idea of Europe, built on the hegemony of Europeans and the subjugation of non-Europeans (2008: 491).

That the retention of the language of 'race' is important for resisting attempts to deny, negate or silence it is articulated most eloquently in Goldberg's (2006: 338) claim that 'race' has been 'buried alive' in post-World War II Europe. This racial erasure, he argues, has come about in the process of making the Holocaust (the victims of which are portrayed as Jews only) the sole referent point for racism in Europe, while colonialism is dismissed as part of European history because it is considered to have taken place outside of Europe and thus be external to it (2006: 336). This burying of 'race' 'in the rubble of Auschwitz', Goldberg warns, obscures its effects in violence and discrimination across a Europe itself forged in the context of 'expansion, enslavement and colonization': 'Race disappears into the seams of sociality, invisibly holding the social fabric together even as it tears apart' (2006: 338). In practice, 'race' is so deeply embedded in what Europe is that European values and ways cannot be accepted or adopted without being inflected with its other – non-Europeanness – and invoking the crimes committed in the name of 'European universals'; no 'common European future' is possible, it follows, while Europe is divided between those with the capacity to racialise and those who must bear the badge of 'race' (Lentin, 2008: 500).

While morally persuasive, these arguments are caught in the theoretical bind of viewing 'race' as socially constituted, on the one hand, whilst imparting ontological value to it on the other (Nayak, 2006: 414). This is not to suggest that socially constructed categories do not have real social effects; they do, and their practices, enactment and consequences are open to study. However, in order to avoid reifying the very categories they seek to abolish, Nayak (2006: 415) argues, 'race' writers need to develop a post-'race' language based on 'an anti-foundational perspective which claims that race is a fiction only ever given substance to through the illusion of performance, action and utterance, where repetition makes it appear as-if-real'. Criticising Lentin's simple dichotomisation of racialised identities–subject positions, Nayak (2006: 417) argues that whiteness is much more complexly constructed, making it difficult to isolate white ethnicity from a 'chequered tapestry of sustained black–white interaction'. This position draws on Gilroy's argument that 'race' is a discursive arrangement emerging out of, not causing, the raciological ordering of the world (cited in Paul, 2014: 703). In this sense, 'raciology' – 'the lore that brings the virtual realities of "race" to dismal and destructive life' (Gilroy, 2000: 1) – does not bury 'race' alive but artificially resuscitates it. 'Post-racialism', in contrast, abandons what is viewed as the false category of 'race' in an epistemological and methodological effort to develop more accurate descriptions and analyses of social life (Paul, 2014: 710).

As noted above, however, there is a strong political argument for retaining 'race' as a social category, while post-racialism has yet to prove it has political teeth. The case for a vibrant post-'race' politics has been subjected to critique on the grounds of its abstract and theoretical nature as well as for glibly calling for the eradication of racial marking that may not be missed by those whose whiteness was not recognised as such but which, for minority ethnic groups, constitutes the erasure of an identity and the silencing of racially marked historical experiences (Nayak, 2006: 423). Indeed, not only the beneficiaries of racial hierarchy but also those who have been subordinated by 'race'-thinking may be invested in its continuation, since ideas of racial particularity are inverted by those subordinated to them to provide racialised populations with hard-won oppositional identities (Gilroy, 2000: 12). These groups, Gilroy recognises, will need to be persuaded that there is something worthwhile to be gained from a deliberate renunciation of 'race' as the basis for solidarity and community that has been created by their protracted subordination along racial lines (2000: 13). Nonetheless, Gilroy argues that racial hierarchies can be countered more effectively when the idea of 'race' is delegitimised (2000: 13). Recognising that his antipathy towards 'race' comes at the risk of being perceived as a betrayal of those groups whose oppositional claims have come to rest on identities and solidarities forged at great cost from the categories given to them by their oppressors, Gilroy insists that:

> our perilous predicament, in the midst of a political and technological sea-change that somehow strengthens ethnic absolutism and primordialism, demands a radical and dramatic response. This must step away from the pious ritual in which we always agree that 'race' is invented but are then required to defer to its embeddedness in the world and to accept that the demand for justice requires us nevertheless innocently to enter the political arenas it helps to mark out. (2000: 52)

Nayak (2006: 423), too, makes a strong case that post-'race' agendas do not constitute post-political ones. Understanding how we 'do' 'race' – not least through representations of racialised excess disseminated through global media technologies – may equip us with strategies and techniques to 'undo' it by 'revealing the racialized body as a highly dubious zone upon which to anchor difference'. A post-'race' attitude, he concludes, 'makes evident that our bodies are thoroughly unreliable sources of "race truth"' (2006: 423). This echoes Gilroy's (2000: 43) argument that new technologies of spectral imaging of the body demonstrate the internal similarity (as opposed to external difference) of bodies and provide the means by which 'we can let the old visual signatures of "race" go'.

In practice, however, marrying post-racialist thinking with anti-racist activism remains challenging and characterised by frustration on both sides. While Gilroy (2000: 51) calls for greater boldness on the part of activists in letting go of 'basic mythologies and morphologies of racial difference', as long as 'race' remains a 'driver for decision making' in social and political life then post-racialism often appears impractical to activists (Paul, 2014: 709). Jettisoning 'race', it is argued, is problematic because without reference to it, there can be no effective and meaningful talk about racism (St Louis, 2002: 65). Most damning of all is the claim that post-racialist critiques legitimate conservative post-racisms (Paul, 2014: 704–5), collude with claims that multiculturalism has failed, deny the lived experience of racism and thus imply that there is no longer a need for anti-racism (Lentin, 2014: 1279). Post-racialism, Lentin (2014: 1269) concludes, 'is in fact the dominant mode in which racism finds discursive expression today'. These distinctions and elisions between racism, post-racism and post-racialism are central to understanding and evaluating understandings of racism and claims to non-racism encountered among EDL activists.

Constructing the non-racist organisation: media lies or a minority within?

Racism is rejected almost universally by activists included in this study and claims to non-racism are made at both organisational and individual levels. At the organisational level, respondents concede that historic links with the BNP and the National Front mean that racist elements are encountered within the movement but remain adamant that this does not signal that the movement itself is racist. Implying that racism has become 'stuck' to the organisation rather than the beliefs and actions of its members, its former Chair notes that 'until I joined the EDL, I never had to … say "I'm not racist"' (Eddowes, 2015). EDL activists articulate their conviction that the movement is 'not racist' through three main narratives: the commitment to kicking out racists; the openness of the EDL to all (regardless of colour, ethnicity, faith, gender and sexuality); and its differentiation from traditional far right parties (especially the BNP).

Kicking out the racists

There is a palpable frustration among grassroots members of the EDL with what they perceive as the media and opposition organisations' misrepresentation of it as 'Nazi' or 'racist' (see Figure 4.2). At the same time, many activists recognise the responsibility of a minority 'within' (Richard) for the continued public perception

4.2 'Racist EDL': counter-demonstrators' placards, Manchester demonstration

of the movement as racist. The continued presence of racists or extremists within the movement was most frequently cited as what respondents 'disliked' about the EDL. There is a certain resignation among activists that the movement would always attract racist 'idiots' (Lisa) or extremist 'nutters' (Chas) who 'turn up doing Nazi salutes and Nazi tattoos' (Ed). While this can carry a somewhat dismissive tone, respondents are also adamant that the EDL as an organisation does not tolerate neo-Nazi elements within the movement and has demonstrated this through its commitment to 'kicking out the racists':

> There's been many occasions when we've been at demos and I did see a lad once and he did a Nazi salute and it wasn't that far away from Tommy on stage and I heard Tommy go absolutely ballistic and in his own words 'get that fucking arsehole out of here, we don't want anything to do with people like that' and they fucked him off basically, they got rid of him cause they don't want that sort of thing. (Jack)

Such actions – alongside the presence of 'Black and White Unite' banners at demonstrations and the burning of a swastika flag at a press conference – have been interpreted as the strategic deployment by a media-savvy leadership of demonstrative opposition to racism, fascism and Nazism while racism and Islamophobia remain commonplace among grassroots activists (Garland and Treadwell, 2010: 27–30). Extended observation of such incidents, however, suggests this is not a wholly top-down process. Whilst waiting for the speeches to start at the Birmingham demonstration (July 2013), Tim approached me, highly agitated, and vented his outrage at someone displaying a swastika tattoo on his chest. He said that he had told this individual that he was not welcome and had reported it also to the EDL national leadership. Minutes later, Tommy Robinson began his address to the crowd with an attack on Nazi elements attending EDL demonstrations, naming suspected individuals and saying that no Nazis were welcome at any EDL event. In a comment that presaged his resignation less than three months later, he asked, angrily, how such people 'could have not got the message in four years?' (field diary, 20 July 2013).

Grassroots activists in this study recount personal stories of encounters with racists where they have personally intervened. Jack – in an incident that at the same time attests to the presence of racism within the ranks of the movement – recalled how, at one demonstration, 'some of the local lads' had verbally abused an Indian member of the EDL and he had stepped in to defend him. Ray also tells how he had 'backed' a Sikh member of the movement who subsequently left the EDL because of racism he had experienced:

> I can't be doing with it. He was coming to demos and people who were new to the thing were being racist and that towards him. Well, because he travels with us lot we was giving it them back ... because he's one of us so we're going to back him. (Ray)

Ray's designation of those responsible for the racism as being 'new to the thing' is indicative of another narrative (discussed below) in which respondents understand the EDL as a mechanism for learning not to be racist or 'growing out of' racism. At the same time solidarity – being 'one of us' – is accorded on the basis of participation in collective action ('he travels with us') rather than skin colour, ethnicity or faith.

Respondents and Local Organisers cite numerous incidents when racist behaviour had led to members being disciplined by being removed from the Facebook group (Matt), getting 'a bollocking' for racist comments (Kane) or being expelled from the movement altogether. At the same time, some members feel that the rooting out of such elements is not conducted sufficiently systematically:

> They need to kick out the racists because there is a few in there and unfortunately you know I've seen it myself at Manchester, Nazi salutes, who's doing anything about it? No one. I think the division ROs need to be sorting it out, not Tommy. They need to be watching what their own groups are doing and saying you know this is not right because it is putting the rest of us in a bad light. You know, I'm not a racist. Nobody I talks to is a racist. (Michelle)

As is clear from Michelle's statement, the claims to non-racism are more complex than a non-racist 'front stage' screening a racist hinterland; rather the non-racist self constructed by grassroots activists is threatened by the failure of the organisation to tackle the racist minority within.

Open to all

A second narrative used to counter accusations of racism is that the movement is open to people of all ethnic and religious backgrounds: 'they might say we're racist but we've got Indian people, Chinese people, black people, and we've got all these different races, so how can we be racist?' (Matt). Statements that the movement welcomes members from many different ethnic backgrounds is heard repeatedly from speakers at demonstrations (field diary, 24 May 2013) and visually demonstrated in the 'We love Hindus and Sikhs' placard displayed at the EDL protest camp set up outside Rotherham police station (September, 2014) (see Figure 4.3).

These claims cannot be taken at face value of course. As important as the *in*clusion of Hindus and Sikhs in the placard in Figure 4.3 is the *ex*clusion of Muslims, while the notion of inclusion itself is saturated with assumptions about power, ownership and access. Such statements serve above all to fuel a particular narrative of distinction from the BNP – since the latter had to be forced to open its membership because its exclusionary rules breached anti-discrimination legislation – and substantiate the EDL's own claims to being 'not racist'.

Openness is institutionalised through a number of 'divisions' for members of different ethnic and religious groups as well as a women's ('Angels') and LGBT division (see Chapter 2) and the movement prides itself on the fact that

4.3 'We love Hindus and Sikhs': EDL placard, Rotherham protest camp

> We've got people from all backgrounds. Even Muslim members are in the English
> Defence League. If a Muslim joins the EDL they are tret [treated] just like one of,
> just like open arms. I'm gay. I was tret with open arms since I first joined. It does
> not matter who you are or where you come from. (Declan)

Other respondents also cited their own experience as confirming the declarations of the movement as open and welcoming. Lisa, who has African and
Italian heritage, describes how initially she contacted the movement via the main
national Facebook page and was a little uncertain as to how she might be received
but had got 'a really nice message back saying, you know, everybody's welcome'
and within less than an hour during the first event she attended (Walsall demo),
she had felt 'comfortable' and 'accepted' (Lisa). Lisa envisages the physical
acceptance of her 'not white' body as evidence of non-racism among EDL activists and thinks those with ethnic minority backgrounds have an important role
in countering media and popular perceptions of the movement as racist, which
she thinks are 'absolutely wrong'. While Ed is not an ethnic minority member
himself, the greater openness of the EDL to members of all ethnic backgrounds
was central to his decision to leave the BNP, which he accused of having 'a token
Sikh' who they paraded around the circuit and contrasted to the EDL, which
he saw as a more genuinely diverse organisation including 'Jews, gays, blacks,
Hindus, Sikhs' (Ed).

Of course accusations of tokenism similar to those made by Ed in relation to
the BNP have been levelled at the EDL itself. The conscious recruitment of ethnic

minority supporters might be interpreted as a cynical strategy to defend itself against allegations 'that the EDL is a group of white supremacist, skinhead, boot boys, or the BNP in disguise' (Copsey, 2010: 21). Indeed, the utilisation of ethnic partners, especially fringe Hindu and Sikh organisations, to construct Islam as a common enemy is a strategy that has been used also by the BNP (Allen, 2011: 288). Observation conducted for this study identified a certain 'trophy' status attached to ethnic minority members. On demonstrations it sometimes appeared that everyone wanted to have their photograph taken with an ethnic minority member while the presence of Abdul Rafiq, a Muslim from Glasgow who frequently attended EDL rallies in England, incited spontaneous applause and a chant 'Abdul, Abdul, give us a song' from EDL participants in the Manchester demonstration (video clip, 2 March 2013). According to the Hope not Hate campaign, Rafiq was so important to the EDL that under the leadership of Tommy Robinson, 'Abdul would threaten people who questioned either his sincerity or his sanity, with a beating from the boss himself' (Collins, M., 2013). However, they warned, under the new leadership, Rafiq (described as a 'self-hating collaborator') had become the target of hatred for the extreme fringe of the movement, suggesting openness to ethnic minorities was superficial only. Indeed, some ambivalence about the ethnic minority divisions was encountered in this study too; Ed complained that they 'segregated' people and he ridiculed the formation of a Travellers' division as 'stupid'.

Nonetheless, in this ethnographic study both Sikh and Muslim members of the EDL were encountered at local demonstrations (field diary, 12 January 2013) and divisional meetings (field diary, 19 October 2012; field diary, 31 August 2012). At one such meeting, one of the agenda items concerned reports of verbal abuse in relation to one of the Sikh members of the division. A number of members spoke of their anger at this and it was resolved to ensure that such abuse was not tolerated (field diary, 31 August 2012). Whether this constitutes tokenism or not, it is certainly symbolically important to EDL members to be able to counter accusations of racism through evidence of being 'open to all' and particular weight is attached to incidents in which respondents feel that the prejudices of others are challenged:

> We done a flash in [names town]. We gone into the town doing our chanting. There was a group of about five black lads. 'You racists. Fuck off out the town.' So a group of us run over 'Why are we racist? Why are we racist? You can come and join us if you want.' 'No, you're racist.' As soon as we've explained and then they've gone on the net, they've gone on the official EDL page, and they've read about it. 'Oh, we thought you was against everyone and everything.' … And then they come and just stand with us. A couple of them still come on demos now. (Chris)

The significance of such narratives, it will be argued in Chapter 8, is not purely symbolic but reflects also the importance attached to 'being heard' or 'getting your point across' by movement activists.

Beyond the racist BNP

Common shorthand for expressing the non-racism of the EDL was to contrast it with the BNP. While much is made of the historical links between the EDL and the BNP, only two respondents in this study had previously been members of the party and although nine respondents said they had or would vote for the BNP, despite reservations about it, the same number said they would never vote for the party. When criticising the BNP, the party is generally dismissed as a 'bunch of racists' or 'Nazis' (Neil, Chris, Connor, Euan, Kane, Lisa, Michelle, Richard, Tim, Tina) with whom respondents do not want to be associated. Brett, when asked why he had become involved in the EDL rather than the BNP or the National Front, stated simply, 'cause the BNP are racist', while, for Chas,

> it's only for like the really extreme. You look at their sort of opinions like they don't like gay people, they don't want black people, they got forced to have multicultural people in their party. Hell I mean it says it all. I'm all for gay people. I got no problems with 'em. I got no problem with black people so no I could never be part of them. (Chas)

This distinction, and its limitations, was observed in action during an informal conversation between an EDL member, one of a group with whom the researcher had travelled to a flash demo in a neighbouring town, and a local BNP member who had come along to the demonstration. In the course of the conversation, the BNP member noted that he thought the EDL 'has got some things right but not the fact that they are not racist'. 'If you're not white', he continued, 'you're not right'. This kind of slogan was never used within the EDL milieu I encountered and the EDL member present at the time responds that for him 'this isn't the issue'. However, he does not challenge the racism of the BNP member and responds with understanding, noting that he is ex-National Front himself (field diary, 18 May 2013).

Thus, in differentiating the movement from the BNP, respondents sought to make a general case that the EDL was not a traditional far right organisation. This is based primarily on the lack of recognition of the gamut of traditional 'far right' ideologies in favour of a 'single issue' focus. However, this only confirms the 'non-racist' status of the movement if Islamophobia is excluded as a form of racism. This is evident in Brett's attempt to define the difference for him between the EDL and the BNP:

> because the EDL stand *for* the country, they [the BNP] stand against just like generally skin colour … we stand for against religion, against their actual religion not their skin colour. I mean you've got Muslim, you've got Sikh, you've got just generally Indian people but it's not like we are targeting at the skin colour, it's at the one religion Muslim. What within the religion is wrong. (Brett)

Here the reduction of racism literally to the colour of one's skin and the inability to recognise the relationship between prejudice on the basis of ethnicity or religion and biological racism is self-evident. This is returned to below since it constitutes the mechanism by which Islam and Muslims are rejected as possible objects of racism as individuals construct their 'non-racist' selves.

Constructing the non-racist self: understandings of racism

Claims made (usually spontaneously) in the course of interviews and informal conversations about the non-racist nature of the movement were followed up by the interviewer with questions about how respondents, as individuals, understood 'racism' and why, in their view, the hostility they extended to Islam and Muslims did not constitute 'racism'. This probing revealed that activists make sense of their own anti-Islam or anti-Muslim views within a wider perception of the individual self as not-racist. Respondents construct these non-racist selves by evidence of their own proximity and comfortableness with non-white bodies whilst excluding their sites of discomfort – with Muslims – as not a question of 'race'. This leaves room within the movement for those who recognise racial 'difference' as more than socially constructed (although not grounds for prejudice or discrimination) or who uphold forms of 'new' or 'cultural' racism in which 'difference' is identified and articulated as presenting a threat to 'our way of life'.

'Some of my best mates are black ... '

The importance of physical proximity and body to the understanding of racism and non-racism is evident in the fact that this self-description is frequently, and spontaneously, substantiated by references to having closeness to non-white bodies. Thus individuals often explain that they are personally not racist by talking about family and friends from ethnic minority groups. Jack states 'my best friend is Indian', Michelle that she had 'good friends that are like Caribbean and stuff like that, a good Chinese friend'. Tim, who named Nelson Mandela and Martin Luther King as among those who influenced him most politically, recounts how one of his best friends – described as a 'big black guy' in a way that marks out the body as a site of embracing 'otherness' – had backed him up when he had been stopped in the street and accused of being racist because of his EDL membership. For Mike, accusations by the UAF of being a racist are undermined by his revelation that his ex-wife is Jamaican while Carlie finds the suggestion that she is racist preposterous: 'I can't be called racist cause I've got that many coloureds in my family. Try telling them that I'm racist' (Carlie). The shared logic behind these statements is that, if you personally are not prejudiced against people of other ethnicities (evidenced by the fact that you have 'black mates' or family) and those same people support, and even join, the EDL, then the organ-isation and its members cannot be racist: 'How can anybody be a racist today? I've got black mates who support the EDL. I've got Sikh mates, I've got Indian mates' (Declan). Moreover, such statements imply that all non-white bodies are the same; lack of racism towards one group is assumed to be evidence of lack of racism towards all.

These narratives are genuine in as much as they are based on real relation-ships. However, public perceptions of the EDL as racist mean that demonstrating non-racism takes on a particular significance. A story told by one of the local 'admins' (but repeated frequently by others, indicating its significance in counter-ing accusations of racism) was designed to illustrate the gap between perceptions and reality. The woman in question had been living at a refuge for victims of domestic abuse and, during a training course organised by the refuge, another resident – a young Muslim woman – had become upset when a video on domestic violence was shown. The EDL activist had looked after her – made her tea, got tissues, tried to console her – and, she said, this had led to an open exchange about 'customs' in the Muslim community around violence to women and about the EDL. Having seen the EDL activist's response to this young woman, the course tutor was reported as saying that though she had been worried initially (when she had seen her EDL tattoo) she now knew that she 'wasn't any kind of racist' (field diary, 1 December 2012). At one level this story is another example designed to demonstrate that the EDL does not conform to its public image. At another level, however, it suggests that not only friendship and kinship but also gender can be a source of solidarity that crosses racialised difference.

Understanding racism: back to bodies?

Neither the existence of 'race' nor of its consequences – racism – is refuted by respondents in this study. They recognise that racist hatred and violence exist, but their practice is universally denied in relation to self or (most) others in the movement. This rejection of any self-ascription of racism is rooted in a simple, and narrow, definition of racism: 'to me to be a racist is to hate another race of people which I don't' (Mike).

Such definitions when deployed by respondents do not engage with the com-plexities of post-racialist arguments. They are underpinned, usually, by what respondents would think of as a 'common-sense' understanding of the exist-ence of bodily inscribed differences between people – in the statement above, for example, Mike talks about 'another race of people' as if 'race' is real rather than constructed – but that these differences should not be the source of rejection, revulsion, hatred or discrimination. The following ironic exchange between two women respondents who were close friends captures this engagement with 'race' as Lisa explains why some people (outside the EDL) do not understand why she is a member of a movement they associate with white racists:

> LISA: They just don't understand cause you know I'm not white. I'm not black but ...
> RACHEL: Aren't ya? You're not white?
> LISA: No. I fucking keep scrubbing it but it's not happening man.

Lisa sees 'race' as inscribed in the colour of one's skin notwithstanding the fact that her mixed heritage means she feels herself neither white nor black and that she can laugh at the racist imagination that black skins can be scrubbed clean to reveal white skins beneath. In this way, respondents treat 'race' – and its consequences in racism – as real rather than constructed. Only in the case of fringe members of the movement, who identify themselves as national socialists and are themselves highly critical of the EDL, however, is 'race' actively mobilised as a biologically rooted category imbued with notions of superiority and inferiority (see below). Most respondents thus, in some sense, adopt a post-'race' stance that imagines solidarities and social bonds overriding 'racial' difference. Mike describes himself as 'colour-blind' and prioritises loyalty over other forms of solidarity: 'I don't care what colour you are cause if you've got my back I'll have your back' (Mike). Declan, whilst again not challenging the existence of 'the white race and the black race', rejects it as a site of belonging or animosity, declaring that 'I'm human race. Nothing to do with colour with me' (Declan).

Of course both Mike and Declan's whiteness affords them the privilege of feeling themselves to be unracialised or colour-free. Indeed, the position most respondents adopt is not that of critical post-racialism but closer to conservative post-racism, of the kind criticised for ignoring continued racial stratification and racist discrimination (Paul, 2014: 704–5). This is reflected also in how they define what constitutes racism. When talking about racism, respondents did not talk about institutional racism or structurally rooted discrimination but most frequently referred to individual expressions of verbal abuse or name-calling directed at those whose bodies mark them out as racially or ethnically 'other': 'Why am I not a racist? Because I don't go round saying … "You're a fucking Paki, I don't like you", you know what I mean? … That, to me, is a racist' (Jason). Tina confirms this definition of racism: 'Racist is like if I was to go out and call a black person a racist name, do you know what I mean? Or call an Asian person a Paki.' For some, the use of such racist language is in fact seen as a reliable indicator of someone who does *not* support the EDL. Discussing how you identify an infiltrator or 'troll' either at a demo or online, two respondents suggested that the use of racist language was indicative: 'Then they say "Pakis" and things like that. Then you know 100 per cent that they ain't one of us' (Ray). As Ray resists the projection of what he considers to be racist terminology onto the EDL and excludes those using such language from 'one of us', the layers of reflexivity in how respondents understand 'racism' becomes apparent. Kane spells this distinction out further, and seeks to mobilise those 'others' he has personal contact with to substantiate his own understanding of what is, and is not, racist. In the following interview excerpt Kane is responding to the researcher's probing of what being 'racist' means to him:

> KANE: Erm, nigger, Muzzie, well Muzzie ain't even bad, Paki, that's bad.
> INT: Why is 'Muzzie' okay and 'Paki' bad? …
> KANE: They take it as alright. Cause I've actually spoke to them and sat down, the name was [names person], Muslim geezer and 'what do you take as racist?' He says 'Paki', Mars bar he has been called in the past. I says if I called you a Muzzie stuff like that, [he] says 'I am Muslim though, Muzzie don't bother me, it's just like a short word in't it?' 'What about Paki?' 'Aye saying that. That's just over the

top.' He was telling me all the different words that people have called him in the past and he just told me he says there ain't no point in it.

What is striking from this exchange is the naivety of this young respondent and the failure to understand how ethnicity and religion intersect or how terms used by different people, and in different contexts, can have different meanings. This is identified by Nayak (2003: 149) also in young people's confusion about why white racial epithets are not construed as forms of racist name-calling in the way that terms such as 'Paki' are saturated with racist power because of the different structural – dominant and subordinate – positions white and black students occupy in racialised social relations. However, it also constitutes a genuine exchange, a way of talking, about racism. In this sense it differs, I would argue, from the strategic dodging of the racist label whilst engaging in homogenising and derogatory representations of groups who are both religiously and ethnically defined. Such lip-service to being 'not racist' can be found also in the EDL. At a demonstration in Rotherham in May 2014, Ian Crossland[3] paused his speech in front of massed EDL demonstrators to respond to a shout from someone in the crowd of 'dirty Paki bastards' to chide the demonstrator for using the term 'Paki' because that is racist and 'we are not racist'. The object of his anger is not 'Pakistani gangs', he says, but 'Muslim gangs'. Not only is this a clear example of 'cultural racism' that produces a racist effect while denying that this effect is the result of racism but within minutes, when recounting a story about a white girl 'used' by a Pakistani lad and then dumped and subsequently murdered, he attributes the problem to what is clearly inferred to be a 'backward' culture, in which elders will not allow relationships with white girls. Crudely mocking a local Pakistani accent, he says 'they have to marry a cousin in Pakistan innit' (field diary, 10 May, 2014).

I was not the only one to notice the gap between the declaration of non-racism and the practice of racism. Rachel and Lisa, with whom I had travelled to the demonstration, staged their own protest that day by not participating in the main demo but listening to the speeches from a distance. They wanted to express their resistance not only to the 'piss heads' attending the demo (a frequent object of complaint) but, with reference to those speaking from the podium, 'the way people they don't agree with are speaking for them' (field diary, 10 May, 2014). For Lisa this proved a turning point and she subsequently left the movement to engage with 'more positive' actions (field diary, 26 June 2015).

Understanding racism: 'what race are Muslims'?

EDL narratives largely exclude Islam or the Muslim community as possible objects of racism. Accusations of racism are frequently deflected by differentiating Islam – 'It's not a race, it's a religion' (Tina) – or Muslims – 'what race are Muslims?' (Declan) – from ethnic minority groups towards whom prejudicial attitudes would be wrong. Connor states this most explicitly. While he considered it unacceptable to hate people for the colour of their skin, seeking to destroy what he perceived to be a hateful ideology (Islam) did not constitute racism: 'It ain't racist to oppose like an ideology what's based on to rape children and like based to cause hate' (Connor). Responding to the researcher's challenge that some anti-Muslim or anti-Islam chants used on EDL marches might be experienced as racist, Declan responds that he would find such chants unacceptable if they were 'Something that was racist. If it said "gassing the Jews" or "kill the blacks", if anyone ever chanted that I'd be out the EDL but it's never against Muslims, just Islam. ... Islam is not a person, it's a belief. It's a religion.' This distinction between anti-Islam and anti-Muslim sentiments is made repeatedly by respondents in this study and is explored in depth in the following chapter. Here it is worth noting that, unlike some other respondents, in this comment Declan recognises the actual or potential racialisation of religious groups – both Jews and Muslims – and their persecution or discrimination on that basis.

Growing out of racism: EDL as a learning process

The finding that EDL members express a specific hostility towards Islam does not mean that it does not co-exist alongside wider anti-Muslim prejudice that has itself a 'generic anti-immigrant component' (Strabac and Listhaug, 2008: 274). Indeed some respondents recognise, and reflect on, the racism, including their own, that they encounter. Kane admits that racism certainly exists in the movement but that being part of the EDL is a process of learning that the expression of racism is wrong:

> My mate, he said one racist comment, I think it was at Bristol and he had a bollocking cause you ain't meant to shout racist stuff. People am probably racist but you don't be racist with the English Defence League cause it don't stand for that cause any colour, any race is welcome. (Kane)

Connor, who comes from a family of active EDL members, admits freely that he had been racist and had joined because he thought the movement would reflect those racist views. In practice, he said, the EDL had brought him into contact with ethnic 'others' as a result of which he had changed his opinions:

> CONNOR: To be honest, when I first joined the EDL and my dad told me about it, I thought it was racist. That is the reason I went. I'm being deadly honest. On the way on the train and that we met up with the Sikhs and people like that and after that got on with it like. And now I am glad that I did join it because it's made me think about their religion and what them think. And like, I do get on with Sikhs, blacks, anything now where I used to. ... When I first joined the EDL I think I was racist and now I've got in with them and when I got on with it I met all black and whites and it was alright man, it was good, now, ever since, I've stuck with black people and everything. ...
> INT: So do you consider yourself racist?
> CONNOR: No, I'm not now, I was.

Older members talk about the process of 'growing out of' racism. Matt (34 years of age at the time of interview) says that, at 25, 'I could say I was racist'.

He recognises that he retains an element of racism but thinks that those on the outside of the movement are often more racist than him. Sean too recognises that while today he keeps an open mind and, unlike others, does not think every Muslim is a potential terrorist, when he was younger, 'I'd probably spout off about "Muslims", "Pakis", "Indians" and all that but that's being younger, being stupid and naive and spouting off crap.'

Notwithstanding this it remains clear that activists in this study retain particular anxieties towards Islam and Muslims. Sean, noting that he has friends of all different ethnicities (black, Thai, South African, Polish) concludes, 'We are all just human beings at the end of the day. But I just can't get my head around the Muslims.' This evokes what Back (1996: 98) describes as a 'strategic' racism practised in multi-ethnic urban environments whereby ethnic groups are ascribed different insider–outsider statuses by white populations. The form this takes among this group of respondents is explored in relation to wider understandings of Islamophobia and anti-Muslim hostility in the following chapter.

'Not racist'? Tracing objects of love and hate

INT: What is a racist? Would you call yourself a racist?
CONNOR: No I'd call myself like … English.

In the final section of this chapter, we consider how EDL members' understandings of themselves as 'not racist' sit in relation to other ideological positions. What objects of love and hate appear in their understanding of the world and how do they relate to broader ideologies associated with the far or populist radical right? The section starts with a discussion of narratives of patriotism. In these narratives, the nation appears as an object of 'love' and pride – opposed, as in Connor's statement above – to the hate-filled identity of the racist. However, narratives of patriotism also carry emotions of fear and threat, which, in some cases, turn positive affective identification with nation into a more exclusive nativism. Precisely what threatens the nation is then traced through views expressed on multiculturalism and immigration. While multiculturality, it is suggested, is largely accepted as 'how it is', multiculturalism, understood as an ideology of the liberal elite, is an object of hatred. A similar pattern is found in discussions of immigration and citizenship where widespread concern with the level of immigration is expressed as anger primarily at a government unable or unwilling to see how immigration affected (threatened) them. Since discrimination and exclusion of sexual minorities are seen to be key markers of traditional far right organisations, respondents' positions on LGBT rights are discussed. Finally, in order to illustrate the diversity and complexity of views encountered within the movement, the position on all these aspects of ideology among a fringe group of respondents (identifying as Infidels) is explored; these are compared and contrasted to views within the majority of the respondent set.

Patriotism: love without hate?

An online survey of EDL supporters found a key motivating factor in support for the EDL to be a 'love of England, commitment to preservation of traditional national and cultural values, and representation of the interests of "real" British country-men'; this was cited as the reason for joining the movement by 31 per cent of those surveyed and was second only to 'views on Islam' (Bartlett and Littler, 2011: 6). This is reflected in narratives of respondents in this study. Although the object of affec-tion is less specifically stated (as 'England'), respondents talk of their love 'for this country' (Declan, Lisa, Michelle, Tina) and understand their activism as 'fighting for' (Declan), 'standing up for' (Connor, Lisa) or 'saving' (Connor) the country. While, in this form, patriotism expresses a positive, self-identification with nation, it can also find expression in resistance to groups and forces perceived as threatening nationhood, national identity or culture and calls to preserve the state (if not territo-rially then at least its resources) exclusively, or primarily, for members of the native group (nativism). Soutphommasane (2012: 19) argues that patriotism – understood as a special concern for the welfare of one's nation and fellow citizens – does not inherently incorporate nativism. This position is expressed in some respondent narratives in this study while, in others, there is a clear drift into nativism.

Patriotism is often articulated by respondents as an emotional response to the nation that encourages activism but pre-exists it. As Matt puts it, 'I'm just a patriotic bastard like. I always want what's best for my country.' In this sense patriotism is the 'given' that identifies 'like minds' and allows the development of affective bonds that sustain activism (Klatch, 2004: 491). Moreover, activism – taking part in demonstrations – provides a space for the expression of shared patriotic sentiments that generate solidarity:

> ... it's nice to be around a bunch of people as patriotic as I am, you know, ... it's the only place that you can actually be patriotic. ... I don't have to be politically correct, you know. I can go there and I can sing 'Keep St George in My Heart', you know. I can be the patriotic person, I can love my country, you know what I mean, and be round a lot of people that love their country too. (Tina)

This like-mindedness is reinforced rhetorically by the use of the term 'fellow patri-ots' (see also Garland and Treadwell, 2011: 630; Busher, 2012) to refer to those in the movement by the leadership during speeches at demonstrations (field diary, 30 June 2012; field diary, 12 October 2013). Grassroots members also spontane-ously link this subject position as 'patriot' with activism in the EDL – 'I'm stand-ing there as an English patriot' (Connor).

For some respondents, loving 'being English', as Soutphommasane (2012: 19) suggests, does not mean hating others. Tim clearly differentiates between negative and positive forms of patriotism and implicitly questions claims to the ownership of 'British values' through a notion of indigeneity:

> I just think the BNP, to me personally, is just like let 'em carry on. No-one's fucking listening to 'em ... they are just saying, 'Oh we wanna protect British

values' and all this and it's like OK protecting British values is OK but you've got to have tolerance to let other people have their own values. ... [I]t's not about white power ... you can love being English and your English heritage. I do. But it doesn't mean I can't love somebody else. To me, if you strip somebody of their skin then we are all people. (Tim)

When respondents talk of being 'proud' of the country (Lisa, Connor), therefore, it is not, in most cases, a racialised 'white pride'. Differentiating her patriotism from that of the BNP and National Front, Michelle seeks to distinguish a feeling of pride from that of superiority:

... they are just pure racialists that's all they are. It's all white power this, and white pride that .... You know I'm a white person, I'm proud to be a white person but I don't need to stick it in other people's face to use it as a, you know, like a 'I'm white you're not, I'm better than you are' ... I just think it's absolute tosh. (Michelle)

Patriotic attitudes and actions are also ascribed to ethnic minority groups by some respondents; examples include Sikhs (who fought in the British army during the war) and Muslims who stand up against extremism within their community (Ian, Tim).

However, there is also evidence in respondent narratives of the drift from positive identification with the country, and concern for its citizens, into a defensive resistance to 'change'. Kyle had joined an EDL flash demonstration against the conversion of a church in his home town into an Islamic prayer centre because he felt there was 'no need to change'. In these narratives, patriotism is associated with the preservation of some imagined (but rarely specified) 'traditional' national and cultural values of a fixed national entity: 'Keeping Britain Britain' (Richard). While nobody is excluded from this mission, what, and who, constitutes the imagined nation remains unclear: 'at the end of the day it ain't about what colour you am, it ain't about what race you am ... It's all about do you agree with Britain to stay as Britain' (Kane).

In some cases this position is articulated as the continuation of a defence of Britain conducted in a more tangible way by previous generations. As Tina puts it, 'The wars weren't won for us ... to give our country away ... Them wars were won for future generations.' Indeed, for Tim, respect for war veterans is an anti-fascist statement that distinguishes the EDL from extreme nationalist groups such as the National Front whom he describes as 'Nazis': 'the whole point of the EDL is about protecting like the honour of troops and respecting like the sacrifice that was made and it's just like for anybody to be a Nazi is an absolutely sworn enemy of Britain as far as I'm concerned' (Tim).

However, resistance to change can slip into a more aggressive racialisation of change. This is evident in Tina's description of her experience in what she calls 'a white British Christian area' in which she had grown up:

... the more I was walking around, and as the years went on, there were, they were just everywhere, you know what I mean? It was literally, 'spot the British person', anywhere I went. Sitting on the bus ... when I used to come from [names home district], like, go on the [names bus route] to go to [names city] city centre, like you wouldn't get Muslims on that bus route. You just wouldn't see it. Not that I've got a problem with seeing Muslims on the [names bus route], it was just how quickly the amount of Muslims on that bus, how quickly it changed. (Tina)

Tina's reflections exemplify what Hage (2014: 233) calls 'numerological racism' in which concern is expressed through the category 'too many'. Of course change – including a growth in ethnic diversity – is taking place. Although the White British ethnic group represents the overwhelming majority (80 per cent) of the population of England and Wales, the total ethnic group population other than White has risen from three million (or 7 per cent) in 1991 to almost eight million (14 per cent) in 2011 (Jivraj, 2012). Moreover, the residential areas with the greatest growth of ethnic minority groups are those areas – like the one Tina refers to – where they were fewest in 2001 (Jivraj, 2012). A similar aggressive racialisation of 'others', who are seen as responsible for disrupting the 'English community', is identified by Leddy-Owen (2014: 1128) in his study of English identities in an ethnically diverse area of South London.

Among EDL activists in this study, anxiety over change is articulated most frequently through a discourse of infringement (see Chapter 7). Carlie feels 'we've basically got no rights in our own country any more' and places blame at the door of the government who she sees as 'failing to protect us British that live in the country, that have grown up in the country'. Her remedy is to 'put us British first because it's our country not theirs'. While Carlie's 'they' remains unspecified, Connor explicitly racialises those he perceives as threatening 'our laws and our beliefs': 'It's England, not Pakistan. You know what I mean? It's up to us what we do, not them. It's our country, if you dow [don't] like our laws and our beliefs [names local city] airport terminal 16. You know what I mean? Pack your bags and go.' At demonstrations this sentiment finds expression in the chant 'We want our country back' and, towards the end of the fieldwork, it began to appear also in nativist statements in speeches: 'This is our country. They are *guests* [my emphasis] in it and they would do well to remember that' (Dave Russell, EDL national demonstration, Luton, recorded in field diary, 22 November 2014).[4]

Ahmed (2004: 117) argues that emotions, in particular of hate and love, are 'crucial to the delineation of the bodies of individual subjects and the body of the nation'. In extreme right ideologies, she suggests, the subject (the ordinary 'white' man) 'is presented as endangered by imagined others whose proximity threatens not only to take something away from the subject (jobs, security, wealth), but to take the place of the subject' itself. Central to this is the emotional reading of others as hateful, which 'works to bind the imagined white subject and nation together' (2004: 118). This is particularly important to understanding narratives of Islam among EDL respondents and is discussed in more detail in the following chapter. However, it is sometimes applied more widely, as evident in Lisa's confirmation of her own patriotism through the identification of 'others' who hate:

> Muslim extremists … I don't care if they are Muslims or fucking if you had an Eastern European party or whatever, if you are going to come over to this country and blatantly hate us, you know, hate our country, hate us as people, fuck off. (Lisa)

Can patriotism's promotion of a special identification with one's fellow citizens exist without an accompanying enmity or lack of sympathy towards all outsiders as Soutphommasane (2012: 38) suggests? Or is such privileging of one's 'own' destined to turn into the excessive or irrational patriotism ascribed to movements like the EDL (Jackson, 2011c: 5)? On the one hand, respondents' own understanding of their EDL activism as the attempt 'to do something for the country' (Casey) or 'making the country a better place to be' (Neil) evokes the sense of 'collective responsibility' and desire to 'promote a common good' identified as characteristic of 'good' (national liberal) patriotism (Soutphommasane, 2012: 17). The political demands associated with 'putting this country first' expressed by activists in this study, moreover, are no more extreme than those included in UKIP's 2015 General Election manifesto. They include: withdrawal of the UK from the European Union (Declan); limiting access to NHS care and social security benefits to those from overseas (Matt); and cutting overseas aid budgets and withdrawing from commitments to military and humanitarian interventions abroad (Euan, Declan).

Notwithstanding this, the patriotism of EDL respondents differs from Soutphommasane's (2012: 19) model of a liberal nationalist approach to citizenship and community where 'patriotism refers to the identification with one's political community, and a special concern for its welfare and the welfare of one's fellow citizens'. This is, first, because of the evident slippage into nativism, and indeed into xenophobia, in the case of some individuals (discussed below). Second, it is because patriotism in the case of the EDL is developed in conditions of a profound *disidentification* with the political community as currently constituted, and populist distrust of liberalism (see Chapter 8). Third, although in his vision, and that of the EDL, patriotism must be 'put into action', for Soutphommasane liberal patriotism is accomplished through a 'national conversation' (2012: 7), while, for EDL activists, the emotional dimension of patriotism is crucial: 'the older I've got the more patriotic I've got and more passionate I've got and I am very passionate about it now' (Lisa). Thus, Soutphommasane's vision of the enactment of patriotism through a 'patriotic mode of deliberation' (2012: 13) appears to have little room for the passions at play within the EDL.

Anti-multiculturalism: racism by any other name?

'Multiculturalism', and its entwinement with the politics of class, 'race' and ethnicity are discussed in detail in Chapter 6. Policies associated with multiculturalism have been subject to a series of 'backlashes' in recent decades, most recently by leading European politicians such as Angela Merkel and David Cameron, for supposedly encouraging the self-segregation of ethnic minority communities and thus contributing to a decline in social cohesion and rise in a range of social problems, including crime and terrorism. This mainstreaming of anti-multiculturalist rhetoric, Lentin (2014: 1273) argues, has enabled the new far right in Europe to appropriate arguments that opposition to multiculturalism is not racist while intolerance of immigrants is justified on the basis of cultural incompatibility rather than biological, racial hierarchy (2014: 1273). In this section the tension in the relationship between cultural diversity and political solidarity in patriotic and multicultural visions of society and community (Soutphommasane, 2012: 12) is explored, and the claims of the EDL to be both patriotic and multicultural are critically examined.

The EDL's claim to be 'not racist', and in this way different from movements of the 'far right', rests on the argument that it is a 'multicultural organisation made up of every community in this country' (Tommy Robinson, cited in Allen, 2011: 287). This study identified some evidence of this broad acceptance of multiculturality. The term 'multicultural' for example is commonly used by respondents to describe society as they experience it: 'we live in a multicultural society. We do, that's a fact and that's never gonna change' (Jack). Lisa explains that she would never participate in actions such as vandalising mosques because 'I think we are a multicultural country'. Tim sees the EDL as reflecting wider society and claims that it was the 'multicultural' nature of the EDL's membership and orientation that had led him to attend his first demonstration:

> ... like looking into it ... one of the main reasons ... I wanted to go was cause I noticed that it wasn't like BNP ... cause it's like I don't know. I looked at it and there was a lot of Indian names on there and like black people and so I was thinking this is like a bit more like a multicultural thing and so it should be. (Tim)

A number of other respondents referred to the benefits of diversity. Tina, for example explicitly said that she thought multiculturalism was 'a good thing' arguing that 'Britain would be a boring place without it'. The advantage of 'multicultural' foods and spices was discussed by younger respondents and approval was given by activists with young children to the benefits of learning different languages at school and introducing pupils to 'different foods' (Casey, Matt). However, the advantages of multicultural society are sometimes qualified with reference to Islam and/or Muslims. Matt resents what he perceives to be the overemphasis on Islam in multicultural education: 'it's always about we got to learn about Islam, it's always Islam, Islam, Islam' (Matt). Tina, despite her positive comments about multicultural society noted above, concludes that, nonetheless, 'there is a really bad issue with Muslims'. This tendency to view Muslims, uniquely, as disloyal and culturally different is discussed in Chapter 5.

The general acceptance of multiculturality, however, is sharply contrasted to a broad rejection of multicultural*ism*. Multiculturalism is understood not as a condition of society but as a 'concept' or ideology and, as such, 'the enemy':

... the Earth benefits from cultural diversity and racial diversity, it makes it more unique, it shapes what humanity is. However, multiculturalism is destroying diversity altogether, which is ironic because the liberals say we need diversity ... the enemy for me is not one race specifically, it's multiculturalism as a concept. (Nick)

As will be seen from further contextualisation of Nick's position below,[5] the argument that multiculturalism 'is destroying diversity' is based on a biologically essentialist and anti-miscegenist position. Ollie, while sharing Nick's national socialist views, sees multiculturalism as divisive because it emphasises difference: 'you just have a lack of shared values now because of multiculturalism' (Ollie). Where these extreme views overlap with those of mainstream EDL members is in the belief that multiculturalism is a 'failure':

> BRETT: The reason our country is in ruins is because since the Second World War we've tried to be multicultural. Well fuck them.
> CONNOR: Multicultural is a thing of the past. Nothing will never be multicultural ever.
> BRETT: We've tried being multicultural and all we've done is fuck up the country cause we've tried too hard and we've ...
> CONNOR: You know this is moving onto racist stuff and multiculturalism for me shouldn't be a thing, do you know what I mean? Don't get me wrong it is probably something what EDL class as extreme views but I don't think like that mixed breeding, things like that, should go on. I really don't.

Here, Connor recognises his own position slipping from the view widely encountered in mainstream discourse that 'multicultural is a thing of the past' into 'racist stuff' – anti-miscegenism – that would not be approved within the EDL. This slippage would seem to lend weight to Lentin's (2014) argument that anti-multiculturalism is, in fact, an expression of anti-multiculture or anti-multiculturality, and as such a form of racism.

Immigration and citizenship

A frequent corollary of anti-multiculturalism is the justification of intolerance of immigrants on the basis of cultural incompatibility; this allows 'race' to be coded as 'culture' and apparently stripped of its racist content (Barker, 1981: 23; Solomos and Back, 1994: 155–56). A distinguishing feature of the EDL at its inception was its lack of reference to immigration in its mission statement (see Chapter 2); at the time, an important indicator of its difference from traditional far right groups. This was reflected in the themes of campaigns and demonstrations throughout most of the fieldwork period and corroborated by respondents: 'I ain't seen immigration being brought up a lot. ... I've never been out to a demo that has been involved with immigration' (Kane). This absence began to appear more anomalous than distinctive when, in the long run up to the 2015 UK General Election, immigration emerged as a key policy debate.[6] Reflecting also the mood of its grassroots membership, in February 2014 the EDL posted that a meeting of the ROs had agreed that mass immigration would be included in the movement's mission statement as a central campaigning issue.[7] However, at the point of writing, no such addition had been made to the mission statement and, in interview, Eddowes confirmed it was still 'in the pipeline' because 'it's not the right time to tackle that'. He goes on to note that he is 'not against immigration' and recognises its benefits but, echoing the UKIP position (see note 6), he was against the volume of unskilled, cheap labour coming into the country, which he sees as 'not controlled' and 'changing the face of *our* country dramatically' (Eddowes, 2015; my emphasis).

Cognisant of the danger of obscuring the racialisation of immigrants through the coding process, in this study attitudes to immigration and references to 'immigrants' were coded for analysis separately: the first under 'political views'; and the second under 'race and ethnicity'. From this it became clear that immigration (as a process and phenomenon) was a matter of considerable concern for respondents and that the vast majority of respondents took an anti-immigration stance. Of a total of 136 codes generated during data analysis on a diverse range of 'political views', 'negative attitudes towards immigration' was the third most populated while only two respondents (in addition to Eddowes) explicitly said they were 'not against' immigration (and even in these cases, the respondents voiced concerns about the capacity of the UK to handle immigration at its current rate and its impact on employment opportunities). Immigration is viewed as bad for the country by respondents primarily for economic reasons, although individual respondents also see it as being divisive in reducing 'shared values'(see above) or the sheer numbers threatening to 'change' what Britain looks like (the racialisation of this notion of change is discussed above).

Given that this chapter explores racisms, old and new, the key question addressed here is whether 'immigrants' are the object of a new, cultural racism. In EDL respondent narratives, 'immigrants' are rarely posited as a single, homogenous group. Usually a distinction is made between 'good' and 'bad' immigrants where 'good' immigrants are those who 'work and pay their taxes' and 'bad' immigrants are those who 'sponge off the benefit system'. Thus when asked if immigrants who have been working in the country for a number of years should be entitled to citizenship and a permanent right to stay in the UK, Michelle responded, 'Oh yeah, if they've worked to pay their taxes and everything then fair enough, absolutely fair enough.' She goes on to qualify this with the proviso that, 'But then if it is people moving here now, before you know it, in a couple of years' time, the whole family is going to be here and they are going to be on benefits and I think they need to stop benefits going to other countries' (Michelle). Complaints about abuse of the benefit system are echoed by others (Euan, Matt, Tina):

> I will not stop anybody from coming here, but if you are just going to come here to sponge the benefit system … We've got Polish people who will work. I'll welcome them with open arms, anyone. But if you are gonna come here just for a house, for water, for money and deprive everyone of a house and a job and all that then that's what I've got the problem with. (Declan)

Richard recognises that, 'I suppose they do come over here and work hard', but the reality for him is that 'they're taking all our jobs and we're suffering for it. That's why there's so much unemployment. Our country's full enough as it is and if they just keep coming over and coming over, where are we going to be in 10, 20 years?' Indeed respondents are often deeply conflicted about immigration; within a single narrative a respondent might suggest that the solution to improving housing and employment 'for white people' is to 'get hold of all the immigrants and kick 'em out' *and* that the vast majority of immigrants had earned their right to housing and other material benefits (Jason). This conflicted attitude may arise from a subconscious recognition of the clash between feelings of anger about the current social and economic situation and the realisation that immigrants themselves are not to blame, and are 'like us'. This is captured in Tim's statement that:

> with like immigration and things like that ... the way I see it there's no problem. It's a shame there aren't enough jobs for everybody really ... those people that come here they just wanna come here and work and kind of provide, put food on the table for their families and they accept the British laws and the British way of life and they enjoy it you know so it's like fair play to 'em. I wish there was enough jobs for the whole world. (Tim)

Steve Eddowes extends this sentiment, arguing that the problem is not migrants coming to the UK to work – 'you can't blame them for coming here to get on' – the problem is the impact it has on others 'because they'll come and they'll work, for a lot lower wage'. On the basis of his own experience working in the transport industry, he says, wages fell by 40 to 50 per cent after EU enlargement. While Eddowes recognises the underlying economic forces at play here – 'That's capitalism ... all over' (Eddowes, 2015) – this position exemplifies how the white working class is constructed as 'victim' while immigrants are seen 'as agents of capital rather than fellow objects upon whom capitalist social relations inscribe themselves' (Clarke and Garner, 2010: 203).

There is relatively little evidence of the racialisation of immigrants, or of cultural differences, being used as a cover for racialised prejudice. In this sense respondents are in line with a wider section of the UK population concerned primarily about the 'entitlement' of immigrants to state resources (social housing, benefit payments) and to which all political parties responded with proposed curtailment of entitlement during the 2015 General election campaign (see note 6). In two interviews reference was made to the failure of immigrants to 'integrate', although this accusation was levelled at differently labelled groups, specifically 'Muslim' communities and 'East European' migrants. This suggests a nativist presumption that recent immigrants have, naturally, less entitlement or, to put it the other way around, 'we' (native people) should have privileged entitlement. Such anxieties about the status of the 'native', 'indigenous' and white population, Ware (2008: 11) argues, are apparent in all European and Anglophone societies where national identities, rooted in colonial histories, are conflated with being 'white, Anglophone and Christian' and expressed in the perception of economic migrants, refugees and asylum seekers as the undeserving beneficiaries of welfare entitlements at the expense of majority ('indigenous') populations (2008: 11).

This raises the question of who constitutes the 'we' assumed here. For the most part (exceptions are discussed below) respondents tend towards an inclusive notion of citizenship, even if they do not question who dictates the terms of that citizenship. When Carlie calls for greater promotion of 'our' rights, she includes in that anyone with a British passport. Tina states unequivocally that British means British regardless of colour and that she had no problem at all with, for example, Asian immigrants being entitled to citizenship and benefits: 'They've probably been … in Britain longer than I've been born, a lot of them. You know, I ain't got a problem with that at all' (Tina). This position is elaborated by Tim:

> How can you … say like the Indian people shouldn't be in Britain. Well why bloody not? Cause if it wasn't for them Britain wouldn't still be called Britain. They came from a different continent to fight for a country when realistically all we did was go in there and take over their country hundreds of years ago and declare that their country was part of our Empire. … So I think for the BNP to say 'well you know we want them to go home', sorry I don't believe that. (Tim)

Tim's rejection of calls for repatriation includes a critique of British imperialism that suggests South Asian immigrant groups are not only entitled to but owed rights as British citizens.

The extremist fringe

There are exceptions to the main thrust of what has been argued above and they are discussed here separately as the views emanate primarily from a group of three young men, Andrew, Nick and Ollie (aged 16–23), who form part of the respondent set for this project and who attended EDL demonstrations but whose affiliation was with a regional organisation of the Infidels movement. By treating their views separately, it is not suggested that there is no continuum in some views between this extremist fringe and the majority of the respondent set and this has been indicated where relevant throughout the text. However, their interview narratives differ significantly from those of mainstream EDL members in terms of both the degree to which they invoke ideological positions and the content of those ideologies.

Andrew, Nick and Ollie's worldviews were characterised by strong Christian beliefs, support for National Socialism, interest in Aryanist ideology and a fascination with white supremacist organisations (such as the Ku Klux Klan) and their leading figures; these are all ideas (including Christianity) that are largely rejected by mainstream members. The suspicion is mutual. All three 'Infidels' expressed severe reservations about the EDL and its members (because they did not follow a 'Christian lifestyle'). Nick said the Infidels were a 'more serious' movement, while the EDL was 'more interested in having a fight with the local Muslims and the pub culture' (Nick). What they shared was 'being against Islamic extremism' (Andrew). The personal ideologies of these three respondents vary, being informed by National Socialism, Christianity and Hindu nationalism. What they had in common was a fascination with Aryanism and thus the failure to live a 'noble life' by members of the EDL sat uneasily with them. In contrast, Ollie was a vegan and didn't drink, smoke or use drugs, Andrew was a kick-boxer and Nick disparaged the EDL as a 'bunch of degenerates'.

Andrew, the oldest of the three, was a former member of the National Front, although he had been ejected from the movement after his exposure in a local newspaper as a Breivik supporter and KKK sympathiser. This incident happened in August 2012, when Andrew had been posting, along with his friends, comments about Anders Breivik and, around the same time, had bought a KKK outfit and posted photos of himself wearing it on social media. The pictures had been reprinted in a local newspaper and then by anti-fascist electronic media 'edlnews'. Andrew reflects in interview that he genuinely 'admires' the KKK while Nick said he was 'attracted to' the white hoods and had investigated their views and 'I started to see well yeah maybe they are right' (Nick).[8] Andrew also expanded on his sympathy for Anders Breivik who, he said, had 'inspired' him. When he watched the trial, he said, 'I could see … his love for his people and for his nation … That he truly cared about his own people. And all he wanted to do was to save his country.' He goes on to state that 'I see myself in him' and to talk in stark terms about the mass killing committed by Breivik as getting 'the job done' without causing 'any pain' to the victims. When challenged about the terror victims must have experienced, he continues to rationalise the atrocity and empathise with the perpetrator as 'a man who had little hope left for his country' (Andrew).

In sharp contrast to the views expressed by mainstream EDL members, for the three Infidel respondents, Britishness was an ethnic category open only to those who are 'English, Scottish, Irish, or Welsh' and excluding, in Nick's view, even 'an Asian family that's been here five generations'. It follows that, for Nick, citizenship should be ethnically rooted and, in his ideal world, immigrants would be 'stripped of' their citizenship and 'repatriated': 'they all deserve their own rights in their own you know … in Africa, they deserve full rights there. … [I]n Britain, the ethnic British, of the white race deserve full rights here. We deserve to be put first, cause it's our country' (Nick).

Andrew also says he thinks that 'multiculturalism is bad', defining it as 'an anti-European hate ideology designed to deconstruct Western values and traditional values of our civilisation'. In his way of seeing the world, neither equality nor cultural mixing is desirable. Thus multiculturalism is criticised for 'teaching that all cultures are equal' and posited as a left-wing/liberal ideology imposed on people against their will:

> I think that segregation is a good thing. I think that people naturally segregate anyway. You can't force people to mix with another people who they don't wanna be mixed with and that's what the Marxists, liberals are trying to force us to do, like in the schools and in the jobs and at work and everywhere. They, they're trying to force us all together. (Andrew)

When pushed on who is responsible for imposing this ideology, Andrew blames 'ideas of multiculturalism, of tolerance, and of political correctness' on the Frankfurt School and 'cultural Marxism'. Nick, however, sees multiculturalism itself as 'the enemy' because it promotes racial mixing, which reduces distinctiveness and risks losing the 'spirituality, and spiritual divineness' of the blessed race of the Israelites.

All three members of this group self-identified as national socialists and emphasise that National Socialism combines left- and right-wing ideas. Nick says his interest in National Socialism started with 'an obsession with Hitler' but he had since learned more about it and explains it as 'Socialism is basically support of the working class, it's the opposite of capitalism, it's a left-wing *economic* ideology, nationalism is a right-wing *political* ideology and that's why they don't clash, cause one's economic, and one's political' (Nick). He does not consider himself far right because that would imply fascist when, in fact, 'fascism is national capitalism, and I'm a national socialist which is left-wing – but right-wing as well' (Nick). For Ollie, who said he had identified with National Socialism since the age of 10, it was more directly linked to 'the revival of like the Aryanist ideology'. In his personal ideology, it was combined with Hindu nationalism and veganism/animal rights activism. The Aryan 'noble man' was a core concept for him – which included not only healthy living but also engagement in charity work – and he tried to live by these principles. However, he recognised that 'it's very unrealistic that it will happen that National Socialism will be achieved in my lifetime' (Ollie).

Gender and sexual equality

Nativism or anti-immigrant sentiment of the far right or newer populist extremist parties is generally seen as rooted in a broader rejection of human equality and desire for a return to traditional values and to remove 'threatening' groups from society (Goodwin, 2011b: 12). This, it is suggested, makes such movements an inhospitable environment for women and sexual minorities. The male-dominated composition of, but also the active female participation and presence of gay men and lesbians in, the EDL was discussed in Chapter 3. Below the movement's ideological position on gender equality and LGBT rights is explored.

Formally women are recognised as equals in the movement and there is a women's (Angels) division at national and many regional levels. Referencing this equality, female EDL members are said to stand 'beside not behind' the men in the movement (see Figure 4.4). While the designation of the division as 'Angels', and the iconography that accompanies the term, would appear to evoke a conservative femininity based on the 'angelic' virtues of purity and innocence, angels are not exclusively male or female and appear in the Bible with male names and forms. Moreover, angels are not passive but play a crucial communication role (carrying messages between heaven and earth), and while they may perform a protective role (which might be associated with a nurturing or mothering function), they are also spiritual and inspirational figures. Angel wings – which are popular tattoo symbols (see Figure 7.2) – symbolise aspiration, speed and elevation. Adopting the title of 'Angel' before one's movement name (used on Facebook and printed on their hoody), therefore, may signify gender transgression rather than conformity. Indeed, as Figure 4.4 illustrates, EDL Angels are not represented as sexually passive.

As discussed in Chapter 3, traditional notions of femininity are challenged or transgressed by women in the movement; in contrast traditional gender roles for men are generally upheld. This is usually captured in the course of observation – especially in the 'banter' on the coach to and from demos and in the pub before and after them – but is occasionally directly articulated. Andrew speaks proudly of coming from a 'traditional nuclear family' in which his mum is 'a traditional housewife'. Jack describes himself as a traditional 'provider'; he works hard all week, brings money home, while *she* manages it (field diary, 1 December, 2012). He also prides himself on being 'the hardest guy' in the area; this is said in the context of explaining why his partner (who had been subject to domestic violence in her previous relationship) does not have to be afraid of anyone (field diary,

4.4 EDL Angels 'stand beside their men'

1 December, 2012). Indeed, this vision of men's role as to protect women is the most frequently referenced attribute of masculinity and is referred to positively by both male and female respondents; a fact that sits uneasily alongside the frequent reporting of the experience of domestic violence. In addition to the childhood experiences discussed in Chapter 3, six respondents reported that they personally had experienced domestic abuse at the hands of a male partner, two reported that current or previous partners had been subject to domestic violence and one respondent said her daughter had been. While as a rule this provoked outrage by male respondents and declarations of their lack of tolerance for violence towards women, the continued sexual objectification of women in EDL images and Angels iconography compounds the undermining of women's role that is expressed in men's everyday talk (see Chapter 3). The same regional Angels division Facebook page that carried the image recreated in Figure 4.4, for example, also carried a photo of *Daily* and *Sunday Sport* glamour model Kelly Bell barely clad in a St George's cross bikini in Page 3 style.

Discussion of gender equality at the ideological level was rare among respondents and confined almost exclusively to the three members of the Infidels taking part in this study (see above). These respondents bemoaned a 'drift' in gender roles. Mirroring the debate on multiculturalism, femin*ism* is pitched as a negative (and imposed) force which has been allowed to go too far and has led to the deformation of 'real' gender equality and the rights of men. These three respondents envisage an ideal society as one in which what they believe to be the innate difference between men and women is recognised:

> My better society would be where women respected men as men, as leaders, as people to be looked up to … and men respected women as like a precious creation which God has made who they will show respect to that they'll always love and care for. Like back in the old days where men showed women respect by opening doors for them. (Andrew)

Feminists are considered to be the source of the problem since 'they want absolute equality for men and women, they want men to become women and women to become men' (Andrew). This is contrasted to their own understanding of men and women as 'different but equal': 'men do need to have their own roles, women need to have their roles, but I don't think either one should play a bigger part in society than the other' (Ollie). Transgression of this – women choosing a career over children – is thus considered 'wrong because it's messing up society' (Nick). For this small group of fringe activists, the biological rooting of gender difference indeed falls within a wider rejection of human equality; as Ollie put it, 'I just completely reject that [attempts to make everyone completely equal in the Soviet Union], not everyone is equal.'

If the movement makes only a partial break with gender norms within the far right, in its creation of an active LGBT division within its structure and promotion of LGBT rights, it has marked new territory. As Allen (2011: 288) notes, 'a far-right LGBT grouping is almost unheard of' and thus the EDL sits among a small number of anti-Islam parties and movements, such as Geert Wilders' Partijvoor de Vrijheid, that incorporate gay rights platforms. Observational evidence suggests, moreover, that the LGBT division of the EDL is more than a cynical attempt by the leadership to distance itself from classic far right groups. The LGBT rainbow flag was visible at every demonstration and at the national demonstration in Newcastle in May 2013, Declan, the 19-year-old leader of the LGBT division, gave a speech, to much applause, about the importance of the division in challenging representations of the movement as 'homophobic fascists' and the failure of what he called the 'far left' to be consistent with their claim to oppose homophobia wherever they encountered it (field diary, 25 May 2013). Declan rejects suggestions of tokenism in EDL policy on LGBT rights and narrativises his own movement into the EDL (he had previously been a member of the BNP) as a conscious search for a party on the radical right that was 'open to all':

> I came to realise that I couldn't be gay and in the BNP and just before I left I thought to myself 'Is there any organisations out there with the same views as me that accept people of all backgrounds?' And that's when I found English Defence League. (Declan)

Gay men and lesbian and bisexual women were all represented within the respondent set in this study and felt comfortable within the movement. A transsexual speaker at the Bristol demonstration was treated with respect and applauded for a speech in which she talked about being proud to be a transsexual EDL member and of the support she had received from the movement (field diary, 14 July 2012). Indeed, the Bristol Gay Pride march was staged simultaneously with the EDL march in the city that day and a number of individuals who would normally have attended the Pride March chose to march with the EDL, sporting their rainbow flags.

This is not to suggest that the EDL is free of homophobia or motivated by an impartial commitment to human rights. Homophobia is an accusation that is strategically targeted at Islamic doctrine which, according to Declan, says 'gays should be taken to the top of a mountain and thrown off'. Moreover, homophobia continues to be demonstrated at the fringes of the movement. Declan recounted how he had left his original EDL division because individuals in it had 'called me an embarrassment being a gay EDL member and they said that the EDL should not allow gays'. The three Infidels members in this study went further. Andrew said in his vision of a better society, he would like to see homosexuality recriminalised because 'even behind closed doors I think that it can be harmful because it spreads disease, and it spreads immorality within communities, and it destroys families' (Andrew). Their arguments often drew on their Christian beliefs. Nick justifies his opposition to the gay marriage bill as 'because again it says in the Bible that homosexuality is wrong' (Nick).

Among the mainstream movement too the researcher observed homosocial banter with elements of sexism and homophobia and Declan conceded that he still had to be 'careful' on demonstrations because he could attract violence from

'UAF bullies', but also from EDL members. Individuals within the movement are often conflicted and uncertain about their views. With regard to the Bristol demonstration discussed above, one respondent met for the first time over a year later, commented that, on that day, he had held the 'gay flag' for some people marching with the EDL until they started kissing next to him; that was enough, he said, 'nothing against 'em … but within limits' (field diary, 7 October, 2013). I encountered a similarly conflicted reaction from one of the young respondents who said that he had a gay friend and no problem with gay members in the movement but had felt uncomfortable when a couple had kissed and cuddled in public. When I ask if it would be alright for him to kiss his girlfriend in public, though, he replied, 'of course' (field diary, 23 March 2013). Even such young members, still struggling to find the right expression for their own masculinity, however, were not closed to other ways of being men and were able to feel a genuine solidarity with LGBT rights campaigners. When asked what they made of the Pride March being held simultaneously in Bristol, members of the local youth division in this study empathised with the LGBT activists whom they see as defending their rights in a similar way to the EDL: 'Respect. Them was out to do what we wanna do. … They are allowed to do what they allowed us to do' (Ray).

Conclusion

The slogan 'Not racist, not violent, just no longer silent' reflects more than the attempts of a media-savvy leadership to strategically distance the EDL from public perceptions of it as 'racist'. The findings of this study suggest that there is a genuine aspiration to non-racism among grassroots members of the movement. At the organisational level this is evident in a commitment to excluding racism from the EDL, making it 'open to all' and marking a clear line between it and those parties and movements considered to be racist. At the individual level, respondents construct subject positions, which they view as not racist, by reflecting on their own past, or even current residual racism, by referencing their own proximity and comfortableness with non-white bodies (the presence of 'black' people among their friends and family) and by excluding their discomfort with Muslims as not a question of 'race', because being 'Muslim' is not a racial but religious identifier. While the discussion of this has been postponed until Chapter 5, it is also evident that anti-Muslim and anti-Islam sentiments are routinely expressed and Muslims are consciously excluded from constituting a racially defined group and thus as a possible object of their own 'racism'.

Thus central to the non-racism claimed by EDL activists is the appeal to a simple, and narrow, definition of 'race' and racism. This position is rooted not in a consistently post-racialist politics but is akin to the 'post-race' argument which does not reject the 'reality' of 'race' but argues that it should not be grounds for prejudice and discrimination. In this sense it is in danger of banishing 'race' and denying the continued impacts of racisms. This is evident in the presence of a range of 'everyday' racisms in EDL milieux and respondents' almost universal failure to recognise the structural conditions and histories of domination and subordination underpinning racism that makes discrimination against one group of people 'racist' and against another, not. This, it is argued, emanates from the fact that the EDL 'maintains an ideological premise that is typically discriminatory but, at the same time, appeals to the typically discriminated' (Allen, 2011: 294). While, of course, feelings of socio-economic dispossession cannot explain participation in far right or populist radical right movements (in the same position the majority do not take this route), there is evidence from other studies that among young men who 'drift' in and out of right-wing politics, racism increases at particular stages of fragmentation and insecurity in both economic well-being and sense of identity (Cockburn, 2007: 551). How these feelings of social and economic exclusion (Chapter 6) and of cultural 'othering' (Chapter 5) are implicated in the activist routes taken by respondents in this study is explored in the following chapters.

Notes

1 This figure refers to three-quarters of those who had heard of the EDL. See http:// extremisproject.org/2012/10/the-english-defence-league-edl-what-do-people-think. Accessed: 05.05.2014.

2 See www.youtube.com/watch?v=9RTa0vmFCAY. Accessed: 14.04.2014.

3 Crossland had been leading the local EDL protest at the failure of Rotherham council to prosecute grooming-gang activity in the town. In December 2015 he took on leadership of the EDL when Steve Eddowes stepped down.

4 See www.youtube.com/watch?v=NCiBrZgP018. Accessed: 06.08.2015.

5 The first narrative is referenced by mainstream EDL members, while Nick, Ollie and Andrew, who refer to multiculturalism as a failed ideology, are members of the Infidels.

6 This debate was driven by UKIP, which promised to stop all immigration for unskilled jobs for a five-year period and end access to benefits and free NHS treatment for new immigrants until they had worked for five years (www.ukip.org/ukip_manifesto_summary). The Conservative Party also pledged to restrict access to tax credits, child benefits and social housing for EU migrants until they had worked in the country for four years (https://s3-eu-west-1.amazonaws.com/manifesto2015/ConservativeManifesto2015.pdf, p. 30), while the Labour Party, although still recognising the net benefit brought to the country by immigration, said they would link access to benefits to those who had contributed to the country through paid employment and stop Child Benefit being claimed for children living abroad (www.labour.org.uk/manifesto/immigration). All online sources accessed: 26.08.2015.

7 See www.englishdefenceleague.org/edl-announces-new-chairman. Accessed: 28.03.2014. A new version of the mission statement was released on 3 January 2016 and included a position on immigration, noting the 'stresses' on infrastructure created by 'uncontrolled immigration'. See https://www.facebook.com/notes/edl-english-defence-league/ edl-mission-statement/1099342593431789'

8 In contrast, Tim, a mainstream EDL member, argued that organisations such as the KKK and any neo-Nazi organisation should be banned.

5

'Their way or no way': anti-Islam and anti-Muslim sentiments

In the previous chapter it was argued that there is an aspiration to non-racism among both grass roots and leadership of the EDL, albeit one that is neither fully achieved nor shared universally among those encountered in EDL milieux. In this chapter it is demonstrated that, in sharp contrast to the importance attached to distancing themselves from racism as they understand it, EDL activists openly articulate the belief that there is a 'problem' with Islam that is not associated with other aspects of multicultural society. This has led to the conclusion that 'the EDL is clearly Islamophobic' (Allen, 2011: 293) and, although having successfully accommodated aspects of the diversity of contemporary multicultural Britain and not espousing a traditionally racist ideology, promotes a form of 'new racism' or 'cultural racism' (2011: 293).

This chapter starts by critically outlining debates about how we define and measure 'Islamophobia', focusing on the question of whether Islamophobia is a new, and distinct, phenomenon or consists primarily in anti-Muslim attitudes, which are adequately understood within the existing notion of cultural racism. The nature and content of perceptions of, and attitudes towards, Islam among EDL activists participating in this research are then explored. After establishing the degree to which Islam is understood as complex and differentiated or as a single, monolithic entity, the dominant tropes of anti-Islam rhetoric encountered among grassroots activists are identified and explored in the context of how they frame campaigns and actions led by the EDL at the time of research. It shows how these views coalesce into a vision of Islam as an ideology (as opposed to a religion) which is (ab)used politically and strategically in the interests of internal oppression ('Islam rules by fear and oppression') and external aggression (extremism and terrorism). This expression of hostility towards 'Islam', rather than 'Muslims' or any particular ethnic group, it is shown, is employed by activists to support claims that the movement is 'not racist'.

The second section of the chapter engages critically with such claims by considering specifically, and separately, hostility or prejudice towards Muslims. Anti-Muslim rhetoric and sentiment is identified among some respondents and found to be indiscriminately applied to all Muslims in everyday talk and reinforced at EDL demonstrations by songs and chants. The question of whether this hostility is directed at Muslims as immigrants and members of particular ethnic groups rather than against Muslims as a religious group – as suggested by Halliday's (1999) preference for the term 'anti-Muslimism' over Islamophobia – is more complex. Explicit racialisation, in the form of abusive rhetoric, is identified among a number of respondents alongside the explicit rejection of any such racialisation by others. Similarly, the strong association of Muslims with violence and terror (Goldberg, 2006: 346) is accompanied by an equally strong rhetoric of differentiation between 'extreme' and 'moderate' Muslims.

Coming to a conclusion as to whether the identified hostility constitutes either a distinct 'Islamophobia' or is the latest form of cultural racism (Meer and Modood, 2009: 344) may bring some definitional clarity but leaves open the question of why Islam and Muslims have emerged as targets of hostility. Given the rhetorical and symbolic reference to Christianity and the crusades, as well as the use of the St George's flag by the EDL, the final section of this chapter opens by exploring the contention that such hostility is rooted in a clash of religious views. Finding widespread indifference to Christianity, beyond its use as a general signifier of 'our' way of life, the discussion seeks other answers. Drawing on Ezekiel's (2002: 54) insight that 'thoughts and feelings about the Self' constitute the emotional centre of the (racist) group, the focus is shifted from the characteristics ascribed to the target 'others' and towards how anti-Muslim sentiments are worked through emotionally-driven, personal and localised experience. Drawing on two strong tropes of anti-Muslim hostility identified in this study – the perception that Muslims seek to 'impose their rules here' and Muslims 'have no respect' – it is argued that fear and hate do not reside in either the individual expressing hostility or the object of hatred and fear, but circulate within an affective economy (Ahmed, 2004: 127). However, the findings challenge assumptions about the location of power within this economy. Switching the analytic lens from 'other' to 'self' reveals the power to 'other' embedded in models of Islamophobia is too simple. Analysing how anti-Islamic and anti-Muslim sentiments are engendered in personal, localised experience reveals such hostility can itself be the product of perceived 'othering'.

Defining and measuring 'Islamophobia'

Islamophobia is sometimes argued to be an entirely new phenomenon but, more usually, to constitute a modern manifestation of historical anti-Muslim or anti-Islamic phenomena (Allen, 2010: 13–15). The historically negative representation of Islam has been understood to sit within a wider 'orientalist' discourse reflecting that 'for Europe, Islam was a lasting trauma' (Said, 1978: 59, cited in Meer, 2014: 501). Goldberg (2006: 344) argues that orientalism became racially historicised in the wake of European colonial domination in the Middle East in the latter half of the nineteenth century when 'The Muslim ... came to be read as inevitably hostile, aggressive, engaged for religious purpose in constant jihad against Europe and Christianity'. In this way, he suggests, the figure of the Muslim, alongside that of the Jew, 'has historically bookended modern Europe's explicit historical anxieties about blackness' and thus is central to the very construction of race in, and of, modern Europe (2006: 344).[1] The consequence of this historical formation of the image of the Muslim, according to Goldberg, is that in the European imaginary, Islam has come to be associated with a lack of freedom, sense of scientific inquiry, civility, love of life, human worth and equal respect for women and sexual minorities while at the same time, it is imagined, it promotes an aggressive religiosity and violent rejection of the perceived sociocultural conditions of alienation (2006: 345). Thus, Goldberg concludes, in Europe the Muslim is perceived 'as the monster of our times' that has come to stand for 'the fear of the death of Europe itself' (2006: 346). At the same time, an overemphasis on historicity is cautioned against by some, less it obscures contemporary forms of Islamophobia or oversimplifies the historical continuity of orientalist categories and generates an unfounded impression of perpetual discursive conflict between Muslims and the West from the Crusades onwards (Meer, 2014: 503).

Recognition of Islamophobia as a distinct and contemporary form of prejudice emerged following the publication of the influential report by the Commission on British Muslims and Islamophobia (CBMI) for the Runnymede Trust (1997) *Islamophobia: A Challenge for Us All*. The report lent Islamophobia public and political recognition and provided a 'shorthand way of referring to dread or hatred of Islam – and, therefore, to fear or dislike of all or most Muslims' (Allen, 2010: 15). Islamophobia is understood as consisting in a 'closed view' on the nature of Islam whereby Islam is seen as: monolithic and static; separate and 'other' to other cultures; inferior to the West (barbaric, irrational, primitive and sexist); aggressive and supportive of terrorism; and a political ideology, used for political or military advantage. This 'closed view' also means that: criticisms made by Islam of 'the West' are rejected out of hand; hostility towards Islam is used to justify discriminatory and exclusionary practices towards Muslims; and anti-Muslim hostility is accepted as natural and 'normal'. This is contrasted to an 'open view' on Islam in which Islam is perceived to be: diverse and progressive; interdependent with other faiths and cultures; distinctively different but equally worthy of respect; an actual or potential partner in the solution of shared problems; and a genuine religious faith, practised sincerely by its adherents. In this mindset: criticisms of 'the West' and other cultures are considered and debated; debates and disagreements with Islam do not diminish efforts to combat discrimination and exclusion; and critical views of Islam are themselves subjected to critique.

The application of this typology, drawn from Milton Rokeach's concept of the 'closed' or 'open' mind,[2] attracts strong criticism from Allen (2010: 67) on grounds of methodological lack of rigour in the derivation of the original typology by Rokeach and with regard to its particular application in the Runnymede Trust report where the 'closed mind' becomes both the foundation for theoretical development *and* the definition of Islamophobia. This, he argues, means the features of 'closed' views are equated to the features of Islamophobia (2010: 69). The 'closed–open' binary establishes a series of dualisms that appear to reinforce many of the 'closed views' themselves and, since 'closed' and 'open' are largely interchangeable with 'negative' and 'positive', it follows that the report appears to suggest that

Islam be both understood and engaged with 'openly' or 'positively', irrespective of whether any 'closed' or 'negative' realities exist (2010: 74). Following this model, Allen (2010: 77–78) argues, disagreeing with or criticising individual Muslims, for being intolerant of other faiths or of preaching messages of hate, could be legitimately construed as being Islamophobic. The Runnymede Trust's report has been criticised also for providing a definition of Islamophobia that fails to sufficiently differentiate between doctrines within Islam or recognise diversity within British Muslim communities (Meer and Modood, 2009: 341; Allen, 2010: 75; Jackson, 2011a: 13); a particularly damning criticism given that this homogenising view of Islam is one of the characteristics ascribed by the report's authors to a 'closed' view of Islam. It is also said to understand Islamophobia in a limited sense – as the aggregate of acts or practices of discrimination or prejudice – rather than as a broader 'ideological phenomenon' that can shape wider discourse and consensus on who 'we' are, through the construction of Muslims as 'the other' (Allen, 2011: 290).

Allen's extensive critique of the Runnymede Trust definition and understanding of Islamophobia leads him to redefine Islamophobia as consisting of three components: the process or phenomenon; the signs and visual identifiers; and the consequences of its enactment (Allen, 2010: 189). In terms of the phenomenon itself, he suggests that 'Islamophobia is an ideology, similar in theory, function and purpose to racism and other similar phenomena, that sustains and perpetuates negatively evaluated meaning about Muslims and Islam' (2010: 189). In terms of the signs and visual identifiers, he suggests that these signs shape and determine understanding, perceptions and attitudes about Muslims and Islam as Other in similar ways to that which they have historically, although not necessarily as a continuum. Finally, he suggests that, as a result of this, there is evidence of the existence of exclusionary practices that disadvantage, prejudice or discriminate against Muslims and Islam in social, economic and political spheres, including their subjection to violence. In arriving at this position, Allen effectively rejects that anti-Muslim sentiment is the same as racism or xenophobia; there is a distinctive phenomenon, he suggests, but, for this to constitute Islamophobia an acknowledged 'Muslim' or 'Islamic' element (explicit or implicit) must be present. Thus he rejects Halliday's (1999: 898) suggestion that a more appropriate term is 'anti-Muslimism' (Allen, 2010: 135) or that Islamophobia is simply a manifestation of 'new racism' ('cultural racism'). Indeed, seeing Islamophobia as cultural racism, Allen (2010: 155) argues, may inadvertently homogenise perceptions and essentialise Muslims by attributing universal importance to characteristics that are in fact specific, for example, to the particular dominant groups within British Muslim communities.

Meer and Modood (2009: 353) also embrace the notion of Islamophobia and argue for the recognition of anti-Muslim hostility as being distinctively rooted in anti-Islamic sentiment, or at least that anti-Islamic sentiment is inseparable from anti-Muslim sentiment. This, they suggest, is evident from the experience of Muslims who, when reporting street-level discrimination associate it with when they appear 'conspicuously Muslim', for example, when wearing

Islamic dress (2009: 341). However, they argue that 'anti-Muslim sentiment' and 'Islamophobia' are valid specifications of a wider cultural racism and racialisation and suggest that resistance to accepting anti-Muslim sentiment as racism among opinion-makers lies in the understanding of religious identity as chosen rather than (like race) involuntarily ascribed alongside a reluctance to sympathise with a minority that is perceived to be disloyal or associated with terrorism (2009: 344).

Since, as noted above, claims to non-racism by EDL activists draw on the direction of their hostility towards 'Islam', rather than 'Muslims', it is worth briefly addressing the question of how we might, in practice, measure whether a particular prejudice towards Muslims, beyond that extended to them as immigrants or members of various ethnic minority groups, exists. To test this, Bleich (2011: 1582) suggests operationalising the concept of Islamophobia as the presence of 'indiscriminate negative attitudes or emotions directed at Islam or Muslims'. This posits Islamophobia as consisting of *attitudes or emotions* rather than behaviour and extends its scope beyond a strict or clinical definition of a 'phobia' – an irrational/unwarranted fear of an object/phenomenon – to include a range of attitudes such as aversion, jealousy, suspicion, disdain, anxiety, rejection, contempt, fear, disgust, anger that range in source, type and intensity (2011: 1586). It also suggests that to constitute Islamophobia, these attitudes or emotions must be *indiscriminately* directed at Islam and Muslims – that is, people must make generalisations about a group of people on the basis of traits that can be ascribed to a minority of its members at best (Helbling, 2012: 7), while negative attitudes or emotions directed at some interpretations of Islam by some Muslim communities does not necessarily constitute Islamophobia (Bleich, 2011: 1585). Third, these negative attitudes or emotions must be directed at Islam or Muslims, not just out-groups in general. This suggests any definition of Islamophobia should include *either* Islam as a religious doctrine, *or* Muslims, as the people who follow it, since Islamophobia is 'multidimensional' and 'Islam and Muslims are often inextricably intertwined in individual and public perceptions' (2011: 1587).

While there are few dedicated surveys of Islamophobic attitudes at the individual level, analysis of the findings from those empirical studies available[3] suggests Islamophobia is hard to distinguish from other prejudices (xenophobia, racism and anti-Semitism) (Helbling, 2012: 8–11) since the same individual-level variables (unemployment and financial difficulties) appear to increase or reduce (higher education, higher socio-economic status and urban residence) anti-Muslim prejudice as anti-minority prejudice (Strabac and Listhaug, 2008: 279–81). However, both Helbling's (2010) and Strabac and Listhaug's (2008) studies employed a single question, asking, 'Which of the following groups [Muslims] would you NOT like to have as a neighbour?' In addition to the dangers of making conclusions on the basis of a single survey question (Bleich, 2011: 1591), this particular question clearly asks about attitudes to Muslims not Islam and since it does not itself differentiate between different groups of Muslims (Sunnis, Shiites) or Muslims from different ethnic backgrounds, it is impossible to know whether those answering the question have *indiscriminately* negative attitudes or not. Moreover, even if the same people show hostile attitudes toward both immigrants and Muslims, it does not imply that Islamophobia is the same as xenophobia; the same people might be xenophobic and Islamophobic for different reasons (Helbling, 2012: 10). In this study, therefore, perceptions and attitudes to Islam and to Muslims are analysed discretely.

Perceptions of Islam

If Islamophobia is to be considered a distinct phenomenon from wider racism, then an identifiably Islamic or Muslim dimension to the prejudice or hostility must be demonstrated (Allen, 2010: 189). Islam is clearly singled out by EDL respondents as a 'problem' in a way that other aspects of multicultural society are not: 'All religions and races get on apart from Islam' (Connor). Islam is understood by respondents as 'separate and other' in a way determined by the Runnymede Trust (1997) to be characteristic of an Islamophobic mindset. According to Matt, 'the bad side of Islam' is 'the biggest threat this country's got', while for Declan, 'Islam … always will be a problem unless like myself and everyone else does something about it.' This appears to confirm Allen's (2011: 293) conclusion that 'the EDL is clearly Islamophobic' in as much as it creates 'a "form of order" that confirms Muslims and Islam as against "our" way of life'. Before considering the particular tropes that underpin this perception of Islam as culturally alien in the narratives of EDL respondents in this study, it is important first to establish exactly what 'Islam' is being referred to.

Islam as monolithic and undifferentiated

In official documents, such as the movement's mission statement,[4] the EDL refers to its object of concern not as Islam per se but 'radical Islam' or 'Islamic orthodoxy'. At EDL demonstrations speakers also distinguished between ordinary Muslims and 'extremists':

> I am not talking about the guy you carpool with. I am not talking about the guy you see at the school gate picking up their children. … I'm talking about the extremists, the loons … the clerics and Imams who want to preach a seventh-century ideology in a twenty-first-century world. (Mark Robinson, Luton national demonstration, 2014 recorded in field diary, 22 November 2014)

Grassroots activists in this study also differentiate within Islam, in particular between 'moderate' and 'extremist' forms of Islam. Thus Matt says he is only against 'militant Islam', while for Euan being an EDL supporter is 'all about the radical Islam'. Some respondents compare Islam with other world religions and conclude that it is no different in having 'extremist' elements: 'you get Christians with different views as well. Same as you get Muslims who are just Muslim by culture and you get extremist ones who that's all they think of all day in their mind' (Andrew). Lisa, who, unlike Andrew, is not religious herself, concurs that 'you'll get extremists from every religion, you know, even Christianity' and, on the basis of her own reading of the Qur'an, suggests that Islam is actually 'a very peaceful religion. Nothing wrong with it at all'. Tim also decouples 'extremist' mindsets from the faith itself. Based on two sets of experiences – with a Muslim man with whom he had 'carpooled' and the family of a Muslim friend – he argues that 'avid Muslims' (those strongly committed to their faith) are not necessarily extremist since, at the same time, they 'embrace other cultures and stuff. They are not on a one way track.' Thus, he concludes, 'It's not Islam I've got a problem with' (Tim). Respondents also recount narratives of differences between Muslim communities of different ethnic origin or branches of Islam, although such discussion is rarely at the theological level but rather describes tensions at a cultural or community level between, for example, Pakistani and Somalian communities (Matt) or positive relations with individual Muslim community groups (Euan).

However, among respondents in this study, there was also routine slippage into talking about Islam or Muslims as single entities and failure to distinguish between different branches of Islam, different ethnic groups among Muslims or between 'extremist' and 'moderate' readings of Islam. The youngest interviewees were the most inclined to see Islam as monolithic, as indicated in the exchange below during a group interview with three local youth division members:

> BRETT: Stuff like, I look at my little sister some days and I think like if it was living under their conditions in their country, which is what they are trying to bring here, my sister would be raped and beaten and I think I couldn't live like that.
> INT: Do you think all of Islam is like that?
> CONNOR: Yeah there's no such thing as moderate is tha?
> BRETT: It's a culture. The way that it's set everybody's like it. So with Catholic, it's a religion so everyone within that religion is set to the same way.
> NEIL: And it's always gonna be that way.
> BRETT: From birth it's brought into your head.

Notwithstanding the official line of the EDL, this kind of statement could also be heard by speakers at EDL events. At the 2014 Luton demonstration, Dave Russell stated that 'There are no moderates. There is only Islam. And Islam is certainly not moderate in its teachings' (field diary, 22 November 2014).[5] Talking about 'Islamic State' (IS), Islam is referred to as a 'supremacist death cult' and Russell cites a number of verses of the Qur'an 'Book of death and slavery' on punishment and the importance of jihad to argue that IS had not hijacked the Qur'an but 'taken it as instruction, exactly how it was written'. As Russell pauses for effect following this claim, he is greeted with a chant from the crowd of 'Stick your fucking Islam up your arse' (field diary, 22 November 2014). The lack of complexity in the understanding of Islam in 'front stage' messages of the EDL noted by Jackson (2011a: 13) thus appears to have strengthened in the recent period.

Islam as backward-looking

In this section, the key tropes that underpin the perception of Islam as culturally alien found in narratives of EDL respondents in this study are outlined. While for the purposes of the analysis they are separated into four themes – Islam as backward-looking, Islam as oppressive and intolerant, Islam as aggressive and supportive of terrorism, and Islam as ideology – in everyday talk negative characterisations or associations of Islam are often interlinked. For example, the perceived anachronistic nature of Islam is central to its characterisation as a 'cult' or 'ideology' rather than a faith. Similarly, attitudes to women in Islam are perceived as evidence of both the 'oppressive' nature of Islam as well as its 'backward-looking' nature.

The discussion begins with the understanding of Islam as anachronistic, or 'backward-looking', not because it is the most frequently encountered but because it underpins a number of more specific narratives and helps respondents make sense of their feelings that Islam is culturally alien whilst not, in their minds, relying on racist constructions of otherness.

A common argument that Islam is anachronistic in nature is that the Qur'an has not been adapted to modern society.

> … the Bible has been updated hasn't it so many times to fit in with society and to fit in with the day. The Qur'an hasn't changed for 1,400 years. That's why you get all your paedophiles and things like that because, that even happened in the Bible years ago, do you know what I mean? But they've moved forward, they've moved forward with society. In Islam they haven't have they? (Rob)

This failure to move with the times rather than Islam itself is blamed for what Euan sees as a cultural clash:

> I mean the modern-day Bible, they update it don't they? … [I]t wouldn't be half as bad if they'd allow them to do that with the Qur'an. … When they want them to worship it in this barbaric form, you know, in our civilised country, you know, then it just doesn't seem like it's gonna be a happy ending in it. (Euan)

Another Local Organiser, chatting informally at a demonstration noted that in his local area a new mosque had been opened by a group who had 'modernised the Qur'an to fit with contemporary English life' and that he doesn't have an issue with them (field diary, 14 July, 2012).

The emotional dimension of EDL activism is particularly evident in discussions of Islam that posit it as non-progressive or backwards-looking. This is important to our understanding of 'Islamophobia' since emotional responses (as distinct from, for example, stereotypes) are stronger predictors of discrimination and social distance (Bleich, 2011: 1586). Brett identifies Islam as allowing people to 'get away with' beating children and raping wives and concludes 'It's just wrong. That's like old-style Britain. It's bringing us back to how we used to be. It's not moving forwards, it's moving backwards.' In the course of discussing whether the Prophet Mohammed should be considered a 'paedophile' as a result of his marriage to Aisha[6] (discussed below), Connor becomes passionate and aggressive: 'All these little Muslims you see round here ain't living in the twenty-first century. They're living in the seventh century where it was all Sharia law and all that bollocks. Well fuck that. You're in England. You live by our rules.' Chas calls Islam 'barbaric, backwards', citing ritual slaughter, the stoning to death of those convicted of adultery and the 'selling off' of child brides. Declan, who heads the LGBT division of the EDL, complains that the problem is that Islam 'needs to evolve' and seeks to 'take us back to that belief that being gay is not normal'. Indeed, the terms 'barbaric' or 'disgusting' are commonly used to describe a range of practices associated in respondents' minds with Islam, including: physical abuse of women and children, sexual violence towards women, genital mutilation, polygamy, paedophilia and 'grooming', forms of punishment permitted under Sharia law (stoning of women found guilty of adultery, 'chopping hands off') and marriage within families (between cousins for example).

The single most frequent association made with Islam by respondents relates to 'paedophilia' and 'grooming gangs' and is expressed collectively in the chant 'Allah is a paedo'. The centrality of this issue in respondent narratives reflects a number of high-profile court cases of such gangs that took place during the course of the research and the fact that it was one of the key campaigning issues of the EDL. For some supporters it was also a very personal issue; Peter recounted that his sister had been a victim of one of the gangs recently prosecuted for grooming. The attention to the 'grooming gang' issue in speeches at demonstrations, in line with wider media coverage, grew considerably over the period of research. If at the start of the fieldwork, speakers might mention, inter alia, the need to 'protect our little girls' (Tony Curtis, Dewsbury National Demo recorded in field diary, 30 June, 2012), by the end it had become the cause for the establishment of an EDL protest camp outside the police station in Rotherham (see Figure 4.3), and a long, impassioned speech by Ian Crossland at the national demonstration in the town (September 2014) in which he attacked both the police and the social services for being 'too scared to offend Muslims' (field diary, 13 September 2014).

A number of respondents qualify the connections they make between Islam and grooming gangs by the recognition that paedophilia and grooming is committed by people of all ethnicities and religions. Lisa, for example, cautions against speeches that link grooming of girls to Muslims because there are 'a lot of white paedophiles'. Matt also makes clear that 'it's not just Muslims ... white people can do that as well, black people, Chinese people can do it, it's happening in any race, any culture' (Matt). A number of respondents said they felt the 'Allah is a paedo' chant was 'wrong' (Tim), although for Rob this was on the technical grounds: 'I don't believe that Allah is a paedo but I believe Mohammed is a paedo so I think that's wrong in how they say it.'

However, a local speaker at the Rotherham demonstration (September 2014), who described himself as 'half-English, half-immigrant', makes explicit the logic that is implicit in many respondents' statements when they insist on 'grooming gangs' being referred to as 'Muslim' rather than 'Asian'. The raping of girls, he says, continues a tradition going back 1,500 years when Mohammed, upon conquering lands, allowed the raping of conquered women (field diary, 13 September 2014). The most consistently cited argument among respondents for the direct link between Islam and the current phenomenon of grooming is that the veneration of the prophet Mohammed in the knowledge of his marriage to Aisha sanctifies sexual activity with underage girls. This, it is argued, provides the basis for the legitimation of groups of men of Muslim faith engaging in sex with girls under the age of consent: 'Mohammed, when he was 73, he married his 6-year-old niece, which is why they think it's okay. They think it's okay to marry a child and do all this child sex and it's not' (Theresa). The problem as Tim sees it is a white paedophile, such as Jimmy Saville, is treated, rightly, as a 'sick bastard', while Mohammed, who 'married a five-year-old girl and had sex with her at like about six or seven', which 'in our day and age that's a paedophile, definitely', is worshipped (Tim). This is expressed more emotionally by Tina: 'when I look at my daughter and think of a grown man, I can't … I just don't understand how you can pray to a man who thinks it's okay to have sex with a nine-year-old girl' (Tina). The logic of this argument is extended to the claim that white girls are the primary target of this grooming activity because attitudes within Islam to non-Muslims make them an object to be treated without respect (see below).

Islam as oppressive and intolerant

Grassroots EDL members make a range of associations of Islam with intolerance and discrimination. Islam is described as anti-Semitic and anti-Christian (Declan) and as 'the only religion that is against all other religions' (Local EDL Organiser recorded in field diary, 14 July 2012). A number of respondents claim that Islam or the Qur'an preaches hate (Connor, Declan) and, at the 2014 Luton demonstration, Islam is described as 'an ideology that preaches hate towards everything else other than Islamic doctrine' (Mark Robinson, cited in field diary, 22 November 2014).[7] Other respondents complain that extremist Muslims (such as Anjem Choudary, co-founder of Islamist organisation al-Muhajiroun) are allowed to make speeches or display placards expressing hate without arrest (Lisa, Michelle).

Islam is described as intolerant also in relation to sexual minorities. Connor associates Islam with 'the executing of gays' while Declan claims Islam preaches that gays should be thrown off the top of a mountain. As leader of the LGBT division, this was a particular source of concern for Declan who also recounted a personal experience of homophobic attack and the failure of the police to act on his complaint:

> Outside Bradford I was attacked by Muslims for being gay and I went to the police … This was after the Bradford march. I didn't have my hoody up, this was when I first started up, and I had the gay flag around me shoulders. They attacked me, called me a fag, I'm dirty, I'm a queer, I deserve to die and all that. I went to the police, 'no evidence'. Black eye, broken nose, cut lip. (Declan)

It is gender inequality and the abuse of women, however, that features most frequently in the characterisation of Islam as oppressive and intolerant. Jack sums this up as 'Women are second-class citizens; they have to walk behind their husband.' The burqa is widely deployed as a symbol of this inequality although it is recognised by a number of respondents that its wearing is a cultural norm rather than a religious requirement. Thus the burqa is described as being imposed by fathers (Jordan) or husbands (Chas, Matt) as a means of control over women:

> ... nowhere in the Qur'an does it say they [Muslim women] have to cover their face. Nowhere. ... I asked a Muslim guy who's a dead religious Muslim like and he said 'No I don't make my wife, that's just men who feel like women shouldn't be seen.' (Tim)

For other respondents, however, the burqa is seen as inherently Islamic and as containing a more sinister meaning. Andrew notes that 'the Islamic faith forces women to cover up, and ... it allows husbands to beat the wives' and that this is one of 'many things that they do which are oppressive to women'. This suspicion that Islamic dress can conceal violence towards women is repeated by Kane: 'It makes me think as well, why does Muslims wear burqas? Do they get beat up underneath there and they are hiding bruises?' (Kane).

This is indicative of a wider association of Islam with systemic violence towards women through the mechanism of Sharia law. Thus Islam is associated with the brutal punishment of women for adultery or disobedience to their husbands (Chas, Connor), legitimising the rape of women and girls (Chas, Connor, Declan, Jack) and of punishing women rather than the perpetrators of rape:

> 'I seen in the YouTube video she is buried chest high cause she is raped by another Muslim man. When she got taken to a Sharia court, her case is half of a man's so they buried her up to her chest and they stoned her to death which I think is barbaric.' (Declan)

The conclusion drawn by Declan is that 'Islam rules on fear and oppression.'

Islam as hostile and aggressive

Another Islamophobic trope, as defined by the Runnymede Trust, found widely among this respondent set is a perception of Islam as hostile and aggressive. This is expressed in concerns that Islam is both a rising power and has imperialistic designs. Declan argues that Islam 'has still kept its old fifth-century sense that we must control the world', while others point to placards carried by Islamist protestors proclaiming 'Islam will dominate the world' (Lisa). A number of respondents discussed conversions to Islam as one means of imperialist expansion.

> ... [T]hey started forcing their laws on the streets on a night, beating people up. ... If you are not Islamic or part of the Muslim community you'll get done over and it installs intimidation and fear into everyone who lives there. So it's easier

for them when they can get someone who can sort of give them leaflets going
'you've gotta join this, you've gotta be a Muslim'. ... [T]hat's why they claim to
be one of the fastest-growing religions and it is only through fear, violence and
intimidation. (Euan)

Respondents and demonstrators talked about members of their family who
had converted (Jordan; field diary, 12 January 2013). For Tina, conversion was
a particular source of anxiety. She recounted how in an area in which she had
previously lived, young Muslims had begun to convert Afro-Caribbean youth
leading subsequently to turf wars over drugs sales. She also talked about the
high rate of conversions to radical Islam in prison, recounted how she had
seen a boy being 'converted' on the street and showed me a YouTube video of
a similar incident. Her fear is for her own children: 'I don't want to be in a situation where my kids are bullied into converting into Islam when they're older'
(Tina).

Islam is felt to be growing in strength, especially in comparison to the decline
in believers in Christianity (Andrew), and to represent a direct threat. The creep-
ing imposition of Sharia law in districts of large multicultural cities is often cited
as evidence of the imperialistic designs of Islam and blamed for pushing out
those who do not conform. Declan claims that the previous leader of the LGBT
division of the EDL had been forced to move out of London after 'being attacked
by that Sharia police'. Jack expects Sharia law to be implemented to some extent
in the UK within the next 10 years and believes politics is increasingly being
infiltrated by those with extremist views. Euan confirms this view, arguing
that 'radical Islam' has 'corrupted near enough every tier of our democracy ...
From the police upwards', and cites the attempted terrorist attack on Glasgow
airport by a British-born doctor of Iraqi background as evidence. Although
not expressed as a 'fear', there is a real sense in respondents' narratives of
Islam as an unstoppable power: 'Islam is the strongest religion in the world.
... [A]nd it does dominate most of the world, Islam, if you look on the maps'
(Lisa).

Natural population growth is also presented as threatening. In the region in
which the research was conducted one-fifth of the population identify themselves
as Muslims and in one town from which respondents were drawn the Muslim
population had grown by over 200 per cent between 2001 and 2011 (Jivraj, 2013).
Fears about Islamisation being an automatic consequence of population growth
are expressed (Connor, Richard) and Theresa predicts 'an Islamic takeover' within
two generations 'because they are out-populating us'.

Islam as ideology

The argument that Islam functions as an ideology rather than a religion is another
characteristic of Islamophobia, according to the Runnymede Trust (1997) definition, that is widely referenced among grassroots EDL members. Connor refers
to Islam as an 'ideology' while Chris notes 'It isn't a religion. It's a cult', and Tina

describes young British Muslims as 'brainwashed'. This is an image invoked in official EDL messages also. In the movement's mission statement, for example, 'radical Islam' is described as a kind of oppressive cult that distorts ordinary Muslim faith:

> Radical Islam keeps British Muslims fearful and isolated, especially the women that it encases in the burqa. It misrepresents their views, stifles freedom of expression, and indoctrinates their children, whilst continually doing a discredit to those who do wish to peacefully co-exist with their fellow Britons.[8]

In his statement at the press conference hosted by Quilliam at which he resigned from the EDL, Tommy Robinson declared that he wanted 'to lead a revolution against Islamist ideology not against Muslims'.[9] This is echoed in Declan's statement that 'I don't hate anybody as a person-wise I just hate the ideology of Islam.' The attempt to distinguish between Islam as a religion practised by sincere, and unthreatening, adherents and Islam as an aggressive ideology is common. It was noted above in Tim's description of a Muslim friend's family as 'avid Muslims' but who embraced 'other cultures'. It is also evident in Matt and Casey's respect for a local pharmacist who is a devout Muslim: 'All he does is pray, pray and pray but with like militant Islam, he's got no time for 'em, he's just a strict Muslim, he doesn't hurt anyone else ... people like that I've got time for' (Matt).

The tenuous nature of this distinction, however, can be seen in discussion of, and activism against, mosques. On the one hand respondents did not articulate a general hostility towards mosques nor challenge the right of Muslims to worship. However, the building of mosques is viewed in some cases as a symbolic incursion (see Figure 5.1); a sign that Islam is 'taking over' or that the Muslim community is treated in a privileged way. Among respondents in this study, this occurred where the building of new or so-called 'super mosques' (Lisa) was proposed in areas that already had mosques, or permission to convert existing buildings into mosques or Islamic prayer centres was sought where there was no significant Muslim community (Peter, Michelle, Tim, Tina). This would appear to be in line with a minority opinion within the wider population; surveys suggest that around one-third of the population objected to any new mosque being erected in their neighbourhood (Field, 2012: 151).

However, one Division Organiser recounted how he had rejected an activist's call to register an objection to a planning application for conversion of a property into a Muslim community centre because there was no reason to object: 'To me, it's a Muslim area, it's owned by a Muslim and he wants to make his shop, which is doing very good, into a Muslim community centre for the local people' (Matt). Objections to the use of public money to finance the building of mosques (when other community projects had not received funding), however, were articulated (Declan, Euan, Matt).

A number of respondents also expressed concerns that extremist preaching took place in some mosques (Michelle, Tim, Tina). When challenged about

5.1 'No more mosques' flag, Leeds demonstration

an EDL chant that threatens 'Burn our poppies and we'll burn your mosques', however, Tina responds that mosques are referenced purely symbolically without any intent: 'I would never burn their mosques, you know what I mean? It's ridiculous really that we sing it … it's just to say this is what's pissing us off, you know, you burning our poppies' (Tina).

Respondents denied that they themselves engaged in the symbolic violation of mosques and other Muslim community sites and complained that the EDL was blamed for graffiti and other attacks on mosques when it was not in their repertoire of actions (Michelle). However, a former NF and Combat 18 activist who attended a number of EDL demonstrations early on in the fieldwork period (until arrested at a demonstration for possession of drugs) had been given a suspended prison sentence for putting a pig's head on the wall of a local mosque in May 2010 (field diary, 30 June 2012). Damon, another ex-NF member, also recounted how a new scar on his face had been the result of having been 'slashed' after he had thrown a pork chop at a mosque (field diary, 18 May 2013). He tells this story on the way to a flash demonstration against a planning application to turn a disused church into an Islamic prayer centre and, whilst protesting in front of the building, he repeated the symbolic violence by throwing a piece of pork (from a sandwich purchased en route) over the wall into the church yard (field diary, 18 May 2013).

'We are not anti-Muslim, we are anti-Islam': Islamophobia or anti-Muslimism?

EDL respondents in this study consistently placed Islam, not Muslims, as the object of their anxiety and hostility: 'We are not anti-Muslim, we are anti-Islam' (Declan). Some respondents talk about their 'Muslim mates' (Ed, Sean, Tim, Tina) and work colleagues with whom you can 'have a laugh' (Kane) or express empathy or solidarity with Muslims as 'the first victims of Islam' (Declan).[10]

While the Demos online survey of EDL supporters confirms that support is motivated first and foremost by views on Islam (not immigration) (Bartlett and Littler, 2011: 6), this rhetorical shift clearly has strategic value; it allows generalised anti-Muslim sentiments to be replaced with a critique of Islamic doctrine or teachings and thus underpin claims to non-racism by the movement. Moreover, being anti-Islam does not exclude being anti-Muslim also. Hostility towards Islam can be used to justify discriminatory and exclusionary practices towards Muslims (Runnymede Trust, 1997) while racialisation of Muslims is not excluded by phenotypical dissimilarity; racialisation takes place because of the unity of the 'gaze' not of the object (Garner and Selod, 2015: 14). Thus Muslims are racialised as 'other' through their interpellation (regardless of physical appearance, country of origin and economic situation) solely as Muslims on the basis of visible markers (such as dress) of their faith (St Louis, 2002: 17).Thus, respondents' claims that their hostility is directed exclusively towards Islam as a doctrine (or 'ideology') rather than towards Muslims, as followers of Islam, or indeed as racialised immigrant groups requires critical assessment.

Indiscriminate hostility? Anti-Muslim sentiment

Notwithstanding claims to be *not* anti-Muslim, generalised or indiscriminately negative attitudes or emotions towards Muslims were found among some respondents in this study. Sean expresses a generalised anxiety exclusively in relation to Muslims: 'I haven't got a problem with any other race, colour whatever' (Sean). Tina is careful to say that she doesn't hate all Muslims but her logic of argument proceeds to generalise about Muslims on the basis of characteristics ascribed to a minority: 'I don't hate all Muslims. I hate extremists, I hate grooming gangs, I hate paedophiles full stop, but when 95 per cent of grooming gangs are Muslims, then I think you've got to deal with the bigger problem first, you know' (Tina). Jack also first qualifies his statement by saying he is not referring to *all* Muslims, before labelling not only Islam but also Muslims as 'filth'.

Jack is not alone in using generalised terms of abuse towards Muslims. Muslims are referred to as 'scummy bastards' by Connor in the context of discussing his concern about grooming gangs and rape. Lisa admits that she has chanted 'scum, scum' at demonstrations, even though she says she is not prejudiced towards Muslims ('I don't treat Muslims any different'). Racist abuse was encountered most frequently at demonstrations, occurring especially when there were direct interactions with local Muslim communities or suspected Muslim

Defence League (MDL) counter-demonstrators. Thus, at the Walthamstow demonstration (September 2012), where the march passed through a heavily populated multicultural area and demonstrators were highly frustrated by the fact that counter-demonstrators had blocked the route of the march and halted the EDL demonstration, spontaneous hostility emerged on sighting groups who were taken to be Muslim. This was articulated in chants of 'You can stick your fucking Islam up your arse', 'Allah, Allah, who the fuck is Allah?', 'Muslim bombers off our streets' or 'Muzzie scum' (field diary, 1 September 2012). Late in the fieldwork, a chant not heard previously of 'If we all hate Muslims, clap your hands' was struck up by a small group of demonstrators on the coach on the way to the Rotherham demo while, during the demo itself, demonstrators were heard to chant, 'If we all hate Pakis, clap your hands' (field diary, 13 September 2014). This was particularly shocking as the term 'Pakis' had been repeatedly described by respondents as racist and unacceptable; Michelle explicitly stated, for example, that she would not use the term 'scum' in relation to Muslims and would object to others chanting if they started 'calling people Pakis'. However, even outside the context of demonstrations, some respondents used abusive language. Driving through their home town with a group of young EDL activists, for example, racist comments and 'jokes' were made constantly as Asians were passed on the street amidst a relentless refrain of 'fucking filthy bastards/cunts' and 'dirty Paki' (field diary, 2 February 2013).

When I challenge respondents on generalisations made about Muslims or use of abusive language such as 'Muzzies', responses tend to reveal contradiction and ambiguity. When I tell Ian for example that I really don't like it when he refers to Muslims indiscriminately, he tells me defiantly that he had 'told the Job Centre that he wouldn't work for a Muslim' but then goes on to recount how he had 'thumped' a new supporter attending the Bristol demo precisely because of racist comments he had heard him make (field diary, 16 June 2013). Significantly, the unacceptable racism Ian intervened against had been directed towards some black people among the UAF counter-demonstration (the new supporter had started to do monkey chants). This confirms the singling out of Muslims as the object of hostility and is most explicitly stated by Jordan who claims, 'I've got every colour relation, religion, friends but one religion I will not be friends with are Muslims.'

Muslims as perpetrators of violence and terror

This contradiction or internal conflictedness is evident in the two most frequently referenced associations with 'Muslims' found among the respondent set, which are, on the one hand, perceptions of Muslims as perpetrators of violence and terror, yet, on the other, the distinction between 'extremist' and 'moderate' or ordinary Muslims.

Speaking at the EDL demonstration in Luton (November 2014), Liberty GB's Paul Weston declared that Islam and terrorism 'go hand in hand', while Mark Robinson used the term 'Qur'animals' to suggest an inherent connection between individual acts of violence and Islamic teaching (field diary, 22 November 2014).

Respondents in this study also associate Muslims with ideologically motivated terror. Sometimes these associations take the form of a simple depiction of all Muslims as potential terrorists or scare stories about the exponential growth of the number of 'terrorists' in the country:

> ... there's fifty-eight *thousand* terrorists in this country, fifty-eight *thousand*. Now that's a lot. Now you imagine every single one of them fifty-eight thousand are having six to eight kids, that more than trebles the amount of terrorists there's gonna be in fifteen, twenty years' time. (Tina; emphasis in the original)

Kane also paints a fearful image of contemporary British society, which he sees as characterised by 'people having their heads chopped off, bomb explosions, kidnapping, rapists'. Sean says he feels 'uncomfortable' near someone wearing a burqa: 'Even stood in a queue or summat I do feel nervous. I do because you're not safe I don't think. Someone could walk in right now and fucking blow this place up, you know' (Sean). Notorious acts of terrorism or violence are mentioned such as the murder of the British soldier Lee Rigby or of Kriss Donald in Glasgow (see Chapter 6) and towards the end of the fieldwork the issue of British citizens heading to Syria as jihadi fighters appeared in speeches at demonstrations (Dave Russell, EDL demonstration, Luton, recorded in field diary, 22 November, 2014).[11] The 'war on terror' is conducted symbolically by respondents in a counting-down song sung at, or on the way, to demonstrations (video clip, Walsall demo, 29 September 2012):

> It starts ... 'There was ten Muslim bombers in the air. There was ten Muslim bombers in the air.' Then it goes, 'Then the RAF from England shot one down.' Then obviously it goes all the way; 'there were nine' and all the way down. (Theresa)

Associations with ideologically motivated terror are less common, however, than reference to localised, everyday 'intimidating' behaviour, threats or violent actions perpetrated by 'Muslims'. Chas attributes this to 'Muslim youth running round streets terrorising local people', and it appears to be an issue primarily for the youngest male respondents, who talk frequently about the threats they receive and how they cannot walk in certain parts of town or they will get 'stamped on' (Chris). This is how Ray describes his passage through one of these areas of his home town:

> If you walk up our area and there's more than five of you you'll get arrested you'll get stopped. They say it's racist. I walked through there and from one end of the street to the other, you couldn't move. It was just full of Muslims and they were all ... shouting things. It was all about intimidation. There was a hundred of them easily and it was about 11 o'clock at night. (Ray)

Ray, and his brother Connor, come from a family strongly associated with the local division of the EDL and they recounted a period when 'they [the Muslims] put five grand on my dad's head' (Ray). Local Organiser, Matt, recounted having received death threats and having a petrol bomb thrown at him in the street. Intimidation and bullying in educational contexts are mentioned frequently and discussed in Chapter 6 as part of a wider discourse of victimhood.

Muslims: extremists and moderates

Sitting incongruously alongside such generalised associations of Muslims with terrorism, the other most frequently coded reference to Muslims relates to the importance of *not generalising*. Sean recognises in himself a tendency when younger to 'spout off about "Muslims"' but that as he has got older he realises 'Not every Muslim is the same. ... I get that. They are not all the same.' As noted above, respondents recognise also that extremism is not inherently associated with Muslims, since 'you get extremists from every religion' (Lisa). When defining what constitutes moderate and 'extremist', Chas suggests extremism emerges when religion is taken 'far too seriously' and means 'you can't sit back and you can't say "Oh yes we can talk about this"' (Chas). The red line for Lisa is the question of attitudes of Muslim communities to the non-Muslim British population; she distinguishes 'extremists' (be they Muslim or not) as those who voice 'hatred' towards the country and its citizens.

In contrast 'moderate' Muslims are described as those who 'adopt British ways' and follow 'our law' (Kane, Chas) or are not 'strict Muslims' (Kylie). However, a number of respondents expressed concern that such moderate Muslims do not resist extremism strongly enough. Talking about conversations he had had in the past with Muslim friends, Tim says:

> If they went and said you know to the extremists out there, if the Muslim community came out in force and just said 'Do not use the word Islam cause you're not what Islam represents.' I said that would kind of squash a lot of things people are saying. (Tim)

Theresa, after making clear that she has no issue with 'moderate' Muslims, goes on to say, 'We can't understand why don't these moderate Muslims then come and demonstrate as well against the extreme ones that we do?' This perceived failure to speak out can lead some back into a position that sees all Muslims as potential extremists: 'Why ain't they [moderate Muslims] saying, "We're nothing to do with those radicals" instead of standing up with them?' (Euan). This is expressed explicitly by Tina, who, reflecting on my challenge that EDL chants that reference Muslims indiscriminately undermine the movement's claim to be against only 'radical' Islam, suggests that power is on the side of extremists:

> ... when Nazis come into power in Germany, they ['most Germans'] weren't gonna stand against them ... because it was either stand with the Nazis or die, what you gonna pick? You're gonna pick to live, ain't you? You know, it's just survival instinct. So these moderate Muslims, they are not gonna put themselves

in a situation against extremists, do you know what I mean? They'd rather join them than go against 'em, the same as what happened in Germany. ... [I]t's like, let's be honest, if ... this turned into an Islamic state, let's just say ... do you think these moderate Muslims would say, 'Oh, no way, I'm going to stand with them guys? The Brits, the infidels.' They're not gonna go and stand with the infidels, they're gonna go with them. It's a survival instinct. ... [A]t least they've got something in common. They've got Allah and Mohammed in common. What they got in common with the infidels? Nothing. (Tina)

Indeed, Tina rejects the idea that there is a clear distinction between 'moderate' and 'extremist' Muslims citing her own extended family experience where she claimed that she had found moderate Muslims sympathised 'with extremists' because of their opposition to the interventions of British forces in Afghanistan and Iraq.

Islamophobia: irrational fear or 'common sense'?

Notwithstanding a diversity of views across the respondent set and the differentiation made by many between 'moderate' and 'extremist' Islam and Muslims, this study of grassroots activists broadly confirms what Jackson (2011a: 13) calls the tendency within the movement to talk about Muslims as a single, 'dangerous and threatening "other"', which, according to the Runnymede Trust (1997) definition, constitutes a key criterion of an Islamophobic outlook. In this final section, therefore, we return to the question of Islamophobia but ask not *what* the object of hostility is, but *why* that hostility has emerged.

It opens by exploring the contention that hostility is rooted in a clash of religious views, given the rhetorical and symbolic references to Christianity in the movement. Finding that, among grassroots members in the EDL there is widespread indifference – sometimes even hostility – to Christianity it seeks answers as to why Islam and Muslims are singled out as targets of hostility in two further tropes of anti-Muslim hostility identified in this study, namely that Muslims seek to 'impose their rules here' and that Muslims 'have no respect'. This discussion moves us away from rationalised, ideological positions into emotionally driven, personal and localised experience. Ezekiel's (2002: 54) insight, that while ideological messages of the (racist) group focus on the characteristics of the target Others, 'thoughts and feelings about the Self' form the emotional centre of the group, is drawn on here. These particular tropes, it is suggested, emerge out of the 'affective economy' (Ahmed, 2004) in which fear neither resides in subjects 'who are scared and who draw important comfort from being members of a group' (Ezekiel, 2002: 54) nor the object (Ahmed, 2004: 127) but is produced through the circulation of signs of fear which, on the one hand become attached to particular bodies, and encoded as profoundly threatening to society but, at the same time, are worked through individual experiences and contexts in a way that is experienced by subjects as threatening to the 'self'. In shifting the gaze to this 'self', moreover, a mismatch is revealed between the empowered subject of 'othering' present in existing models of Islamophobia and the way in which anti-Islamic sentiments emerge in individual respondents' narratives in a more complex process of 'othering' and feeling 'othered'.

A new crusade?

Given that the 'other' for grassroots activists in the EDL is constituted as 'Islam' or 'Muslims', it might be anticipated that the 'self' that feels 'infringed' is also defined religiously. Indeed, the rhetorical and symbolic reference to Christianity, the crusades and the use of the St George's flag in EDL messages would appear to confirm this (Busher, 2012: 20). Official messages also posit Christianity as underpinning 'our' morality and contrast its 'truly ancient values' with Islam, which is described as 'some half-baked concept from a warmongering paedophile' (Dave Russell, Luton demonstration, recorded in field diary, 22 November 2014).[12]

However, evidence from this study found that among grassroots members of the movement there is widespread indifference to Christianity beyond its use as a general signifier of 'our' way of life and as such an object of preservation. Only two respondents (both members of the Infidels fringe) had strongly Christian identities and only four respondents in total called themselves 'Christian'. The most common position was ambivalence – 'I don't believe but I don't disbelieve' (Ian) – or a vague belief in 'something', alongside a high degree of scepticism about both biblical teachings (Tim) and the pretension of the Church to 'tell you what to do' (Kylie).

Thus Christianity is invoked rarely in relation to 'self' and almost always with reference to the imagined 'other' of Islam that is aggressive and threatening. Connor, for example, does not identify as Christian; when asked if he is religious he responds, 'English, that's my religion.' However, he sees the mission of the EDL as being to 'stand up against' any attempt of other faiths or ethnicities to 'impose other laws … to impose something on us' (Connor). This invocation of Christianity in conjunction with national belonging ('Englishness') to suggest a civilisational boundary with an alien 'Islam' is found also in the symbolic displays and rhetoric of EDL organisers and supporters in Busher's (2012) study (see Chapter 7).

'Their way or no way': everyday experiences of infringement and 'othering'

One of the key characteristics attributed to the Muslim 'other' by respondents in this study is itself the practice of 'othering' (of non-Muslims). Expressions of anti-Muslim sentiment thus include perceptions that the Muslim 'other' constitutes a direct infringement of, or sets itself in a superior position to, respondents' 'self'.

This sense of infringement or imposition is expressed as the belief that Muslims seek to impose their own laws rather than to integrate, do not help the community and are 'more segregated' than other cultures (Tim). While survey data suggest around one-third of the UK population share this perception that Muslims do not fit into British society and tend towards self-segregation (Field, 2012: 158), among EDL supporters in this study, the perceived problem is not simply lack of integration but of imposition – 'It is their way or no way' (Lisa). This articulation of the issue illustrates the frequent reference by respondents to concerns that unacceptable practices and rules (including aspects of Sharia law, attitudes to women and the ritual slaughter of animals for meat) were being gradually incorporated into British society[13] without discussion or the possibility of objection. As Connor puts it, 'the way them chuck their laws on us' fosters anger and resistance. The narratives of respondents are replete with examples of everyday encounters of the infringement into 'our life' that this engenders. Rather than summarise or seek to generalise from these examples, two are selected, from the narratives of Jordan and Michelle, to explore how, at the individual level, the formation of Islamophobic sentiments takes place through the process of experiencing the self as 'othered'.

Jordan is the only respondent in this study to accept that he was Islamophobic. It was when he moved from 'a white primary school' to a secondary school where there were 'so many different colours' that he became conscious of the fact that he 'had a thing with Muslims'. The move is articulated as a major turning point in his life; a 'shock' that he can 'never forget' (Jordan). The trauma is experienced in a highly corporeal way. Conscious of an unfamiliar minority status – he says around a third of his class were 'English'[14] – Jordan becomes acutely aware of his white body and what it felt like to 'sit with people in class' and 'have breaks with them'. His self-consciousness and sense of exclusion is communicatively as well as physically experienced:

> … they'd speak in their own language and you'd know … if it was about you kind of thing because they don't make it discreet, they are staring at ya, they are pointing and it was just like at the end of the day, yeah speak however you want outside of school in your own houses but when you are in a community school you should all speak the same. … There'd be a lot of fights over language issues. (Jordan)

These language issues were intensified when, subsequently, school policy on language options meant that Jordan was obliged 'to learn like a Muslim language or an Arabic language' as a second foreign language alongside French. While, logically, this might have overcome the communicative barrier that had developed between him and other pupils, Jordan experienced this rule as a further infringement of his rights and refused to study one of the prescribed languages. As a result he was suspended from school although was later reinstated following an appeal by his mum to the local council. Winning this battle did not alleviate the sense of isolation; although he was allowed to return he felt that the school 'didn't want me there' and that he was 'always singled out'. The outcome was that Jordan 'hated school' and, by the time he left, was fully convinced that he was the discriminated minority. In his mind, it was to his body that the label of 'other' was attached.

The turning point for Michelle is recounted as a single incident rather than a life-changing move but articulates a similar resentment at what is perceived to be the imposition of 'others'' norms and values. Michelle recounts the following incident has having triggered her decision to join the EDL:

> I got dressed up ready to go to the England–Germany game in the town, got my flag and my face painted and I got on the bus and you know put my money in the machine and of course there was a Muslim guy behind the steering wheel and I put my money in and he says, 'Sorry you can't get on the bus.' I says, 'Why?' He says, 'cause your flag offends me'. And then of course I saw red and thought, you know what, oh I'm not having that, you know, if you are gonna be here like it or lump it, it's the World Cup. So of course I went to sit down and he refused to move and I said, 'You've got a few options really, you carry on driving or you get off and walk cause I ain't going nowhere, I've got a football match to get to.' ... And I sat there and eventually he kind of just drove off on his way but I got a bit of a cheer from the crowd in the back. (Michelle)

Michelle experiences the bus driver's comment about her flag as an attempt to impose 'other' rules on territory that is as much hers as anybody else's. At one level, therefore, her story 'others' Muslims as aggressive and imperialistic (see above). In the context of her whole life, however, it tells a tale of the displaced self as much as the hostile 'other'.

Michelle had been physically and emotionally displaced when she moved, at the age of 21, from a small town in a neighbouring county to the city where she now lived. On arrival she had been housed in a women's refuge and had broken all ties with her family. Her move from what she describes as the 'white countryside' to the city was experienced as 'a complete smack in the face'. Like Jordan, she felt acutely aware of her physical 'otherness' in an urban space where, she said, '90 per cent of the chip shops in the area are probably Halal' and, on the street, 'all you see is Somalians and Asian women, burqas, left right and centre'.

Michelle's 'self' was, in any case, tenuously secured. She describes herself as somebody who does not 'mix very well with people' and is nervous of attending meetings and events where she does not know people. She eschews friendship with other women in the local divisions of the EDL and states categorically that 'I wouldn't class myself as an EDL Angel in any way shape or form.' Michelle had had almost 50 Facebook accounts and jokes that her record for the shortest time an account lasted was 15 minutes. She attributes this to accounts being disabled by Facebook but it is evident that she feels more comfortable with multiple identities and she takes pleasure from creating contentious or sexualised names for her virtual persona.

In this context, the 'cheer from the crowd in the back', whether real or imagined for narrative effect, is a central element in Michelle's rendition of her encounter with the bus driver. It constructs the incident as an act of defiance – the assertion of her right to display support for her national football team – and a symbolic reclamation of space. It is illustrative of many everyday incidents recounted by respondents in which they experience what it is like to be 'other' and her response to it compensates, although does not overcome, what she experiences as the devaluing of a gendered, classed and racialised self. In the following chapter how this sense of being 'othered' develops at the collective level into the claiming of victim status is discussed.

'If they had respect, there wouldn't be an EDL'

The second trope in respondents' narratives of Islam in which they present themselves as 'othered' centres on the feeling that they, as 'infidels', are looked down on, lied to and not respected by Muslims. At the individual level, respondents most frequently complain that 'as a Muslim you are allowed to lie to an infidel but you cannot lie to another Muslim' (Mike). For Tina this undermined trust and confidence in personal relationships and interactions with members of the Muslim community. She illustrates this with a story she tells about having 'made friends' with a young Muslim woman on her course at university who, the following week, 'just acted like I didn't exist, like she'd never met me' (Tina). Her greatest concern, however, is what she believes to be a policy among 'extremist preachers' who are 'telling Muslim men to marry the infidel women … make them have your kid and then leave them' (Tina). To substantiate her argument she uses the example of a young female neighbour who had converted to Islam when she had married a Muslim man but had been subsequently 'dumped'. This perception of Muslim men's exploitation of non-Muslim young women clearly draws on other associations of Islam with the oppression and sexual exploitation of women and children discussed above. In contrast, Tim (citing a BBC 3 documentary *Inside Britain's Mosques*) argues that Islamic doctrine tells Muslims to 'stay away from non-Muslims as they are a serpent or a snake'. He contrasts his perception of Islam as a religion that seeks not to contaminate itself with 'others', to religions such as Sikhism and Christianity, which reach out to others.

Islamic doctrine is perceived by EDL grassroots activists to underpin a superior attitude towards 'others' among the Muslim community, which is described most frequently as manifesting itself in a 'lack of respect' towards others and for society, and its norms, in general. A meta-analysis of public opinion surveys on attitudes to Islam suggests that a third of the British population share this view that Islam 'lacked respect for other cultures' (Field, 2012: 149). A Sikh member of the division, when invited to talk about 'the differences between Sikhs and Muslims' at a divisional meeting, also chose to forefront the issue of 'respect'. He says England is a tolerant country; if you come and treat it with respect, then you are respected also. The problem, he says, is that Muslim communities do not respect others and this has to be addressed (field diary, 19 October 2012).

Respect is found lacking among the Muslim community for things held dear in British memory, especially those associated with sacrifices made in war by army personnel and symbolised by the poppy. The burning of the poppy as a protest against British interventions abroad is denounced as 'so disrespectful' (Rachel). Incidents in which poppies have been burned are recounted often prior to wider discussions of the lack of respect shown by (some) parts of the Muslim community to 'our law' (Chris), the British armed forces (Chris, Ryan, Jordan, Kane, Matt), 'elders' (who fought in the war) (Connor, Carlie, Tina), 'the community' (Chris), 'us as people' (Lisa), 'our homeland' (Lisa) and 'the heritage of this country' (Tina). It is of course the objection to the demonstration of 'disrespect' for returning British forces that was the original impulse for the founding of the EDL (see Chapter 2) and thus Chris says, 'If they had respect, there wouldn't be an EDL.'

Disrespect is experienced as personal infringement by some respondents as a perceived lack of respect for the country and is mapped onto 'immigrant' bodies that are understood as taking resources from, or undermining, individual respondents themselves. Rob, for example, complains,

> I mean you got them all that come here and when they come here all they do is diss the place and we are the people that are putting them up probably saving them from death and then, you know, they are putting banners up 'Behead those who insult Islam … Islam will take over the world.' Hang on we just give you a place to live. We've given you security, we've given you money, we've given you houses. … That really gets up my nose because me as a person I've got nothing, my family have got nothing, and these people have got more than I will ever have and that really, really winds me up. … [V]ery disrespectful. (Rob)

For Lisa, who refers to her experience of working alongside migrants from eastern European countries, the fact that 'they have no respect for us' is a characteristic of eastern European migrants – who 'don't want to talk to you' – as well as Muslims. The way these feelings of not being respected at a personal level are collectively experienced as 'second-class citizenship' is explored in the following chapter.

'Islamophobic and proud': racist or rationalist?

Finally, it should be noted that there is a minority position in which the Islamophobia label is appropriated and individuals declare themselves 'Islamophobic and proud'. At the Dewsbury national demonstration, Tony Curtis referred to himself as an 'Islamophobe' in that, although he had nothing against the religion per se, he did have issues with elements of it, including Sharia law (field diary, 30 June 2012). Within this study, only one respondent – Jordan, whose story is discussed above – accepted that he was Islamophobic after I challenged his generalised hostility towards Muslims:

> INT: I mean does that worry you, would it bother you that someone said to you that you were an Islamophobe, you hated all Muslims?
> JORDAN: No, because I do.
> INT: You do?
> JORDAN: I do and it's, I'll never change. They can be the nicest person in the world, but I just won't like them. You can be anything else, any Sikhs, Jamaicans …

However, images declaring pride in being Islamophobic were displayed on respondents' Facebook pages (see Figure 5.2), suggesting this position attracts broader sympathy. The logic of this position is often that Islamophobia is not an irrational fear of Islam but a 'common sense' understanding of a real threat. This is most clearly articulated in the oft-repeated phrase which Jack attributes to former BNP leader Nick Griffin: 'something that Nick Griffin said once always stuck in my head and he said and I quote "It's not all Muslims who are suicide bombers but all suicide bombers happen to be Muslim"' (Jack). Indeed, as Allen (2010: 171) points out, the rise in fear towards, and mistrust of, Muslims following 9/11 might be 'entirely logical, rational and justifiable by those who feel increasingly fearful or at risk' even though the ideological content of the rationale for this fear 'might be inappropriate, inaccurate and without empirical justification'. A representative of the Sikh Awareness Society, invited to speak at a regional 'meet and greet' event, provides a variant of this rationale when he notes that 'no other religion has a "phobia"' attached to it. Making the point that nobody talks about Sikhophobia, for example, he implies, simultaneously, that there is no smoke without fire and that Muslims are given special protection (field diary, 4 October 2010). This illustrates Meer and Modood's (2009: 338) argument that while Muslims are increasingly the subject of hostility and discrimination, as well as governmental racial profiling and surveillance, paradoxically, complaints about anti-Muslim racism

5.2 Islamophobic and proud

and Islamophobia have not highlighted and alleviated anti-Muslim discrimination but frequently invited criticism of Muslims themselves.

In this respect, we might ask whether anti-Islam and anti-Muslim sentiments expressed by EDL respondents in this study are qualitatively different from those found across a growing proportion of the wider British public? Population surveys in the UK suggest that up to a fifth of the adult population are strongly Islamophobic, and up to a half think Muslims need to do more to integrate, perceive the face-veil as a barrier to integration, see Muslim immigration as a threat to British identity and think that Muslims have too much political power (Field, 2012: 158). Up to three-quarters oppose the subordinate status of Muslim women and press for tougher action against Muslim extremists (2012: 158). Most notoriously, Polly Toynbee, writing in *The Independent* in 1997, declared, 'I am an Islamophobe and proud of it!' (cited in Meer and Modood, 2009: 345) and later defended her right to challenge the legitimacy of the idea of Islamophobia as well as calls to make criticism of a religion a crime akin to racism (Toynbee, 2004) on the grounds that this was the 'rationalist' position. In such examples, according to Helbling (2012: 5), Islamophobia is employed to articulate 'a critical and reflexive position toward Islam' and distrust of Islam as a doctrine rather than hostility towards Muslims.

Conclusion

Islamophobia is, for many, the most powerful new form of racism. Islamophobia is seen as operating as a form of racialisation (Vakil, 2010 : 276; Klug, 2012: 675) enacted through ideas and practices that amalgamate all Muslims into one group and treat characteristics associated with Muslims (violence, misogyny, political allegiance/disloyalty, incompatibility with Western values, etc.) as if they are innate (Garner and Selod, 2015: 13). Islamophobia is dangerous because it provides a common ideological basis and programmatic platform for right-wing populist parties in Europe (Hafez, 2014; Skenderovic, Späti and Wildmann, 2014: 439) and the EDL is widely considered to be such an Islamophobic movement (Copsey, 2010: 5; Allen, 2011: 293).

This study suggests that, in contrast to a genuine aspiration to non-racism among grassroots activists in the EDL, they openly single out Islam as a 'problem' not associated with other aspects of multicultural society. In order to sustain claims to non-racism, therefore, a strategic distinction between Islam and Muslims is drawn; the object of hostility is (some) Islamic doctrine or teachings, not its followers as individuals or racialised groups. By analysing data on associations with Islam and associations with Muslims separately, this chapter has attempted to show how, in practice, these distinctions are made by grassroots EDL activists. It has found, first, that differentiation between Islam and Muslims is common among grassroots activists as well as in official EDL statements, although such distinctions are not consistently made within respondent narratives. It revealed, second, that EDL activists' talk about Islam is distinct from Islamophobic associations found among the general UK population (for whom Islam is associated

primarily with 'extremism', 'terrorism' and 'violence')[15] in its use of strongly political motifs (Islam is associated with oppression, intolerance and non-progressive-
ness). This is encapsulated in the understanding of Islam as an 'ideology' rather
than a religion and appears to support the position that the movement is anti-Islamist not Islamophobic. While viewing Islam as an ideology is itself, according
to the Runnymede Trust (1997), characteristic of an Islamophobic outlook, for
most respondents in this study, the use of the term 'ideology' is not intended to
demonise Islam per se but highlight the dangers of allowing religion to be appropriated for radical and violent political ends.

But how far is such a distinction possible? Since neither Islam nor Muslims
can exist without the other, the insistence on their separation is hard to sustain
(Klug, 2012: 676). Moreover, in practice, being anti-Islam does not exclude being
anti-Muslim also. This chapter has demonstrated, drawing on observational evidence as well as interviews, that among grassroots activists there is considerable
slippage in distinctions between Islam and Muslims as the object of hostility as
well as, especially in the context of demonstrations, the use of generalised terms
of abuse towards Muslims. These expressions take the form of both generalised
demonisations (in chants such as 'Muslim paedos off our streets') as well as more
localised references to everyday 'intimidating' behaviour, threats or violent actions
perpetrated by 'Muslims'. This suggests that alongside the critique of Islam as an
ideology there is a racialised anti-Muslim sentiment that is expressed through
more everyday encounters and community relations and in which Muslims are
seen as particularly problematic and unwelcome immigrants and in which Islam
is a contributing factor.

If we accept that hostility to Islam and to Muslims are intertwined, what
purpose does it serve to see them as independent variables that are related rather
than expressions of the same underlying process of racialisation (Klug, 2012: 677)?
Indeed, for those on the receiving end of hostility, the differentiation is immate-
rial; the message received is the same (Allen, 2011: 292). In contrast, there are
important advantages in seeing Islamophobia as another form of racialisation not
least in exposing that it is more than religious intolerance and invokes discourses
and practices that are, in effect, 'racist' (Klug, 2012: 677). Notwithstanding this,
the evidence from this study points to the value of a definition of Islamophobia
that recognises its multidimensionality and includes both Islam as a religious
doctrine and/or Muslims (Bleich, 2011: 1587). The argument for this is that in
some cases, it may be possible to identify differences between anti-Islamic and
anti-Muslim attitudes or emotions (which can aid our understanding of both) and
their analytic separation is the first step in understanding how they are related.

In this chapter this has been demonstrated through the exploration of the
practice and experience of 'othering'. In this study two tropes of anti-Muslim hostility were identified among grassroots EDL activists that do not reflect back familiar media images or ideological positions but emerge out of emotionally-driven,
personal and localised experience: Muslims seek to 'impose their rules here'; and
Muslims 'have no respect'. Analysis of these tropes reveals that one of the key characteristics attributed to the Muslim 'other' by respondents in this study is itself the

practice of 'othering' (non-Muslims). Expressions of anti-Muslim sentiment thus include perceptions that the Muslim 'other' constitutes a direct infringement of, or sets itself in a superior position to, respondents' 'self'. This draws, on the one hand, on associations of Islam as an ideology rooted in intolerance and imperialism while, on the other, it is expressed as feelings of incursion by racialised bodies. Through the analysis of a small number of everyday encounters and how they fit in individual respondents' stories, it has been suggested that 'thoughts and feelings about the Self' are highly implicated in the formation of associations of the 'other' (Ezekiel, 2002: 54). It is suggested that these particular tropes emerge out of the 'affective economy' (Ahmed, 2004) in which fear resides in neither subjects (themselves seeking shelter from fear in group membership) (Ezekiel, 2002: 54) nor the object that is feared. It is produced, rather, through the circulation of signs of fear (Ahmed, 2004: 127), which, on the one hand become attached to particular bodies, and encoded as profoundly threatening to society but, at the same time, are worked through individual experiences and contexts in a way that is experienced by subjects as threatening to the 'self'. In shifting the gaze to this 'self', it is argued, a mismatch is revealed between the vision of the empowered subject of 'othering' found in existing models of Islamophobia and the more complex process of 'othering' and being 'othered' in which anti-Islamic and anti-Muslim sentiments emerge in individuals' narratives. What might appear to be the aggressive assertion of a powerful majority subjectivity is exposed as the further destabilising of already insecure selves.

Notes

1 Indeed, the shift in Europe's dominant concern from the figure of 'the black' (and before that 'the Jew') to that of 'the Muslim', for Goldberg, only confirms the continued significance of 'race' and that race extends beyond false views about biology or skin colour (Goldberg, 2006: 349).

2 Rokeach's *Open and Closed Mind* (1960) was devised as the basis for a general psychology of totalitarianism (extending beyond that specifically related to fascism) and divided individuals into 'dogmatic' and 'open-minded' types (Billig, 1978: 50–51).

3 The studies cited by Helbling include: Sniderman and Hagendoorn (2007), Kalkan, Layman and Uslaner (2009), Stolz (2005) and Strabac and Listhaug (2008).

4 See http://englishdefenceleague.org/about-us/mission-statement. Accessed: 26.06.2012. The revised mission statement released in 2016 does not make this distinction but states the EDL's mission to be one of 'struggle against global Islamification'. It makes clear that the issues the movement have are with 'problems deriving from Islam' not only particular interpretations of it whilst also explicitly denouncing the 'demonisation of Muslims' and 'the unjust assumption that all Muslims are complicit in or somehow responsible for the actions of other Muslims'. See https://www.facebook.com/notes/edl-english-defence-league/edl-mission-statement/1099342593431789

5 See also: www.youtube.com/watch?v=NCiBrZgP018. Accessed: 06.08.2015.

6 The age of Aisha at the time of betrothal and consummation of marriage as well as the implications of taking the marriage out of context remain disputed (see Francois-Cerrah, 2012).

7   See also: www.youtube.com/watch?v=4naC3dhyhIs. Accessed: 06.08.2015.

8   See http://englishdefenceleague.org/about-us/mission-statement. Accessed: 26.06.2012.

9   See www.youtube.com/watch?v=9RTa0vmFCAY. Accessed: 14.04.2014.

10 The EDL mission statement also positions Muslims as 'the main victims of some Islamic traditions and practices' (see http://englishdefenceleague.org/about-us/mission-statement. Accessed 26.06.2012).

11 See also www.youtube.com/watch?v=NCiBrZgP018. Accessed: 06.08.2015.

12 See also www.youtube.com/watch?v=NCiBrZgP018. Accessed: 06.08.2015.

13 In fact the Islamic Sharia Council and Muslim Arbitration Tribunal have used the framework of the Sharia to resolve disputes within the British Muslim community since 1982 (Meer and Modood, 2014: 659).

14 In this instance, Jordan clearly uses this term as a metaphor for 'white' as he goes on to say that many of the 'others' (non-English) had been born in the UK.

15 When asked which words they associated with Islam, those surveyed in a YouGov poll (2010, n=2,152) were most likely to link Islam to extremism (58 per cent), terrorism (50 per cent) and violence (33 per cent) (Field, 2012: 150).

6

'Second-class citizens': reordering privilege and prejudice

Castells (2012: 14) argues that anxiety is a response to an external threat over which the threatened person has no control. Anxiety leads to fear, and has a paralysing effect on action. However, anxiety can be overcome and lead to action if it develops into anger, usually through the perception of an unjust action and the identification of the agent responsible for it. In the previous chapter, the anxieties held by EDL supporters about Islam, and about Muslims, were detailed. It was shown how these anxieties construct a threatening 'other' that compounds and reinforces anti-Muslim and anti-Islam sentiments in wider society. It was argued, however, that the empowered subject of 'othering' assumed in existing models of Islamophobia needs rethinking in the light of how anti-Islamic and anti-Muslim sentiments emerge in individuals' narratives as a feeling of themselves being the object of 'othering'. In this sense anti-Islam or anti-Muslim sentiment is as much a narrative of 'self' as 'other'. In this chapter, attention turns to the exploration of the most consistent and emotionally charged narrative of 'self' identified in this study; that of 'second-class citizen'.

Urban deprivation manifests itself not only in poverty but also community fragmentation, loss of meaning and the fracturing of individuals' sense of self (McDonald, 2014: 4–5). In that context, justice is understood as equality and its violation as inequality whose intimate experience may take the form of resignation, shame and fear but also resentment and resistance (2014: 4–5). Among respondents in this study there was a universal perception that the needs of others were privileged over their own. While the perceived beneficiary of that injustice might be racialised (as 'immigrants' or 'Muslims'), the agent responsible for this injustice is understood to be a weak-willed or frightened government that panders to the demands of a minority for fear of being labelled racist.

In the first part of this chapter, expressions of resentment and injustice and its links to class and racialised identities are traced through the literature on the backlash to multiculturalism in the UK. This is followed by a detailed exploration of accounts of respondents' experience of injustice and the 'preferential treatment' afforded to ethnic minorities in terms of access to benefits, housing and jobs. The third section considers the perceived institutionalisation of this injustice through a 'two-tier' justice system, which, respondents claim, allows 'them' to get away with things and fails to protect or recognise injustices towards 'us'. Finally, EDL activism is analysed as a mechanism for resisting this perceived second-class citizen status. How this is accomplished through a discursive reordering of privilege and prejudice – in which 'we' are seen as the discriminated and those in power are dismissed as liberal elite 'do-gooders' who have little understanding of the everyday worlds they inhabit – is discussed here. In Chapters 7 and 8, attention turns to the more tangible practices of resistance in strategies of being seen ('standing together') and being heard ('getting your message across').

Whiteness, class and the backlash to multiculturalism

The views of EDL activists can be broadly situated within the series of backlashes against multicultural politics that have taken place in the UK in recent decades (Busher, 2013: 72). 'Multiculturalism' was promoted in many countries in the last quarter of the twentieth century as a proactive policy to recognise and realise the positive social and cultural impact of interaction and communication between diverse 'cultural' communities (defined, usually, as 'ethnic minorities') alongside legislative and educational measures to expose the 'scientific' underpinnings of racism as erroneous and protect individuals against racist acts that had characterised initial Western, post-imperial attempts to combat ethnic and racial intolerance. Multiculturalism has ensured that post-war migrants, arriving as citizens of the United Kingdom and Commonwealth, have been recognised as ethnic and racial minorities requiring state support and differential treatment to overcome barriers to their exercise of citizenship (Meer and Modood, 2014: 658–59), while 'multicultural citizenship' provides an antidote to the cultural assimilation traditionally demanded of migrants and minorities (including religious minorities) by nation states (Modood, 2013: 2).

'Multiculturalism' has been criticised, from an academic perspective, for both being too radical and for being not radical enough. The former criticism suggests that multiculturalism equates cultural diversity with cultural relativism, while the latter accuses multiculturalism of failing to eliminate the implicit hierarchies of biologically rooted racial doctrines in favour of cosmetically replacing the uncomfortable notion of 'race' with that of 'culture' or 'identity' (Lentin, 2004: 98). The replacement of the language of race and racism by that of 'different but equal' culture, Lentin (2014: 1275–76) argues, has obscured the experience of racism and reduced the struggle for equality and justice to a fight for the recognition of cultural identity.

From a political perspective, in the post-9/11 context, multiculturalism is increasingly interpreted as 'part of the problem not the solution' (Kundnani, 2004: 108) to racism and ethnic discrimination. In this understanding the 'problem' is not inequality or deprivation of 'minority' communities but self-imposed cultural barriers between communities that hinder the full participation in British society of ethnic minorities and foster racism (Kundnani, 2004: 108; Abbas and Akhtar, 2005: 134). To its critics, therefore, multiculturalism constitutes a practice of excessive tolerance and benevolence towards disloyal, unassimilable, culturally different others and has been blamed by leading European politicians for a range of sociopolitical problems including crime, terrorism and urban segregation (Lentin, 2014: 1272–73). This thinking is epitomised in the Blair government's adoption of 'community cohesion' as a new social priority in the wake of the 2001 'race riots' in Burnley, Bradford and Oldham while, more recently (February 2011), David Cameron (cited in Meer and Modood, 2014: 659) claimed that 'the doctrine of "state multiculturalism" has encouraged culturally different people to live apart from one another and apart from the mainstream'.

The backlash to multiculturalism in the UK has deeper roots, however, and is bound up in tensions between the politics of class and the politics of anti-racism. Viewing Labour-controlled local authorities as a potential site of resistance to the newly elected Conservative government under Margaret Thatcher (1979), the Labour Party initiated the creation of a structure of equalities-related posts within local government and anti-racist policies and racism-awareness training, which generated resentment among local authority staff whilst feeding central government and right-wing media attacks on local government multicultural and anti-racist initiatives (Hewitt, 2005: 30–32). This led, Hewitt (2005: 33) argues, to a growing disconnect between Labour and the concerns of the white working class (particularly in areas bordering on racially mixed communities) who, at a time of a rapidly widening gulf between the rich and the poor, 'felt themselves to be unheard and neglected by the local politicians they would once have looked to for support'.

This problem reflected a wider failure to connect issues of racism and class rather than set them in unhelpful competition with one another. This is evident also in early sociological writing on race in the UK where migrant workers are seen either as an 'underclass' outside of the working class in the employment of the 'race relations' problem (Rex, 2000: 179) or, alternatively, 'race' is rejected as no more than a mask which hides real economic relationships (Miles, 2000: 195) and racial differentiations are seen as taking place always in the context of class differentiations (Meer and Nayak, 2013: 8). Thus, through the 1980s, Hewitt (2005: 33) argues, real concerns that made some whites receptive to the interpretations of racist political groups 'frequently went unanswered or were dismissed as racist talk', resulting, by the 1990s, in white working-class backlash to equalities policies (2005: 34).

Today, multiculturalism is challenged by critiques from the right and left alike (Hewitt, 2005: 151; Bygnes, 2012; Meer and Modood, 2014). This, Hewitt suggests, is not due to a problem with the philosophy of multiculturalism per se but the everyday management of its politics such that local authorities have come to be perceived as promoting a special interest group 'against the will of a victim white community' (2005: 152). This is identified by Lone and Silver (2014: 177–78) in their study of the white working-class community of Higher Blackley (Manchester) where residents felt things had become palpably worse for working-class communities in recent years, while local politicians had failed to address the issues that mattered to them and took their support for granted.

Recognising the entwinement of class and race/ethnicity in patterns of contemporary inequality and marginalisation is central to understanding the context of activism in movements such as the EDL. Wacquant (2008: 163) suggests contemporary forms of 'advanced marginality' (in western Europe and North America) are not explained by a single dynamic but by 'two closely interwoven trends': the unexpected resurgence of a range of inequalities and the crystallisation of novel forms of socio-economic marginality widely perceived to have an 'ethnic' component; and the spread of racialising ideologies and xenophobic tensions as a result of the simultaneous increase in persistent unemployment and the permanent settlement of immigrant populations (2008: 163). While differently construed in each context, politics – state structures and policies – always plays a decisive role in how inequalities of class, place and origin are woven together, while the reticence of governments to address the accumulation of economic hardship, social dissolution and cultural dishonour gives rise to civic alienation and chronic unrest capable of challenging the institution of citizenship itself (2008: 5–7). Indeed, the Lone and Silver (2014: 181) study noted above, found a marked decline in democratic engagement and participation and a cultural divide between white working-class communities and the socially liberal world of individuals and institutions in positions of power (termed the 'do-gooders'). This lack of trust in public institutions, they argue, is, in large part, the cause of decreasing social cohesion since a perception that such institutions favour immigrants over the majority population often stems from a lack of transparency in the decision-making process and a concomitant tendency to believe things heard through public conversation. This widens the opportunities for populist parties to enter the debate with simpler messages that resonate with certain issues and anxieties, thereby creating further tensions in the community (2014: 181).

How this works in a particular spatial and historical context is analysed in Rhodes's (2011) exploration of working-class support for the far right in the Lancashire town of Burnley. On the back of the urban disturbances (labelled 'race riots') in the town over the summer of 2001, the BNP gained three councillors during the 2002 local elections and went on to win 10 per cent of the vote in the town in the General Election of 2005 (Goodwin, 2011a: 11, 71). Exploring the reasons for this support, Rhodes demonstrates how, in conditions of high deprivation,[1] local council resource allocation came to be understood as unfairly skewed to the benefit of areas of the town which were 'predominantly "Asian"', leaving the town's 'white' areas neglected (Rhodes, 2011: 108). At one level, this is a classic manifestation of the 'white backlash' towards policies aimed at equality and the promotion of multiculturalism discussed above; BNP voters constructed what was interchangeably termed 'the "Asian"/Pakistani/Muslim' population as a group undeserving of local government resources since, it was imagined, they refused to adhere to the dominant values of British society, engaged in criminal activity and 'benefit-scrounging', and represented a material, political and cultural threat to locality and nation (2011: 108). However, Rhodes warns against seeing this as solely an issue of the scapegoating of ethnic communities by an undifferentiated 'white working class' since BNP voters not only distanced themselves from ethnic and racial 'others', but also from those 'poor' whites – single mothers, drug addicts, welfare-dependent 'dossers' and 'alkies' – whose entitlement to resources was viewed by the more affluent BNP voters as equally unmerited.

White working-class resentment is often cited as an explanation for racist or anti-social attitudes and represented as an unfortunate but inevitable outcome of inequality and injustice frequently related to the proclaimed failure of multiculturalism (Ware, 2008: 2). Ware argues that since such resentment towards immigration is often found among the poorest sections of the population (and compounded by fear and insecurity as a result of rapid economic and social change) policy-makers feel compelled to respond with understanding and 'manifest fairness' (2008: 3). In fact, she suggests, resentment is rarely alleviated by removing the source of the grievance, since it often involves 'a kind of pleasure inherent in self-pity or victimhood' and thus does not necessarily expect or want a remedy (2008: 11). The construction of economic migrants, refugees and asylum-seekers as the undeserving beneficiaries of social resources, claiming and receiving welfare entitlements at the expense of majority ('indigenous') populations, in fact reflects a 'paranoia' – a pathological form of fear based on a conception of the self as excessively fragile, and constantly threatened – on the part of the 'native', 'indigenous' and white population about the potential loss of Europeanness or whiteness and of the lifestyle and privileges that are seen to emanate directly from that (Hage, 2003, cited in Ware, 2008: 12). Resentment, no matter how genuinely felt, therefore must be understood in the context of societies where whiteness has historically conferred some sort of guarantee of belonging and entitlement.

Second-class citizens: perceptions of privilege and prejudice

Steve Eddowes understands the anger EDL supporters feel as 'a natural thing'. Anger is not something you choose but 'things make you angry, and at the end of the day, if people don't get angry sometimes then things don't get done' (Eddowes, 2015). Castells's formulation of the process of the transformation of anxiety into anger and anger into action is illustrated in Tina's story:

> It makes you angry. It's like you're always angry. It's like when that happened with the door. I was so angry, I was livid. When I was going to view houses and Somalians were getting them, I was absolutely livid, because I know for a fact they haven't been in the country as long as I've been on that waiting list. I know for a fact they're not sharing a house with their dying dad, you know what I mean? And my kids had to watch that because they were first priority over me and the council knew that, what the situation was, you know? (Tina)

The anger Tina recalls feeling relates to two moments in her life when she felt acutely aware that 'others' were being prioritised or privileged over her. The first incident – what she refers to as what 'happened with the door' – refers to a recent occasion when she had lost the keys to her front door. A neighbour (a white woman who had converted to Islam) advised her to call the council because, in the same situation, she said, 'within an hour' the council had changed the locks free of charge for her. Tina had taken her advice but, she recounts, she had been given no help beyond a list of telephone numbers for locksmiths who would allow her to pay the bill in weekly instalments. When she rang them, however, none would agree to anything but immediate payment. As she continues the story, her anger grows and becomes physically articulated in a struggle to breathe as she relives the humiliation. In its retelling, the experience becomes framed as an example of the council's preferential treatment of ethnic minorities for fear of being labelled racist itself:

> I couldn't get my breath at it. I was just so angry about it. I just thought, I mean, if I'd have said to them, 'Right, you're being racist. I'm Muslim' or whatever, you know, 'You're discriminating against me 'cause I'm a Muslim' without them actually seeing me, they'd probably have come out … and it just got me so angry. (Tina)

The second story she refers to is a more significant turning point in her personal narrative when she had had to move out of privately rented accommodation because her landlord did not renew her contract. She moved, she thought temporarily, into her mum's house. The conditions were difficult. The whole family, that is, her, her partner and her four children, had a single room in a three-bedroom house shared also with her mum, her brother and his two children and her dad, who had terminal cancer. She had spent almost a year trying to access social housing and her memory of being 'always second' in the priority list for any house is extrapolated to an understanding of her status as 'second-class':

> So I was on that bidding site. Ten months I had to live at my mum's house in that one bedroom that was full of mould, and damp, and I was always second on the bidding list, and the number one always has first refusal of that house. Every single property that I went to view, Somalians got it, you know, and I was thinking … my kids have to watch their granddad die, do you know what I mean? The house is totally overcrowded. Why are they getting this house, do you know, like, it really got me angry … I was actually first-hand witnessing that I was a second-class citizen in this country. (Tina)

Tina's account reflects her own interpretation of specific personal and traumatic events and could not be verified by observational data. However, the belief that the government gives preferential treatment to ethnic minorities in terms of access to benefits, social housing and jobs is commonplace among respondents in this study and the notion that immigrants and minority ethnic groups constitute a threat in that they compete for scarce economic resources is central to the 'racial threat' paradigm of understanding support for extreme right and populist parties (Goodwin, 2011a: 99; Rhodes, 2011: 108).

Housing is the most contentious issue. Like Tina, others cite personal experience to evidence privileged treatment of ethnic minorities. Carlie (who has three children) said that only Asian families were given housing in her area while Casey recounts how, despite being a single parent from the age of 16, it had taken twelve to thirteen years 'to get a house out of the council'. As a basic right, access to social housing is surrounded in particularly emotive discourse about belonging and entitlement and, while boundaries of 'us' and 'them' are deeply localised and far from always related to the colour of skin, housing has come to be perceived as a question of the redirection of state resources away from the white working class towards migrants and ethnic minority groups rather than as a question of shortage per se; it has in this sense become 'racialized' (Garner, 2009: 48). Dancygier (2010: 26–27) argues that this is a historical failing of the post-war UK immigration regime; the failure to prepare for the arrival of immigrants by setting aside vacant housing or building new houses meant that by the late 1960s (when many immigrants came to fulfil the minimum residency requirements to apply for council housing) there was intense competition over housing. However, the lack of affordable or social housing has been a core issue for populist radical right parties and movements in other countries too (for example CasaPound in Italy) (Bartlett, Birdwell and Littler, 2011: 96).

In this study, among respondents there also circulated an urban myth that ethnic or religious minority groups are privileged within the benefit system. Thus, Brett claims – based on comparing the £100 per fortnight he receives with the £160 he says a young Muslim woman (also single and without children) who lives on his mum's estate gets – that '*They* get paid more than I do on the dole … because of their religion, race' (my emphasis). Tina also said seeing immigrant families who were on benefits with top-notch phones had made her ask, 'Are they entitled to more than what the average person is entitled to?' She goes on to complain that 'when they come into this country, they get given everything, absolutely everything', whereas she herself, as a single mum, had worked long, overnight shifts stacking shelves at a supermarket yet struggled to afford even to clothe her children:

> I couldn't afford to treat the kids to even just some extra goodies in the shopping. I couldn't afford nothing. If they needed a new pair of trainers, I used to have to scrimp and save for about a month just to get one pair, and they're out shopping, you know, living it up. Bags from Primark and … River Island and God knows what, and I'm just thinking, 'How can they afford that when I'm working five nights a week?' I was knackered all the time. … I was missing out on my kids growing up, and when I did see my kids, I was nothing but snappy because I was exhausted, you know. … I mean, my kids were like, what, eleven, ten and nine at the time, so I'd been in the housing system and on that housing waiting list for ten years before I could get anything. They come in this country, bam, house, house done up, money to get everything they want … about five or six years ago, they even used to get free driving lessons … Can you get your breath at that? Their kids used to get free cricket lessons, about five, six years ago. … and I couldn't afford to get my son into the local football team, do you know? It's just the two-tier system. (Tina)

Similar outrage was vented by respondents in a study of racist violence in Manchester by Ray, Smith and Wastell (2004: 352) who claimed that the local South Asian community received targeted help for starting businesses and 'free driving lessons'[2] as well as special deals on their council rents and higher social benefit payments.

The prominence of this discussion of benefits should be seen in the light of the recent shift in the base electoral support for the extreme right in the UK from skilled workers (who might be concerned about competition for jobs from immigrant workers) to unskilled manual workers and those dependent on state benefits who are 'more concerned over competition for state benefits' (Goodwin et al., 2010: 199–200). Indeed, Tina's reference here to what she perceives as the injustice of the prioritisation of the needs of those recently arrived in the UK over her own appears to confirm the 'undeserving' beneficiaries discourse identified among BNP voters in Burnley (Rhodes, 2011: 108). Its expression, however, barely conceals its roots in the unacknowledged shame associated with feeling neglected, overlooked and undervalued (Ray, Smith and Wastell, 2004: 361–62). The anger, bitterness and resentment that appear as the personal disposition of Tina are rooted in structural relations of inequality whose experience is intensified by the feeling of being 'misrecognized as valueless and judged unjustly by those considered undeserving of authority' (Skeggs and Loveday, 2012: 482).

Privilege: racialised, naturalised or politicised?

A racialised discourse of the 'unjust' allocation of resources is an established component of extreme right ideology. In the mid-1980s the BNP youth wing distributed leaflets claiming 'young Whites' had been left on the scrapheap while 'Britain's coloured racial minorities' received 'specially favoured treatment' (Goodwin, 2011a: 40). This sentiment is found in some respondents' narratives in this study. Nick questions, 'Why should we come second to foreigners in our own land?' and links this 'second-class' status to an imagined (white) minority status resulting from the country's immigration policy. Other respondents single out Muslims as being particularly privileged by the system:

> Like a young English male like myself ... we're not counted any more, we haven't got as much rights as say a young Islamic 28 year old, I think he's got more rights than me. You know, he can get more off the government than me. Say if I was not working. ... And I just think it's wrong. (Richard)

When asked what would be a 'better society' in her view, Tina echoes this belief, saying she would like to see 'systems within government that are fair for everyone, not just Muslims. I mean, 'cause I'm not being funny, even Sikhs don't get the same treatment. No other religion or culture gets the same treatment that Muslims get.' This perception is found more widely among the UK population; surveys in 2007 and 2008 showed Muslims were the most frequently cited group to receive – allegedly – preferential treatment by public services (Field, 2012: 152).

At the same time, Tina's stories speak not to anger towards 'Muslims' in general or 'Somalians' in particular but a sense that 'our rights' have been forgotten or undermined by the rights accorded to others. In a reflection that answers the question Skeggs and Loveday (2012: 488) pose as to 'What happens when the affects of anger and anxiety produced through injustice are not attached to their proper object?', Tina recognises that it is not the beneficiaries of what she perceives to be privilege that are at fault but wider inequality and social division:

> There's just no fairness in this country. And another thing, another thing, fairness between the poor and the rich, you know, close these gaps up. Just close 'em up, because what, the main thing I can see in society that causes these divides, is when people are struggling, and they can see other people being treated so much differently. Like me, I hated them Somalians that got them houses because I had to go back and watch my dad die, with my kids, while I'm sleeping in a room full of damp in the middle of winter. (Tina)

Carlie also blames the government: 'it is the government at the end of the day who is buggering everything up not EDL not BNP not the Muslims not us whites'. The negative impact for social cohesion of the lack of trust in public institutions to represent 'us', and the belief that they favour immigrants over the majority population, identified by Lone and Silver (2014), is noted above.

That political discourse inverts the reality they perceive around them is evident in the narratives of respondents in this study. While what they hear and read is that ethnic minority groups are underprivileged and discriminated against, what they experience themselves is a privileged treatment of those groups and their own 'minority' status. This is encapsulated in Tina's outrage at a fellow student who had expressed a desire to work with Muslims as he perceived them to be a discriminated community:

> Why can't you work in the community with all, with everyone? ... I think it's the systems in this country, and the two-tier systems, and people like him that actually cause so much friction, do you know what I mean? ... [I]t's supposed to be a country of equality, treat everyone the same then, you know what I mean? (Tina)

Thus the government and its agencies are accused of protecting 'them' over 'us', even at the cost of denying real issues that need to be resolved. Michelle, for example, accuses the police and social workers of 'covering' grooming gangs while Tim vents his anger at the fact that treatments are sometimes deemed too expensive to provide on the NHS yet large sums of money are spent on counter-terrorism, 'to keep a terrorist like Abu Qatada walking our streets freely'. Another strong motif of concern is the government's perceived failure to adequately protect armed services personnel both in action and after they return (Michelle, Tim, Jordan).

The incapacity, or reluctance, of governments of advanced industrialised countries to address the accumulation of economic hardship, social dissolution and cultural dishonour in the deteriorating working class and/or ethnoracial enclaves of their cities fuels civic alienation and social protest (Wacquant, 2008: 7). Wacquant (2008: 6) argues that state structures and policies play a decisive role in the differential stitching together of inequalities of class, place and origin. How this is translated into different outcomes in terms of local ethnic conflict is explored in detail in Dancygier's (2010) comparative study of national and local immigration regimes and responses in the UK and Germany in the post-World War II period. At the country level, she argues, local conflict involving postcolonial migrants in Britain was greater than local conflict involving guest workers in Germany because policies that guided guest-worker migration (e.g. the provision of local resources, or the conditionality of migration and settlement on employment and housing) in Germany reduced the likelihood of competition over economic goods and lowered the incidence of immigrant conflict in the areas of settlement (2010: 9). At the same time, poorer economic rights for migrants in the UK were compensated by greater political rights since most New Commonwealth migrants were entitled to participate in local and national elections and their settlement in concentrated areas meant the political parties had to pay attention to their interests (2010: 82).

While, on the one hand, it can be seen here that for many respondents it is government agencies rather than immigrant communities that are 'to blame', there is a danger that accepting this discourse of second-class citizens naturalises assumptions of racially based inequality, that is, that 'we' should be prioritised and 'they' should be poorer; any other situation is evidence of discrimination against 'us'. This, according to Rhodes (2009), is reflected in wider discursive tendencies to present racialised inequality 'as reflective of a natural order' embedded either in the market or in the tendency to self-marginalisation of ethnic minority communities. Despite perceptions of respondents in this study, Pakistanis and Bangladeshis are the most deprived social groups in the UK. In 2011, more than one in three members of the Bangladeshi and Pakistani community lived in a deprived neighbourhood,[3] which is considerably more than any other ethnic group (the proportion is around 7 per cent for the White British population) (Jivraj and Khan, 2013). Indeed, the region in which this study of EDL activism was conducted showed the highest ethnic inequality in the country. This calls into question the notions of 'fairness' – based on constructing an equivalence between ethnic minority groups and whites as an endangered ethnic group (Ware, 2008: 9) – invoked by some respondents in this study. In the context of the historically conferred guarantee of belonging and entitlement that whiteness brings (2008: 12), Connor's resentment that 'it feels like we're fucking immigrants in our own country … like the English don't at all matter' might be interpreted as a the understanding of racialised inequality as the natural order while poverty or disadvantage for the white majority is its inversion and perversion.

The two-tier system of justice

Injustice is perceived as determining not only the social but also the legal sphere. A central narrative of injustice – mentioned by more than half the respondents in this study – is the sense that there is no longer a 'universal' justice system but a 'two-tier' system which is weighted against 'people like us' (see Figure 3.9). There are two principal dimensions to this form of injustice. The first is the perception of a privileged sensitivity to the rights and needs of ethnic minority (especially Muslim) communities and is not exclusive to the respondent set. Muslims were thought to be unfairly advantaged by 39 per cent of the general population surveyed (2009) and to enjoy greater freedom of speech and action than British Christians by 56 per cent (2010) (Field, 2012: 151). The second element is more specific to those studied here and consists in: the sense of discrimination or persecution of 'us' – as EDL supporters – by the justice system and law enforcement agencies; and a wider construction of whiteness as a site of discrimination and victimisation.

The rights of 'others'

A key symbol of the two-tier system for respondents is the 'right' afforded to Muslim women to wear the burqa. Nine respondents called directly for the burqa to be banned in public places; some noted their approval of the French decision to do so (Sean). Respondents objected to the wearing of burqas because they were 'intimidating' (Connor), degrading to women (Matt) or facilitated the conceal-ment of criminals or terrorists (Sean). Others objected not to the burqa in and of itself but the *right* to wear it. For Theresa those who wore it were effectively 'prac-tising Sharia law' and, in so doing, undermined the principle of the universality of the law. This, it is argued, goes unchallenged because the government is 'scared' to take a stand:

> if you go to a petrol station you are not allowed to go in with your motorbike helmet on but if you've got a burqa on you are allowed to walk in there. ... It's just different rules for different ... people and I don't like the fact that the gov-ernment are pussyfooting around with it and they are scared and that's what annoys me. (Lisa)

The same example is given by Jason and Chas, while what Ray finds unfair is that you are not allowed to wear a balaclava or scarf around your face on the street (so they 'can see your face on the cameras') but wearing a burqa is permitted. Jordan complains that the government has advised troops that wearing uniform outside of barracks might be provocative, yet burqas are deemed acceptable: 'it can't be one rule [for some] and one rule for another' (Jordan). Tim cites his own experience of rules being applied differentially at an EDL demonstration in Bolton:

> ... we were coming under heavy fire and I mean the police weren't really doing anything and I noticed one person who stood out in this crowd was a man wearing a burqa and he kept pulling it up ... and when everyone was wearing face

masks on our side they were going, 'take them off'. And I said to the police, I says like, 'look you see that man over there, turn' and he goes, 'oh I'm not prepared to turn round' and I said, 'but there's a man over there who's covering his face, wearing a burqa'. And he was throwing things over and I was just like disgusted by it. (Tim)

Another site of resentment was that Muslims were allowed to conform to Islamic rather than British law in the case of ritual slaughter. One respondent, who had joined the EDL originally over the halal meat issue, argued that it was unfair that, for religious reasons, Muslims can bypass UK laws stating that all animals should be stunned before being killed (field diary, 18 May 2013).[4]

The 'privileged' rights of 'others' are always seen in relation to the perceived injustice towards the self. In this instance, EDL activists argued that religious or cultural symbols for ethnic minority and faith communities are viewed as a 'right' while symbols important to them are deemed 'offensive' or provocative. Jordan points out a sticker on the front windscreen of his car showing the six members of the Royal Engineer Fusiliers based in the area killed in a single incident in Afghanistan (one was his friend). He tells me he was asked by a policeman to remove it because it might incite criminal damage to his car (field diary, 24 July 2013). Kane cites having been 'kicked out' of the local Asda supermarket for wearing his EDL hoody and recounts a story of 'an old bloke' having been beaten up by 'three Muslims for no reason, just for having the England flag round his waist'. Another common complaint is that 'the council come round my house and tell me to take my England flag down' on the grounds that 'it offends people' (Eddowes, 2015). Perhaps most frequently mentioned are concerns about the per-ceived uneven justice meted out to those who offend Islam and those who violate what is held dear in Britain, symbolised by the poppy. Tim's conviction that a 'two-tier system' was in operation had been strengthened when he had taken a seat in the public gallery of a Westminster court to hear a case brought in relation to the public burning of the poppy:

> ... it's a two-tier system ... a man burns a poppy which represents every single man and woman who's gave a sacrifice ... and yet they just do nothing about it. They give 'em a fifty pound fine and I went to that court down in Westminster ... and I was sat there and ... first of all they disrespected the British law by when they asked them to stand there they stayed seated and when they finally like did stand they told 'em to sit and they just laughed .... I had to like sit by these Al-Qaeda supporters and they were laughing about it in the courtroom and ... and they gave 'em a fifty pound fine and they all like burst out laughing ... laughing in the face of the law. (Tim)

He goes on to contrast this with the case of a man who had burnt a copy of the Qur'an not 'out of disrespect to Muslims' but in protest at this case and 'our justice system' and was sentenced to twelve months in prison (Tim). Expressing disgust at acts of poppy-burning, members of the local youth division compare the '£50 fine' given to those prosecuted for it with the six-month prison sentence handed out to 'two of our lads' for spray-painting a poppy on the side of a mosque (Ray, Connor, Chris). Lisa complains that the EDL gets abused for the placards it carries at demonstrations when Islamist clerics like Abu Hamza are 'standing on a box, you know, in the middle of our fucking city, saying that we are all scum and we should all die'. Declan also complains that 'One of my mates in Dudley had a banner that said "Muslim paedophiles off our streets", he had the flag confiscated off him because of a racial hatred crime' yet, he says, 'they' are allowed to hold 'placards saying "this soldier is going to hell" … "Islam and Sharia will dominate the UK"', which, in his mind, was equally 'a hate crime'. Tim sees this as making a mockery of the principle of the freedom of speech:

> … it's like freedom of speech has to apply like equally or not at all … It's like if I walk down the street holding a Nazi flag I would be arrested and done, which quite rightly so, I should be imprisoned like. But they can walk down the street waving a … Al-Qaeda flag or a jihadi flag praising … the death of British soldiers and like you know almost rejoicing in British soldiers dying in our streets but nothing, that's freedom of speech. (Tim)

EDL activists understand injustice to arise out of the uneven application of rules and laws. In expressing this injustice, Muslims are the object of 'othering' – 'they are so protected in this country' (Declan) – but it is the government which is at fault. As Declan continues, 'The government will appease Islam just to make them happy. Like we have got Sharia courts now just for their benefit'. He concludes that this has resulted in the unacceptable situation in which there are 'two laws for two communities'. Tim goes further to suggest that this attention to the rights of religious groups undermines the basic principles upon which the rule of law is founded: 'the law should be absolutely neutral', he says, rather than being 'bent around religion'.

Demonstrations, violence and the full force of the law: the two-tier system in action

Personal experience of the 'two-tier system' is, for most respondents, associated with their participation in demonstrations and other EDL activism. Participants in this research described this experience as illustrating a differential treatment of them and 'the opposition' (UAF, MDL). According to Connor, 'The police treat you like you're fucking animals. … The first sign of anything kicking off you get bent. We get battered, while UAF or MDL get the run of the town.' The metaphor used to describe this differential treatment is often that EDL are treated 'like animals' (Richard, Connor, Chris, Tim, Chris) and it is cited as partially responsible for ensuing violence at demonstrations. 'If you treat us like animals we're going to act like animals', says Connor. The failure to control counter-demonstrators is also blamed for encouraging violence and, when violence does occur, respondents say, the police are concerned only with the protection of the opposition.

> I mean we had dogs set on us and things like that. There was, a lot of times as well the police would face us and so ... the missiles were coming over, we were all getting hit. There's people bleeding and then we say like to the police, 'do something about it'. ... You are being penned in and they might as well have put a big target over us. ... [W]e were treated like animals a lot of the time (Tim).

In contrast to the routine use of police dogs to push back the EDL, respondents claimed that the police have a policy of not deploying dogs against counter-demonstrators because it would be offensive to the Muslim community (Richard, Jason).[5]

Alongside many accounts of the experience of police violence, respondents also praise and often empathise with officers policing demonstrations. As one of the most seasoned of demonstrators, Tim had seen both the good and bad in policing: 'I've seen some coppers do some disgusting things ... but seen some police officers who have been great and sometimes right within seconds of each other' (Tim). Police 'liaison' officers were often excellent at moving around the crowd, chatting and reducing tension, treating demonstrators with respect and receiving it in return. It was routine at EDL demonstrations for leaders or Local Organisers to thank the police, sometimes with a round of applause, and stress the importance of acting peacefully (field diary, 12 October, 2013). This is more than a token gesture; during the course of research numerous everyday, respectful, humorous interactions between EDL members and police officers were observed and recorded including the following excerpt from the field diary entry on a flash against a proposed plan to open a Muslim prayer centre:

> While we are standing there a late middle-aged woman comes up and tells the group that she thinks what they are doing is 'despicable' and that they are 'bigots'. Ian and another respondent talk to her and put forward their concerns about 'creeping Islamisation'. The police watch on and afterwards comment that they thought the EDL had handled the situation well and that they are not there to intervene in a peaceful exchange of views. This seems to breed good will between the two sides. (field diary, 18 May 2013)

Given the quite different story that follows about the Walsall demonstration, it is important to acknowledge that animosity and violence are the exception rather than the rule.

On 29 September 2012, an EDL demonstration in Walsall descended into prolonged violence. The events of that day, or more accurately, the arrests, prosecutions and narrativisation of events that followed, illustrate how their experience at demonstrations cements the EDL's sense of being treated 'differently'. It is not entirely clear why a relatively small demonstration should descend into violence. Factors differentiating it from previous or subsequent largely peaceful demonstrations include the fact that demonstrators had not been allowed to march, so a static protest was held and the pubs in the designated area for the demonstration were left open throughout the event. There was also a significantly higher proportion of young people than usual, although observations recorded in the diary suggest that it was not these young people who were in the thick of the violence (field diary, 29 September 2012). Over the course of around 45 minutes, missiles (beer cans, placards, wooden planks, pieces of flag stone and even a drain cover) were thrown from the EDL side of the demonstration towards the police and the counter-demonstrators beyond, while the police, deployed in full riot gear, launched baton attacks and used police dogs to push back the EDL line.[6] A number of casualties – especially head wounds – were sustained by EDL demonstrators (see Figure 3.10), although it was impossible to tell at the time whether these were from missiles thrown or baton attacks. Interviewed after the events Connor was adamant that the violence had ensued not from EDL aggression but police (in)action: a failure, first of all to keep the counter-demonstrators out of the line of vision; and a subsequent overreaction to the EDL response to taunts from behind the police lines.

> The coppers kicked that demo off, not us. It was the Muslims and the police who done that. And the copper specifically let that Muslim who was dressed in Adidas with a bandana around his face, it's a bit obvious what he is there for you know. ... [T]hem coppers day give a shit about him but as soon as we reacted they battered us. We walked out with cuts on our heads. That's like proper police brutality. (Connor)

Euan confirms Connor's claim that it was the counter-demonstrators who had sparked the violence but goes on to argue that the special protection afforded 'them' leads the police to 'wade into us':

> You can see it, you know, that there is a two-tier system going on. It's like up there at Walsall there was a group of about thirty Asians come past and was throwing bottles. That was what started it all off originally. ... There is footage of it and all. The police do absolutely nothing about it. They just turn on us and start hitting us. It's almost like they are not allowed to hit them, you know, but they are allowed to just wade into us. 'We can't hit them so I'm just going to vent my frustration on these white lads here because I'm allowed to do that' and it just don't seem right. (Euan)

It is also true, however, that the police were being bombarded with missiles from a group of people who had congregated outside the Wetherspoon's pub. They started by throwing gravel before proceeding to trash the outside furniture and plant pots and throw large planks of wood and pieces of plant pot at the police. They then began to dismantle the wall, breaking stone flags into smaller pieces by dropping them on the ground before throwing these too (field diary, 29 September 2012). The people in this group were not familiar to me nor those I had attended the demonstration with – many of whom spent much of the time wandering around shaking their heads at the unfolding violence and muttering 'this isn't good' (field diary, 29 September 2012). I noted also in my diary that those throwing missiles were not in EDL colours and Rachel later commented that she had noticed people wearing T-shirts with '13–12' ('All Coppers Are Bastards') on them, which she had not seen before at EDL demonstrations. It is possible that the violence, or at least this element of it, was caused by outsiders or local criminal elements rather than EDL demonstrators.

A total of thirty arrests were made on the day, with subsequent arrests in dawn raids in March 2013. There followed a series of 'group' prosecutions, mainly for 'violent disorder'.[7] One of the respondents in this study, Jack, was charged with this offence and I attended his trial in Crown Court in October 2013. Despite the police having reviewed 300 hours of CCTV and other video footage, there was no clear evidence of Jack (or his co-defendant) having used violence. The video evidence placed him at the police lines when the violence took place but did not capture any direct use or threat of violence. One of two police officers gathering intelligence from within the EDL demonstration, however, stated that Jack had been heard 'inciting' others to violence by calling them down to the police line to 'go get' counter-demonstrators (UAF). Jack was found guilty.

After the verdict, as those in court were preparing to leave but the defendants were still in the dock, the judge, who was responsible for sentencing those prosecuted on this 'collective' charge, asked counsel to clarify which people precisely he would be sentencing. In particular, he asked, referring to the footage shown during the trial of the man in the bandana described by Connor above, if he would also be sentencing the 'Asian man who provoked the EDL from the wall'. He was told by Jack's counsel that this young man 'had already been dealt with in the Magistrates' court'. The judge frowned and said 'I don't think he should have been, it should have been sent to Crown Court.' Outside, Jack asked his barrister to confirm if he had understood correctly; he responded that he had and the young man in question had been sentenced to twelve weeks and would serve six (field diary, 9 October 2013). On 17 December, Jack was sentenced to thirty-six months in prison.

The colours of racism: whiteness as a site of discrimination and victimisation

As discussed in earlier chapters, EDL activists in this study maintain that they 'don't really see what skin colour matters' (Tim) and, in some cases, reject classification as 'white' when asked to state their ethnicity on official forms (Carlie, Declan). 'Colour' or 'whiteness' *is* voiced, however, where it is seen as a site of discrimination or victimisation. This perception of white victimisation results from a failure on the part of respondents to identify as members of a privileged 'majority' and an understanding of themselves rather as a discriminated minority. Power relations are inverted, in their minds, as they confront a 'system' weighted against them by the ability of others to 'play the racist card' (Chris). Non-whiteness, it follows, is transformed into a powerful tool, institutionalised in the law and used against 'us' who are rendered victims of the process.

Claims of discrimination are encountered in the context of the competition for limited resources discussed above. Carlie claims that she has not been able to access social housing because she is white: 'I mean I've been on homes lists for five years and I had to go private in the end because I couldn't get a house off the council. ... I'm the wrong colour, put it that way.' Discrimination is sometimes also perceived in the cultural, or even emotional, sphere. Thus Casey complains that a teacher (who she describes as 'Asian') at her daughter's primary school had demonstratively discriminated against the 'white kids' by giving presents to the Chinese and Asian children 'on their Christmas' but refusing to participate in Christmas events for 'the white kids'.

Ian's account of his struggle to avoid eviction from his house provides a vivid illustration of victimisation narratives framed in resentment towards ethnic 'others' perceived to be (undeservedly) successful and in positions of power in relation to them. In this account, perhaps because of a more deeply rooted shame at his inability to get out of debt and long-term unemployment (see Ray, Smith and Wastell, 2004: 362), Ian turns his anger on an individual housing officer whom he perceives as illegitimately exerting her power over him:

> IAN: My housing officer has decided to put in for eviction for me. ... [S]he's a Muslim ...
> INT: But she's not making the law, I mean she's applying rules that she is given ...
> IAN: Is she? ... I've had her drive up my street, stop, and I caught her walking up to my house looking through my living room window. I went out and says 'What the hell do you think you'm doing?' Her went 'I can come and look in your house any time I want. I can look through your living room window any time I want.' I actually threatened to set the dogs on her if her day jog on ... then the police get a report that I've got a racist poster up in my living room window. ... It had 'no more terrorist training mosques' on. It was a demo poster which has been okayed by the chief of police cause they check all of the posters before you carry 'em ... police turned up, raided my house ... turned round and went 'I can't see nothing racist about the poster but we know you have got a problem with the neighbour-hood officer I will suggest you take it down just to keep yourself from harm'. (Ian)

An eviction notice had been issued nonetheless, he claimed, on the grounds that he had not completed the necessary form regarding a discretionary payment, even though he had hand-delivered it (witnessed by a friend who had accompanied him) and had it stamped and photocopied in the neighbourhood office. This Ian attributes to a deliberate act of racialised victimisation on the part of his housing officer, concluding 'and then people expect me to trust Muslims. Everybody says they want my house, even the police have turned round and said "Wind your neck in, they want your house".'

Such stories are often told in the form of a David and Goliath narrative in which respondents position themselves as the underdog fighting the system, as is illustrated in the conclusion to Ian's story of his eviction struggle:

> He tells me he had been in court again last week over his house. He had been sent another eviction order by [names housing association] even though his total arrears are around £500 only and he has a court agreement about paying them back at £14 per month. He says he had sought legal help and eventually got a court hearing. The magistrate had immediately said that it was a ridiculous sum

to evict for and quashed the order and told him to go back and tell the housing association that they should not be doing this. His solicitor, after the hearing, apparently said to him 'tell me what's really going on' because he had had two calls from [names housing association] prior to the hearing saying they would fight the appeal tooth and nail. According to the solicitor this was the smallest arrears he had ever seen an eviction order over and so he thought something else must be wrong. Ian then told them that he was EDL and the solicitor immediately replied 'And they are all Asians in that office' and then, apparently, congratulated him on winning. (field diary, 3 September 2013)

Narratives of victimhood of course cannot be treated uncritically and, in this case, a different interpretation was encountered in an interview with Kylie (Ian's daughter) who was sceptical about her father's version of events, commenting that her dad had a tendency to 'blame the world for everything'.

It is the judicial system which features most frequently in narratives of victimisation, however. Respondents routinely claim that the law is applied differentially on the basis of the 'skin colour' of the perpetrator and victim.

BRETT: Say I go for a fight, with someone that's from Pakistan, I hit them it's a racial attack. If they batter the hell out of me it's a fight.
NEIL: It's just common assault.
CONNOR: It's wrong. Just because of their skin colour it gets taken different. I mean all I want really is equal rights, cause it ain't equal.

Narratives of white victimisation combine reference to personal experience and 'notorious' cases, which circulate in social media and become celebrated causes. There is frequent reference, for example, to incidents of racist abuse, bullying, violence or murder perpetrated against people who are white, which, it is claimed, are neither reported by the media nor punished appropriately. A small number of respondents complain that they have experienced racist verbal abuse. Tina cites an incident when a group of Asian and 'Afro-Caribbean lads' had shouted 'White slag!' at her while she was waiting at the bus stop while Lisa reports that she has 'been called a stupid black bitch' by 'East European' immigrants. A classic example is provided by Kevin Carroll who, in his speech to demonstrators in Dewsbury in 2012, cited the case of a local man who, while out with his girlfriend, had been beaten up 'by Muslims' and died of his injuries. The perpetrators, he says, were sentenced to just twenty-one months in prison in the case of one and six months suspended with community service in the other (field diary, 30 June 2012). This kind of incident, which respondents perceive as racially motivated but not recognised as such by the judicial system, is referenced thirty times.

These Muslim girls kick the absolute shit out of this white British girl. I mean, even, she's on the floor unconscious and they're kicking the fuck, and they got off with it in court, because they drank and, because of their religion, they wasn't used to alcohol, so they got off with it. No cautions, got off with it. Nothing done, no punishment at all. Now, if that was me and a couple of my mates that went out and beat the shit out of a Muslim girl, I'd be getting 5 years, if not more ... Do you know what I'm saying about two-tier system? (Tina)

The same case is cited by Jack, who, complaining at the acquittal, notes,

If ... five of us would of attacked a Muslim it would have been affray, it would have been a racist attack and we'd have been jailed for it. There is now double standards in this country. If you are a white, ethnic British person and you do something like that you're a racist. (Jack)

However, such accounts do not go unchallenged. When a demonstration is called in June 2013 in Ashton-under-Lyne supposedly in response to the attack by a group of Asians on 'white kids' outside a mosque, Ian expresses his doubt, seeing the incident as 'more of a gang against gang thing and that there had been an earlier altercation and the white kids had deliberately gone to the mosque to provoke. Not surprising they got thumped' (field diary, 16 June 2013).

The most frequently cited example of what is perceived to be 'double stand-ards' is that of the murder in March 2004 of Kriss Donald, a 15 year old from Glasgow, by 'three Asian gang members ... because he was white'.[8] Although, as *The Guardian* report cited here makes clear, in this case the racial motivation of the murder was recognised, the length of the minimum sentences were crit-icised by respondents for being too short (Declan). The real injustice, however, is seen to be the relative lack of attention this murder received, 'Yet Stephen Lawrence even now after ten years later, he gets headlines, headlines, headlines' (Mike).

Issues around unrecognised ethnic bullying are raised routinely. A local inci-dent in which a 9-year-old schoolboy had committed suicide apparently because of bullying at school by 'Asian' pupils is mentioned frequently. Andrew had organised a flash demo outside the school to protest at it:

... the boy was bullied for being white by an ethnic minority and it was in his own country as well and we think that that was very wrong, and also it was wrong how he didn't get much media attention, and how nobody seemed to care. Whereas if that was the other way around then they'd all be demonstrating and protesting. It'd be all over the news. (Andrew)

These incidents, circulated via social media, often spark uncomfortable associations with respondents' own personal experience:

It's like Newcastle MDL they posted a video of a young British lad walking back home from school, the MDL was videoing 'em bullying the British kid. He was just walking home and they was just throwing stuff at him, bullying him, calling him words, and you could tell he day wanna be there. He day know what to do or anything. I felt sorry for him cause I got bullied in school myself and there's young Muslims that go off round here at the moment. They think they own the place pretty much. (Kane)

School is frequently mentioned as a site of the experiencing of discrimination and victimisation. These accounts are often rooted in one's own 'minority' status and an accompanying sense of powerlessness. Brett, for example, explains that his nephew and nieces attend a school which is 'Muslim run' and there are just four white pupils in a school of 500:

> And like they all terrorise my nephew and niece, and when my nephew and niece hit 'em back and they've removed them from the school cause of it. I mean there's a group of lads hitting my little nephew and he hits 'em back and he gets kicked out of school for it. It's wrong. It's like me when I was in [names school] a few years ago, year eight, a Muslim lad smacked me over the head with a chair so I grabbed his head and smashed his head on the table. I got kicked out the school for it, and it was on camera him hitting me over the head with a chair. ... I got kicked out of school for a racial attack. (Brett)

This expression of injustice among white pupils, who claimed that name-calling by black students was ignored while white students were expelled for using racist taunts, was found by Nayak (2003: 146–48) also in schools in the West Midlands and North East of England. A number of other respondents reported being bullied at school by pupils of other ethnic groups (Andrew, Jordan, Nick). Nick says he was 'picked on' by Asian and black kids at school and, when he had reported it to teachers 'they weren't really that interested in it ... they said, "Oh you caused the problems yourself", trying to call me a racist'. Nick continues to explain 'that's why I started to dislike them [the 'non-white' kids]'. Both Nick and Brett (whose story is noted above) were 16 years old at the time of interview and these incidents, in which they perceive themselves to have been labelled racists when they were actually the victims of racist bullying or violence, signal a 'turning point' in their narratives reminiscent of a similar case cited by Garland and Treadwell (2011: 628) of an EDL supporter who had got involved in football firm violence after he had been 'battered by a load of Pakis at college'. Kimmel (2007: 209) also found that all but one of the Scandinavian participants interviewed in his study of former neo-Nazis passing through the EXIT programme had been bullied while other studies of EXIT participants suggested 'bullying was a common unifying theme' among the participants and that those bullied felt they had not received the support they needed to stand up to it (2007: 209). The disregard for their own distress confirms their own sense of devaluation (Skeggs and Loveday, 2012) and is compounded by the feeling that the assumption of the police in Asian–white incidents of violence would always be that any racist motive was to be found in the white party to the conflict (Ray, Smith and Wastell, 2004: 359). Complaining that three EDL organisers had been arrested for posting 'racial tweets' in the run up to the Newcastle demonstration (May 2013), Tommy Robinson notes ironically that he had made the police aware of over 200 death threats he had received against himself and his family but none had been followed up. Nobody, he said, had ever been prosecuted for hatred or violence towards EDL members (field diary, 25 May 2013).

The right to grievance? Resisting second-class status

Less than a week after the Conservative Party won the 2015 UK General Election, Prime Minister David Cameron announced new laws ostensibly designed to strengthen legal options to ban groups, individuals and events that promote hatred and intolerance, making it 'harder for people to promote extremist views'.[9] The UK's 'passively tolerant society', he argued, however, has bred not only the harmful 'narrative of extremism' but also that of '*grievance*'.[10] The right to grievance, it appears, is also under review.

As has been detailed in this chapter, a key motivation for EDL grassroots activists is the articulation of grievance – understood as the hardship and injustice they perceive themselves to experience – through the emotionally charged narrative of 'self' as 'second-class citizens'. EDL activism provides a mechanism for resisting this perceived second-class status through a discursive reordering of privilege and prejudice in which 'we' are seen as the discriminated and those in power are exposed as a liberal elite of 'do-gooders' who have little understanding of the everyday worlds of ordinary people. Activism is a way of saying 'I don't want to be a second-class citizen in my own country' (Connor). People join the EDL 'because they can see like our community is basically being neglected while other communities get, you know, gold-card treatment. So they're angry and they want to do something about it' (Euan). In this final section of the chapter we ask what class is second-class? And whom are EDL activists angry with?

Interviewed on BBC's *Newsnight* programme, Tommy Robinson stated that the EDL is a movement of the *working class* whose voices need to be listened to (BBC *Newsnight*, 8 October 2013).Those who are prepared to 'stand up', Tim suggests, are those who have little to lose: 'the kind of people who are gonna stand up, you know, the working class' (Tim). Theresa makes the same connection between class and EDL activism: 'working-class people are less afraid of saying what they think'. The EDL is experienced as a space for working-class people to 'stand up'; 'you wouldn't see posh Eaton boys become part of the EDL', jokes Chas alluding to the educational background of the current political elite. Indeed, the anger at their perceived second-class status is levelled precisely at politicians who wield huge power, yet 'don't know what it's like to live at this end of the spectrum'.

> In fifteen years' time, my kids ain't gonna have a leg to stand on in this country. … [T]hat same divide will still be there even though the British will be the minority then. They will still be getting nothing, and *they*'ll be getting everything. Do you know what I mean? It's just fairness, and this is why I want to go into politics. Not only because of Muslims obviously, but just because, like, government just cause [there are] so many divides. It's like, they decide on things, they decide on the life of people when they've never walked in the shoes of them people living that life. … They just, they've got no real life experience at all. They don't know what it's like to live at this end of the spectrum. They just don't understand it. (Tina; emphasis in original)

In this context, the struggle becomes a broader one in which the opposing sides are politically as well as economically defined. 'We' are 'just like the common people like the people fighting back you know just saying "look we've had enough"' (Tim) while 'they' (the political class regardless of party affiliation) are 'just do-gooders' who 'act like … everything's for the people when nothing is' (Tina). EDL activism is thus also a form of refusal by a devalued and ridiculed section of the working class to authorise the 'do-gooders' who claim the authority to judge them in distinctively moral ways (see: Skeggs and Loveday, 2012). Notwithstanding the very real and divisive forms of racialised self-understanding and hostility to multiculturalism such resistance can take, it is possible that some such grievances deserve to be heard rather than immediately dismissed as motivated by narrow-minded prejudice (Kenny, 2012: 24–25). Whether one agrees with Kenny or not, the case of the EDL suggests that the outlawing of the expression of 'grievance' can only exacerbate social division and thus fuel rather than tackle extremism.

Conclusion

In this chapter the focus has shifted from unpacking anxieties about the 'other' to a distinctive narrative of self as 'second-class citizens'. It has detailed the everyday encounters respondents interpret as evidence of the privileging of the rights and needs of 'others' – in terms of concrete goods such as social housing, benefits and jobs as well as looser cultural needs for self-expression and respect for tradition – to the direct detriment of their own interests. The anger elicited at the everyday level is reframed in a wider discourse of injustice in which the object of frustration is sometimes a racialised 'other' but primarily political actors, who fail to protect the rights of 'people like us', and a 'two-tier' justice system, which institutionalises this injustice.

It has been argued that this narrative of second-class citizenship reveals the way in which sections of the white working class fail to recognise 'self' as the privileged majority. They perceive themselves rather as the victims of discrimination and in some cases violence or abuse; the anger at this is amplified by the conviction that such discrimination and abuse goes unrecognised by the media, police and political system when the victims are white. 'Whiteness' is invoked here as a site of discrimination where, as we saw in earlier chapters, respondents had been keen to expunge colour from their discourse, denying the significance or pertinence of 'race' and positioning themselves as 'not racist'. It is important therefore that we recognise that even when respondents target anger and 'blame' for their perceived 'second-class' status at government and its agencies rather than immigrant communities, they nonetheless naturalise assumptions of racially based inequality; that 'we' not 'they' should be prioritised is the natural order (Rhodes, 2009).

EDL activism is experienced by respondents in this study as a means of resisting this perceived second-class citizen status. At the discursive level this is accomplished through a reordering of privilege and prejudice and a collective understanding of the EDL as a movement of 'the common people' prepared to 'stand up' and 'fight back' against the government and wider circles of power controlled by liberal elite 'do-gooders' who have little understanding of the everyday worlds they inhabit. Does this mean that movements like the EDL are locked within a politics of resentment, racism and grievance? Or are there grounds to understand arguments made on behalf of white working-class communities as a form of recognition politics (Kenny, 2012: 24)? The question of how we interpret and respond politically to this articulation of grievance is returned to in Chapter 8.

Notes

1 Parts of Burnley rank in the most deprived 1 per cent of boroughs in the country (Rhodes, 2009).
2 Although Ray, Smith and Wastell refer to this as urban folklore, and its formulation bears the hallmarks of such, there is some evidence of the introduction of pilot schemes to improve the employability of those on benefits by providing a package of driving lessons (see www.telegraph.co.uk/news/uknews/1478175/Migrants-to-get-free-driving-lessons.html. Accessed: 30.0.2015). There is no evidence to suggest such schemes were exclusively for migrants and asylum-seekers.
3 This is based on 2011 Census data using the Index of Multiple Deprivation (2010) to determine deprived neighbourhoods based on seven factors: income, employment, health, education, barriers to housing and services, crime, and living environment (Jivraj and Khan, 2013).
4 In fact, the Food Standards Agency estimates that 88 per cent of animals in the UK killed by halal methods are stunned beforehand. See www.theguardian.com/lifeand style/2014/may/08/what-does-halal-method-animal-slaughter-involve.   Accessed: 27.08.2015.
5 For a discussion of the reasons for this see http://guide.muslimsinbritain.org/guide9. html. Accessed: 5.05.2014.
6 Photographs and video footage of events can be found at www.birminghammail.co.uk/ news/local-news/edl-protest-in-walsall-video-more-4925. Accessed: 0.05.2014.
7 'Violent disorder' is point 2 of the Public Order act 1986 and is used in a case when there are three or more people who use or threaten violence that might cause people to fear for their safety.
8 See www.theguardian.com/uk/2006/nov/09/race.ukcrime. Accessed: 05.05.2014.
9 Extremism is defined in the government's Prevent strategy as 'vocal or active opposition to fundamental British values including democracy, the rule of law, individual liberty, mutual respect and tolerance of different faiths and beliefs. In addition, calling for the deaths of members of the armed forces.'
10 See www.bbc.co.uk/news/uk-politics-32714802 (my emphasis). Accessed: 13.05.2015.

7

'One big family': emotion, affect and the meaning of activism

Following discussion of the ideological dimensions of EDL activism (Chapters 4 and 5) and of the particular 'injustice frame' (Jasper, 1998: 398) of 'second-class citizens' underpinning the rationalised meanings attached to EDL activism (Chapter 6), attention turns here to the emotional and affective dimensions of activism. The recent rehabilitation of 'the emotional' in the field of social movement studies has led to a recognition that emotionality does not equate to irrationality (1998: 398) and that the rational and the emotional may be entwined in social movement participation rather than constituting alternative explanations of motivation to engage (Crossley, 2002: 50). Indeed, Jasper (1998: 398) argues many aspects of collective action in social movements that have been viewed as primarily cognitive in fact have emotional dimensions to them.

This chapter starts with a brief discussion of theoretical debates on emotion and affect in relation to social movements and adopts the notion of 'affective practice' (Wetherell, 2012: 4) as a means of understanding and exploring the role of emotion in EDL activism as more than the social expression of feelings that drive or accompany rationalised action. The second section of the chapter considers the principal form of EDL activism – participation in street demonstrations – as one such site of affective practice. Demonstrations, it is suggested, are experienced by respondents as not only a place for achievement of the rational goal of 'getting your message across' but also, emotionally, as 'a good day out'. The associated pleasures of the 'demo buzz' and, for some, of violence or 'disorder' are also discussed. The third section engages with the contention (Virchow, 2007) that, in the case of far right movements, 'collective emotions' are consciously generated at demonstrations and other events to integrate supporters and sustain movements. In this section the forms and means – the use of symbols, colours, chanting and other performative acts – by which the emotional collective is formed within the EDL are considered, in particular whether these emotions are instrumentally orchestrated from above or generated bottom-up. Finally, what Goodwin, Jasper and Polletta (2001: 20) call the 'reciprocal emotions' – rooted in participants' ongoing feelings toward each other and including the close, affective ties of friendship, love, solidarity and loyalty – generated within social movements are discussed. They are articulated in this study in respondents' understanding of the EDL as 'one big family'. These emotions are shown to both arise out of, and enhance, the pleasures of shared activism. They also ameliorate risk and, for some respondents, evoke an onto-logical security missing in their past or wider lives. The emotional sustainability of movements is far from assured (Brown and Pickerill, 2009: 33), however, and these same emotions can work to undermine as well as strengthen groups of activists. The chapter thus concludes with a discussion of the limits of affective ties within the group studied.

Emotions and social movements: from irrational behaviour to affective practice

The original 'collective behaviour' approach to understanding social movements in both its symbolic interactionist form (developed by Blumer) and its later struc-tural functionalist variant (in the work of Smelser) share an understanding of collective behaviour as emotionally driven rather than deliberative and thus as different from normal, 'rational' behaviour (Edwards, 2014: 37). Emotions were considered central to understanding extra-institutional political action; crowds and their dynamics were conceived as the heart of protest movements; and a political 'type' was constructed of an individual alienated, predisposed to violence and seeking, through activism, to compensate needs unfulfilled in private life (Goodwin, Jasper and Polletta, 2001: 2–3). In this way, those involved in social protest were viewed as being motivated less by a particular 'cause' than the need to participate in and of itself (2001: 2–3).

In a conscious attempt to move social movement theory away from viewing activism as the manifestation of protest by the irrational, usually marginal, few, 'resource mobilisation theory' (which emerged in US social movement studies in the 1970s) focused not on 'grievances' and 'beliefs' as the key to the emergence of collective action but the ability to mobilise resources (money, participants, communications infrastructure, skills and public support). Resource mobilisation theorists (drawing on rational action theory) argue that both decisions to join a movement and the ensuing collective action (participants' behaviour in protests) are rational in nature (Edwards, 2014: 44). From the end of the 1960s, emo-tions played almost no role in theories of social movements and collective action (Goodwin, Jasper and Polletta, 2001: 5).

The published literature on social movements and their collective action has shown that the collective behaviour approach was wrong to understand collective action as irrational group behaviour in which the individual is overwhelmed by the emotion associated with the cause and ceases to act rationally. However, empirical research also suggests that it is equally problematic to eradicate emotion from the understanding of the motivations and actions of social movement actors and reduce their collective action to an instrumental activity designed to achieve particular objectives or promote specific interests. The field of social movement studies has been characterised recently, therefore, by what might be said to be the rehabilitation of 'the emotional'. This is not to dismiss rational, political or ideological motivations or to suggest that a social movement can be reduced to no more than 'the sum of its members' personal preoccupations and inadequacies' (Billig, 1978: 8). It is rather to seek to understand how the emotional and the rational are intertwined in collective action. Here it is worth returning to Blumer's understanding of the role of emotions as the glue that holds the acting group together by generating what he calls 'esprit de corps' through: the identification of common enemies, which cements the existence of the group and loyalty to it; the formation of personal relationships within the group; and group rituals such as meetings, rallies, parades and demonstrations that reconfirm commitment to the group (cited in Edwards, 2014: 26–27). While this first and foremost has an emotional outcome – generating a sense of solidarity and feeling among participants of belonging to something bigger than themselves – it is not disconnected from the rational dimension of engagement. This same esprit de corps is identified by Klatch (2004: 491), in her study of affective bonds among members of the Students for a Democratic Society, as initial feelings of 'relief and enthusiasm on discovering others of "like minds", with shared values and perspectives' develop into a deepening sense of attachment to the movement through the affirmation of activists' views of the world.

In studying the role of emotions in contemporary social movements, an important distinction is made by Goodwin, Jasper and Polletta (2001: 20) between the different roles played by 'reciprocal' emotions and 'shared' emotions. Reciprocal emotions concern participants' ongoing feelings towards each other – friendship, love, solidarity and loyalty – and the more specific emotions they give rise to, that are the substance of the affective ties binding the group and that generate much of the pleasure of collective action and protest. In contrast 'shared' emotions are held in common with other group members but are directed externally; these emotions include anger, outrage and so forth. How such emotions are turned into action is elaborated by Collins (Collins, R., 2001) who draws on Durkheim's concepts of collective ritual and 'collective effervescence' to suggest a process by which collective rituals generate 'emotional transformations' through amplifying the original emotion (for example outrage) or transforming the initiating emotion into an 'emotional energy' arising out of consciousness of collective engagement and solidarity. However, emotions do not always produce positive 'affective solidarity' (Juris, 2008: 66) and emotions and relationships can also be destructive to movements (Klatch, 2004: 489).

A further crucial contribution to the debate has been the recognition of the role of 'affect' alongside emotion. The distinctive role of 'affect' is rooted in the differentiation between feeling (as a personal sensation), emotion (as the social display of feelings) and affect (as the pre-personal or non-conscious movement between one experiential state of the body to another) (Massumi, 2004: xvii; Shouse, 2005). While much recent literature on affect has emphasised its non-human dimensions (Thien, 2005: 451), understanding it primarily as the process of 'becoming' as a result of impact and change rooted in the body (Massumi, 2004), for the purposes of this study, the notion of 'affective practice' (Wetherell, 2012: 4) is employed. 'Affective practice' focuses on the emotional as it appears in social life and concrete activities. It asks how people are moved and move others in the context of particular affective performances, scenes and events (2012: 3). Affective practice recognises that affect can be held inter-subjectively across a few or many participants and can thread across a scene, a site or an institution (2012: 13). This is important for this study of EDL activism because it allows a fresh look at the question of collective (or 'crowd') behaviour by asking how affect moves from one body to another. Rejecting notions of transmission as 'contagion' or chemically induced 'entrainment' (2012: 146), it is argued that affect is not generated randomly or universally but is communicated in crowds with shared identity and social practices; this makes actions and affect intelligible to those inside the crowd whilst not being transmitted automatically to onlookers (2012: 148). The notion of affective practice thus also allows for the reconnection of emotion, affect and *meanings* attached to activism at the cognitive level.

A 'good day out': love at first demo

Twenty-eight different forms of activism were mentioned by respondents in this study; from leafleting and writing to MPs to violence and vigilantism. However, narratives are heavily dominated by references to participation in national, regional and 'flash' demonstrations. This reflects the fact that the EDL is a self-consciously 'feet on the street' movement, and while each demonstration has a formal rationale – in line with the official 'awareness raising' mission of the movement – in practice for many participants it means 'a good day out with a load of friends'[1] (Richard). Demonstrations allow people to travel to different parts of the country, making 'connections all over the place' (Tim), and, in this way, forge the substance of solidarity; the feeling of being 'one big family'. Thus in contrast to the frequent scepticism expressed about social media communication (see Chapter 2), the embodied communication with other EDL members that takes place at demonstrations evokes pleasure: 'I love demos, do you know what I mean? You can't beat a good day out' (Connor). Even remembering demonstrations is pleasurable: 'Walsall was a great day. [It] sparked back memories … of all these years gone by' (Chas). Through the evocation of memories, affect is passed from the body past and present as one demonstration becomes pleasurable through memories it triggers of an earlier one.

Chemical reactions? The demo buzz

A 'good day out' starts with the build-up. Posts to Facebook record emotions in the 'countdown' to the day of the demonstration: 'you kind of psych yourself up over the week before and then it comes to demo eve and that's it, nobody can sleep, so yeah it's proper exciting' (Michelle). In practice, 'demo eve' often runs into demo day:

> People go on the drink because it's Friday the night before … it's like an early start, people think, 'Oh, it's 1, 2 o'clock, I'd better get my head down, I've got to

get up for 6'. Then they look, think, 'Oh I'll have one more' and before you know it half of 'em just stop up. (Matt)

Activists in this study generally travelled to national demonstrations together on a hired coach and the journey is an important part of the build-up. This is where you 'get in the mood' (Rachel) and engage in the 'singing' and 'banter' (Tina), story-telling and practical jokes (Tim). Of course the mood is enhanced, for some, synthetically through consumption of alcohol, cannabis and cocaine. Ray's description of the coach on 'a good day out' evokes the noise and atmosphere of a crowd embarked 'on a big mad 'un'; the coach 'literally does bounce down the street like' (Ray).

Notwithstanding this steady build-up of emotions, the demo itself sometimes generates an 'affect' that is experienced in a physically embodied way. While it is almost impossible to capture this adequately in narrative data, there are a number of cues in the stories told that signal these affective moments. The first is the use of the word 'whoa' by respondents to mark the moment when one bodily state is interrupted or taken over by another, more intense, one. Jordan, for example, describes emerging from the train station into the crowd at his first demonstration: 'When we landed into the street I was just like "whoa".' While prior to this he had been emotionally charged – he talked of being 'psyched' about meeting people he had only met online before – this 'whoa' signals the moment when he becomes physically overwhelmed by the presence of others. On reflection, when he has processed the affect into a feeling that he can articulate, he says the demo experience 'was the best thing … I've ever done'. In the following excerpt, Theresa also indicates a change of bodily state she experiences with the same 'whoa' as she describes the sensation of 'all marching together' at a demonstration in Tower Hamlets:

> Well, there was like nearly 3,000 people that did turn up for the demo. The police didn't know what to do with us, so … they walked us for four miles. We got taken over Tower Bridge all marching together on this lovely hot day and like, the Japanese tourists and everything and all the boats waving to us and we were like, 'whoa!' just singing England songs. It was like St George, 'English until I Die' and all of that. It was a fantastic demo. (Theresa)

A second cue indicates being taken over by a physical sensation, often described in similar ways to the effect of drugs or alcohol, as a 'buzz', 'adrenaline rush' (Nick) or being 'wired' (Richard). This sensation of being overtaken by chemical agents lends itself to understanding through theories of affect that view emotions as transmitted from one body to another by chemical reactions, or 'entrainment', as a result of the effect of pheromones[2] (Brennan cited in Wetherell, 2012: 146). Thus Richard describes being nervous when he attended his first demonstration but then experiencing 'an adrenaline buzz, which I liked because you don't know what's going to happen'. Wetherell is sceptical, however, of the evidence that pheromones and chemical signals are the missing mediating link in affective contagion since it explains neither why some bodies are entrained while others resist or why one emotion, for example anger, evokes anger in some while evoking other emotions, such as anxiety, laughter, indifference or sadness, in others (2012: 146). Moreover, actors themselves experience the 'buzz' as an emotional response to concrete, not mysterious or unseen chemical, stimuli. This is evident in Tim's description of the moment of stepping off the coach and being overwhelmed visually (by 'a sea of England flags') and audibly (by the 'roar' of the crowd) when he arrived at his first demo in Stoke (2010):

> ... you could just see a sea of England flags, there was all different kinds, of like mixed races and whatever, there and it was just, I stepped off ... this bus, and every bus that turned up got a roar and ... I was just like, 'yes, finally!' It just felt like ... people of England was finally standing up, saying like we've had enough of this bullshit that's been pushed on us all the time and it's just like right we are standing up. (Tim)

While Tim's experience is strongly embodied, it remains associated with the meaning he attaches to his activism; the sensations made him feel 'like the people of England was finally standing up'. Rachel too becomes animated as she describes the sensation of feeling part of a mass of bodies at a large demonstration in Luton:

> It was massive. It is unbelievable. It was hundreds and hundreds. Police always say something like there was 300. There wasn't three *hundred*. There was three *thousand*. Do you know what I mean? But the police always say there was three *hundred*. I mean if you've got somebody standing up the road like with the camera and you can see bodies for as far as the eye can see that's not 300 people. (Rachel; emphases in original)

As Malbon (1999: 22, 185–87) has shown from the study of clubbing crowds, however, while participants in such gatherings may take deep pleasure in ceding their body to the crowd and atmosphere, in fact what is experienced is a fluctuation between belonging to the crowd and 'differentiation' from it, between 'losing oneself' and having a heightened awareness of self. In this way, the pleasure of collective immersion does not replace but embodies, sensitises and enhances rationalised meanings of activism. This is reflected in the feeling among respondents that 'A good demo is when you get there and you get a turn-out' (Ray, Chris), while demos where '20, 30 people turn up' are 'a total waste of time. ... [Y]ou want thousands to turn up and make yourselves heard' (Rob).

The pleasure of disorder?

> I ain't even going to lie about it. That is part of the demo buzz. It makes it more violent. Makes you more proud of what you're there for. (Ray)

The 'buzz' of demonstrations discussed above cannot be detached from the thrill of the potential for, and actuality of, aggro with the opposition and even violence. The thrill of the eruption of violence between EDL and MDL or UAF counter-demonstrators at a demo is described by Tim as 'just like Braveheart', while Connor talks of the 'adrenaline rush' of 'having a good scrap'.

Reference to violence as 'having a kick off' (Ray, Connor) or 'having it off' (Chris) is indicative of the links between this kind of fighting and football hooliganism. Peter and Kyle, who identified primarily as Casuals, describe the 'excitement' of the moment before violence kicks off at a football match and how 'that adrenaline lasts for days' (Peter). Although they attended EDL events, this was primarily motivated by the search for a similar pleasure in 'a bit of disorder' (Kyle): 'I wouldn't say I have an interest about the EDL, well … only in the violence like' (Peter). This pleasure in violence ('disorder') is what Peter and Kyle think motivates EDL activists, too: 'I think the EDL are just banned football hooligans, lads that aren't allowed to go to football, what else are they looking for to do on a Saturday, they go there for their disorder, don't they?' (Peter). This trajectory is not uncommon and is discussed in Chapter 3.

However, the pleasure in 'disorder' or 'chaos' is not confined to those with a football background:

> Best thing I've ever been to erm wow Stoke was just chaotic. It was wild. There was fireworks, there was smoke grenades going off. You were just coming through clouds, you just got caught, horses running charging at ya. There's riot vans getting knocked over and that was chaotic. (Tim)

Some respondents thus associate violence and trouble at demonstrations not with football hooliganism but with life-stage; being young. These respondents attribute their own earlier participation in violence to their youth (Jordan, Tim, Matt). As Sean puts it, 'Maybe a few years ago, if I'm honest, … I would have got in with the ruck, but no. From some of my friends dying in the war and what not my views have changed on it. I just wanna go along, peaceful demo, get your word heard' (Sean). Connor admits, 'if you say it is definitely going to go off, you know a hundred percent there is going to be more youths there. Cause … youths are going there for a fight. Know what I mean?' (Connor). At the same time, his brother Ray confirms that the EDL's reorientation away from its Casuals roots and violence had led many younger members to leave the movement:

> Most youth – them are out for violence … Whereas you come to the EDL, you aren't getting no violence. You get the odd one but apart from that, you ain't getting no violence. You're there to do your peaceful protesting and things like that. But if you go to a football match, you've got 50 times more chance of having a kick-off and having a bit of violence, like. (Ray)

There is active discussion and disagreement within the EDL on the efficacy and acceptability of the use of violence. The efforts of the leadership to rid the movement of the 'thuggish' element and improve the public perception of it have been decisive in the decisions to leave of many of what Jack refers to as the 'hard-core' that 'look for the violent side of it'. For those that choose to stay the attraction of the EDL is that it offers more meaning than football violence. Jordan says he used to be in a local football firm and thus 'I've been there done that and it gets you nowhere to be honest. You don't get your point across.' Tim, talking about an early demonstration at which there had been significant violence, describes this process as the struggle between the emotional and rational dimensions of activism:

> All hell broke loose and I mean like we'd already had a few beers and that and it just got outta hand, and the thing is the police didn't anticipate that many people. … [I]t was almost like the first raw emotion. … [W]hen a fight breaks out, at first you can go crazy but then … after a while the energy starts to, you know, you've released that anger so you calm down and then you have to start thinking about the real … ways. (Tim)

For Tim, it seems, violence or fighting is an affective practice – raw emotion or energy release – that *precedes* the rationalisation of activism. Others, however, find rationality *in* violence in as much as it is the most effective way of gaining publicity for the movement:

> Like if you stood there in the town chanting 'E, EDL' you ain't making nothing. You know as soon as you chuck something bang you am on worldwide news man, for rioting. … I think it promotes our event. It says that we have been out there and we are proving our point, that we aye gonna bow down to the police. (Connor)

This reflects what Juris (2008: 63) sees as a trade-off that social movements have to make between 'scripted' and peaceful demonstrations, which may win sympathy from the media but feel mundane to protestors and 'generate diminishing returns with respect to visibility and affective solidarity', and more spectacular, confrontational free-form actions, which are 'particularly potent in emotional terms' but 'often contribute to media frames that stigmatize or belittle protesters'.

This is not only a question of tactics. At the grassroots level pleasure in violence was rejected as a matter of principle by some. Ollie says, 'I've never had a proper violent fight' and when trouble kicks off, 'I don't get adrenaline at all, sometimes I get really angry by it'. For others the movement's continued association with violence is a source of deep frustration: 'You do get the odd few that kick off but you know, that spoils it for the rest of us like' (Jason). In these cases, meanings attached to EDL activism are quite different. Kane states, 'I dow like getting involved with the fighting and that cause we ain't there to fight. We ain't there for violence. I'm just there to show my respect and that.' Indeed, even for those described as enjoying a 'kick off', violence was not necessary for 'a good demo'.

> CHRIS: A good demo is when it all goes peaceful and you get your point across. That's what you're meant to be there for.
> CONNOR: You can be loud and proud at the same time and it comes under peaceful.

At the same time those who are reluctant to engage in fighting the opposition directly may have the most tolerant attitude to extreme violence. In the same breath Andrew says he would not attack members of the opposition unless in self-defence yet condones Anders Breivik's mass murder on the grounds that 'He didn't cause them any pain … he didn't stop them and shout abuse at them or torture them or whatever, he just shot them' (Andrew).

In understanding these debates around violence, it is important to distinguish between violence and 'aggro' or 'banter'. Pre-planned violence was not encountered in the course of fieldwork. The only exception was a planned flash demo that, it was said, would involve tables (on which Islamic literature was displayed) being overturned in the city centre. This led some core respondents to refuse to take part and the action in fact never took place (field diary, 1 December 2012). Fighting was also unplanned and is recounted as being responsive or opportunistic: 'every demo I've been to, … it's never been us who's kicked off. It's always been someone confronting us for us to kick-off' (Connor). Notwithstanding this, Connor adds, 'if you get confronted then obviously you prove your point, you aye gonna run off you know. You stand there and you be heard for who you am.' Moreover, what counts as 'confrontation' varies and can include taunts, chants, bottle- or egg-throwing by counter-demonstrators. 'Banter' with counter-demonstrators is routine and ritualised and jibes about the opposition as 'the great unwashed' or suggestions that 'we all want a go at them' are delivered occasionally by speakers from the podium (field diary, 10 May 2014). Organised violence, however, is replaced by routinised scuffles which occur at easily identifiable trigger points. Corners along the route of a demonstration are one such point; as this is where the opposition often comes into view and the 'banter' starts. The police push forward at these points to keep order, fuelling antagonism and a sense that EDL demonstrators are being unfairly treated. These incidents are characterised by rumours and multiple interpretations, even amongst demonstrators themselves (field diary, 13 September 2014). Whatever the 'truth' is, observation at more than twenty demonstrations suggests the most peaceful marches are those where the opposition is kept consistently out of the line of vision.

The fine legal line between banter and violence was brought home to EDL demonstrators prosecuted following the Walsall demonstration. At the trial of two of them, one of the police officers giving evidence noted that prior to the violence, the mood had been 'good-natured', although there had been a two-way exchange of 'banter' or 'obscenities' between EDL demonstrators and people behind the police line. The EDL, he said, had chanted 'E, E, EDL' and 'Muslim bombers, off our streets'. Counter-demonstrators had used similar ripostes to the EDL. Jack (one of the defendants), he said, had encouraged others to move towards the police line, saying, 'UAF are down there, let's go and get them.' The mood became more agitated, the police officer says, and when a counter-protestor jumped up onto the wall and gave a 'Come on' motion to EDL supporters, the latter surged towards the police line and a violent confrontation between police and EDL demonstrators ensued (see Chapter 6). The prosecution's case against Jack and his co-defendant was not built on evidence that they had committed any violence themselves but that their participation in the chanting among the front lines of the EDL supporters and, in particular, Jack's alleged encouragement of others to move up to the police line constituted incitement to violence. While both defendants freely admitted that they had been stupid to choose to go to where the trouble was and join in the chanting rather than stay listening to the speeches, for both the notion that 'banter' was incitement to violence was completely alien. As the second defendant noted 'there is "no malice in banter"; it is just tit for tat'. When the prosecutor insists that the purpose of banter is to encourage violence, he responds, 'No, it's banter', and that they expect only that the opposing groups shout back (field diary, 7 October 2013). Jack's understanding of a good demonstration as having a bit of a laugh and 'a shout at the opposition', as he put it, ended in a thirty-six-month prison sentence.

The management of emotions and the creation of affective solidarity

The build-up to, experience of and stories told about demonstrations create a sense of 'togetherness' that binds members of the movement. It is these affective bonds that are central to sustaining activism and they are saturated with emotion. Virchow (2007: 148) argues that the creation of 'emotional collectives' and 'collective emotions' is an objective of these events as 'leaders of far right organisations carefully plan these emotions to integrate sympathisers'. That emotion is not 'an incidental aspect of activism' but 'strategically deployed and fostered by organisers to engender sufficient commitment amongst activist collectives to maintain their on-going participation' is recognised by Juris (2008: 65) too. This is achieved, he argues, by building affective attachments (to the cause, and among activists) and creating particular emotional moods during protests. In this section the forms and means – the use of symbols, colours, chanting and other performative acts – by which the emotional collective is formed within the EDL are considered. It is argued that, while much might be read into the symbols deployed in EDL communications and demonstrations, understanding signs, in this case, is not the key to understanding activism; action is not a public display of representation of identity but an embodied practice (see also McDonald, 2006: 196). It is suggested also that, in contrast to Virchow's findings, these emotions are largely generated bottom-up rather than instrumentally orchestrated from above. Indeed, for former EDL Chair Steve Eddowes the 'raw emotion' he sees among some supporters is a constraint rather than an asset, since it inhibits their capacity for rational engagement ('they won't grasp what you're saying to them') (Eddowes, 2015).

Symbolic markers: style and tattoos

Busher (2012: 420) draws on the notion of 'civil religion' to understand the use by EDL organisers and supporters of rituals and symbols of national and Western 'civilisational' belonging – articulated and performed during demonstrations, meetings, online discussions and other activities – to evoke a sense of a clash of civilisations between a Christian Europe and an Islamic Middle East. This is epitomised for Busher in the adoption of symbols and nomenclature of the crusades, such as the cross of St George, the motto *in hoc signo vinces* (associated both with the adoption of Christianity by Emperor Constantine I and with the order of the Knights Templar), and images of medieval crusades and crusaders in the formal and informal promotional materials that circulate among activists and their supporters.

Such symbols and references were encountered in this study but primarily at national demonstrations and sported by demonstrators who were not respondents. A Knights Templar battle flag – a black cross on white background with red St George's cross in the centre – was encountered at the Rotherham demo in 2014 (field diary, 13 September 2014). At Tower Hamlets a demonstrator had used the EDL hoody design on the back of a crusader-style cloak and personalised his division name to 'Crusaders' (see Figure 7.1) while a participant at a local demonstration in Leeds had a tattoo featuring a cross and sword with the motto 'English by the Grace of God' displayed that covered his back.

The one exception among respondents in this study was Ed, who also said that, when having a tattoo himself, he would prefer 'a Crusader leaning on his sword ... or an England tattoo, bulldog, Knights Templar' rather than, for example, 'EDL', since the longevity of organisations could not be guaranteed. Indeed there was also significant scepticism about some symbolism; on a number of occasions respondents quipped that only the English would have a patron saint who was actually 'a Turkish Muslim who never came to England' (field diary, 21 April 2013).

However, in general, in this study it was national belonging and EDL affiliation that dominated symbolic displays. Rachel had a large tattoo indicating her 'Angel' status on her calf (see Figure 7.2) and always wore shorts to demonstrations so it was visible. She was frequently complimented on it and often passed the number of the tattooist to other demonstrators, making it a sign literally passed from one body to another (field diary, 30 June 2012). Less permanent visual symbols included Lisa's St George's cross contact lenses (see Figure 3.8).

Symbolic performance on demonstration days centres around the display of EDL flags. These are hung across the windows of the coach on the way to demonstrations to provoke reaction from passing cars. Positive responses – beeping of horns or thumbs-up signs – are celebrated with cheers and chants of 'E, E, EDL', while negative responses are met with jeering and abusive gestures. While demonstrations themselves were experienced as a 'sea of England flags' (see above), in fact a range of flags were encountered on demonstrations. The Union Jack was often displayed or wrapped around demonstrators as they marched. The well-known Muslim Scottish Defence League member Abdul Rafiq (see Chapter 4) demonstrated in Walthamstow draped in a Union Jack and with a Rangers bag over his shoulder while Chas, a respondent in this study, sported a Union Jack onesie to the Norwich demo (see Figure 7.3). This speaks to a strong Unionist agenda (alongside the promotion of a specific 'Englishness'), which is evident also in the slogan 'No surrender' chosen for Louise's tattoo (see Figure 7.2) and

7.1 Crusaders?

featuring frequently on EDL hoodies and in chants (see below). Matt and Casey's house was adorned with both a St George's flag and a Union Jack doormat. At demonstrations the Israeli flag was often seen (field diary, 20 July 2013) as well as the LGBT flag (see Figure 3.2). Bandanas, neck scarves and face masks to cover the nose and mouth were also sported in both St George's flag and Union Jack colours (field diary, 29 September 2012).

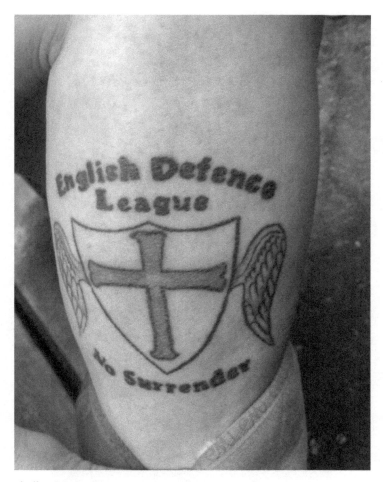

7.2 Rachel's EDL tattoo

Performative dress was the exception rather than the rule at demonstrations, however, and most EDL members cared little about style, declaring that they just 'dress normal' (Tina).

> To tell the truth, I don't give a fuck what I wear as long as I'm there. Someone can look at me and say I'm UAF. ... At the end of the day, I wear what I want to wear. I can be trackied up. Little fucking chavvy look ... I don't care. I'll wear what I wanna wear. (Chris)

7.3 Chas in his Union Jack onesie

The only exceptions to this rule were those with primary identifications or ongoing links with local football firms. Peter and Kyle discussed style at length as well rituals of buying new clothes and deciding what to wear as part of the build-up to a match. Ray and his brother Connor also referred to themselves as having a 'Casuals' or 'hooligan' look, including iconic brands such as Stone Island and Sergio Tacchini as their preferred style.

On demo days, most respondents wore 'colours', usually an EDL hoody, exchanged for a polo shirt in the summer. Political colours are known to play an important role in the emotional life of social movements, helping to create and sustain collective identities (Sawer, 2007: 39). The EDL standard was a black hoody (a pink one was also available) with a red cross on the back, which created four squares into which text or symbols could be added. This allowed individuals to personalise the garment. Most added the words 'English Defence League' and their divisional belonging. Some were more ambitious and cited postcodes (indicating symbolic turf wars between rival divisions), nicknames for divisions ('Anti-social division') or EDL logos and chants ('No surrender') (see Figure 7.4).

In the case of the EDL the significance of 'colours' is more akin to the meaning attached to football colours than political colours, however. Wearing colours demonstrates pride in your 'side' and the importance of 'being seen for who you are', while the semiotic significance of the colour is ambiguous. Black has a long tradition in both anarchist and fascist movements and is more recently associated with autonomist movements, again of both left and right (Sawyer, 2007: 42). In this sense the colour draws something from its association with the 'street' identity of such movements. However, at the grassroots level, meaning is more likely to be attached to the hoody (in particular its hood) than its colour. As indicated in Chris's statement above, wearing a hoody signals the appropriation of 'chav' style as a reassertion of class status (see Chapter 6), while raising the hood can help disguise appearance and mark an act of defiance against police

7.4 Being seen for who you are: personalised hoodies

7.5 Performance in protest

and other authorities. Thus, some respondents wore their hoodies around town to show they would not be intimidated and to indicate their pride: 'I'm proud to wear this hoody cause … it's just who I am … I'll wear it and I'll feel proud to wear it because every little bit of stitching is who I am' (Declan). Others chose not to wear colours even at demonstrations because of the potential risk to safety this entailed moving around the city before joining the coach or demonstration (Tina). Those who adopted this approach said they were never made to feel excluded because of this (Richard).

Performative acts at EDL demonstrations are limited in comparison to those found at larger anti-globalisation or anti-austerity demonstrations. Most frequent was the use of face masks, especially pig masks but also those representing hate figures such as Osama Bin Laden (see Figure 7.5). This performativity and embodiment of protest can serve to sustain emotional experiences for activists (Brown and Pickerill, 2009: 28). However, it is not always successful. An attempt to deliver a speech from the podium in a white EDL-logoed 'burqa' descended into farce as the speaker was unable to see her written speech through the headdress, which also made it difficult for her to be heard (field diary, 29 September 2012).

There is sometimes a fine line between performativity and symbolic violence. In general EDL members denied their engagement in actions such as the violation of mosques and at demonstrations grand acts of symbolic violence (such as burning the Qur'an) are avoided by official speakers – not least because of the beliefs about 'two-tier justice'. However, 'desires' to violate the Qur'an (to burn or use it as toilet paper) are expressed and badges sold at demonstrations are often intended to offend; for example badges with images of pigs alongside the words 'EDL infidels' (field diary, 30 June 2012). At a local demonstration attended in a district of Leeds, one demonstrator marched wearing a pig mask while, later, as the speeches came to an end, a whole pig's head was retrieved from a bag and thrown towards the police line (see Figure 7.6) (field diary, 4 May 2013).

Indeed such performative displays could arouse criticism within the movement. Ed expressed his disdain for those with highly provocative tattoos such as 'Allah's a paedo'. Commenting on a particular individual who had had such a tattoo done, he notes, 'God forbid he never gets sent to prison cause he ain't gonna fucking come out. When he's in the shower, and then people see that, he's dead.' Awareness of the potential danger of sporting EDL-related tattoos was noted by others (Richard, Kane). One respondent, nonetheless, during the course of fieldwork, had 'Infidel' in Arabic tattooed on the back of his head (field diary, 7 September 2013).

'We're coming': creating an emotional collective

While much discussion in extreme right studies is concerned with the role music has in disseminating ideology and attracting people, especially young people, into extreme right movements (Langebach and Raabe, 2013) the extreme right music scene in general was barely referenced by respondents in this study. Ian posted YouTube clips of the Swedish singer Saga (known to many for her Skrewdriver tributes) to his Facebook page, but when challenged about this (since he rejected white supremacism), he claimed to like the songs but not the ideas behind them (field diary, 18 May 2013). Other respondents dismissed what they called such

7.6 Symbolic violence in protest

'Nazi music' (Lisa) and expressed preferences for punk or ska music. Rachel attended a local punk music festival annually while Kurt talked excitedly about a ticket he had to a Specials gig in a nearby town. The role music plays in the EDL is thus less about recruitment to an ideology than about creating an atmosphere, self-affirmation and community-building. When the EDL set up a 'camp' outside the police station in Rotherham to protest at institutional inaction against child grooming in the town, one of the tents was named the 'EDL community singing tent' (field diary, 13 September 2014).

In contrast to performative dress and actions, chanting and singing are well-developed affective practices among the EDL, taking place: on the coach and at the muster point in the build-up to a demonstration; as demonstrators march; and as the whole crowd gathers at the main demonstration point prior to the speeches. The most frequently heard recorded music is the band Alex and the Bandits, many of whose songs consciously reference the EDL. Some of the lyrics carry ideological content. 'We Must Resist', for example, picks up on the discourse of injustice discussed in the previous chapter, claiming the EDL are 'the only people to defend your rights'. However, more commonly heard and enjoyed songs are those that simply reference and affirm the movement itself. 'Famous EDL', for example, contains the refrain 'Tommy Robinson's barmy army' and was frequently played through the sound system prior to the beginning of speeches (before Robinson's resignation). Probably most frequently heard, however, is 'We're Coming' which declares, 'We're the infidels of the EDL and we're coming down the road'. Whether sung along to when played from the sound system (video clip, Walsall demo, 29 September 2012) or unaccompanied as demonstrators set off through the streets (video clip, Dewsbury demo, 30 June 2012), there is an embodied pleasure in losing oneself in collective motion or song even when amongst strangers (Goodwin, Jasper and Polletta, 2001: 20). Indeed, in the process these 'strangers' cease to be so and singing becomes an embodied way to both create and confirm the emotional collective.

'We're Coming' carries not only emotion but meaning. It declares presence and intent and signals what is perhaps the most important meaning attached to EDL activism: being seen and being heard (see Chapter 8). This is echoed in other chants that assert the rights of demonstrators to make their presence felt, for example, 'Whose streets? Our streets' (video clip, Dewsbury demo, 30 June 2012). The connection between chanting and the core meanings of EDL activism is captured by Connor:

> That's why you travel together. Because you've got to get your point across. On the way there, we'd stop at services and chant like … Well, we give a chant and make it loud and proud of who we am. (Connor)

A visual performance of the assertion of this right is also sometimes staged, for example through the physical occupation of space. At the Birmingham national demonstration, demonstrators climbed onto the roof of the bar designated as the muster point, members of one division scaled the statue outside the Registry office (see cover photo) while those from another found their way onto the top of a bus shelter (field diary, 20 July 2013).

The form and content of chants and songs at EDL demonstrations also show this combination of functions of building and sustaining the emotional collective and expressing the shared values and beliefs of the group. Such songs and chants fall into three main types: anti-Islam, 'patriotic', and identity-affirming. The first two types clearly prioritise ideology over collective identity in terms of their content. However, their context of use and their form – often sung to the same tunes and rhythms of the football terraces – mean they function to create atmosphere prior to a demonstration or to rally support and speak with one voice in the face of 'opposition'.

Anti-Islam chants and songs may take the form of extended songs, often sung in the pub or at the muster point prior to the demonstration. Classic examples of such songs include, 'There were ten Muslim bombers in the air' (see Chapter 5). A variation of the song heard at a local demonstration in Leeds, and referring to the failed attempt to attack the EDL demonstration in Dewsbury, began with 'There were six Muslim bombers at Dewsbury' who, instead of being shot down by the RAF from England, 'saw the EDL and fucked off home' (field diary, 4 May 2013). There are also shorter and more aggressive anti-Islam chants, which are struck up particularly when counter-demonstrators come into vision, for example 'Allah, Allah, Who the fuck is Allah?' and are consciously offensive to all Muslims. This is true also of the particularly controversial chant 'Allah is a paedo' or 'Muzzie bombers off our streets'. This kind of chanting is a ritual of collective action which confirms common commitments among protestors, stirs up strong emotions and reinforces a sense of solidarity with the group (Jasper, 1998: 417). As an affective practice, however, this is not emotionally transformative but rather reinforces anger or outrage and, most importantly, offends and insults others.

The category of 'patriotic songs' includes renditions of the national anthem and of 'Keep St George in My Heart, Keep Me English' (sung to the tune of the hymn 'Give Me Joy in My Heart'). Other chants shout defiance in the face of aggressors: 'No surrender, no surrender, no surrender to the Taliban. Scum! Scum! Scum!' The latter can be chanted independently or at the end of a rendition of 'Keep St George in My Heart, Keep Me English' and has its history on the football terraces where it was chanted as 'no surrender to the IRA'. This confirms the Unionist hue to much EDL symbolism despite the apparent assertion of Englishness. As discussed in Chapter 5, chants such as 'Burn our poppies and we'll burn your mosques' are claimed to contain rhetorical rather than real threats (Tina).

One of the first changes introduced by the new collective leadership following the resignation of Tommy Robinson and Kevin Carroll, was non-tolerance of anti-Muslim chants. This was announced by Ivan Humble (East Anglia Regional Organiser) speaking at the Bradford demonstration shortly after the leadership resignations. He stated, 'there will be no 'Allah' songs sung at demonstrations any more – we don't need them. We have plenty of English songs to sing' (field diary, 12 October 2013). Indeed, the speeches themselves at this demonstration were interspersed with chants and songs – 'E, E, EDL', 'We're Coming, We're Coming …' and 'Keep St George in My Heart' – led from the stage in a way not previously encountered at demonstrations. This appeared to signal a strategy to encourage unity and a sense of collective spirit at a difficult time for the movement and is, perhaps, a relatively benign example of the attempt to create and manage 'collective emotions' (Virchow, 2007: 148).

The last category – identity-affirming chants – includes the frequently heard 'E, E, EDL', which is chanted on the move during a march but also often erupts at the end of longer songs or chants as a kind of signature or 'tag'. These chants are low and aggressive in tone, designed, just as on the football terraces, to signal strength and numbers and to intimidate the opposition. EDL demonstrators also borrow football chants with which to taunt the opposition such as 'Who are you?' And, if the counter-demonstration looks small, the chant 'We're your famous EDL' is often complemented by the taunt, 'Where's your famous, where's your famous, where's your famous MDL?' Alternatively, if counter-demonstrators are heard booing or seen making gestures to marching protestors, the call of 'You're not English, You're not English, You're not English any more' may be heard. Performative demonstrations of this include pogo-ing to a rendition of 'If you canna do the bouncy[3] … You're not English any more' (video clip, Dewsbury demo, 30 June 2012).

While these chants and songs are certainly identity-affirming, they are far from instrumentally orchestrated by the movement leadership. At the Tower Hamlets demonstration there was a steady flow of jibes and banter between demonstrators and counter-demonstrators lining the streets through which the march passed including counter-demonstrators greeting EDL marchers with monkey noises. At one place, from within the midst of such a group of counter-demonstrators, an EDL supporter emerged and unfurled his flag; a cheer from the EDL march went up amidst chants of 'Who are you?' and, answering their own rhetorical question with, 'You're not English anymore' (field diary, 7 September 2013). For grassroots activists, these moments epitomise 'a good day out'.

'It's like one big family': reciprocal emotions

The emotions discussed so far have been those engendered by shared feelings, which take on particularly affective forms through activism. However, social movements are characterised also by 'reciprocal emotions', that is, emotions generated by the feelings participants have towards each other (Jasper, 1998: 417). The two, of course, are connected. The unpredictability, confrontation and imminent danger of mass direct actions produce 'powerful affective ties' between participants 'amplifying an initiating emotion, such as anger or rage, and transferring it into a sense of collective solidarity' (Juris, 2008: 63). Emotions in this sense are the glue that holds the group together (Blumer, cited in Edwards, 2014: 27). However, as this study of the EDL shows, while moments of confrontation or risk produce particularly memorable days and bonding moments, more routine or mundane 'togetherness' experienced on 'a good day out' also generates affective bonds. Indeed these affective bonds are cited more frequently than anything else when respondents talk about what it means to be active in the EDL. Two related but distinct kinds of bonds were referenced: friendship and loyalty; and the sense of belonging and family. While the former are quite closely linked to the 'style' of the group (that is their rituals and behaviour in the course of actions) and reflect the values of the group in an almost homological way (Clarke, 1993: 179), the latter are underpinned by a more diffuse affective solidarity based in feelings of care and concern.

Friendship, loyalty and standing together

Friendship, loyalty and standing up for one another are the most frequently cited meanings attached to activism. This is reflected in the repeated claim that EDL members look after each other. Reflecting on the experience of attending his first demonstration, Jordan remembers 'everyone made me so friendly, everyone made me so welcome … I was just like, do you know what, I felt safe. I felt safe there … I lost someone a few times and they'd ring me and they wouldn't let me go on my own and I thought that was really nice.' Kurt played an important role in creating this sense of security. His divisional flag was hoisted on a fishing rod, making it invariably the tallest flag at a demonstration (see Figure 3.11) and guiding demonstrators to a safe place during or at the end of the demonstration (field diary, 29 September 2012).

This ethos is demonstrated primarily in practices of sticking together at demonstrations: 'Well, when you are going out as a division, you stay together so no one gets separated just to watch each other's backs' (Chris). This is not meant metaphorically but in a literal, embodied, sense: 'we all stand together. We come as like a big army, we leave as an army' (Matt). However, watching each other's backs can take place in the virtual as well as the real world. At the end of a long discussion of 'trolls' and how to recognise their approaches via social media, members of the local youth division conclude that they have never been seriously infiltrated or exposed because 'We're too close and we watch each other too much. … We just have to keep an eye on one another' (Chris).

The strength of such interpersonal relationships is vital for sustaining activism and energy (Brown and Pickerill, 2009: 32) and has often kept people in the EDL. Responding to a question about whether he might 'burn out' or give up EDL activism, a Divisional Organiser explained that he had thought about it but it was hard to contemplate leaving, 'Because you've made friends, some real good friends, you know. People who you'd genuinely miss' (Euan). Thus even if 'you always get the prats' (Matt) in the movement, activists felt that beneath that 'there's a solid like loyalty to it' (Tim). Kane compares his earlier 'mates', who had let him down badly at a time of need, with EDL friends who 'keep me out of trouble':

> These are my real mates. I class these as family now. The EDL are my family. …
> My mates what I knew before the EDL they ran off and left me. But the EDL they
> stay by each other's side. I class them more as family than mates now. First I
> classed them as friends, then besties, now family. (Kane)

The loyalty and care that comes with this friendship, for Kane, makes his EDL friends are no longer only 'mates' but 'family'.

Family and belonging

EDL activists in this study spontaneously refer to the EDL as their 'family' or extended family. Lisa, after attending her first demo, describes the feeling as 'It's like a family, you are all there for the same reason aren't you at the end of the day'. This is something, as Connor identifies, that cannot be captured in the media:

> Like when you am at a demo the media only show like the actual demo. They dow show like what goes on behind the scenes like the meetings. Like when you meet up at the coach park it's like *one big family*. Everyone is there for each other and that's how it should be to be honest. (Connor; my emphasis)

Matt also says that now the connection with Casuals has receded, family and friends have become more involved: 'I think a lot of the football thing is gone out of it now, it's more, it's like a big family' (Matt).

A crucial role performed by the family is providing a sense of where you belong and caring in times of need. Demo days for Jack bring pleasure because 'it's a great atmosphere, it's a great feeling to belong'. Declan and his partner at the time, Ryan, are treated almost as adopted sons by local EDL organisers in a neighbouring town where they spent a lot of their time after Declan had been made to feel unwelcome by members of his own EDL division (field diary, 23 March 2013). Simply caring for one another is an important aspect of the politics of affect (Brown and Pickerill, 2009: 33) and this caring atmosphere can bring respite to difficult and troubled lives. Kurt, who had been suffering from depression during a very difficult period of his life, was visibly lifted by getting out on a demo (field diary, 2 March 2013) while Rachel had found EDL activism an important part of rebuilding her life after an abusive relationship and a period of ill health (field diary, 6 June 2012).

For some respondents, this family means even more; providing a 'safe space' and ontological security absent in childhood. Rob describes this sense of feeling 'part of a family' both when he joined the National Front in the late 1970s and again from his activism in the EDL and EVF:

> Growing up my family wasn't like a proper family, do you know what I mean? … [I]t was shit basically … It didn't give me the fun that I was getting at these demos … And plus, I felt part of a family … Like I do now, I feel part of a family, you know? (Rob)

This was very much true for Kane too who felt 'more safe with the EDL than what I do at home' (see Chapter 3).

The limits of loyalty

It is important not to romanticise reciprocal emotions and the affective bonds they generate. The sense of collective belonging and emotional support described above are not universal. Chas and Michelle talked about gaining acceptance as a long process rather than an immediate experience of 'belonging'. Indeed, Chas talks about EDL activism not as a collective endeavour but a personal, psychological journey: 'It's like my personal like space' (Chas). His relative isolation on demonstration days was noted in the field diary and confirmed by Connor who complains that Chas fails to 'assert himself at demos' in a way that leads to doubt that he would 'come through' if you were ever dependent on him to 'watch your back' (field diary, 1 December 2012). The three respondents whose affiliation was primarily with the 'Infidels' rather than EDL are also exceptions to the rule. Ollie does not mention friends or loyalty in the movement while Nick talks about affective bonds as being of 'comradeship' rather than friendship or family. The caring function of the movement sometimes also appears more an aspiration than a consistent practice. Connor complained that 'nobody cares' about division members serving prison sentences (field diary, 2 February 2013) while Ian notes that the movement had failed to act like a supportive family towards the widow and children of a well-respected RO who had died recently (field diary, 16 June 2013).

EDL activists also qualify their talk about the friendship and family they find in the movement through reference to the fact that alongside the 'real friends' made in the movement, it is also a place where you meet 'clowns', 'nutters', 'pricks', 'idiots' and 'backstabbers'. Referring to recent conflicts with the leadership of neighbouring divisions over their behaviour when travelling to demonstrations, as well as the language used in some posts to Facebook pages, members of a local youth division complained that 'We were all meant to stick together but some people like to be like the UAF' (Chris). Disloyalty was also ascribed to those who moved out of the movement. Connor noted that a member of another city's youth division had left the movement and gone 'straight to the Left'; if he tried to get back in, he said, he will 'not get out alive' (field diary, 23 March 2013). He also dismissed a former member of his own youth division, who had moved to the National Front and then set up a local branch of the Infidels as 'a racist prick'. Indeed there is some evidence of mutual surveillance practised by Division Organisers and 'admins'. Discussing a recent spate of 'troll' scares, Rachel clarifies that warning messages had circulated about an individual who was rumoured to be a police infiltrator and that a newly appointed division leader had been 'put on watch' due to concern about his activities with other (more radical) groups (field diary, 4 October 2014).

By far the most destructive force in the movement, however, arises from the very same emotions that serve to sustain it. In the absence of 'supportive spaces for emotional reflexivity', the affection and emotion rooted in interpersonal relationships that fuel activism can also undermine it (Brown and Pickerill, 2009: 32–33). For Euan it is romantic relationships that are the source of most tension:

> A lot of things what I've found that causes the fallouts is the relationships. …
> You know, somebody was going out with so and so and they fall out and then her
> goes out with so and so. Then they're fighting and they're fighting and everyone's
> fighting. (Euan)

This is confirmed by numerous field diary entries in which bitter arguments often involve accusations of 'shagging around'. In these tales, the web of 'who said what about whom' is often unfathomable (and sometimes farcical). But these tales have real consequences; individuals are removed from Facebook pages, stripped of admin positions and no longer feel welcome to attend demonstrations (field diary, 4 October 2014). They were a source of frustration to insiders too. Rachel, who found herself falsely accused of having a relationship with a Local Organiser, said she hated 'the way everybody is interested in who's sleeping with whom rather than the cause' and chose not to socialise with other members outside demonstrations to avoid entanglement in the rumour mill (field diary, 29–30 April 2013).

Disputes and fallings out were often caused also by the entwinement not only of activist and personal relationships but also of financial or informal economic ties. Sometimes such disputes developed precisely out of the caring and supportive ethos of the group. The coach journey to the Manchester demonstration was tense, for example, as Rachel finally spoke her mind to another member of her division whom she felt had betrayed her trust and friendship and exploited her financially after she had supported him emotionally and economically over a period of time (field diary, 2 March 2013; field diary, 20 July 2013). Ian's offer to put up Damon at his place ended in Damon moving out amidst mutual recrimination (field diary, 28 May 2013; field diary, 12 October, 2013). Suzy related how she had been beaten up badly after she had recognised on CCTV footage that one of the people responsible for a burglary at the pub where she was working at the time was her lodger. This individual, she said, was a fellow EDL member whom she had taken in and acted 'like a second mother' to. Indicative of the ethos of 'watching each other's backs' noted above, the incident had been 'sorted' not by the police but a group of EDL from a town in another region who had been dispatched specifically to 'do them' (field diary, 4 October 2014). Thus, while leaders may seek to foster affective bonds in order to encourage integration and the internalisation of ideology among grassroots members, those bonds have a dynamic of their own and can generate frustration, annoyance and hurt as well as solidarity, loyalty and security.

Conclusion

The role of emotions has been rehabilitated in social movement theory and received new theoretical impulse from the 'affective turn' in the social sciences. This has facilitated the distinction between different types of emotions in movements – shared and reciprocal (Goodwin, Jasper and Polletta, 2001: 20) – as well as between emotions as the social expression of feelings and affect as non-conscious movement between one experiential state of the body to another. In studies of anti-globalisation protests, this has led to nuanced discussion of how activists perform their networks through diverse bodily movements, techniques and styles, generating distinct identities and emotional tones (Juris, 2008: 89). In contrast, in studies of extreme and populist radical right movements, an instrumental approach continues to dominate in which it is suggested that collective emotions are consciously orchestrated by leaders among masses in order to construct emotional collectives (Virchow, 2007: 148).

Such an instrumental approach is questioned by the findings of this ethnographic study, which suggest that affective bonds within the EDL are generated from the bottom-up, emerging from a sense of 'togetherness' generated through shared activism – primarily in the form of participation in street demonstrations – that binds members of the movement. At the same time these bonds – experienced as being 'like one big family' – enhance the pleasures associated with activism and thus are central to sustaining it. This confirms Goodwin, Jasper and Polletta's (2001: 20) argument that, while distinct, reciprocal and shared emotions reinforce each other, thereby building a movement's culture. At the same time, it has been demonstrated that those interpersonal relationships central to the formation and maintenance of the emotional collective can also undermine it (Jasper, 1998: 419).

While a nuanced study of the role of affect in social movements would require more focused attention than it was given in the design of this research, as well as a more sensory ethnographic approach, in this chapter moments during activism are captured where affect becomes tangible and articulated. These moments – when senses are overwhelmed by the crowd, when respondents feel the 'buzz' or 'rush' of the demonstration or are lost in the pleasures of communal singing, chanting and marching – are moments when bodies affect one another and transpersonal intensities emerge (Anderson, 2009: 78). Notwithstanding the acceptance of the importance of the pre-personal and bodily dimensions of affect, however, the findings of this study confirm the importance of understanding affect as a 'practice' rooted in social life and concrete activities (Wetherell, 2012: 3) rather than as a 'contagion', virtual or transhuman process that takes place outside the subjectivities of those experiencing them (Shields, Park and Davidson, 2011: 318). This approach reconnects emotion to affect and recognises that affect is neither generated nor experienced randomly but communicated in crowds that have a shared identity and social practices (Wetherell, 2012: 148). This also allows for the reconnection of emotion, affect and *meanings* attached to activism at the cognitive level and is epitomised in the understanding of EDL activism as standing 'loud and proud', as explored in the following chapter.

Notes

1 The exception to this rule is Infidel respondents for whom EDL activists' treatment of demonstrations as a 'good day out' was a source of criticism and further evidence that they were not 'serious' (Andrew).
2 According to this theory, pheromones emitted by one body cause the release of hormones in the blood of another body and thus a change in the body state.
3 A football chant associated most frequently with Glasgow Rangers fans (and often accompanied by an anti-Irish tag line) but appropriated by fans of other Scottish and English football clubs.

8

'Loud and proud': piercing the politics of silencing

The response to inroads into the political system by right-wing populist movements has been to establish a *cordon sanitaire* around them in a 'moralization' of politics that denies social division and silences the multiplicity of voices that constitute politics (Mouffe, 2005: 120). Conducted as it is from a viewing point on the 'other' side of that *cordon*, this study explores this reframing of the political sphere in the moral register (2005: 5) through the concrete – and embodied – experience of it by EDL activists. In this chapter, that experience is shown to be one of a politics of silencing in which attempts to articulate grievances are met with accusations of racism and respondents learn to 'keep your mouth shut'. This constraint on political space compounds a wider disengagement from the formal political sphere and a denial of the 'political' nature of activism. Such disengagement, it is argued here, is not rooted in a traditional far right, anti-democratic ideology, however, but in an experientially based scepticism about the functioning of contemporary formal democracy that has much in common with a disavowal of politics among the population more broadly (Beck and Beck-Gernsheim, 2002: 157–58). That this is a radical variant of views found in wider society rather than 'a normal pathology unconnected to the mainstream' (Mudde, 2007: 297) is demonstrated through the absence (with rare exceptions) of anti-democratic alternative ideologies in respondents' narratives.

EDL activism provides a response to the politics of silencing beyond 'keeping your mouth shut'. In contrast to the formal political realm, this activism is experienced not as a site of meaningless debate but a space to 'tell it like it is'. It does not require compliant listening but allows respondents to stand 'loud and proud'. This understanding of activism constitutes a form of embodied agency that defies the 'social weightlessness' that the political (including the radical democratic political) might assume (McNay, 2014: 20). On the contrary, it is deeply socially constituted because it starts from the concrete experience of powerlessness and injustice (the removal of 'our issues' from the realm of the political) and addresses this exclusion and silencing through embodied practices of 'being seen' and 'being heard'. These practices, however, signal also a demand for recognition by, and on behalf of, sections of white working-class communities who feel their problems have been overlooked, their grievances dismissed as motivated by narrow-minded prejudice and who, as a group, have been culturally marginalised and vilified (Kenny, 2012: 25–26). The chapter thus concludes by considering whether EDL activism constitutes a 'potentially legitimate demand for "recognition"' (2012: 32) or simply the loud proclamation of the wrong kind of pride.

The politics of silencing

Attempts by white working-class communities to articulate their worsening position, Kenny (2012: 25) argues, have been ignored or their grievances dismissed as the product of ethnically charged nationalism or narrow-minded prejudice (2012: 25). This politics of silencing is recognised by the EDL and referenced in its slogan 'Not racist, not violent, just no longer silent' (see Figure 4.1). It is kept in place through the legal and cultural circumscription of 'legitimate' political discourse – what constitutes 'acceptable' issues for discussion – and is socially and politically reproduced through the social distance between 'politicians' and 'people like us'. In this section, the first of these dimensions is considered through activists' experiences of the politics of silencing in their institutional interactions (with the police and the education system) and in the inculcation of a fear of being labelled 'racist'. The second dimension is considered in the following section through discussion of activists' experiences of disassociation and exclusion from the political sphere.

Keeping your mouth shut

The experience of cultural marginalisation and hostility to their EDL affiliation (see Chapter 2) leads many respondents to 'keep their mouth shut' about their political views. Tina had made a conscious decision not to let fellow university students know she was in the EDL, 'not because ... I'm ashamed of it, but purely because ... I don't want things getting back to tutors and ... people being judgemental of me, or even worse kicking me out.' For Tim hostility had affected relations at work and he had come to realise that it is better to keep quiet and maintain work and other social interactions as 'a separate life from EDL'. Chas says that he tries to avoid getting into discussion about his views because, from past experience, 'it can get you into a lot of problems. ... But keep your mouth shut, keep your head down. Be alright.' Since at grassroots level, EDL members have little direct engagement with political institutions, the politics of silencing is primarily experienced through institutions with which they have regular interaction: the police and educational establishments.

The attitude of the police to the EDL is 'shut your mouth or you'll get a slap' (Matt). This is echoed by Ray, who notes that the officers policing the Bristol demonstration had said 'as long as we kept our noise down they wouldn't arrest us'. The response to such silencing is often external compliance but internal defiance: 'I don't care if the coppers batter us basically. I'm standing there as an English patriot. I'm allowed to stand there. I'm allowed to say my views. He can't shut me up' (Connor).

Another regular political encounter for the EDL is the 'opposition', who are described not as agents of silencing but as people whose own unwillingness to listen closes down the space for a politics of genuine debate and contestation. Members of the local youth division had tried to engage counter-demonstrators in discussion when they found themselves mistakenly directed by police to the other side of the police lines at a demonstration in Bristol. They were interested in finding out more about the counter-demonstrators because they 'wasn't just UAF' (Ray) but a broader coalition ('We are Bristol'). However, when Ray went into the pub to talk to one of them, he says, 'She didn't want to debate. She just wanted me to get off their streets.' This failed attempt to engage served to confirm that the minds of others were closed:

> They don't want to listen. They don't want to listen to our point of view. Then later on, they come to you and say 'We don't want you here'. 'Why don't you want us here?' 'Because you're racist.' 'No we aren't racist.' 'Yes you are.' ... As soon as you start going around trying to explain. 'You're a racist.' Boom. They don't have none of it. Get the camera. Take a picture of the racist. Put it on the Internet. (Connor)

While, as Back (2002: 47) found in the course of research with a skinhead gang in the West Midlands, an articulated desire to 'have a debate' with the object of hostility (referred to by the respondents as 'Pakis') might simply create another opportunity in which to assert 'white selfhood', what is telling in Connor's statement is his construction of self as powerless and the *object* of hostility. While his subjective experience of powerlessness may not be reflected in his objective structural position (and is a consequence of his choice to identify himself as an EDL activist), it remains a crucial factor in understanding activism.

Former EDL Chair Steve Eddowes also expresses frustration that past attempts 'to enter into dialogue with Muslim communities' had failed. As an example of this he cites the case of EDL engagement with Conservative parliamentary candidate for Dudley North, Afzal Amin. Amin was forced to resign his candidacy in March 2015 when tapes were released exposing an apparent plot to stage an EDL demonstration in Dudley against the planned new mosque for which Amin would later take credit for having persuaded the EDL to call off.[1] Amin's claim that he had been the victim of a 'sting' by the EDL is dismissed by Eddowes (2015) who had attended meetings with him on the understanding that Amin would facilitate dialogue with those leading the new mosque project.

The institutionalisation of silencing is experienced by respondents also through the education system. Chas explains how he was excluded from college for wearing an EDL hoody. Brett also recounts how he had been 'kicked out' of religious education lessons in school in Year 10 for objecting to studying Islam and that he had been prohibited from talking about the EDL:

> ... in one of my lessons in science I was talking about the EDL to another lad ... and then one of my teachers just got me removed from the lesson ... There was no-one in that room that was Muslim and there was no way it could have

hurt anybody – me talking about the EDL. It's my view, it's freedom of speech.
I should be allowed to say it. So I got pulled out in front of four teachers being
questioned about my views. It's my view, respect my view. (Brett)

A number of respondents suggest that their experience in the EDL is indicative of the wider abandonment of the principle of 'freedom of speech'. The media
is a particular object of criticism. Declan complains that the host of the official
EDL radio show, Geoff Mitchell, had given an interview to ITV news, but the
substance of what he said had been excluded from the broadcast:

It's like Geoff who does the radio show … he actually did a TV interview for ITV
news. He was there for 10 minutes but they only played 30 seconds of this interview and that was talking about why we were in Norwich that day. And she asked
him 'What are your views on Islamic influence?' and all that. So he told them
honestly but it did not make it onto the news. He was oppressed. His freedom of
speech was oppressed but when they interviewed a UAF woman [*in angry voice*]
'We don't want racist and fascist groups like English Defence League marching
through our city.' (Declan)

The experience of the Walthamstow demonstration, when counter-
demonstrators occupied the space designated for the EDL rally and prevented
speeches taking place (Pilkington, 2012) was described by one demonstrator as
effectively 'taking our freedom of speech away' (Jason). Explaining her anger at
attempts to prohibit EDL marches, Lisa says she feels 'very strongly that we just
need to be heard, you know, and respected'. Recognition, in the form of political
voice, is thus central to EDL activism.

The 'racism' label

The politics of silencing is discursively implemented through what respondents
refer to as the application of the label of 'racism'. As Peter puts it, 'People are so
scared of that word, and being called a racist … when half the things people say
and do isn't racist.' He illustrates this by recounting how, when he was at school,
a Sikh pupil, with whom he was friends, was distressed (due to family problems)
and 'this other lad was sort of taking the piss out of him cause he was crying in
school'. The response of the school had been to warn other pupils to 'be careful
what we say' lest it be interpreted as racist. From this Peter had concluded that 'if
you're bullying someone that's black, or Asian or whatever, in school, you're not
told off because it's wrong, you're told off because you're branded a racist'. Peter
does not doubt that the boy needed understanding not teasing, and that those
taunting him had to be told to stop; his objection was to the inappropriate framing
of the issue as one of racism.

When it comes to political dialogue, respondents express their experience in
ways that illustrate Mouffe's (2005: 5) claim that the political sphere has taken on
a moral register. Tina complains that one of her fellow students, who was active
in the youth section of the Labour Party, dismissed her views simply as 'You're

wrong and that's the end of it'. Chas, although perhaps deluding himself that his interlocutors fundamentally agree with him, imagines attempts at political dialogue as interrupted by a set of moral equivalences that 'block' engagement:

> Sometimes people are hearing the message and agreeing with me but it's like a mental block in their head. 'We don't, we can't agree with it, they're right wing, they're fascists, they're Nazis. We can't agree to it. It will be classed as racist if we agree to these people.' (Chas)

The fear of being labelled racist, according to Jack, inhibits people from engaging in activism:

> I would say millions of people that agree with what we do, including police officers ... can't say it or move in a circle where they are too worried about offending people or too worried about being attacked by people because they believe in something. People are too frightened to stand up ... They won't come out on the streets and start demonstrating with us because they are too frightened of getting their faces shown on TV or they are too frightened of what people might think, 'Oh you are a racist', because we live in a multicultural society. (Jack)

The government is also accused of not addressing issues for fear of being perceived 'racist' (Tim) whilst using its power to block institutional access to the political sphere such that any political route becomes impossible for the EDL because 'they just won't be allowed to. They'll be shunned off. They'll have a national newspaper find something about them, even if it hasn't happened, to try and break the EDL down' (Jack). Matt complains that, in his experience, the response to any success by the far right (citing past electoral successes of the NF and BNP) is that they 'mix the wards up' to prevent it happening again. In a shocking statement, Andrew blames the actions of Anders Breivik in Norway on precisely what he calls a 'silencing of the right':

> ... people weren't ready to listen, because the right were silenced, if anyone spoke out about immigration or about these rape issues or these crime issues, these left-wing people, these so called innocent people who got killed, they would silence them and they would accuse them of being racist, they would contact ... the jobs and the clubs and the churches or wherever else that they go and accuse them of racism, bigotry, and, all the other '-isms', then it would jeopardise their future like it has done mine. (Andrew)

Andrew had lost his job following exposure of his support for Breivik and the KKK in the local newspaper, and he goes on to claim that, after the publication of the article, 'four big black men came to my kickboxing club looking for me. And one of them had a weapon. But luckily I wasn't there that day, but if I had have been there, they could've made sure that I was silenced for good' (Andrew). While Andrew's views are deeply disturbing and not typical of the EDL mainstream (see Chapter 4), this feeling of being silenced is shared more widely among the respondent set and indeed in wider society. Lone and Silver (2014: 179–80) found that residents in a white working-class community in Manchester felt that they were not able to talk freely about immigration and that articulating concerns and opinions that differed from 'the mainstream' risked being seen as 'a racist'. Similarly, research with ordinary young people (not activists) undertaken as part of the larger MYPLACE project, of which this study of the EDL is a part, found evidence that young people felt issues such as immigration were excluded from mainstream political discourse.[2] Making the connection between structural forms of inequality, cultural stigmatisation and political marginality, one respondent in the UK understood this was because immigration was an issue of concern for working-class people: 'It just seems to be questions that affect MPs and things and people of the class of politics as it were that seem to get discussed rather than the things that generally affect the working person' (Grimm and Pilkington, 2015: 216). Thus while Ware (2008: 3) warns against accepting claims that the issue of immigration has been silenced in the past, and it is certainly true that these anxieties are exploited by anti-immigration and far right political parties,[3] that sections of the population experience the political realm as silencing some issues cannot be denied.

'Politics ain't us'

> I'm not interested in politics. … I don't want to be another man putting a suit on, sitting there lying and bound by political correctness. … I'm interested in change for this country. (Tommy Robinson on BBC, *Sunday Politics*, 16 June 2013)[4]

In this extract from an interview with Andrew Neil on the BBC's *Sunday Politics* show, Tommy Robinson is explaining why he would not stand for election and why the EDL will not put up candidates. Andrew Neil interprets this as evidence that he is 'not interested in democratic politics … It's the politics of the street that you're interested in which is the hallmark of extremism.' Robinson's rejection of the formal political system, however, is far from radical. It has been widely demonstrated on the basis of population surveys that there is an erosion of trust in politicians, disidentification with mainstream parties and growing criticism of key political institutions and the performance of democracy across European societies (Hay, 2007). Hay (2007: 39), however, rejects the tendency to explain trends towards political disaffection, disenchantment and disengagement as a result of problems in 'the demand side', that is, a lack of responsiveness and engagement by voters. He argues, on the contrary, that it is 'the supply side' that is the problem as the politics on offer to the electorate has been downgraded through: the 'marketization' of electoral competition and the narrowing of the range of the policy spectrum; and the embracing of public-choice theory and the consequent projection onto politicians, political elites and public officials more generally of narrowly instrumental assumptions (2007: 56–57). Not only does this fuel the negative characterisation by the public of politicians as self-interested but also an increasing tendency to 'depoliticise' public policy as politicians shift responsibility for policy-making and/or implementation to independent public bodies and constrain still further the sphere for policy-making. It is hardly surprising, he argues, that in a context in which even politicians concede that politics is something we need rather less of, public political disaffection and disengagement are rife (2007: 58). Indeed, the impact of this downgrading of politics as the pursuit of the collective good is intensified given that it coincides with the rise of the 'critical' citizen, resulting in a growing 'democratic deficit' emerging from the divergence between levels of satisfaction with the performance of democracy and public aspirations (Norris, 2011: 4–6). These deeper political processes underpin surface manifestations of 'disengagement' from conventional politics.

Scepticism about the electoral process is common among grassroots members of the EDL. Many respondents said they do not vote because 'they're all a waste of time' (Matt). Chas said that he would vote, but only 'when there's actually a party out there where I can relate to', while Michelle was waiting to vote until she 'had a good reason to'. Others simply have not even thought about voting (Kyle) or see 'no point' (Ray, Connor) in doing so: 'if they're not EDL, I'm not voting for them' (Connor). Two respondents were not on the electoral register (Chris, Sean); for Sean, this had been a conscious choice since he feared registering would mean 'they'd know everything about ya'.

The disengagement of EDL respondents from the formal political sphere is generally active rather than passive. Three respondents had spoiled their ballot paper or advocated doing so rather than not voting (Mike, Ryan, Euan).

> EUAN: Yeah I've voted. I've voted Labour a few times. I've voted UKIP and I just think they are all lying, spineless arse wipes. You know. If you could have a vote of no confidence I'd vote for that. ...
> INT: So when did you stop voting then? Was there a particular turning point where you thought 'that's enough'?
> EUAN: The last one. ... To be honest I just writ 'EDL' on my ballot paper. I just writ 'EDL' over it. That's all I could do.

Ian, who had been a member of the Labour party for three to four years in his early twenties, said that he had left after being disgusted at the way in which the local electorate was taken for granted. He recounts, to illustrate this, an occasion when he was standing at the bar next to a local Councillor who declared to anyone listening that 'the people am that thick on these estates that Labour could ... put up a pig for election, they'd still vote for it' (Ian). This feeling is echoed in Lone and Silver's (2014: 178) study of a white working-class district in Manchester where local politics had been dominated by the Labour Party for decades.

Others do vote, because it is important to, but have no greater trust in the system or confidence that their vote will 'change anything' (Jordan, Carlie). Lisa explains that she votes not out of a sense that it will have any impact but in recognition of the fact that it is a right that 'women died for' and 'because there are countries in this world where they are told they are not allowed to vote or if you don't vote for me … then we will kill you basically'. Others say they do, or would, vote, but qualify this with an express antipathy for the three main parties (Ed, Declan, Andrew, Ollie). Michelle repeats a common sentiment that mainstream parties do not deliver on their promises: 'what they are saying and what they do is two different things. … They are just ripping people off really' (Michelle). That is not to say that some respondents, usually out of family tradition, did not vote for the main parties: four respondents (Tina, Ed, Lisa, Jason) had voted in the past, or said they would vote in the future, for the Conservative Party; one respondent (Kane) said he would vote Labour while another had in the past (Euan) and one had been a member of the Labour Party (Ian).

The lack of formal political engagement is extended to other forms of activism. Participation in EDL actions is reported to be the first real political or civic engagement for most respondents. Exceptions are involvement in animal rights campaigns (Ollie), street preaching (Andrew), charity work (Jason, Ollie, Andrew, Kane) and campaigns against cases of miscarriage of justice (Euan) as well as membership of the BNP (Ed, Declan) or National Front (Rob).

More remarkable than the expression of common disillusionment with the party political system is that, despite their current active political engagement in the EDL, many respondents deny any interest in 'politics' per se.

> CHRIS: I don't follow politics.
> RAY: Nor me. I can't answer no questions about politics.
> CHRIS: Politics are bollocks. I don't know nothing about politics. I don't follow politics.
> RAY: Ask me a question about politics, and I'll phone me granddad. …
> CHRIS: I don't follow them. I don't read about them. So I can't answer … I don't know anything about politics.

Michelle claims she has neither understanding of, nor interest in, politics while Richard articulates his antipathy in a common expression of distrust in politicians:

> … never really been into politics, I don't really understand like … I just think they're all bullshitters, politicians. I just think, you know, gonna tell as many lies as they can to get into you know, government, or into power or whatever then just do what they want and fuck the country up even more. (Richard)

The disavowal of politics voiced by EDL respondents thus appears marked by a clear distinction between the politics of talk and the not-politics of action. This is epitomised in discussion within the movement about whether the EDL should seek a more political route forward (via electoral representation) or remain true to its roots as a 'street movement'. There was a gut rejection of the political among the youth division respondents who associated being 'political' with 'debating with other fucking parties' (Chris). The implications of the rejection of 'debate' for understanding EDL members' wider views on democratic (or non-democratic) ways forward are discussed in the following section. Here it is important to note the concern of many respondents that taking 'the political route' would signify the prioritisation of words over action. Connor argues that 'We don't want to debate. We want to do something about it.' And, as is evident in the following discussion between Connor and an older respondent (who had recently moved from the EDL to the EVF), Connor rejects arguments that being 'political' is necessary to make an impact:

ROB: You need to be political to get anywhere.
CONNOR: Yeah but what do you get out of sitting in a room voicing your opinion, shouting at each other? You know what I mean? If you don't agree with something you are arguing with someone over a table. You know what I mean? Or pointing fingers.
ROB: Which is exactly what we are doing now.
CONNOR: Not really. We are going to the streets and we are doing it, proving that we can go to the streets and not sit in a room, do you know what I mean?

Specifically on the question of whether a, at the time of interview, recently formed alliance with the British Freedom Party (BFP) was a good thing, there was also split opinion. When I interviewed Chas, Tommy Robinson had just stepped down as Co-Chair of the BFP to concentrate on his EDL role and this met with Chas's approval. He did not agree with those who said 'we need to go down the political route … We don't. There's nothing wrong with the street movement.' Tim was also unsure about the rationale for a political route and erred towards prioritising action:

I preferred it when there was like mass street movement. Look, actions speak louder than words because I reckon they'll just see it as another BNP and it's just like I don't know. … I'm just unsure. … But I'm not political. … I'm just more action. Just get on the streets. Let's get on the streets make ourselves be heard. (Tim)

Others, however, are positive about a political route for the EDL. Euan states unequivocally that 'I think we need representation'. Jason also says 'I hope that eventually the EDL will get someone elected. … I reckon it'd be a big step forward for us.' He goes on to suggest that he thought Kevin Carroll and Tommy Robinson would make good MPs 'because they speak their minds, they tell the truth' (Jason). Some respondents go further and recognise the EDL, and their own activism in it, as definitively 'political' (Jason, Lisa). Lisa clarifies that she is not political in the sense of being interested in what the government says – 'because … they are all going to do the same thing just different ways' – but she is interested in what is going on in the world and sees herself as 'political in my views'. Others are less ambivalent about their political interests and ambitions. Nick said he had 'always been interested in politics and the right wing and all of that' and intended, when he was older, to get involved in a political party because 'it's purely political isn't it? It's not just about demos here and demos there, it's about appealing to the British people.' Ollie said he did something 'political' several times a week and saw himself as different from his peers: 'I'm a lot more politically minded than everyone else' (Ollie). Ed had stood for election (for the BNP) in the local council elections in his area three times. Tina was studying politics at university and hoped to enter local politics after she graduated because 'One voice may, might make a difference ... I don't wanna be doing marches for the rest of my life to try and be heard. I wanna actually be in there, trying to be heard' (Tina). Looking to the future, the former Chair of the EDL does not rule out 'a political wing' of the EDL but sees the way forward as one of continuing to hold street protests and demonstrations whilst pursuing, in parallel, strategies that are targeted at the government more directly, including lobbying and using the Freedom of Information Act (Eddowes, 2015).

Both for those who oppose a political route for the EDL, prioritise 'action' over 'talk' and deny they themselves are 'political' and for those who embrace the political, however, activism is above all about needing to 'be heard'. Politics in general holds no interest for Michelle 'as long as our voices get heard, that's what counts'. Connor sees the point in demonstrations as being a way to do politics authentically: 'You stand there and you be heard for who you am. It don't matter who you are but you should just be heard for who you are like and your views' (Connor). In this sense EDL claims for recognition are not dissimilar from those pursued by other movements – such as the LGBT rights or anti-racist movements – who have linked structural forms of inequality, discrimination or exclusion to their own political marginality (Kenny, 2012: 26). What is sought – notwithstanding the different content of the message – is political voice.

Being heard: piercing the silence

Activism in the EDL provides a way of cutting through the politics of silencing and finding a political voice. This is evident in the meanings respondents attach to their participation in actions and what they feel it achieves. These meanings range from the predominantly rational – 'getting your point across' – to the cathartic and emotional – acting 'loud and proud'. Underpinning this activism is the distinction it reinforces between the duplicitous chatter of formal politics and the practice of 'telling it as it is' in a non-politics of action.

Getting your point across

Reflecting on the meaning of their activism in the EDL, primarily through participation in street demonstrations, respondents repeatedly refer to the importance of 'getting heard' (Sean, Tina), 'getting your voice out there in the public' (Michelle) or 'getting your point across' (Chas, Jason, Jordan, Richard, Connor, Chris). As Kane puts it, 'We're there for a reason. We ain't there for the fun of it, we are always there for a reason.' This rationalisation of activism is reflected in Andrew's description of how his small group of Infidels had mobilised their resources in the form of skills and equipment in order to stage a flash demo against ethnic bullying outside a local school:

> Ollie written up a fantastic speech ... which we took it in turns on the megaphone to speak out, and ... there was a couple of teachers and a couple of other

parents who stopped to listen to us and they and they shook our hands and says 'well done', the reception that we got was genuinely positive. (Andrew)

Demonstrations are worthwhile, therefore, if 'You've got your word out. So more people know what you am about. ... [A]s long as only one person listens to what we said, and thought "that's right that is"' (Chris). Connor had taken this aim off the street and onto the airwaves by setting up his own EDL radio show on BlogTalkRadio (mirroring the East Anglian EDL Radio Show), which, he said, 'voices our opinion'.

Speaking out also carries a cathartic dimension. Eddowes (2015) says he experienced 'a great sense of release from being at demos'. Chas, who admits that he often keeps his views to himself because talking has led to him being 'de-friended' and disowned by certain members of the family, thinks it is important to talk about the difficult issues that the EDL raises: 'There is definitely a problem out there. No one was speaking about it. People were too scared to speak about it. So why not speak about it? Get it off your chest and get it all out' (Chas). Others are aware of the psychodynamics of their EDL participation. Lisa is conscious that EDL activism is a way of channelling her anger. Tim had experienced his participation in one of the early EDL demonstrations as the release of a long-standing 'pent up anger', which he traces back to an incident when he was 16 years old and the police 'beat the living shit out of me':

> ... basically just a lot of pent up anger and it was just like we finally felt like ... we was in this unstoppable force and it was just like ... people had to listen and it was just like we keep being loud and like wild. Not so much wild but ... for me it was just like this massive built-up anger just screaming out of me. (Tim)

EDL activism therefore not only provides a platform to speak or have your voice heard. Passions remain a key moving force in politics (Mouffe, 2005: 24) and there is a real pleasure and release experienced in letting go and 'being loud'.

Being loud

RAY: When we first started EDL ... we always got told it would never be a politics thing. But now all of a sudden they want to be in politics and they want to do this and that.

CHRIS: The day it goes to politics, that's the day I come out.

RAY: That'll be the day that I come out because if we're in politics it's going to look bad when we go to a demo or we go on a march and all that's going to stop. We am going to end up being peaceful. Yes, we are peaceful but when you're a proper official peaceful protester, you can't drink, you can't do nothing. You all just stand there quiet, listening. That ain't EDL. EDL's loud.

CHRIS: Loud and proud.

RAY: If I've got to go there and read the *Sunday Times*, like, that ain't happening. Know what I mean?

As argued above, EDL activists experience the current political sphere as a politics of silencing. This silencing produces a deeper sense of disenfranchisement, which is evident in respondents' wider disengagement from, and populist critique of, the formal political sphere, envisaged by Ray as a space where you 'go ... and read the *Sunday Times*'. EDL activism creates a space to resist this silencing. This can involve 'being loud' in a very literal sense. Chanting (as discussed in the previous chapter) is central to EDL activism because when you chant you 'make it loud and proud of who we am' (Connor). But almost any opportunity to make noise is relished: chanting, singing, laughing, stamping, banging, rattling. As a crowd escorted by the police across London on the tube came up the escalator at Blackhorse Road station to reach the muster point for the national demo at Walthamstow, people begin banging on its sides, making as much noise as possible (field diary, 1 September 2012). At a demo in Rotherham, younger demonstrators backed up against steel barriers erected to protect the social services building opposite the police station (outside which the demonstration was held) started to bang against the metal to maximise the noise being made by the demonstrators who had started to clap and stamp their feet, physically enacting the call from the podium that it was time to 'stamp out abuse' (field diary, 13 September 2014). Being loud is given rationalised meaning also in official EDL statements. In the European Defence League's 'Memorandum of Understanding', for example, being 'loud' is seen to be an important way of voicing support for reformist Islam in its battle against fundamentalism: 'The more we capitulate, the more we appease, the harder the reformer has to fight. The more we abandon our own principles, the more we forget our pride, the more confident the fundamentalist becomes. That is why we need to be loud.'[5] When Tommy Robinson fronted the first event of the (official) Pegida UK movement outside Birmingham (6 February 2016), the new movement was symbolically distanced from the EDL by designating it a 'silent walk' and banning chants and colours.

The notion of 'loud and proud' is used most widely to refer to EDL activism by younger respondents and can become a site of tension, especially intergenerational. Members of a local youth division had been criticised for chanting at a service station during the journey to the national demonstration at Dewsbury in 2012. In interview afterwards Connor says he had resisted the call to keep their noise down since, for him, being heard and seen is what EDL activism is about:

> Well we went on their coach yeah to Dewsbury and obviously what do you do when you are out on a demo? You chant. You be proud of what you are doing. Well we went to the Services yeah and we was chanting 'E, EDL' and like they [older members] was calling us dickheads and that cause we had our photo took with the flag and that cause we weren't scared to show who we fucking was man. But it was them lot and they was all just sat there on the coach man reading the Sunday fucking Times having a glass of wine. Fuck that. You don't do that on demo day. You go out man, you are bawling, you are ready for it, do know what I mean? You are ready to prove your point. Them weren't man. They was just dead boring. Fuck that man. [*gets passionate*] You wanna be loud. You wanna be proud. (Connor)

In similar vein, another young respondent recounted how he had started an 'anti-front seat' campaign on the coach to Bradford as he had been annoyed by those 'at the front' with their rules and complaints about behaviour' (field diary, 9 November 2013). In this sense younger members experienced the practice of 'silencing' as coming not only from outside but as exercised also by those with more power within the EDL: 'The youths don't really get an opinion, do you know what I mean? If you travel with the olders you listen to them, what them do, you've gotta do' (Connor). However, as the response of both Chas and Connor indicate, younger members are not afraid to challenge the right of older members to dictate behavioural norms within the movement. In an attempt to redefine authority in the movement, Chas points out that one of those in the front seats trying to dictate how the young ones behave 'hadn't even been on a demo for two years'. Moreover, when they have the opportunity to organise events for themselves, such as a 'meet and greet' for the local youth division, Connor resists the adults' practice of holding such recruitment drives inside and away from trouble and insists on the importance of not only being heard but being seen:

> Who'd wanna sit in a pub talking bollocks? You gotta be out on the street. They wanna be active. They [young people] wanna be like putting their face across so that's why I called the meet and greet in the middle of [names town]. Literally in the middle. And we *will* be doing it public, and it can attract people. It probably will kick off and I'll get my head kicked in and that. But it is still gonna attract a crowd, do you know what I mean? They will know that the EDL have touched down. (Connor)

For the most part being 'loud and proud' has meaning in and of itself (being heard and being seen). However, the emotional and rational dimensions of activism are intertwined:

> See that's when you feel you are doing a cause, yeah? I mean when you've got 3,000 people there all for the same reason, not there for throwing bricks or what not you know we are there we are marching that's when you feel proud. It's like being in the army at the end of the day. You are there and you are there for a good cause. (Lisa)

Where a particular object or substance is attached to the 'pride' expressed it is related to Englishness: 'We are loud and proud about being English' (Chris). 'English and proud' was also seen emblazoned on a T-shirt worn by a demonstrator at a demonstration in Rotherham (field diary, 13 September 2014). As discussed in Chapter 3, Englishness is primarily defensively articulated, being constructed, in a similar way to white working-class identity, as a loser from post-war changes in society (Clarke and Garner, 2010: 203). Respondents thus recognise that it is 'a bit dodgy' to talk about being 'English' and defensively assert that it is 'not racist' to call yourself English. Asserting pride in one's Englishness in this way can act to overcome or demonstratively reject a perceived 'shame' attached to it. Ray, Smith and Wastell (2004: 36) argue that racist violence 'represents an attempt to re-establish control, to escape from shame into a state of pride' where shame is experienced by the perpetrators because they feel weak, disregarded and unfairly treated while they imagine their Asian victims as powerful, successful and arrogant. It is conceivable that 'being loud' and standing 'proud' play a similar role of seeking to reinstate a perceived 'natural order', although caution is exercised here since in this study 'shame' was not an articulated emotion and interviews were not analysed for verbal and paralinguistic cues for shame (as in the Ray, Smith and Wastell study). Certainly there is some evidence that milder forms of intimidation – through visibility and strength in numbers – are important elements of activism. A street demonstration 'lets people know we are out there' (Jack) and being able to 'put men there' is a sign of the strength of the movement (Ray). Chants of 'Whose streets? Our streets' and 'We'll do what we want' provide the soundtrack to the visual display of presence and clearly seek to assert control and 'rights'. These rights are not always at the expense of an Asian 'other' but might be claims made against the police, the government, local authorities or the wider public. Such visibility also generates notoriety that can act as a (dubious) sort of pride. Andrew claims that 'I'm a little bit of a celebrity because of what happened last year when I was exposed for supporting Anders Breivik ... I can try and change my appearance a little bit but there'll always be somebody in that crowd who will spot me.' Respondents repeatedly note that police officers recognise them and often know them by name (Ian, Connor, Ed, Matt, Kurt, Declan). Locally people are recognised frequently from media reports of demonstrations (Tim, Connor, Chris, Ray) and, Tim recounts how he had been congratulated and shaken by the hand by a bouncer at a club on a night out. In this study only male respondents took pride in notoriety; women respondents tended to avoid being known for fear of the consequences for work, study and family.

'We ain't debating': anti-politics = anti-democratic?

Politics has failed; it is time for action now because politicians have never listened to us. (Declan)

Feeling themselves silenced by constraints on legitimate issues for discussion and marginalised, through class position, from the formal political realm, EDL activists seek alternative ways to gain recognition and claim political voice. As detailed above, these include both attempts to engage in political dialogue ('get your point across') as well as more emotional demonstrations of the desire to be heard ('loud and proud'). The point of this activism, however, is to 'be heard'; for politics to work, it has to be conducted in a public sphere governed not by disembodied, rational deliberation but in which the experience of listening is central (McDonald, 2006: 200). The sense that this is not happening leads to a rejection of politics and call for 'action'. The extent to which such 'action' might go beyond the norms of democratic politics, or involves a vision of a non-democratic political system, is discussed in this final section.

Mudde's (2007: 30) distinction between the populist radical right, which remains broadly democratic despite opposing some fundamental values of *liberal* democracy and the extreme right, which is in essence anti-democratic, is helpful for considering views within the EDL. The leadership and vast majority of grassroots members are highly critical of the contemporary working of democracy. The criticism voiced by respondents in this study, however, is directed primarily at governments (past and present) rather than at the democratic system in principle. Anger is expressed at the perceived failure by the government to deal with issues of terrorism and, in particular, at the response to the murder of Lee Rigby. Another common complaint is that the government deals with trivial issues while the really important problems, such as poverty, are ignored (Euan), or buries its head in the sand rather than being honest with people about the state of affairs (Michelle). Government cuts are seen as targeting the wrong people (Ray, Euan, Declan, Jordan, Tim) and generating an ever-growing divide between rich and poor (Tina, Michelle).

These criticisms bring forth some suggestions for how the system might be made more responsive. One proposal was for a mechanism for withdrawing a government's mandate mid-term if it was not delivering what it had promised (Chas). Jordan expresses the sentiment behind this argument: 'every government promise you this, promise you that and as soon as they are in power everything is forgot about. You are just another number that's got them there.' Declan went further, suggesting that the current political system did not constitute democracy. He was careful, however, to preface this with the explicit statement that he was not 'anti-democratic' in as much as 'I don't believe in dictatorship and a one-party system' (Declan). Lisa, implicitly drawing on the notion of hegemonic rule, was critical of the way that the system works to prevent change: 'you are brainwashed from a very early age into believing that there is no better way to run the country'. She suggests a presidential system would be preferable to a parliamentary democracy on the grounds that it involved 'less people'. However, respondents fall short of expressing support for any authoritarian mode of government.

The exception here is the three respondents identifying as Infidels (see Chapter 4) who openly declare that they are national socialists. Nick claims that history shows that 'the successful nations have never really been democratic' and cites Germany under Hitler and Spain under Franco as successful non-democratic states. Ollie also declared that 'I don't agree with democracy' and argued that a single-party system (gaining power through revolution rather than election) was preferable to parliamentary democracy since his primary concern was the establishment of a socialist system, and 'you can't have democracy and socialism'. However, there is no support for fascism among mainstream respondents (two respondents explicitly denounce it) and even one of the Infidels respondents makes a point of distancing himself from fascism since it is rooted in 'national capitalism' rather than National Socialism (Nick).

Mainstream EDL rhetoric at grassroots level is thus almost completely devoid of any vision of an alternative to democratic governance. This might be anticipated given the concerns among respondents, and the leadership of the movement, to distance the EDL from traditional 'far right' associations with fascism or National Socialism. However, it is somewhat surprising when set in the context of the wider

MYPLACE project where the survey of young people revealed surprisingly high levels of support for authoritarian rule[6] in the UK research locations; support for a strong leader not constrained by parliament was expressed by 56.1 per cent of young people across the two locations and for army rule by 27.7 per cent (Grimm and Pilkington, 2015: 220). EDL visions of alternatives to parliamentary democracy seem mild against such 'mainstream' attitudes. Comparing the relative value of politicians and armed services personnel in the context of widespread government cuts, Connor states, 'I'd rather drop the 400 politics [politicians] and have that one soldier. Because that one soldier can make a difference.' However, although demands for greater protection (material and moral) for the armed forces and a tougher stance against demonstrations of 'disrespect' towards them are central to EDL ethos and activism, no respondents suggested the army might be an acceptable alternative to democratic government. Moreover, while over half of the MYPLACE survey respondents in the UK locations supported a strong leader unconstrained by parliament, the EDL has promoted a populist message about the direct connection between people and political power but has sought to avoid an organisational structure dependent on a strong charismatic leader and encourages a sense among members that 'every single one of you is a leader' (see Chapter 2).

The only alternative suggested to parliamentary democracy by EDL respondents in this study was the restoration of the powers of the monarchy: 'I don't believe there should be like a Parliament. I just reckon it should be Queen and country' (Neil). In preferring a monarchy to democracy, Nick also points to the prioritisation of action over the 'talk' he associates with current politics:

> ... probably just go back to the monarchy, complete monarchy ... I'd rather have that, cause at the moment democratic societies ... they all appear quite weak in all of this, you know they have to talk about everything first instead of doing it, as long as it's in the interests of the state and the people ... it doesn't really matter. (Nick)

The point of convergence of Nick's anti-democratic (national socialist) views and those of mainstream EDL respondents who do not reject democracy per se, is a shared frustration with the political process as a space for 'talk' rather than action. As Connor puts it, the EDL 'ain't debating'.

It was argued above that this rejection of 'debating' constitutes a critique of the formal political system characterised by meaningless and self-serving 'chatter'. This positioning distinguishes EDL activism not only from traditional political parties, however, but also from other social movements which put the process of debate and deliberation centre stage in the constitution and reclamation of democracy. Castells (2012: 125), discussing the Indignadas movement in Spain, argues that the forms of deliberation and decision-making within the movement aimed explicitly to prefigure what political democracy should be in society at large. By constructing a free community in a symbolic place, social movements that occupy public spaces create a space for deliberation, which ultimately becomes a political space (2012: 11). However, such deliberative democracy, at the heart of which lies 'talk' and 'rational argumentation' (Della Porta, 2013: 61–62), is not necessarily attractive to those who perceive what is bad about the current political system is that it is 'all talk'. Indeed, the valorisation of the method of consensus central to deliberative democratic approaches may be experienced by others as equally exclusionary. For those for whom formal politics is associated with meaningless debate, the centrality of 'talk' to deliberative democratic alternatives undermines its 'alternative' status and constructs it as an extension of the Habermasian understanding of the public sphere as a sphere of rational, disembodied communication in which freedom is envisaged as an 'endless meeting' (McDonald, 2006: 200).

The question then is whether this rejection of deliberative democracy reduces EDL activism to the articulation of politicised grievance or might speak to a different radical democratic critique, which questions claims that 'consensus', as the outcome of deliberation, ensures democratic inclusion. Mouffe (2005: 3) argues that understanding politics as the search for a universal rational consensus can reduce it to attempts to design institutions capable of reconciling all conflicting interests and values, when the essence of democratic politics is, in fact, the legitimate expression of such conflict. Theorists who want to eliminate passions from politics and envisage democratic politics only in terms of reason, moderation and consensus, she argues (2005: 24), fail to understand the dynamics of the political; politics has always had a 'partisan' dimension and for people to be interested in politics they need to have the possibility of choosing between real alternatives. Rancière (1999: 96–97) too points to the importance of contestation for the vibrancy of democracy; when the institutions of parliamentary representation were being contested by generations of militant socialists and communists, he suggests, they were cherished and protected more vigilantly (1999: 97). As a consequence, Mouffe (2005: 66) argues, right-wing populism has made inroads precisely in those places where traditional democratic parties have lost their appeal to the electorate who can no longer distinguish between them in the 'stifling consensus' that has gripped the political system. Bitter arguments over multiculturalism in the 1990s, Hewitt (2005: 153) suggests, is 'the regular fare of democratic politics'. Rancière (2011: 1) argues simply, 'There is politics because the common is divided' and thus 'dissensus', not consensus, lies at the heart of politics.

There is no doubt that 'the point' the EDL seeks to get across generates dissensus not consensus. The question is whether screening out the claims to be heard by groups like the EDL, through a politics of silencing, may not only be increasingly unpalatable given their rising volume and intensity (Kenny, 2012: 32), but whether it is actually in the long-term interest of reclaiming politics and strengthening democracy. If radical democratic critiques are to defend themselves against McNay's (2014: 8) claim that they fail 'to realize their own stated aim of challenging settled political orthodoxies in the name of excluded and oppressed groups', they need to address directly the challenges posed by the embodied politics of the populist radical right.

Conclusion

In this chapter the relationship between EDL activism and the external political environment has been considered. It has illustrated how EDL activists experience the external political realm as a politics of silencing in which the expression of their views, as well as government policy, are constrained by the application of the 'racism label' and learn the best strategy for negotiating this realm is to 'keep your mouth shut'. Lone and Silver's (2014) recent study of a white working-class community in Manchester shows that this experience is far from confined to an extremist minority. This raises the dilemma that while, on the one hand, opening up debate about issues – such as immigration – can be exploited by populist and far right political parties, there is a danger also that allowing 'a growing authoritarian consensus against offensive speech' to develop effectively closes down debate, infantilises the public and marginalises nonconformist ideas (Furedi, 2005: 157).

In light of increasingly assertive arguments made by, or on behalf of, white working-class communities, Kenny (2012: 24) has asked whether we should rethink our tendency to treat them as expressions of 'resentment, racism and grievance' and consider whether they might be thought of as a form of recognition politics and, in some cases, as demands which have a 'rational' basis and 'merit a more sympathetic hearing by the state'. This raises a deeper question in relation to our understanding of democracy of the possibility that populist radical right movements such as the EDL may themselves 'articulate albeit in a very problematic way, real democratic demands which are not taken into account by traditional parties' (Mouffe, 2005: 71). The failure to recognise the impacts of wider structural change on white working-class communities, who have experienced decreasing wages, reduced employment opportunities and declining social mobility for their children over the last three decades, is at least one important factor in a significant decline in democratic engagement and participation (Lone and Silver, 2014: 178). Indeed this goes beyond a disillusionment with formal political institutions and agents; it is reflected in a cultural divide between 'people like us' and the 'do-gooders' (the socially liberal world of individuals and institutions in positions of power) who are perceived not to live in the real world but 'somewhere very secluded, where nothing ever happens' (2014: 179–81). Such a divide runs deeper than 'the angry white men' (older and economically insecure and lowly educated working-class men in particular regions of the country) identified as the core constituency of far right parties such as the BNP (Goodwin, 2011a: 118). It draws on a broader constituency not only alienated from mainstream parties but believing that public institutions are not representing them or their needs and prone to accept unsubstantiated 'public knowledge' as well as messages from populist parties that resonate with pre-existing anxieties (Lone and Silver, 2014: 181).

Notes

1 See www.theguardian.com/politics/2015/mar/23/afzal-amin-quits-conservative-candi date-edl-plot-allegations. Accessed: 28.08.2015.

2 This is drawn from the semi-structured interview element of the project. Approximately thirty semi-structured interviews were conducted in each of the thirty locations with young people aged 16–25 recruited from the locally representative sample of young people participating in the survey element of the project. The two UK locations were Coventry and Nuneaton.

3 Lone and Silver (2014: 172) note that a local BNP candidate in the Manchester area in which their research was conducted played on this sense of being silenced by claiming that anyone 'who has ever dared to mention immigration has been condemned as "racist"'.

4 See www.youtube.com/watch?v=sZHbXhstXG4. Accessed: 28.08.2015.

5 See http://englishdefenceleague.org/european-defence-leagues. Accessed: 26.06.2012.

6 Support for authoritarian rule is constructed from four markers of support for: a strong leader; military rule; a multiparty system; and freedom of speech for the opposition. The survey is based on a representative sample of 16–25 year olds in two locations in each participating country (see note 2).

Conclusion: passion and politics

This book is political. Not because it started with an explicit commitment to a particular political project but because it did not. Not because the author took the position of 'activist-scholar', but because the 'ugly' politics of the movement studied rendered such a role inappropriate. But must research on activism always take the form also of political action? If so, do we not exclude the possibility of close-up research of those political causes and movements that we find, personally, most difficult to comprehend and, socially, most pernicious? And does not such self-imposed constraint on what and how we research not weaken claims to the systematic creation and critique of knowledge (Gillan and Pickerill, 2012: 136)? This is not to dismiss the political implications of choosing to conduct an ethnographic study of a movement widely perceived to actively perpetuate racism. It is to take the position that there should be no areas of social life that are unfit for scientific study (Kirby and Corzine, 1981: 15) and to argue that such studies extend our, very limited, understanding of the meanings individuals in movements of the populist radical right attach to their activism. It is also to suggest that such studies have political as well as academic value.

Ethnography: a choice between politics and knowledge?

Traditional studies of the far right tend to forefront the analysis of ideological frames and organisational effectiveness and take little account of the people who maintain such movements; individuals appear largely in the form of agglomerated socio-demographics of 'supporters' or 'voters' or as an undifferentiated mass following a charismatic leader. Ethnography, in contrast, allows the researcher to approach and present members of such organisations 'as individuals with real lives' (Ezekiel, 1995: xxxv). This is not to underestimate the contentiousness of what that implies; understanding the meanings attached to activism requires a sustained presence in activists' lives. When the individuals concerned are active in 'distasteful' groups, this is both difficult and controversial. But, it is argued here, it is necessary.

> It would be simpler – and pointless – to simply reinforce the reader's stereotypes and pander to the reader's pre-existing images. It takes no effort to speak glibly about a stereotype. ... To present white racists as humans is not to approve their ideas or their actions. But to picture them only in stereotype is to foolishly deny ourselves knowledge. Effective action to combat racism requires honest enquiry. (1995: xxxv)

Over the course of conducting and writing this research, I came to understand this as a political as well as an academic stance. Of course Kalra (2006: 466) is right to argue for the importance of research that goes beyond 'acknowledging the role of racism in racialized minorities' lives'. But I take issue with his suggestion that ethnography is always an inappropriate method for challenging racialisation because it is compelled 'towards the dead-end of cultural difference' (2006: 459). Ethnography can, and does, explore the nuances, slippages and conscious and unconscious transgressions of cultural boundaries (ascribed, appropriated or resisted); indeed this is its value. Ethnography is 'an indispensable tool, first to pierce the screen of discourses ... which lock inquiry within the biased perimeter of the pre-constructed object' (Wacquant, 2008: 9). It is also an appropriate tool for researching 'distasteful' groups if ethnography is understood as unpicking rather than enacting moral simplifications – as more than a question of 'whose side are we on?' (Duneier and Back, 2006: 553). It is this understanding of ethnography that is adopted in this study. It is an approach which prioritises not 'documenting the ways in which capitalist pigs exploit subalterns, but being able to see the ways that different kinds of victims confront one another' (2006: 553). As Duneier and Back indicate, referring to interactions between black, homeless street vendors and white middle-class women, it is these moments that challenge our understandings of the world and extend our knowledge of it:

> ... what I was seeing on the street was a group of liberal white women who are victims of these black men as women. They were wealthier, but the poor black men were able to subvert their race and class position by using their position as men to undermine these women with their taunts and with the things that they say to them and the way that they would undermine conversations with them, and they would apparently feel power at those moments. So those women were victims. It was one group of victims confronting another in public space. (Duneier and Back, 2006: 553)

While I would not choose to designate those who are the focus of the current study as 'victims', their actions in public spaces have contexts that require analysis and interpretation rather than a priori moral condemnation. In seeking to make sense of activism in movements like the EDL, the potential of ethnography to get at the humanity of people (Duneier and Back, 2006: 554) is a powerful tool for revealing the intersections of oppression and thus also the potential sites of cross-cutting solidarities. The exclusion of such groups from such scrutiny in the interests of the researcher's own political or ethical comfort thus denies us important knowledge and constitutes not the enactment of an active political stance but, on the contrary, a form of political 'faintheartedness' (Laclau, 2005: 249).

Understanding the EDL: representation, self-ascription and critical interpretation

This book is about the meanings individuals attach to activism rather than about the EDL as an organisation. If we start from the assumption that action is mean-ing-making, then it follows that a variety of meanings are made by activists in any movement (Beck, 2015: 93). Indeed, one of the findings of this study has been the diversity of people, positions and meanings attached to activism within the EDL. However, given the political sensitivity surrounding the EDL, its characterisation as an organisation cannot be evaded. The default position for an interpretivist social scientist would be to describe the movement as it is understood by the indi-vidual activists studied. In the case of research with 'distasteful groups', however, we are compelled to subject this understanding to the critical perspective of the outsider. Treading a fine line between the conflicting demands of capturing the meaning of the movement for its supporters and employing critical judgement of the movement arising from observation, the EDL has been characterised here as an anti-Islamist movement. This is in tune with other academic studies that con-clude that the EDL is distinct from the 'archetypal far-right party' (Copsey, 2010: 25) and operates as a social movement (Copsey, 2010; Jackson, 2011a). Describing it as 'anti-Islamist' reflects the single-issue focus – protesting against 'militant Islam' – of the movement as well as its defensive (politics of fear) rather than visionary (politics of hope) stance. At the same time it is recognised that there is slippage at movement level, and among individual supporters, into a broader anti-Islam or anti-Muslim position.

As an organisation, the EDL makes for a slippery object of study. This, it has been argued here, is not only because of the diversity within its ranks but because the movement is constituted in reflexive engagement with its own external rep-resentation. This representation as racist (as well as thuggish, drunken and uned-ucated) is a constant concern of activists. At one level these media representations of the movement confirm a sense of victim status and 'conspiracy' between polit-ical and cultural elites to silence 'ordinary' voices and concerns; in this sense they serve a bonding function. At the same time, exclusively negative portrayal of the movement is demotivating and undermines individuals' sense of efficacy. It is also materially damaging; the failure to rid the movement of its racist image is ostensi-bly the reason for the resignation of its founding leaders.

In contrast to the victim relationship the EDL perceives itself to have in relation to traditional media, it has used digital media – especially Facebook – extensively to organise, network and disseminate. However, the relationship between the EDL and the media, new and old, is more complex than suggested in existing literature. While social media have been employed relatively effectively to circumvent 'media blackout' in the traditional mass media, it remains a site of tension. Although significant control over Facebook use is devolved to local divisions, the right to 'say it as it is' emerges as a source of conflict between older and younger supporters and between 'admins' and grassroots activists. Many individual activists are sceptical and often hostile to the medium, prioritising face-to-face interactions that are better able to evoke the trust and loyalty central to the meanings individuals attach to their activism. Thus, the traditional media remain symbolically and politically important to the movement as it juggles the desire to get its message heard and its experience of engagement as one in which 'the only attention is bad attention'.

Real lives

Approaching this study as one that looks beyond organisational ideology to the individuals, with real lives, that constitute the movement, respondents are introduced as rounded individuals whose diverse trajectories in and out of activism are embedded in personal life stories. Activists, it is argued, are neither born, nor aggressively recruited, into the EDL. They are neither duped by a charismatic leader nor are they working-class anti-heroes. Their trajectories in and out of the movement are prosaic rather than heroic. Moreover, in contrast to the decisive entrances and exits into and from classic far right movements, activism in the EDL resembles rather a 'hokey-cokey' in which activists repeatedly engage and 'step-back' as they marry the costs and consequences of participation with their wider lives.

In tracing individual trajectories into extreme right activism, Linden and Klandermans (2007) elucidate a number of 'types' ('revolutionaries', 'wanderers', 'converts' and 'compliants'). While these are useful for distinguishing between experiences of activists, evidence from this study suggests that at both organisational and individual level, elements of more than one type are usually combined. Many activists participating in this research, for example, might be classified as 'converts' (2007: 184) in as much as they narrate their decision to join the EDL in terms of their experience of, or resistance to, injustice. However, post-hoc narrations cannot be equated with motivations for participation, and the emphasis on a life-changing moment in charting paths into the movement is not an accurate reflection of the longer and more multi-factorial process of joining the EDL encountered in this study. Thus, it is concluded, there is not one 'type' of person that is attracted to a movement like the EDL; rather decisions to start, continue and draw back from activism are set within a complex web of local environment, familial socialisation and personal psychodynamics.

For the ethical and methodological reasons discussed in the Introduction, full justice cannot be done in this book to the structural factors – especially environmental factors related to changes in local communities – that help explain paths into activism. However, the structural locations individuals inhabit are explored through respondents' perceptions and narrations of them. Traumatic and abusive experiences in childhood, as well as the experience of being bullied, are identified as persistent themes of personal and family psychodynamics. Political socialisation into the extreme right within the family is identified in some cases but is absent in others while friends and acquaintances rarely 'recruit' participants into the movement. Activism, rather, appears to be a site of the formation of new affective bonds of 'family', 'friendship', 'loyalty'.

Ideological dimensions of activism

The EDL claims to be a single-issue movement protesting against 'radical Islam' and disrespect for British troops. While, as noted above, academic studies tend to confirm the movement's own claims to being 'different' from traditional far right parties, they are sceptical about its insistence that it is 'not racist' and interpret it as 'clearly Islamophobic' (Allen, 2011: 203). This study, focusing as it does on the self-understandings and behaviour of grassroots activists concludes that individual activists (mainly) demonstrate a genuine aspiration to non-racism. At the organisational level, respondents concede that historic links with the BNP and the National Front mean that racist elements are encountered within the movement but remain adamant that this does not mean the movement itself is racist. They point to the commitment to 'kicking out racists' and to making the movement 'open to all' (regardless of colour, ethnicity, faith, gender and sexuality) as evidence of this aspiration. Central to respondents' understanding of the movement's non-racism is its hostility towards traditional far right parties (especially the BNP).

At the individual level, activists construct a non-racist self by mobilising a narrow definition of racism as prejudice based on skin colour. Their own non-racism is then confirmed on the grounds of their lack of such prejudice towards, and personal relationships with, non-white people. This 'non-racist' subject position is sealed by excluding any acknowledged discomfort with Muslims as not a question of 'race' because being 'Muslim' is not a racial but religious identifier. This allows individuals to hold, or condone others', anti-Muslim and anti-Islam sentiments since Muslims are consciously excluded from constituting a racially defined group and thus being a possible object of racism.

Thus central to the non-racism claimed by EDL activists is the appeal to a simple, and narrow, definition of 'race' and racism rooted not in a consistently post-racialist politics but akin to the 'post-race' argument, which does not deny the 'reality' of race but argues that it should not be grounds for prejudice and discrimination. This, of course, leaves the movement and its participants open to the accusation that they underestimate the continued impacts of racisms. This is evident in the presence of a range of 'everyday' racisms in EDL milieux and respondents' almost universal failure to recognise the structural conditions underpinning racism.

In sharp contrast to the importance attached to distancing themselves from racism as they understand it, EDL activists openly articulate the belief that there is a 'problem' with Islam that is not associated with other aspects of multicultural society. The findings of this study demonstrate that Islam is understood by EDL activists as 'separate and other' in a way determined by the Runnymede Trust (1997) to be characteristic of an Islamophobic mindset. While amongst activists there are those who explicitly distinguish only 'radical', 'extremist' or 'militant'

Islam as the object of their concern, there is also routine slippage into talk of Islam or Muslims as single entities and a failure to distinguish between different branches of Islam, different ethnic groups among Muslims or between 'extremist' and 'moderate' readings of Islam.

Central to respondents' claims that the EDL is 'not racist' is that hostility is expressed towards 'Islam' rather than 'Muslims' or ethnic groups of Muslim faith. For this reason, data on associations with Islam and associations with Muslims were analysed separately in this study. This revealed that respondents frequently emphasised that their hostility was towards Islam rather than Muslims and that generalised anti-Muslim sentiments were often replaced by criticisms of what respondents understood to be Islamic doctrine or teachings. Moreover, in contrast to the most frequent associations of Islam with extremism, terrorism and violence found among the UK general population (Field, 2012: 150), the primary tropes in associations with Islam among EDL activists in this study are that Islam is 'backward-looking', oppressive and intolerant (as well as aggressive and supportive of terrorism). This is encapsulated in the understanding of Islam as an 'ideology' rather than a religion and of the EDL as an organisation as anti-Islamist rather than Islamophobic.

Being anti-Islam, however, does not exclude being anti-Muslim also. Evidence from this study shows slippage, especially in the context of songs and chants at demonstrations, into the use of generalised terms of abuse towards Muslims. The question of whether this hostility is directed at Muslims as members of particular ethnic groups or 'immigrants' rather than against Muslims as a religious group – as suggested by Halliday's (1999) preference for the term 'anti-Muslimism' over Islamophobia – is more complex. Explicit racialisation, in the form of abusive rhetoric, is identified among a number of respondents alongside the equally explicit rejection of any such racialisation and abuse among others. Similarly, the association of Muslims with violence and terror by some is accompanied by a rhetoric of differentiation between 'extreme' and 'moderate' Muslims by others.

When talking about 'Muslims' (as opposed to 'Islam'), it is important to note, associations with ideologically motivated terror are less common than reference to localised, everyday 'intimidating' behaviour, threats or violent actions perpetrated by 'Muslims'. This suggests that alongside a non-racialised anti-Islamist ideological agenda runs an anti-Muslim sentiment that is expressed through more everyday encounters and community relations and in which Muslims are perceived as particularly problematic and unwelcome immigrants. Islam is a contributing but not exclusive factor in this. Thus, this study suggests that Bleich (2011: 1587) is right to argue for a definition of Islamophobia that recognises its multidimensionality and includes both Islam as a religious doctrine and/or Muslims.

Two strong tropes of anti-Muslim hostility identified among grassroots EDL activists in this study – that Muslims seek to 'impose their rules here' and that Muslims 'have no respect' – suggest that one of the key characteristics attributed to the Muslim 'other' is itself the practice of 'othering' (of non-Muslims). Expressions of anti-Muslim sentiment thus include perceptions that the Muslim 'other' constitutes a direct infringement of, or sets itself in superior position to, respondents' 'self'. Recognising that 'thoughts and feelings about the Self' are highly implicated in the formation of associations of the 'other' (Ezekiel, 2002: 54) opens the way to questioning the rather one-dimensional vision of the empowered subject of 'othering' found in existing models of Islamophobia.

The most consistent and emotionally charged narrative of 'self' identified among respondents in this study is that of 'second-class citizen'. This narrative is rooted in a sense of profound injustice based on the perception, almost universally expressed among respondents, that the needs of others are privileged over their own. While the perceived beneficiaries of that injustice might be racialised (as 'immigrants', 'Muslims' or ethnic minorities), and it is claimed that they are afforded preferential treatment in terms of access to benefits, housing and jobs, the agent responsible for this injustice is understood to be a weak-willed or frightened government that panders to the demands of a minority for fear of being labelled racist. This injustice is understood to be institutionalised through a 'two-tier' justice system which privileges minorities whilst discriminating against 'us'.

The narrative of second-class citizenship reveals the way in which sections of the white working class fail to recognise 'self' as privileged majority. They perceive themselves rather as the victims of discrimination and in some cases of violence or abuse; the anger at this is amplified by the conviction that such discrimination and abuse go unrecognised by the media, police and political system when the victims are white. This suggests that even when respondents target anger and 'blame' for their perceived 'second-class' status at government and its agencies rather than immigrant communities, they nonetheless naturalise assumptions of racially based inequality; that 'we' not 'they' should be prioritised is the natural order (Rhodes, 2009).

EDL activism is experienced by respondents in this study as a means of resisting this second-class citizen status. This is accomplished through a discursive reordering of privilege and prejudice and a collective understanding of the EDL as a movement of 'the common people' prepared to 'stand up' and 'fight back' against the government, and wider circles of power controlled by liberal elite 'do-gooders', who have little understanding of the everyday worlds they inhabit.

Emotional and affective dimensions of activism

The recent rehabilitation of the role of emotions in social movement theory alongside new theoretical impulses from the 'affective turn' in the social sciences, has led to an increasingly nuanced discussion of different types of emotions in movements (Goodwin, Jasper and Polletta, 2001: 20) and how activists perform their networks through diverse bodily movements, techniques and styles, generating distinct emotional tones (Juris, 2008: 89). This shift in the field has largely bypassed studies of extreme and populist radical right movements, however, where collective emotions are seen as consciously orchestrated by leaders among masses in order to construct emotional collectives (Virchow, 2007: 148). This instrumental approach has been questioned by the findings of this study, which suggest that affective bonds within the EDL are generated from the bottom-up through a sense of 'togetherness' that emerges from shared activism and that binds members of the movement.

Previous academic studies of the EDL have focused almost exclusively on the ideological dimensions of activism. However, this study found friendship, loyalty and the sense of belonging to a 'family' to be the most frequently cited meanings attached to activism. This is reflected in the repeated claim that EDL members stand up for, and look after, each other and in the practice of mutual care both during and outside of actions. These bonds – experienced as being 'like one big family' – enhance the pleasures associated with activism and thus are central to sustaining it. This confirms Goodwin, Jasper and Polletta's (2001: 20) argument that, while distinct, 'reciprocal' and 'shared' emotions reinforce each other in the formation of a movement's culture. It is important, however, not to romanticise reciprocal emotions and the affective bonds they generate. The sense of collective belonging and emotional support described above is not universal and interpersonal relationships central to the formation and maintenance of the emotional collective can also be a site of tension that ultimately undermines the movement (Jasper, 1998: 419).

While recognising the limitations of the data gathered for a nuanced study of the role of affect in the EDL, an attempt was made in Chapter 7 to capture and analyse moments during activism where affect – understood as non-conscious movement from one experiential state of the body to another – becomes tangible and, sometimes, articulated. These moments included points at which senses are overwhelmed by the crowd, when respondents feel the 'buzz' or 'rush' of the demonstration or are lost in the pleasures of communal singing, chanting and marching. Drawing on Wetherell (2012), it has been suggested here that affect is best understood as a 'practice' rooted in social life and concrete activities rather than as a 'contagion', virtual or transhuman process that takes place outside the subjectivities of those experiencing them (Shields, Park and Davidson, 2011: 318). This approach reconnects emotion, affect and the *meanings* attached to activism at the cognitive level (Wetherell, 2012: 148).

The entwinement of rationalised and emotional dimensions of activism is epitomised in the understanding of EDL activism by respondents as standing 'loud and proud'. This affective practice – manifest primarily in participation in street demonstrations – is one of a battery of means of 'getting your point across' and 'being heard' in a political system that is perceived to be set up not for dialogue with people but for their compliant listening. EDL activists in this study experience the external political realm as governed by a politics of silencing in which the expression of their views, as well as government policy, are constrained by the application of the 'racism label'. They learn that the best strategy for negotiating this realm is to 'keep your mouth shut'.

This shutting down of political space compounds a wider disengagement with the formal political sphere and a denial of the 'political' by respondents. While such disillusionment with the party political system is increasingly common across the general population, it is striking that, despite their active political engagement, EDL activists in this study often articulated a rejection of politics per se, characterising it as meaningless 'debate'. In contrast to the duplicitous chatter of formal politics, activism in the EDL is understood as 'telling it as it is', practised as part of a wider 'non-politics' of action.

This disengagement on the part of EDL activists, it has been argued, is a radical variant of views found in wider society rather than 'a normal pathology unconnected to the mainstream' (Mudde, 2007: 297). This is demonstrated through the absence (with limited exceptions) of alternative anti-democratic ideologies typically associated with traditional far right parties and movements. While activists in this study are highly critical of the contemporary working of democracy, that criticism is directed primarily at governments (past and present) rather than at the democratic system as a whole. The only alternative suggested to parliamentary democracy by respondents (with the exception of the three fringe Infidels activists) was the restoration of the powers of the monarchy.

The politics, and humanity, of research

This book is political because its original quest for honest enquiry became, in the course of research, a political position. That position might be framed, first, as the recognition that such research is essential, even in fields of study where the need to tackle continued oppression and injustice is evident and urgent. Transgressing the *cordon sanitaire* erected around movements like the EDL in order to mark out the moral high ground from which the political grievances of others can be safely ignored, dismissed or condemned is to take a political stance. If that transgression is driven not by self-interest (in vicarious living or notoriety) but by the conviction that effective action to combat racism requires honest enquiry (Ezekiel, 1995: xxxv), then, it is, notwithstanding its potential to offend, politically progressive.

Second, dismissing individuals participating in movements such as the EDL as blinded by 'fascist' or 'racist' ideology, and thereby excluding them from what constitutes the political, is, in contrast, politically non-progressive. This is because it fails to recognise the impact of wider structural change on white working-class communities (alongside its impact on often even more impoverished ethnic minority communities) (Lone and Silver, 2014: 178) as well as the underlying frustration with the contemporary constitution of politics among those communities. Ashe (2014), considering the collapse of electoral support for the BNP, draws the opposite conclusion. The labelling of the BNP as fascists, Nazis and racists, he argues, is, at least partially effective, since this association of the party is the principal reason voters choose not to vote for the BNP, even if they hold racist points of view themselves. While I would agree with Ashe that an anti-racist ethos and inter-ethnic solidarity are best promoted by sustained, local community-based campaigning and organisations, I am less convinced that 'condemnation strategies' are politically effective in more than particular localised and short-term contexts. The disagreement reflects the insights derived from different observational positions of research. From the viewing point of anti-fascist activism, mainstream political parties appear to 'have pandered to, and legitimised, the politics of the BNP' (Ashe, 2014). In contrast, this study of EDL activists, as well research among the kinds of communities from which the movement draws its support (see Lone and Silver, 2014), suggests that the external political environment is experienced as a sphere of condemnation and silencing. From this perspective 'condemnation strategies' are likely to be counterproductive in that they act to consolidate the sense of exclusion and reify resentment. There is widespread agreement that this resentment exists and growing empirical understanding of its contours; the question that continues to divide is how, politically, it should be treated. While Ware (2008: 2) argues that white working-class resentment is used too frequently in current political and media discourse in the UK to explain, and excuse, racist or anti-social attitudes, Kenny (2012: 24) suggests that at least some of the grievances expressed might 'merit a more sympathetic hearing by the state'.

Third, this position is one that views the 'moralisation' of politics as not strengthening but weakening democratic politics. Responding to right-wing populism by labelling it 'extreme-right' and dismissing it through a discourse of moral condemnation is indicative of a wider shift of the political terrain from a struggle between 'right and left' to that between 'right and wrong' (Mouffe, 2005: 4–5), which, for those deemed 'wrong', reinforces the experience of the external political realm as a 'politics of silencing'. This, Mouffe (2005: 71–72) argues, facilitates the potential for right-wing populist movements to exploit popular frustration whilst simultaneously providing people with some form of hope that things could be different; although this is an 'illusory hope', founded on unacceptable mechanisms of xenophobic exclusion, when it is the only channel for the expression of political passions, it is seductive. If 'societies are mechanisms for the distribution of hope' (Hage, 2003: 3, cited in Ware, 2008: 9) it is essential that all are included in the distribution chain.

Finally, this position understands the potential of ethnographic research conducted from the 'other' side of the cordon to get at the humanity of people (Duneier and Back, 2006: 554) and to have political as well as academic significance. Engaging with activists as individuals with real lives allows for the articulation and observation of those lives in all their human dimensions. It provides insight into how and why individuals fail to recognise 'self' as the privileged majority, how this contributes to the racialisation of both 'other' and 'self' and how this acts to discourage the formation of alliances across ethnic, cultural or religious lines. The sustained presence in the lives of others opens us to capturing those fleeting moments when the oppression of others *is* recognised and solidarity that cuts across perceived cultural and ethnic differences becomes imminent. To see and hear this requires the researcher to take a stand on the moral low ground, behind the *cordon sanitaire*, and to practice 'the art of listening' (Back, 2007: 12) in a way that does not silence race but pushes us, often painfully, towards a way of talking about the effects of racialisation that might enable us to move beyond its oppressive force.

Appendix 1 Observed events

Type of event	Name of event	Date of event	Recorded data
National demos			
1.	EDL demo, Dewsbury	30 June 2012	diary entry visual data
2.	EDL demo, Bristol	14 July 2012	diary entry visual data
3.	EDL demo, Walthamstow	1 September 2012	diary entry visual data arrest docket
4.	EDL demo, Walsall	29 September 2012	diary entry visual data
5.	EDL demo, Norwich	10 November 2012	diary entry visual data
6.	EVF demo, Birmingham	26 January 2013	diary entry visual data
7.	North West Alliance/EDL demo, Manchester	2 March 2013	diary entry visual data
8.	EDL demo, Newcastle	25 May 2013	diary entry visual data
9.	EDL demo, Birmingham	20 July 2013	diary entry visual data
10.	EDL demo, Tower Hamlets	7 September 2013	diary entry visual data
11.	EDL demo, Bradford	12 October 2013	diary entry visual data
12.	EDL demo, Rotherham	10 May 2014	diary entry visual data
13.	EDL demo, Rotherham	13 September 2014	diary entry visual data
14.	EDL demo, Luton	22 November 2014	diary entry visual data
Local demos			
1.	EDL demo, Solihull	12 January 2013	diary entry visual data short video interviews
2.	EDL demo, Leeds (Moortown)	4 May 2013	diary entry visual data
Flash demos			
1.	Protest against conversion of public building into Islamic Cultural Centre	18 May 2013	diary entry visual data

Type of event	Name of event	Date of event	Recorded data
2.	Sit down protest on main road, post Lee Rigby murder	24 May 2013	diary entry visual data
3.	Protest at Council Planning Committee meeting against building of new mosque	28 May 2013	diary entry
4.	Protest against refusal to allow poppy sellers at shopping centre	9 November 2013	diary entry

Divisional meetings

1.	Divisional meeting, pub HQ	31 August 2012	diary entry
2.	Divisional meeting, pub HQ	19 October 2012	diary entry
3.	Divisional meeting, new pub HQ	4 April 2013	diary entry
4.	Divisional meeting, new pub HQ	31 August 2014	diary entry
5.	Regional 'Meet and greet', pub HQ	4 October 2014	diary entry

Other events

1.	St George's Day march and carnival	21 April 2013	diary entry visual data
2.	Trial of two EDL members accused of violent disorder, Crown Court	7–10 October 2013	diary entry
3.	Meeting with EDL leaders and police contact to plan forthcoming demonstration	24 July 2015	diary entry

Appendix 2 Respondent set

Pseudonym	Gender	Age	Ethnicity (self-declared)	Educational status	Employment status	Family status	Residential status
1 Andrew	male	23	White/English	completed university	unemployed	single	lives with parents
2 Brett	male	16	White/English/ Northern Irish	currently in secondary education	in full-time education	single	lives with parents
3 Carlie	female	25	British [rejects 'White' British]	n/k	not employed (carer)	married/living with partner and children	lives with partner and children
4 Casey	female	29	White/British	completed vocational education to age 18	unemployed/ (later) employed part-time	living with partner/ child	lives with partner and child
5 Chas	male	18	White	currently in vocational education	in full-time education	single	lives independently alone
6 Chris	male	18	White/English	completed general academic education to age 16	unemployed	single	lives independently alone
7 Connor	male	15	White/English	currently in general academic education	in full-time education	single	lives with grandparents
8 Declan	male	19	English	completed general academic education to age 16	unemployed	single	lives with parents
9 Ed	male	42	White/English	completed vocational education to age 18	not employed (carer)	divorced	lives with own children

Pseudonym	Gender	Age	Ethnicity (self-declared)	Educational status	Employment status	Family status	Residential status
10 Euan	male	33	White/British	n/k	irregularly employed	living with partner/child	lives with partner and child
11 Ian	male	49	White/English	completed general academic education to age 16	unemployed	divorced/separated	lives independently alone
12 Jack	male	47	White	completed general academic education to age 16	irregular self-employment	living with partner/child	lives with partner and child
13 Jason	male	25	White/English	completed vocational education to age 18	employed/(later) unemployed	living with partner	lives with partner and other relatives (in-laws)
14 Jordan	male	23	White/English	completed general academic education to age 16	in full-time employment	living with partner/child	lives with partner and other relatives (in-laws)
15 Kane	male	17	White/British	currently in vocational secondary education	in part-time education	single	lives with father
16 Kyle	male	20	White/English	did not complete secondary education	in full-time employment	single	lives with parents
17 Kylie	female	23	White/English	completed general secondary education to age 18	not employed (carer)	living with partner/children	lives independently with own partner/children
18 Kurt	male	49	White/English	completed vocational secondary education to age 18	employed/(later) unemployed	single	lives independently alone

Pseudonym	Gender	Age	Ethnicity (self-declared)	Educational status	Employment status	Family status	Residential status
19 Lisa	female	39	British/ White/ Black African	completed general academic education to age 18	unemployed	living with partner	lives with partner
20 Matt	male	34	White/British	completed general academic education to age 16	irregularly employed	living with partner/ child	lives with partner and child
21 Michelle	female	29	White/English	did not complete secondary education	in full-time employment	single	lives independently alone
22 Mike	male	n/k >46	n/k	n/k	unemployed (disability)	living with partner	lives independently with partner
23 Neil	male	19	White/British	did not complete secondary education	unemployed	single	lives independently alone (about to move in with relatives)
24 Nick	male	16	White/British	did not complete secondary education	unemployed	single	lives with grandparents
25 Ollie	male	18	White/English	currently in general academic secondary education	in full-time education	single	lives with parents
26 Peter	male	23	n/k	completed vocational secondary education to age 18	in full-time employment	single	lives independently alone
27 Rachel	female	48	White/British	completed general academic education to age 16	irregular self-employment	separated	lives independently alone

Pseudonym	Gender	Age	Ethnicity (self-declared)	Educational status	Employment status	Family status	Residential status
28 Ray	male	18	White/English	currently in vocational education	in full-time education	single	lives with grandparents
29 Richard	male	28	White/English	completed general academic education to age 16	in full-time employment	single	lives independently alone
30 Rob	male	45	White/English	did not complete secondary education	unemployed/ irregular self-employment	separated	lives independently alone
31 Ryan	male	19	White/British	completed vocational education to age 18	in full-time education	single	lives with parents
32 Sean	male	28	White/English	did not complete secondary education	unemployed	separated	lives independently alone
33 Theresa	female	n/k >46	n/k	n/k	n/k	separated	lives with own children
34 Tim	male	25	White/English	completed secondary education to age 16	irregular self-employment	single	lives with father
35 Tina	female	31	White/English	currently in higher education	in full-time education	living with partner/ children	lives with partner/ children

References

Abbas, T. and Akhtar, P. (2005) 'The new sociology of British ethnic and cultural relations: the experience of British South Asian Muslims in the post-September 11 climate' in H. Henke (ed.) *Crossing Over: Comparing Recent Migration in Europe and the United States*, Lanham, MD: Lexington Books, pp. 130–46.

Adorno, T.W., Frenkel-Brunswik, E., Levinson, D.J. and Sanford, R.N. (1950) *The Authoritarian Personality*, New York: Norton.

Ahmed, S. (2004) 'Affective economies', *Social Text*, 22(2): 117–39.

Allen, C. (2010) *Islamophobia*, Farnham: Ashgate.

Allen, C. (2011) 'Opposing Islamification or promoting Islamophobia? Understanding the English Defence League', *Patterns of Prejudice*, 45(4): 279–94.

Alexander, C. (2013) 'The Muslim question(s): reflections from a race and ethnic studies perspective' in C. Alexander, V. Redclift and A. Hussain (eds) *The New Muslims*, London: Runnymede Trust, pp. 5–7.

Allport, G. (1979) *The Nature of Prejudice*, New York: Basic Books.

Anderson, B. (2009) 'Affective atmospheres', *Emotion, Space and Society*, 2: 77–81.

Ashe, S. (2012) *The Electoral Rise and 'Fall' of the British National Party in Barking and Dagenham*, PhD thesis, Glasgow: University of Glasgow.

Ashe, S. (2014) 'Why the British National Party didn't get more votes', available at: http://blog.policy.manchester.ac.uk/featured/2014/07/why-the-british-national-party-didnt-get-more-votes. Accessed: 04.08.2015.

Atton, C. (2006) 'Far-right media on the Internet: culture, discourse and power', *New Media Society* 8(4): 573–87.

Back, L. (1996) *New Ethnicities and Urban Culture: Racisms and Multiculture in Young Lives*, London: University College London Press.

Back, L. (2002) 'Guess who's coming to dinner? The political morality of investigating whiteness in the gray zone' in V. Ware and L. Back, *Out of Whiteness: Color, Politics, and Culture*, Chicago and London: University of Chicago Press, pp. 15–32.

Back, L. (2007) *The Art of Listening*, Oxford and New York: Berg.

Back, L., and Solomos, J. (1993) 'Doing research, writing politics: the dilemmas of political intervention in research on racism', *Economy and Society*, 22: 178–99.

Back, L., Keith, M. and Solomos, J. (1998) 'Racism on the Internet: mapping neo-fascist subcultures in cyberspace' in J. Kaplan and T. Bjørgo (eds) *Nation and Race: The Developing Euro-American Racist Subculture*, Boston: Northeastern University Press, pp. 73–101.

Barker, M. (1981) *The New Racism*, London: Junction Books.

Bartlett, J. and Littler, M. (2011) *Inside the EDL: Populist Politics in a Digital Age*, London: Demos, available at: http://www.demos.co.uk/files/Inside_the_edl_WEB. pdf?1331035419. Accessed: 28.08.2015.

Bartlett, J., Birdwell, J. and Littler, M. (2011) *The New Face of Digital Populism*, London: Demos, available at: www.demos.co.uk/publications/thenewfaceofdigitalpopulism. Accessed: 06.06.2015.

Beck, C. (2015) *Radicals, Revolutionaries and Terrorists*, Cambridge: Polity Press.

Beck, U. and Beck-Gernsheim, E. (2002) *Individualization: Institutionalized Individualism and Its Social and Political Consequences*, London: Sage.

Billig, M. (1978) *Fascists: A Social Psychological View of the National Front*, London and New York: Harcourt Brace Jovanovich.

Blee, K. (2002) *Inside Organized Racism: Women in the Hate Movement*, Berkeley and Los Angeles: University of California Press.

Blee, K. (2007) 'Ethnographies of the Far Right', *Journal of Contemporary Ethnography*, 36(2): 119–28.

Bleich, E. (2011) 'What is Islamophobia and how much is there? Theorizing and measuring an emerging comparative concept', *American Behavioral Scientist*, 55(12): 1581–1600.

Bleich, E. and Maxwell, R. (2012) 'Assessing Islamophobia in Britain' in M. Helbling (ed.) *Islamophobia in the West: Measuring and Explaining Individual Attitudes*, London and New York: Routledge, pp. 39–55.

Bottero, W. (2009) 'Class in the 21st century' in K.P. Sveinsson (ed.) *Who Cares about the White Working Class?*, Chichester: Runnymede Trust, pp. 7–14.

Bourdieu, P. and Wacquant, L. (1992) *An Invitation to Reflexive Sociology*, Oxford: Polity Press.

Brown, G. and Pickerill, J. (2009) 'Space for emotion in the spaces of activism', *Emotion, Space and Society*, 2: 24–35.

Bucerius, S.M. (2013) 'Becoming a "trusted outsider": gender, ethnicity, and inequality in ethnographic research', *Journal of Contemporary Ethnography*, 42(6): 690–721.

Busher, J. (2012) 'From ethnic nationalisms to clashing civilizations: reconfigurations of (un)civil religion in an era of globalization', *Religion Compass*, 6(9): 414–25.

Busher, J. (2013) 'Grassroots activism in the English Defence League: discourse and public (dis)order' in M. Taylor, P.M. Currie and D. Holbrook (eds) *Extreme Right Wing Political Violence and Terrorism*, London: Bloomsbury, pp. 65–84.

Bygnes, S. (2012) 'Ambivalent multiculturalism', *Sociology*, 47(1): 126–41.

Castells, M. (2012) *Networks of Outrage and Hope: Social Movements in the Internet Age*, Cambridge: Polity Press.

Clarke, J. (1993) 'Style' in S. Hall and T. Jefferson (eds) *Resistance through Rituals: Youth Subcultures in Post-war Britain*, London: Routledge, pp. 175–91.

Clarke, S. and Garner, S. (2010) *White Identities: A Critical Sociological Approach*, London: Pluto Press.

Clifford, J. (1986) 'Introduction: partial truths' in J. Clifford and G. Marcus (eds) *Writing Culture: Poetics and Politics of Ethnography*, Los Angeles: University of California Press, pp. 1–26.

Cockburn, T. (2007) '"Performing" racism: engaging young supporters of the far right in England', *British Journal of Sociology of Education*, 28(5): 547–60.

Collins, M. (2011) *Hate: My life in the British Far Right*, London: Biteback.

Collins, M. (2013) 'Sunderland drug dealer threatens Muslim EDL member', *The Insider's blog*, 5 November, available at: www.hopenothate.org.uk/blog/insider/sunderland-drug-dealer-threatens-muslim-edl-member-3162. Accessed: 07.05.2015.

Collins, R. (2001) 'Social movements and the focus of emotional attention' in J. Goodwin, J.M. Jasper and F. Polletta (eds) *Passionate Politics: Emotions and Social Movements*, Chicago: University of Chicago Press, pp. 27–44.

Copsey, N. (2010) *The English Defence League: A Challenge to Our Country and Our Values of Social Inclusion, Fairness and Equality*, London: Faith Matters.

Crossley, N. (2002) *Making sense of social movements*, Buckingham: Open University Press.

Crowley, J. (2007) 'Friend or foe? Self-expansion, stigmatized groups, and the researcher–participant relationship', *Journal of Contemporary Ethnography*, 36(6): 603–30.

Dancygier, R. (2010) *Immigration and Conflict in Europe*, Cambridge: Cambridge University Press.

Della Porta, D. (2008) 'Research on Social Movements and Political Violence', *Qualitative Sociology*, 31: 221–30.

Della Porta, D. (2013) *Can Democracy Be Saved?* Cambridge: Polity Press.

Di Nunzio, D. and Toscano, E. (2014) 'Taking everything back: CasaPound, a far right movement in Italy' in A. Farro and H. Lustinger-Thaler (eds) *Reimagining Social Movements*, Farnham and Burlington, VT: Ashgate, pp. 251–63.

Duncombe, J. and Jessop, J. (2002) '"Doing rapport" and the ethics of "faking friendship"' in M. Mauthner, M. Birch, J. Jessop and T. Miller (eds) *Ethics in Qualitative Research*, London: Sage, pp. 108–23.

Duneier, M. and Back, L. (2006) 'Voices from the sidewalk: ethnography and writing race', *Ethnic and Racial Studies*, 29(3): 543–65.

Eddowes, S. (2015) Interview with author, 18.07.2015.

Edwards, G. (2014) *Social Movements and Protest*, Cambridge: Cambridge University Press.

Esseveld, J. and Eyerman, R. (1992) 'Which side are you on? Reflections on methodological issues in the study of "distasteful" social movements' in M. Diani and R. Eyerman (eds) *Studying Collective Action*, London: Sage, pp. 217–37.

Ezekiel, R.S. (1995) *The Racist Mind: Portraits of American neo-Nazis and Klansmen*. New York: Penguin Books.

Ezekiel, R.S. (2002) 'An ethnographer looks at neo-Nazi and Klan groups: the racist mind revisited', *American Behavioral Scientist*, 46: 51–71.

Field, C.D. (2012) 'Revisiting Islamophobia in contemporary Britain, 2007–10' in M. Helbling (ed.) *Islamophobia in the West: Measuring and Explaining Individual Attitudes*, London and New York: Routledge, pp. 147–61.

Fielding, N. (1981) *The National Front*, London: Routledge and Kegan Paul.

Fielding, N. (1993) 'Mediating the message: affinity and hostility in research on sensitive topics' in C. Renzetti and R. Lee (eds) *Researching Sensitive Topics*, Newbury Park, CA: Sage, pp. 146–59.

Ford, R. and Goodwin, M. (2014) *Revolt on the Right: Explaining Support for the Radical Right in Britain*, London and New York: Routledge.

Francois-Cerrah, M. (2012) 'The truth about Muhammad and Aisha', *The Guardian*, 17 September, available at: www.theguardian.com/commentisfree/belief/2012/sep/17/muhammad-aisha-truth. Accessed: 06.08.2015.

Furedi, F. (2005) *Politics of Fear: Beyond Left or Right*, London and New York: Continuum.

Garland, J. and Treadwell, J. (2010) '"No surrender to the Taliban": football hooliganism, Islamophobia and the rise of the English Defence League', *Papers from the British Criminology Conference*, 10: 19–35.

Garland, J. and Treadwell, J. (2011) 'Masculinity, marginalization and violence: a case study of the English Defence League', *British Journal of Criminology*, 51(4): 621–34.

Garner, S. (2009) 'Home truths: the white working class and the racialization of social housing' in K.P. Sveinsson (ed.) *Who Cares about the White Working Class?*, Chichester: Runnymede Trust, pp. 45–50.

Garner, S. and Selod, S. (2015) 'The racialization of Muslims: empirical studies of Islamophobia', *Critical Sociology*, 41(1): 9–19.

Gillan, K. and Pickerill, J. (2012) 'The difficult and hopeful ethics of research on, and with, social movements', *Social Movement Studies: Journal of Social, Cultural and Political Protest*, 11(2): 133–43.

Gillies, V. and Alldred, P. (2002) 'The ethics of intention: research as a political tool' in M. Mauthner, M. Birch, J. Jessop and T. Miller (eds) *Ethics in Qualitative Research*, London: Sage, pp. 32–52.

Gilroy, P. (2000) *Against Race: Imagining Political Culture beyond the Color Line*, Cambridge, MA: Belknap Press of Harvard University Press.

Goffman, E. (1990) *The Presentation of Self in Everyday Life*, London: Penguin Books.

Goldberg, D.T. (2006) 'Racial Europeanization', *Ethnic and Racial Studies*, 29(2): 331–64.

Goodwin, J., Jasper, J.M. and Polletta, F. (2001) 'Why emotions matter' in J. Goodwin, J. M. Jasper and F. Polletta (eds) *Passionate Politics: Emotions and Social Movements*, Chicago: University of Chicago Press, pp. 1–24.

Goodwin, M. (2011a) *New British Fascism: Rise of the British National Party*, London and New York: Routledge.

Goodwin, M. (2011b) 'Right response: understanding and countering populist extremism in Europe', *A Chatham House Report*, London: Royal Institute of International Affairs (Chatham House).

Goodwin, M., Ford, R., Duffy, B. and Robey, R. (2010) 'Who votes extreme right in twenty-first-century Britain? The social bases of support for the National Front and British National Party' in R. Eatwell and M. Goodwin (eds) *The New Extremism in 21st Century Britain*, London and New York: Routledge, pp. 191–210.

Gover, D. (2012) 'EDL leader Tommy Robinson faces trial for passport allegation after 9/11 US Speech', *International Business Times*, 22 October, available at: www.ibtimes.co.uk/english-defence-league-arrests-robinson-extradition-396866. Accessed: 23.03.2014.

Grimm, R. and Pilkington, H. (2015) '"Loud and proud": youth and the politics of silencing', *Sociological Review*, 63(S2): 206–30.

Hafez, F. (2014) 'Shifting borders: Islamophobia as common ground for building pan-European right-wing unity', *Patterns of Prejudice*, 48(5): 479–99.

Hage, G. (2003) *Against Paranoid Nationalism: Searching for Hope in a Shrinking Society*, London: Merlin Press.

Hage, G. (2014) 'Continuity and change in Australian racism', *Journal of Intercultural Studies*, 35(3): 232–37.

Hallet, R. and Barber, K. (2014) 'Ethnographic research in a cyber era', *Journal of Contemporary Ethnography*, 43(3): 306–30.

Halliday, F. (1999) '"Islamophobia" reconsidered', *Ethnic and Racial Studies*, 22(5): 892–902.

Hann, D. and Tilzey, S. (2003) *No Retreat: The Secret War between Britain's Anti-fascists and the Far Right*, Lancashire: Milo Books.

Hay, C. (2007) *Why We Hate Politics*, Cambridge: Polity Press.

Heath, A. and Demireva, N. (2014) 'Has multiculturalism failed in Britain?', *Ethnic and Racial Studies*, 37(1): 161–80.

Helbling, M. (2012) 'Islamophobia in the West: an introduction' in M. Helbling (ed.) *Islamophobia in the West: Measuring and Explaining Individual Attitudes*, London and New York: Routledge, pp. 1–18.

Herring, S. (2001) 'Computer-mediated discourse' in D. Schiffrin, D. Tannen and H. Hamilton (eds) *Handbook of Discourse Analysis*, Oxford: Blackwell.

Hewitt, R. (2005) *White Backlash and the Politics of Multiculturalism*, Cambridge: Cambridge University Press.

Hogg, M. (2012) 'Self-uncertainty, social identity, and the solace of extremism' in M. Hogg and D.L. Blaylock (eds) *Extremism and the Psychology of Uncertainty*, Oxford: Wiley-Blackwell, pp. 19–35.

Ignazi, P. (2003) *Extreme Right Parties in Western Europe*, Oxford: Oxford University Press.

Jackson, P. (2011a) 'The English Defence League: anti-Muslim politics online' in P. Jackson and G. Gable (eds) *Far-Right.Com: Nationalist Extremism on the Internet*, Northampton: Searchlight Magazine and the Radicalism and New Media Research Group, pp. 7–19.

Jackson, P. (2011b) 'Conclusions' in P. Jackson and G. Gable (eds) *Far-Right.Com: Nationalist Extremism on the Internet*, Northampton: Searchlight Magazine and the Radicalism and New Media Research Group, pp. 70–75.

Jackson, P. (2011c) *The EDL: Britain's 'New Far Right' Social Movement*, Northampton: RNM Publications, University of Northampton.

Jackson, P. and Gable, G. (eds) (2011) *Far-Right.Com: Nationalist Extremism on the Internet*, Northampton: Searchlight Magazine and the Radicalism and New Media Research Group.

Jasper, J. (1998) 'The Emotions of Protest: Affective and Reactive Emotions in and around Social Movements', *Sociological Forum*, 13(3): 397–424.

Jivraj, S. (2012) 'How has ethnic diversity grown 1991–2001–2011?', *Centre on Dynamics of Ethnicity (CoDE)*, University of Manchester, available at: www.eth-nicity.ac.uk/medialibrary/briefings/dynamicsofdiversity/how-has-ethnic-diversi-ty-grown-1991-2001-2011.pdf. Accessed: 25.06.2015.

Jivraj, S. (2013) 'Muslims in England and Wales: evidence from the 2011 Census' in C. Alexander, V. Redclift and A. Hussain (eds) *The New Muslims*, London: Runnymede Trust, pp. 16–19.

Jivraj, S. and Khan, O. (2013) 'Ethnicity and deprivation in England: how likely are ethnic minorities to live in deprived neighbourhoods?' *Centre on Dynamics of Ethnicity (CoDE)*, University of Manchester, available at: www.ethnicity.ac.uk/medialibrary/briefingsupdated/ethnicity-and-deprivation-in-england-how-likely-are-ethnic-mi norities-to-live-in-deprived-neighbourhoods%20(1).pdf. Accessed: 30.06.2015.

Jivraj, S. and Simpson, L. (2013) '2011 Census: Muslims and Sikhs most likely to feel British', available at: www.manchester.ac.uk/discover/news/article/?id=10147. Acces-sed: 22.04.2015.

Juris, J. (2008) 'Performing politics: Image, embodiment, and affective solidarity during anti-corporate globalization protests', *Ethnography*, 9(1): 61–97.

Kalkan, K.O., Layman, G.C. and Uslaner, E.M. (2009) '"Band of others?" Attitudes toward Muslims in contemporary American society', *The Journal of Politics*, 71(3): 847–62.

Kalra, V.S. (2006) 'Ethnography as politics: a critical review of British studies of racialized minorities', *Ethnic and Racial Studies*, 29(3): 452–70.

Kelly, N. (2012) 'A boycott of the police commissioner elections could let in extremists',

The Guardian, 22 October, available at: www.theguardian.com/commentisfree/2012/oct/22/police-commissioner-election-extremists. Accessed: 05.05.2014.

Kenny, M. (2012) 'The political theory of recognition: the case of the "white working class"', *British Journal of Politics and International Relations*, 14(1): 19–38.

Kimmel , M. (2007) 'Racism as adolescent male rite of passage: ex-Nazis in Scandinavia', *Journal of Contemporary Ethnography*, 36(2): 202–18.

Kirby, R. and Corzine, J. (1981) 'The contagion of stigma: fieldwork among deviants', *Qualitative Sociology*, 4(1): 3–20.

Kitschelt, H. (2007) 'Growth and persistence of the radical right in postindustrial democracies: advances and challenges in comparative research', *West European Politics*, 20(5): 1176–1206.

Klandermans, B. and Mayer, N. (2006) 'Right-wing extremism as a social movement' in B. Klandermans and N. Mayer (eds) (2006) *Extreme Right Activists in Europe: Through the Magnifying Glass*, London and New York: Routledge, pp. 3–27.

Klatch, R. (2004) 'The underside of social movements: the effects of destructive affective ties', *Qualitative Sociology*, 27(4): 487–509.

Klug, B. (2012) 'Islamophobia: a concept comes of age', *Ethnicities*, 112(5): 665–81.

Kundnani, A. (2004) 'The rise and fall of British multiculturalism' in G. Titley (ed.) *Resituating Culture*, Strasbourg: Council of Europe, pp. 105–12.

Laclau, E. (2005) *On Populist Reason*, London: Verso.

Langebach, M. and Raabe, J. (2013) 'Inside the extreme right: the White Power music scene' in A. Mammone, E. Godin and B. Jenkins (eds) *Varieties of Right-wing Extremism in Europe*, London: Routledge, pp. 249–64.

Leddy-Owen, C. (2014) 'Reimagining Englishness: "race", class, progressive English identities and disrupted English communities', *Sociology*, 48(6): 1123–38.

Lentin, A. (2004) 'The problem of culture and human rights in the response to racism' in G. Titley (ed.) *Resituating Culture*, Strasbourg: Council of Europe, pp. 95–104.

Lentin, A. (2008) 'Europe and the silence about race', *European Journal of Social Theory*, 11(4): 487–503.

Lentin, A. (2014) 'Post-race, post politics: the paradoxical rise of culture after multiculturalism', *Ethnic and Racial Studies*, 37(8): 1268–85.

Linden, A. and Klandermans, B. (2007) 'Revolutionaries, wanderers, converts, and compliants: life histories of extreme right activists', *Journal of Contemporary Ethnography*, 36(2): 184–201.

Lone, A. and Silver, D. (2014) *Europe's White Working Class Communities: Manchester*, New York: Open Society Foundations.

McDonald, K. (2006) *Global Movements: Action and Culture*, Oxford: Blackwell.

McDonald, K. (2014) *What Could a Sociology of the Subject Look Like?*, available at: www.academia.edu/10139839/What_could_a_sociology_of_the_subject_look_like, DOI:10.1177/20568460023. Accessed: 15.06.2015.

McNay, L. (2014) *The Misguided Search for the Political*, Cambridge: Polity Press.

Malbon, B. (1999) *Clubbing. Dancing, Ecstasy and Vitality*, London: Routledge.

Massumi, B. (2004) 'Translator's foreword: notes on the translation and acknowledgements' in G. Deleuze and F. Guattari, *A Thousand Plateaus*, London and New York: Continuum.

Meer, N. (2014) 'Islamophobia and postcolonialism: continuity, orientalism and Muslim consciousness', *Patterns of Prejudice*, 48(5): 500–15.

Meer, N. and Modood, T. (2009) 'Refutations of racism in the "Muslim question"', *Patterns of Prejudice*, 43(3–4): 335–54.

Meer, N. and Modood, T. (2014) 'Cosmopolitanism and integrationism: is British multiculturalism a "zombie category"?', *Identities: Global Studies in Culture and Power*, 21(6): 658–74.

Meer, N. and Nayak, A. (2013) 'Race ends where? Race, racism and contemporary sociology', *Sociology*, E-special Issue 2: 1–18.

Miles, R. (2000) 'Apropos the idea of "race"... again' in L. Back and J. Solomos (eds) *Theories of Race and Racism: A Reader*, London and New York: Routledge, pp. 180–98.

Minkenberg, M. (2013) 'The European radical right and xenophobia in West and East: trends, patterns and challenges' in R. Melzer and S. Serafin (eds) *Right-wing Extremism in Europe: Country Analyses, Counter-strategies and Labor-market Oriented Exit Strategies*, Berlin: Friedrich Ebert Stiftung, pp. 9–34.

Minkenberg, M. (2015) 'Profiles, patterns, process: studying the East European radical right in its political environment' in M. Minkenberg (ed.) *Transforming the Transformation? The East European Radical Right in the Political Process*, London and New York: Routledge, pp. 27–56.

Modood, T. (2013) 'Multiculturalism and religion: a three part debate. Part one: accommodating religions: multiculturalism's new fault line', *Critical Social Policy*, 22.10.2013. DOI: 10.1177/0261018313501826, pp. 1–7.

Mouffe, C. (2005) *On the Political*, London and New York: Routledge.

Mudde, C. (2007) *Populist Radical Right Parties in Europe*, Cambridge: Cambridge University Press.

Mudde, C. (2014) 'Introduction: youth and the extreme right: explanations, issues, and solutions' in C. Mudde (ed.) *Youth and the Extreme Right*, New York, London and Amsterdam: IDebate Press, pp. 1–18.

Nayak, A. (1999) '"Pale warriors": skinhead culture and the embodiment of white masculinities' in A. Brah, M.J. Hickman and M. Mac an Ghaill (eds) *Thinking Identities: Ethnicity, Racism and Culture*, Basingstoke: Palgrave, pp. 71–99.

Nayak, A. (2003) *Race, Place and Globalization: Youth Cultures in a Changing World*, Oxford: Berg.

Nayak, A. (2005) 'White lives' in K. Murji and J. Solomos (eds) *Racialization: Studies in Theory and Practice*, Oxford: Oxford University Press, pp. 141–62.

Nayak, A. (2006) 'After race: ethnography, race and post-race theory', *Ethnic and Racial Studies*, 29(3): 411–30.

Norris, P. (2011) *Democratic Deficit: Critical Citizens Revisited*, Cambridge: Cambridge University Press.

O'Reilly, K. (2005) *Ethnographic Methods*, London and New York: Routledge.

Paul, J. (2014) 'Post-racial futures: imagining post-racialist antiracism(s)', *Ethnic and Racial Studies*, 37 (4): 702–18.

Pilkington, H. (2012) 'When is a kettle not a kettle? When it is on slow boil', MYPLACE blog, 4 September, available at: http://myplacefp7.wordpress.com/2012/09/04/when-is-a-kettle-not-a-kettle-when-it-is-on-slow-boil. Accessed: 30.03.2014.

Pilkington, H. (2014a) '"My whole life is here": tracing journeys through "skinhead"' in D. Buckingham and M.-J. Kehily (eds) *Rethinking Youth Cultures in the Age of Global Media*, Basingstoke: Palgrave Macmillan, pp. 71–87.

Pilkington, H. (2014b) 'Ethnographic Case Studies of Youth Activism: Introduction', WP7: Interpreting Activism (Ethnographies). Deliverable 7.1, *MYPLACE Deliverable Report*, available at: http://www.fp7-myplace.eu/deliverables.php. Accessed: 06.06.2015.

Pilkington, H. (forthcoming) 'Can qualitative data speak beyond the individual case? Employing meta-ethnography for the synthesis of findings in transnational research projects' in H. Pilkington, G. Pollock and R. Franc (eds) *Understanding Youth Participation across Europe: From Survey to Ethnography*, Basingstoke: Palgrave Macmillan.

Pilkington, H., Omel'chenko, E. and Garifzianova, A. (2010) *Russia's Skinheads: Exploring and Rethinking Subcultural Lives*, London and New York: Routledge.

Quilliam (2013) 'Quilliam facilitates Tommy Robinson leaving the English Defence League', 8 October, available at: www.quilliamfoundation.org/press/quilliam-facili-tates-tommy-robinson-leaving-the-english-defence-league. Accessed: 26.07.2015.

Rancière, J. (1999) *Dis-agreement: Politics and Philosophy* (transl. Julie Rose), Minneapolis: University of Minnesota Press.

Rancière, J. (2011) 'The thinking of dissensus: politics and aesthetics' in P. Bowman and R. Stamp (eds) *Reading Rancière: Critical Dissensus*, London: Bloomsbury, pp. 1–17.

Ray, L. Smith, D. and Wastell, L. (2004) 'Shame, rage and racist violence', *British Journal of Criminology*, 44(3): 350–68.

Rex, J. (2000) 'Race relations in sociological theory' in L. Back and J. Solomos (eds) *Theories of Race and Racism: A Reader*, London and New York: Routledge, pp. 174–79.

Rhodes, J. (2009) 'Revisiting the 2001 riots: New Labour and the Rise of "colour blind racism"', *Sociological Research Online*, 14(5)3, available at: www.socresonline.org.uk/14/5/3.html. Accessed: 06.08.2015.

Rhodes, J. (2010) '*White backlash*, "unfairness" and justifications of British National Party (BNP) support', *Ethnicities*, 10(1): 77–99.

Rhodes, J. (2011) '"It's not just them, it's whites as well": whiteness, class and BNP support', *Sociology*, 45(1): 102–17.

Rokeach, M. (2015) *The Open and Closed Mind: Investigations into the Nature of Belief Systems and Personality Systems*, Eastford: Martino Fine Books.

Runnymede Trust (1997) *Islamophobia: A Challenge for Us All (Summary)*, available at: www.runnymedetrust.org/uploads/publications/pdfs/islamophobia.pdf.   Accessed: 2.03.2014.

Said, E. (1978) *Orientalism*, New York: Pantheon.

Sawer, M. (2007) 'Wearing your politics on your sleeve: the role of political colours in social movements', *Social Movement Studies: Journal of Social, Cultural and Political Protest*, 6(1): 39–56.

Shields, R., Park, O. and Davidson, T. (2011) 'Conclusion: a roundtable on the affective turn' in T. Davidson, O. Park and R. Shields (eds) *Ecologies of Affect: Placing Nostalgia, Desire, and Hope*, Waterloo, ON: Wilfrid Laurier University Press, pp. 317–26.

Shouse, E. (2005) 'Feeling, emotion, affect', *M/C Journal*, 8(6), available at: http://journal.media-culture.org.au/0512/03-shouse.php. Accessed: 09.06.2015.

Skenderovic, D., Späti, C. and Wildmann, D. (2014) 'Past and present expressions of Islamophobia: an introduction', *Patterns of Prejudice*, 48(5): 437–41.

Simi, P. and Futrell, R. (2010) *American Swastika: Inside the White Power Movement's Hidden Spaces of Hate*, Lanham, MD: Rowman and Littlefield.

Simpson, P.A. and Druxes, H. (eds) (2015) *Digital Media Strategies of the Far Right in Europe and the United States*, Lanham, MD: Lexington Books.

Skeggs, B. and Loveday, V. (2012) 'Struggles for value: value practices, injustice, judgment, affect and the idea of class', *The British Journal of Sociology*, 63(3): 472–90.

Smyth, L. and Mitchell, C. (2008) 'Researching conservative groups: rapport and under-standing across moral and political boundaries', *International Journal of Social Research Methodology*, 11(5): 441–52.

Sniderman, P.M. and Hagendoorn, L. (2007) *When Ways of Life Collide. Multiculturalism and Its Discontents in The Netherlands*, Princeton, NJ: Princeton University Press.

Sobolewska, M. (2010) 'Religious extremism in Britain and British Muslims: threatened citizenship and the role of religion' in R. Eatwell and M. Goodwin (eds) *The New Extremism in 21st Century Britain*, London and New York: Routledge, pp. 23–46.

Solomos, J. (2013) 'Contemporary forms of racist movements and mobilization in Britain' in R. Wodak, M. KhosraviNik and B. Mral (eds) *Right-Wing Populism in Europe: Politics and Discourse*, London: Bloomsbury, pp. 121–34.

Solomos, J. and Back, L. (1994) 'Conceptualising racisms: social theory, politics and research', *Sociology*, 28(1): 143–61.

Soutphommasane, T. (2012) *The Virtuous Citizen: Patriotism in a Multicultural Society*, Cambridge: Cambridge University Press.

St Louis, B. (2002) 'Post-race/post-politics? Activist-intellectualism and the reification of race', *Ethnic and Racial Studies*, 25(4): 652–75.

Stolz, J. (2005) 'Explaining Islamophobia: a test of four theories based on the case of a Swiss city', *Swiss Journal of Sociology*, 31(3): 547–66.

Strabac, Z. and Listhaug, O. (2008) 'Anti-Muslim prejudice in Europe: a multilevel analysis of survey data from 30 countries', *Social Science Research*, 37: 268–86.

Team Members (2006) 'Writing life-histories: interviewing extreme right-wing activists' in B. Klandermans and N. Mayer (eds) *Extreme Right Activists in Europe: Through the Magnifying Glass*, London and New York: Routledge, pp. 51–64.

Thien, D. (2005) 'After or beyond feeling? A consideration of affect and emotion in geography', *Area*, 37(4): 450–56.

Toynbee, P. (2004) 'We must be free to criticise without being called racist', *The Guardian*, 18 August, available at: www.theguardian.com/world/2004/aug/18/religion.politics. Accessed: 25.05.2015.

Trilling, D. (2012) *Bloody Nasty People: The Rise of Britain's Far Right*, London: Verso.

Vakil, A. (2010) 'Whose afraid of Islamophobia?' in A. Vakil and S. Sayyid (eds) *Thinking through Islamophobia: Global Perspectives*, London: Hurst, pp. 271–78.

Virchow, F. (2007) 'Performance, emotion, and ideology: on the creation of "collectives of emotion" and worldview in the contemporary German far right', *Journal of Contemporary Ethnography*, 36(2): 147–64.

Wacquant, L. (2008) *Urban Outcasts: A Comparative Sociology of Advanced Marginality*, Cambridge: Polity Press.

Ware, V. (2008) 'Towards a sociology of resentment: a debate on class and whiteness', *Sociological Research Online*, 13(5)9, available at: www.socresonline.org.uk/13/5/9.html.

Wetherell, M. (2012) *Affect and Emotion: A New Social Science Understanding*, London: Sage.

Willis, P. (1997) 'Theoretical confessions and reflexive method' in K. Gelder and S. Thornton (eds) *The Subcultures Reader*, London: Routledge, pp. 246–53.

Williams, S. and Law, I. (2012) 'Legitimising racism: an exploration of the challenges posed by the use of indigeneity discourses by the far right', *Sociological Research Online*, 17(2)2, available at: www.socresonline.org.uk/17/2/2.html.

Wodak, R. (2013) '"Anything Goes!" – the Haiderization of Europe' in R. Wodak, M. KhosraviNik and B. Mral (eds) *Right-Wing Populism in Europe: Politics and Discourse*, London: Bloomsbury, pp. 23–37.

Index

Note: 'n' after a page reference indicates the number of a note on that page.

activism
    affect and 9, 11, 14, 57, 162, 177, 179–80,
        181, 197, 199, 201, 202, 228–30
    affective economy 32, 126, 143, 152
    affective practice 177, 179, 180, 184,
        195, 196, 202, 229
    see also violence, as affective practice
    affective solidarity 10, 21, 75, 90, 109,
        177, 178, 179, 184, 186, 196, 197,
        198, 199, 200, 201, 203, 226, 228,
        229
    research and 17, 18, 32, 33
    see also demonstrations, affect and
    costs of 60, 85–89, 90, 173, 225
    embodied 180, 181, 182, 186, 195, 198,
        203, 216, 219
    see also politics, embodied
    emotion(s) and xiv, 3, 8–10, 11, 30, 56,
        89, 109, 112, 132, 143, 177, 178–80,
        181, 184, 186, 193, 196, 201, 212,
        213, 215, 216, 228–9
    destructive role of 178–79, 200–1,
        202
    emotional collective 177, 186, 193,
        195, 202, 228, 229
    emotional transformation 10, 179,
        196
    reciprocal 177–78, 179, 197, 201, 202
    shared 179, 201, 202
    transmission of 181–82
    effectiveness of 51, 53–55, 56, 184, 212,
        213, 224, 230
    forms of 180
    grassroots 8, 38, 40, 41, 42, 46, 47, 48, 51,
        54, 97, 99, 114, 130, 174, 184, 191,
        197, 201, 204, 225, 226, 227

    leadership 39–42, 44, 45–47, 49, 54–55,
        62, 122, 183, 196, 197, 200, 218, 222
    see also Robinson, T.
    left-wing 27, 63, 122, 191, 200
    performance and 98, 177, 180, 186, 187,
        189, *190*, *192*, 193, 195, 197, 201,
        228
    rationality and 3, 8, 9, 11, 20, 35, 45,
        56, 57, 82, 118, 143, 149, 150, 177,
        178–80, 182, 184, 186, 212, 214,
        215, 216, 219, 220, 229
    right-wing 8, 27, 56, 75, 78, 89, 191
    trajectories into 11, 60, 69, 89, 90, 225
        family background and 80–81
        material circumstances and 85
        traumatic experience and 69, 82–83
        types of 75, 78
        see also women, trajectories
    trajectories out of 11, 60, 85–89, 90
    youth 10, 20, 61, 206, 215
    see also Islamist, activism
al-Muhajiroun 37, 134
anger 9, 10, 40, 56, 74, 76–78, 83, 101, 106,
        108, 116, 129, 145, 154, 158–59,
        161–62, 170, 174, 175, 179, 182,
        184, 196, 197, 206, 213, 217, 228

Back, L. 1, 13, 25–26 *passim*, 28, 31–32
        passim, 34, 60, 94, 108, 114, 205,
        223, 231
banter 29, 31, 44, 181, 185
    homophobic 122
    racist 28,
    sexist 28, 66, 120
    sexual 30, 62, 128
    with opposition 52, 85, 185–86, 197

being heard 51, 101, 155, 195, 203, 212–16,
    229
being seen 20, 155, 191, *191*, 195, 203,
    215
Blee, K. 13, 17, 24, 64, 70, 75, 78–79 *passim*,
    83, 90
BNP *see* British National Party
British National Party 12n.2, 12n.3, 33, 51,
    230
    activism in 38–39, 42, 63, 78, 100, 102,
        122, 210, 211
    Britain First and 41
    EDL and 38–39, 42, 48, 97, 99, 101,
        102–3, 113, 211, 226
    homophobia and 78, 122
    ideology 2, 3, 8
    racism and 38, 74, 78, 99, 100, 102–3,
        109, 110, 117, 161, 221n.3, 226
    support for 2, 8, 12n.3, 61, 77, 78, 102,
        207, 220, 230
    see also Robinson, T. and
Britain First 39, 49
    EDL and 41–42, 55
    see also British National Party and

Castells, M. 9, 45, 51, 60, 154, 158, 218
Casuals 37, 61, 183, 190
    see also football, casual subculture
chants 29, 50, 101, 111, 184, 195–97, 214
    anti-Muslim 107, 125, 131, 133, 138, 139,
        140, 141, 151, 185, 196, 227
    as affective practice 79, 177, 186, 195,
        202, 229
    counter-demonstrators and 31, 185, 196,
        197
    football 196, 197, 202n.2
    identity-affirming 40, 45, 185, 187, 197,
        216
    patriotic 196
    Unionist 56, 188, 191, 196
Choudary, A. 134
Christianity
    EDL and 126, 143, 144, 187
    extremism and 130, 131
    identification with 117, 118, 122,
        144
    UK and 13, 110, 136, 164
    Western civilisation and 116, 126, 144,
        187
citizen
    critical 209
    second-class 135, 148, 154, 155, 158–61,
        163, 174, 175, 177, 228

citizenship 108, 112, 157
    entitlement to 117, 118
    immigration and 114–17, 155
    multicultural 155
class 34, 156
    identity 32, 147, 154, 191, 215
    inequality 8, 156–57, 163
    middle 70, 80n.6, 223
    political 175, 208
    politics of 112, 119, 156, 174
    underclass 156
    upper 70
    working 163, 225
        EDL and 8, 48, 61, 70, 174, 175, 191,
            216
        concerns 57, 156, 208
        racism and 5, 7, 70, 156, 157, 158,
            220, 231
        white working class 3, 7, 8, 11, 116,
            156, 157, 158, 160, 175, 176, 203,
            204, 208, 215, 220, 228, 230, 231
    see also politics, class and; racism, class
        and
Combat 18 48, 55, 138

democracy xiii, 220
    contestation and 219
    critique of 217, 218, 219, 230
    deliberative 112, 178, 216, 218–19
    EDL and 46, 220
    in Islam 58n.6, 136
    liberal xiv, 4, 12n.1, 58n.6, 216–17
    parliamentary 217, 218, 230
    participation in 157, 220
    radical 203, 219
    rejection of 4, 176n.9, 203, 216, 217, 218
    socialism and 217
    support for 7, 38
    see also populist radical right and; social
        movement, democracy and
democratic
    anti-democratic 4, 203, 216, 217, 218,
        230
    deficit 208, 209
    politics 208, 216, 219, 231
demonstrations
    affect and 18, 181
    as 'a good day out' 14, 177, 180, 202n.1
    attendance at 39–40, 66, 67
    bonding at 18, 109, 179, 180, 184, 186,
        198
    build up to 14, 180, 186
    buzz of 62, 177, 181–82, 202, 229

counter- 36n.6, *97*, 140, 166, 185, 197, 206
flash 14, 15, 39, 43, 51, 110, 138, 180
LGBT at *63*, 64, 122–23
local 14, 64, 101, 180, 187, 193
national 14, 39, 40, 64, 180, 181, 195
policing of 18, 23, 42, 88, 164, 166–69, 185, 204, 205
purpose of 38, 172, 177, 180, 212, 216, 229
travel to 43, 80, 181, 187
violence at xi, 15, 23, 44, 48, 51, 53, 84, 166–69, 182–86
women at 30, 62, 64, 66, 73

employment
EDL activism and 52, 88
opportunities xiii, 7, 60, 70, 77, 115, 163, 220
status xii, 22, 25, 48, 64, 65, 69–70, 72, 80, 85, 90, 170, 234–37
unemployment 33, 70, 116, 129, 157
equality 4, 118, 119, 121, 155, 162
government policy and 156, 157, 163
in EDL 44, 45, 62
see also gender, equality and rights; inequality; LGBT, equality and
ethics xii-xiii, 14, 20–21, 22, 24, 29, 33, 34, 223, 225
ethnography x, xii-xiii, xiv, 1, 10, 11, 13n.10, 14, 15, 17, 20, 21, 22, 25, 28, 30, 31–33, 34, 35, 222–23, 231
militant 33
sensory 202
extreme right 5, 69, 75
definition of 4, 217
EDL and 4, 11, 89, 225
ideology 5, 111, 159, 161
research on 13, 35
support for 2, 61, 62, 66, 70, 74, 78, 89, 90, 159, 161
see also far right; women, in extreme right
Ezekiel, R.S. 11, 13, 31, 33, 35, 36n.9, 58n.12, 64, 70, 91n.9, 126, 143, 152, 222, 228, 230

family
background 65, 72, 76, 80–84, 90, 146, 148, 159
EDL as 11, 51, 90, 178, 180, 197, 198, 199, 200, 202, 226, 229

ethnic and religious diversity in 103, 123, 136, 143
impact on 45, 87, 88, 91n.9, 142, 173, 213, 216
support for extreme right 78–79, 90, 107, 141, 225
status 71, 234–37
views on 120
see also activism, trajectories into, family background
far right xii, 1–4, 8, 11, 12n3, 37, 51, 59n.21, 60, 74, 76, 78, 113, 119, 124, 157, 207, 208, 220
definition of 4, 12n.1
EDL and xiii, 1, 3–4, 11, 37, 38, 41, 45, 49, 54, 55, 78, 85, 90, 92, 97, 102, 113, 114, 119, 121–22, 203, 217, 224, 225, 226, 230
ideology 1, 2–4, 8, 10, 15, 34–35, 48, 50, 55, 75, 89, 92, 94, 102, 108, 111, 117–19, 12, 124, 125, 143, 149, 150, 152, 157, 161, 201, 222, 226–28
music and 193–95,
research on 1, 2, 8, 10, 11, 13–14, 17, 24–25, 32–36, 85, 222
see also extreme right; social movement, far right and
fear 9, 17, 56, 76, 77, 93, 108, 125, 126, 127, 129, 135–36, 141, 143, 149, 152, 154, 158, 159, 204, 207, 224, 228
Fielding, N. 13, 30, 34–35
football 59, 68, 77, 146, 147, 160, 183–84
casual subculture 37, 183
see also Casuals
colours 191
EDL and 37, 38, 65, 79, 173, 184, 199
firms 38, 61, 79, 173, 184, 190
hooligans xii, 65, 68, 69, 183
see also violence, football

gender
equality and rights 4, 119, 121, 127, 209
femininities 119, 120
ideology 4, 97, 119–23
masculinities xi, 121, 123
research and 30–32
status 234–37
see also inequality, gender
grievance
motivation for activism 174, 178, 219
political response to 158, 174, 175, 176, 203, 204, 220, 230, 231
Griffin, N. 32–33, 50, 149

hate 10, 55, 56, 101, 104, 106–7, 108, 111,
    112, 118, 126, 127, 128, 134, 137,
    139, 140, 142, 148, 162, 166, 173,
    174, 193
hope 9, 10, 50, 56–57, 118, 224, 231
Hope not Hate 101

immigrants 115, 157, 159
    as unfairly privileged 7–8, 160–62, 228
    negative attitudes to 2, 11, 12n.4, 12n.5,
        113
        in EDL 115, 116, 118, 148, 151, 227
    positive attitudes to 117
        in EDL 115–16
immigration 55, 70, 115, 124n.6, 157,
        221n.3
    attitudes to 2, 150, 208
    EDL and 37, 58n.3, 108, 114–16, 139,
        207
    government policy and 157–58, 160,
        161, 163
    racism and 93–94, 107, 113, 114, 115,
        116, 126, 129–30, 139, 163, 175,
        227
inequality 1, 8, 154, 157, 158, 161, 162, 208,
        212
    class 8, 156
    ethnic 163
    gender 135
    of Muslims 12n.7
    racial 8, 155, 156, 163, 175, 228
    see also equality
Infidels (organisation) 29, 54, 55, 61,
        66, 75, 83 108, 117–19, 121, 122,
        124n.5, 144, 200, 212, 217, 230
infidels 143, 147, 193, 195
injustice 1, 7, 8, 18, 75, 158, 172, 175, 177,
        195, 203, 228, 230
    experience of 89, 154, 165, 173, 174, 225
    government and 154, 161, 162, 166, 228
    institutionalisation of 154, 164, 175, 228
    racialised 154, 175, 228
    struggle against 75, 155, 195, 225
    see also justice
IS see Islamic State
Islam
    abuse of children and 133–34, 144, 147
    as aggressive 127, 131, 135–36, 144, 152,
        227
    as backward-looking 13, 132–34, 151,
        227
    as barbaric 127, 133
    as ideology 58n.6, 106–7, 125, 127, 130,

        132, 134, 136–38, 139, 141, 151,
        152, 227
    as intolerant 134, 151, 152, 227
    as monolithic 125, 127, 128, 130, 131,
        227
    as oppressive 125, 132, 135, 137, 151,
        227
        see also women, and Islam
    as peaceful 131
    as progressive 127
    as religion 6, 106, 107, 127, 129, 137
    as violent 76, 140, 151, 153n.15
    conversion to 135–36, 147, 158
    debate about 38
    demonisation of 3, 151
    extremism and 31, 37, 117, 130, 131,
        134, 142, 143, 151, 153n.15, 227
    in UK 6, 37, 77, 151, 153n.15
    militant 1, 11, 130, 137, 224
    moderate 130, 131, 143, 227
    radical 4, 38, 82, 130, 136, 137, 142, 226
    representation of 126–27
    terrorism and 127, 140, 151, 153n.15,
        227
    threat of 3, 38, 101, 130, 144
    see also democracy, in Islam; LGBT,
        Islam and
Islamic
    courts 38, 58n.5
    cultural centres 39, 232
    dress 129, 135, 137, 139, 141, 146,
        164–65, 193
    orthodoxy 130
    prayer centres 110, 137, 138, 167
    teachings 38, 63, 122, 139, 140, 147, 150,
        227
Islamic State 131
Islamisation 136, 167
Islamist
    activism, 37, 134, 135
    anti-Islamist 1, 4, 12n.6, 151, 224, 227
    clerics 166
    ideology 43, 137
    videos 82
Islamophobia
    definition of 4, 5, 74, 125, 126–30, 150,
        154, 227–28
    EDL and 4, 5, 39, 92, 98, 102, 125,
        130–38, 150, 151, 226, 227
    in UK 1, 5, 6, 150, 151
    racism and 5, 6, 11, 102, 125–26, 128–29,
        150, 151
    self-identification with 145, 148–50, *149*

justice xiii, 1, 96, 154
  Criminal Justice Act 17
  miscarriage of 210
  social 10
  two-tier system of *81*, 154, 164, 165, 173,
    175, 228
  see also injustice

KKK *see* Ku Klux Klan
Klandermans, B. 8, 24, 36, 62, 75–78
    passim, 89, 225
Ku Klux Klan 117, 118, 124n.8, 207

Laclau, E. 35, 224
Lentin, A. 5, 94–96 *passim*, 113–14 *passim*,
    155–56 *passim*
Lesbian, Gay, Bisexual and Transgender
  attitudes towards 23, 63, 122, 134
  EDL division xii, 23, 43, 58n.15, 64, 99,
    121–22, 133, 188
  equality and 119, 127
  Islam and 38, 63, 134, 136
  rights 4, 55, 108, 119, 122, 123, 212
  see also, demonstrations, LGBT at;
    respect, for LGBT
LGBT *see* Lesbian, Gay, Bisexual and
    Transgender
loud and proud xiv, 11, 184, 195, 202, 203,
    212, 213–16, 229

MDL *see* Muslim Defence League
media
  lack of coverage in 23, 49, 171, 172, 175,
    206, 224, 228
  exposure by 19, 20, 29, 39, 118, 216
  representation of EDL in xii, 19, 20, 23,
    24, 26, 27, 49, 50–51, 57, 62, 97,
    100, 199, 206, 224
  see also Muslim(s), representation of;
    social media; social movement, new
    media and
mosques 147, 172
  attacks on 39, 113, 137, *138*, 166, 193,
    196
  building of 13, 55, 137, 138, 205, 233
  extremism and 137, 170
Mouffe, C. 1, 56–57 *passim*, 203, 206, 213,
    219–20, 231
Mudde, C. 4, 11, 12n.1, 61, 62, 70, 75, 203,
    216, 230
multiculturalism
  anti-multiculturalism 112–14
  as ideology 119, 121, 124n.5

backlash to 8, 108, 112–14, 118, 154,
    155–56, 157, 175
failure of 7, 96, 114, 124n.5, 158
policy of 112–13, 155–56, 219
support for 113,
Muslim(s)
  activists in EDL 100, 101, 102
  anti-Muslim attitudes 5–6, 54, 125,
    128–29
    as racism 92, 99, 102–7, 123, 125, 128,
      129–30, 139, 150, 151, 226, 227
    in EDL 3–4, 11, 29, 38, 40, 67, 79,
      102–7, 108, 113, 117, 123, 125–26,
      133, 134, 139–43, 148, 151, 152,
      154, 224, 227
    in UK 6, 8, 12n.4, 78, 127, 150, 164
    rejection of 139, 150–51
  anti-Muslimism 5, 126, 128, 139, 227
  as unfairly privileged 8, 133, 137, 150,
    154, 159–62, 164–65, 167, 168,
    170–72, 228
  as victims 137, 139, 153n.10
  attitudes to non-Muslims 134, 143,
    144–48, 152, 154, 172, 173, 227
  see also infidels
  British foreign policy and 40, 79
  communities in UK xi, xiii, 6, 7, 37,
    127–28, 131, 153n.13, 205
  extremist 112, 126, 131, 134, 139,
    142–43, 227
  gangs 106, 124n.3, 133, 136, 139
  moderate 126, 130, 137, 142–43, 227
  Muslim Arbitration Tribunal 58n.5
  Muslim Council of Britain 12n.7
  patriotism and 110
  population growth 6, 111, 136
  representation of 6, 126–27, 128, 152n.1
  rights of 137
  violence by 67, 88, 126, 134, 135,
    140–42, 149, 227
  see also inequality, of Muslims; chants
    and songs, anti-Muslim
Muslim Defence League 140, 166, 172, 182,
    197

National Front 59n.21
  activism in 78, 102, 118, 138, 199, 200, 210
  EDL and 50, 54, 55, 59n.21, 97, 226
  racism and 110
  support for 207
National Socialism
  identification with 66, 105, 114, 117,
    118, 119, 217, 218

National Socialism (*cont.*)
  ideology of 3, 105, 114, 117, 119, 217,
    218
  rejection of 217
Nayak, A. xi-xiv, 5, 31, 34, 78, 93, 95–96
    passim, 106, 156, 173
NF *see* National Front

patriot 55, 109, 112, 113, 204
patriotism
  chants 196
  ethnic minorities and 110
  national liberal 112
  understanding of 109–12
  ultra-patriotism 4, 37
  see also Muslims, patriotism and
Pegida UK 41, 42, 214
political correctness 31, 109, 119, 208
political socialisation 75, 78, 80, 90,
    225
politics
  British xii, 2, 3, 7, 11, 209, 231
  class and 57, 112, 156, 157, 175, 208
    see also class, political; class, politics
    of consensus in 219
  contention in 78, 203, 205, 219
  distrust of xiv, 46, 136, 203, 204, 208–12,
    216, 218, 220, 229
  EDL and 10, 42, 45, 46, 48–9, 57, 103,
    174, 208–12, 220, 229
  embodied 203, 216, 219
  failure of 216
  formal xiv, 4, 10, 204, 207–13, 216, 218,
    220, 230
  left-wing 27, 63, 118, 119, 231
  meanings of 1, 203, 210–13, 219, 229,
    230
  moralisation of 203, 206–7, 231
  multicultural 7, 155, 156
  non-democratic 216
  non-politics of action 203, 211, 212, 218,
    230
  of resentment 3, 176, 220
  of silencing 57, *93*, 203–8, 212, 214, 219,
    229, 231
  passion and xiv, 1, 3, 213, 219, 231
  progressive 5, 230
  'race' and 94–96, 123, 156, 226
  recognition 127, 176, 220
  research and 1, 4, 5, 11, 13, 14, 20,
    26–27, 31–36, 222–24, 230
  right-wing 38, 42, 119, 124, 203, 208,
    219, 220, 231

  youth and 210
  see also democratic, politics;
populism 3, 4, 7, 12n.1, 12n.10, 42, 47, 56,
    112, 119, 150, 157, 159, 203, 214,
    218, 219, 220, 231
  see also UKIP; populist radical right
populist radical right 1, 160
  definition of 4, 12n.1, 216–17
  democracy and 4, 216–17, 220
  EDL and 1, 4, 11, 78
  ideology 108, 160
  research on 2, 42, 222
  support for 2, 3, 11, 124, 157–58

Quilliam Foundation 4, 12n.6, 40, 41,
    58n.1, 58n.7, 85, 137
Qur'an 131, 132, 134, 135, 140, 165,
    193

'race'
  'post race' 95, 96, 105
  theories of 1, 5, 11, 93–96, 114, 152n.1,
    155, 156
  understanding of in EDL 92, 103, 104–7,
    123, 175, 226
racism xii, xiv, 5–8, 155, 223
  anti-racism 5, 26, 28, 34, 96, 156, 212,
    230
  cultural 11, 93–94, 103, 106, 115,
    125–26, 128, 129
  EDL and 71, 97–108
  experiences of 74, 98, 155, 171, 173
  Islamophobia and 5, 6, 106–7, 125,
    128–29, 130, 150–51, 226, 227
  new 11, 93–94, 103, 115, 125, 128
  numerological 111
  post- 105
  rejection of 42, 53, 77, 97–99, 107, 123,
    140, 226
  socialisation and 78–79
  strategic 108
  struggle against 5, 28–30, 34, 93, 94, 96,
    155, 223, 230
  theories of 1, 11, 93–96,
  understanding of 102–5, 123, 226
  victims of 33,
  whiteness and 169–73
  see also class, racism and
racist
  EDL and language 28–29, 99, 105, 139,
    140
  'not racist' 1, 11, 29, *93*, 97, 99, 100,
    102, 103, 104, 106, 108, 113, 123,

125, 129, 139, 150, 204, 215, 226, 227
  perceived as 3, 4, 5, 50, 57, 62, 88, 92, 97–101, 103, 104, 123, 205, 206, 222, 224
  racists within 29, 97–99, 107–8, 226
  label 154, 159, 173, 203, 204, 205, 206–8, 220, 221n.3, 228, 229, 230
respect 56
  for British culture and tradition 38, 148, 165, 175
  for British soldiers 37, 110, 147, 148, 218, 226
  for LGBT 122, 123
  for Muslims 127, 137, 165
  for police 167
  lack of respect
    by Muslims 126, 143, 147–48, 151, 227
    for non-Muslims 134
Rhodes, J. 8, 35, 70, 78, 157, 159, 161, 163, 175, 176n.1, 228
Robinson, T.
  'barmy army' 37, 40, 45, 57, 195
  BNP and 38–39
  criticism of 49, 54
  ideology of 40, 98, 113, 137, 174, 208
  imprisonment 39, 45, 54, 58n.13
  leadership style of 42, 45–46, 101
  resignation of 40, 41, 46, 92, 98
  support for 45, 54, 211

Sharia law 133, 148
  in UK 38, 58n.5, 136, 145, 153n.13, 164, 165, 166
  punishment under 133, 135
social media
  alternative to mainstream 49, 57, 224
  communication via 15, 51, 57, 118
  dangers of 52, 89, 198
  organisation and 13, 35, 51, 57, 224
  scepticism towards 52, 57, 180
  source of conflict 52, 224
  source of information 76–77, 171, 172
social movement xii-xiii, 1, 4, 8–10, 13, 33, 51, 55, 60, 75, 89, 177–80, 184, 194, 197, 201–2, 218, 224
  democracy and 218
  emotions and 8–9, 55, 89, 177–80, 191, 197, 201–2, 228–29
  far right and 8, 177, 186, 201, 222
  new media and 13, 51–52, 224–25
standing together 54, 155, 198, 200

togetherness 9, 10, 186, 197, 202, 229

UAF see Unite Against Fascism
UKIP see United Kingdom Independence Party
Unite Against Fascism 36n.6
  as enemy 31, 36n.6, 52, 123
  association with 19, 27, 29, 31
  debate with 27
  funding of 48
  tactics of 50, 52, 88
United Kingdom Independence Party 2, 49, 61, 112, 115, 124n.6, 209

violence
  as affective practice 184
  conviction for 15, 23, 40, 84–85, 86, 169, 173, 176n.7, 233
  disorder and 177, 182–86
  domestic 25, 65, 69, 76, 81–83, 104, 120–21
  efficacy of 51, 53, 183, 184, 185
  football 173, 183, 184
  homophobic 122
  incitement to 85, 169, 185–86
  pleasure in 177, 182–84
  police 167, 168
  racist 95, 104, 128, 161, 171, 173, 175, 215
  rejection of xiii, 44, 53, 62, 92, 93, 123, 168, 184, 204
  symbolic 138, 193, 194
  threat of 52, 88, 89, 168, 173
  youth and 167, 183
  see also demonstrations, violence at; Muslims, violence by; Islam, as violent; women, violence towards

Wacquant, L. 35, 60, 70, 157, 163, 223
women
  in EDL
    Angels division 43, 66, 80, 99, 119–20, 120, 121, 146, 187, 189
    proportion of 62
    representation of 119, 121
    roles 45, 58n.15, 62, 64, 66, 121
    trajectories 30, 64, 83
  in extreme right 58n.12, 62, 64, 66, 78, 79, 83, 119
  Islam and 13, 38, 104, 127, 132, 133, 134, 135, 137, 145, 147, 150, 164
  violence towards 104, 121, 133, 134, 135, 146
  see also demonstrations, women at

youth
   in EDL
      attitudes to 43, 48, 53, 67, 214–15
      division 19, 20, 27, 28, 43, 48, 52, 53, 67,
         89, 123, 131, 165, 200, 205, 214, 215
      proportion of 10, 61–62
      racism and 77, 106, 108, 113, 117–19,
         140, 142
      roles 43, 45, 47–48, 57, 67, 214–15,
         225
      solidarity, 198, 200

in extreme right 61, 69, 70, 124, 161,
   193
Muslim 7, 104, 136, 137, 141, 147, 160,
   161, 169, 172
research and 10, 20, 27, 28, 33,
   34
socio-economic position of 70, 77, 85,
   124, 161
see also activism, youth; violence, youth
   and